An Introduction to Modern Economics

London · New York · St Louis · San Francisco · Düsseldorf · Johannesburg
Kuala Lumpur · Mexico · Montreal · New Delhi · Panama · Paris · São Paulo
Singapore · Sydney · Toronto

An Introduction to Modern Economics

Joan Robinson
Emeritus Professor of Economics
Cambridge University

John Eatwell
Fellow of Trinity College
Cambridge

A/330

Published by McGRAW-HILL Book Company (UK) Limited

MAIDENHEAD · BERKSHIRE · ENGLAND

07 084024 5 Hard
07 084025 3 Soft

MADE AND PRINTED IN GREAT BRITAIN

Contents

Book One   Economic Doctrines

CONTENTS

Book Three   Modern Problems

Acknowledgements

During the eighteen months that this book was being drafted we have had a great deal of help and support, and many useful suggestions as well as objections and criticism, from the friends and colleagues whose names are listed below. None of them, of course, is to be held responsible for any errors that remain, or for the tone and emphasis of the argument.

Mahmoud Abdel-Fadil, Brian van Arkadie, Tom Asimakopulos, Adrian Blundell-Wignall, Allan Braff, Monojit Chatterji, Hélène Eatwell, Martin Fetherston, Jack Firestone, Keith Frearson, Harvey Gram, Frank Hahn, Geoff. Harcourt, Mike James, Richard Kahn, Denzo Kamiya, Alfredo Medio, Geoff. Meeks, Don Moggridge, Robert Neild, Ron Peters, Jean Sargent, Thanos Skouras, Jim Street, Bob Wallace

As well as general help and advice, Michael Ellman provided us with appendix 1 to chapter 11; Roger Tarling provided the numerical examples for the appendix to chapter 3, and appendix 2 to chapter 11; and Sue Howson compiled the index.

JOAN ROBINSON
JOHN EATWELL

Cambridge
January 1973

Preface

The book is offered, in the first instance, to students who are beginners in economics, but some parts of it may be of wider interest.

The three topics, Economic Doctrines, Analysis and Modern Problems, might be the subject of concurrent courses or they may be studied consecutively.

Book 1 surveys the main lines of economic thinking from the eighteenth century to the present day. Here, the reader should not be held up by details of theoretical argument; the analytical points involved are explained or exposed in the course of Book 2.

In Book 2, Analysis, the first chapter examines the manner in which various systems of property affect production, when there are no differences in technical requirements.

The following nine chapters are concerned with the operation of capitalist economies. At first, a highly simplified model is used to discuss effective demand, the short-period distribution of income between wages and profits, and technical progress. In successive chapters, the subject matter grows more complex and the specifications of the models are relaxed. Chapters 5, 6 and 7 cover the ground of what is usually called micro economics, including a brief treatment of public finance. The next three deal with various aspects of the monetary system, of the growth of corporations and of trade, from national and international points of view. The final chapter in Book 2 introduces some theoretical problems of planning in a socialist state.

In the Introduction there is some discussion of methodology and a synopsis of each chapter in Book 2, with suggestions of one or two passages that may be omitted without much loss at a first reading.

Pure economic logic may be regarded as a minor branch of applied mathematics, but we have not found it useful to put much of the argument into symbolic form. The reason is that economic relationships, such as the share of saving in national income, the influence on output of the land to labour ratio, or changes in productivity following technical innovations, cannot be adequately represented in simple, smooth functions. To cut them down to fit into algebraical formulae may be seriously misleading. We have found it better to use the method of constructing numerical examples and diagrams; this is not so fashionable, but more enlightening.

Mathematical methods are required when actual data are to be manipulated for practical purposes (an example drawn from Soviet experience is referred to in Appendix 1 to 2 11) but then the mathematics is much more advanced than that generally used for the exposition of elementary theory, and, indeed, it is still in the course of being invented.

Book 3 touches upon problems that involve political judgement and they cannot but be seen from some particular point of view. The authors intend their own prejudices to be sufficiently obvious for the reader to discount them as he feels right.

Book One

Economic doctrines

Introduction

The development of a theory of political economy was an element in the growing self-consciousness of intellectual opinion that followed the scientific revolution of the seventeenth century. If the order of society was not divinely ordained, but part of the natural world, then it was a proper subject for philosophical inquiry. The religious view of social relations, which taught that there is a *just price* for every commodity and which condemned the taking of interest as usury, had given way before the requirements of commercial life. Long before there was a systematic theory of economics, actual economies had reached a high degree of complexity. The philosophers were, so to say, gazing at a rich, confused and complicated scene, trying to make sense of it.

The free-thinkers of the eighteenth century found a substitute for religion in the concept of *natural law*. They sought to find principles of harmony and justice in human life corresponding to the regularity of the physical universe that Newton had revealed.

As thought developed, natural law gave way to the principles of the *Utilitarians* who supported the doctrine of Jeremy Bentham (1748–1832) that social arrangements can and should be judged by their consequences. The criterion for judging the consequences of any policy was taken to be the contribution that it made to the 'greatest good of the greatest number'.

This was a sharp break with the theological view of life which had been transmuted into the conception of natural law. Actions were to be judged by their results, not by appeal to some general scheme of morality. Despite its humanitarian slogan, Utilitarianism quickly turned, as we shall see, into a hard-headed devotion to expediency in which the conception of social class became more rigid than ever.

(a) Problems and functions of economic philosophy

Among the questions which confronted the philosophers was, first, where does wealth come from? It is easy enough to see that work creates wealth while nature provides the kindly fruits of the earth, but there are also profits. Where does profit come from? Does capital create wealth, like labour, or are profits merely a levy upon the wealth that labour creates?

Then, there was the problem of prices. The prices of commodities are the most obvious surface phenomenon of economic life that has to be explained, but prices may vary erratically from day to day under the influence of chance events—surely there must be some underlying principle of *value* that accounts for them?

Then, the problem of money: what is the role of money in an economy? What is the relation of money income of individuals to the wealth of society as a whole? If everyone had more money to spend while the goods available to be bought were unchanged, who would be any better off?

Then, social justice: can it be right that some families live in extravagant luxury while others can scarcely find food for their children? This is a hard question indeed, to which no school of thought (even in the Soviet Union) has found a satisfactory answer.

Finally, the question of effective demand, i.e., the demand, at a remunerative price, for the volume of products that could be produced with existing capacity. Will there be enough demand to keep all available resources, men and machines, fully employed? Wealth grows with specialization and specialization grows with wealth. The subsistence farmer, who feeds his family with his own crops, neither produces much nor demands much from others. With specialization comes the problem of sales. Every producer—cultivator, artisan, or employer of labour—is normally in the situation of looking for a market; he can always produce a bit more if he can find buyers at a reasonable price. Where does demand come from, and why is there rarely enough to keep everyone fully occupied?

From the seventeenth century onwards, each school of economic thought has concentrated on one or other of these questions. They all remain open today.

Actual economies have developed within national states. Philosophy has been bound up with patriotism. From the first, the study of the wealth of nations was the study of the wealth of *my* nation, and how to enhance it. The performance of various elements in the economic system was evaluated according to the contribution they could be shown to make to the growth of national wealth. Theory was involved with advocating policy; philosophy came into the argument mainly to justify the view of society on which policy was based. Even to the present day, economics has three aspects or functions—to try to understand how an economy operates, to make proposals for improving it, and to justify the criterion by which improvement is judged. The criterion of what is desirable necessarily involves moral and political judgements. Economics can never be a perfectly 'pure' science, unmixed with human values. Often, the moral and political viewpoints from which economic problems are seen have become so inextricably entwined with the questions asked, and even with the methods of analysis used, that these three elements of political economy are not always easy to keep distinct.

(b) Metaphysics and science

There is a kind of reasoning, common in the social sciences, that may be called *metaphysical*. This word has been used in various senses. Here, it is applied to a use of language that conveys no factual information, describes no logical relations nor gives precise instructions and yet is calculated to affect conduct.[1] The appeal to natural harmony was metaphysical, for it offered no evidence of what natural order is. The 'greatest good of the greatest number' is a metaphysical concept, for it proposes no criterion for judging what is 'good' nor any means of setting more 'good' to a few against a smaller 'good' to the many.

A metaphysical statement conveys no information, for its terms are not defined by reference to anything outside itself. Harmony is what is harmonious, and goodness is what is good. Such a statement has no scientific content: it is impossible to say that anything would be in any way different if it were not true, yet it is by no means empty. It expresses a certain attitude of mind, certain political sympathies or moral values, and it may crystallize opinions in a way that has important practical consequences.

Since political economy was mixed up with patriotism, slogans about the general good often concealed the advocacy of national interest, and since theories were worked out in societies stratified into classes, slogans expressed sympathy with a particular class and, under cover of promoting national wealth, advocated policies in its interest.

In the following chapters, we give an outline of the doctrines of political economy propagated over the last 200 years, and attempt to distinguish the elements of fact and logic, in each, from the elements which are metaphysical in the special sense in which we are using that term. The analytical part of the argument is expanded and explained in Book Two.

---

1. See Joan Robinson, *Economic Philosophy*.

Chapter One

Before Adam Smith

1. Leading ideas
(a) Effective demand

The first problem out of which political economy developed was concerned with international trade.

The *Mercantilist* school, which flourished along with the growth of British overseas trade in the seventeenth and eighteenth centuries, had one clear doctrine—that exports bring wealth to the nation. Its proponents supported and advocated devices by which the government could protect the balance of trade. Adam Smith mocked them, saying that they mistook gold for wealth, but they were not really so foolish.

Before a system of international finance was highly developed, a country which had a deficit on its balance of foreign payments—paying more abroad than it received—had to cover the difference in cash, and the main element in the balance of payments was the value of goods exported and imported. Individual traders were buying and selling goods to make profits for themselves. The possibility of making profits from imports depended on the demand for exotic goods at home—muslin from India, or spices from Ceylon—and profits from exports depended on prices abroad of home-produced goods—cloth from England. Summing up all the trans-actions for one country over a year, we find that the greater part of the value of imports and of exports offset each other, but there was no mechanism to make them match exactly. When importers, taken together, owed more to foreign sellers than exporters earned from foreign buyers, there was a corresponding excess of payments over receipts for the country as a whole. The only internationally accept-able forms of cash were gold and silver, thus a 'drain of treasure', a flow of precious metal overseas, was a symptom of a deficit in the balance of trade.

The Mercantilists were concerned about the problem of effective demand. They realized that a deficit in the balance of trade is, in general, bad for production. The deficit is an influence depressing effective demand. Imports represent supply without demand. Home incomes are spent on them, but no home income is generated in producing them. Exports, on the other hand, represent demand without supply to offset it. Incomes earned in producing goods for export are largely spent in the home market, thus giving a boost to home demand. The Mercantilists were correct in arguing that a surplus of exports tends to make the home economy buoyant while a surplus of imports tends to depress it.

Concern with the balance of trade made the Mercantilists favour protection to keep out imports and they sought to justify all kinds of government regulations intended to promote national prosperity, though often having the opposite effect.

(b) Money and wealth

There was another element in the Mercantilists' objection to a loss of gold. Without quite understanding why, they could see that a reduction in the volume of gold, and thus in the supply of money, caused a fall in effective demand over and above the depressive effect of a deficit in the balance of trade. But it must be admitted that they left the subject in a state of confusion.

The philosopher David Hume (1711–76) opened up a number of questions that were later dealt with by Adam Smith. Among other things, Hume tried to clear up the confusion between money and wealth. His essay *Of Money* opens as follows:

> Money is not, properly speaking, one of the subjects of commerce; but only the instrument which men have agreed upon to facilitate the exchange of one commodity for another. It is none of the wheels of trade: It is the oil which renders the motion of the wheels more smooth and easy.[2]

In an essay, *Of Interest*, there is a passage which has often been misinterpreted:

> For suppose, that, by miracle, every man in Great Britain should have five pounds slipt into his pocket in one night; this would much more than double the whole money that is at present in the kingdom; yet there would not next day, nor for some time, be any more lenders, nor any variation in the interest. And were there nothing but landlords and peasants in the state, this money, however abundant, could never gather into sums; and would only serve to increase the prices of every thing, without any farther consequence.[3]

Taken literally, this is obviously incorrect. Suppose that you have an income of £7 a week, paid on Friday, and spend £1 a day. Then your annual income is £365 and, on average, you have £3·5 in your pocket. If you wake up one Wednesday morning and find £7 in your pocket, or even if you wake up on Saturday and find

2. A convenient edition is *David Hume's Writing on Economics* (editor, E. Rotvein), Nelson, 1955; see p. 33.
3. ibid., p. 51.

£14, it does not mean that your annual income and annual spending will go up to £730. There might be a once-for-all wave of spending but there is no reason why there should be a permanent rise in prices.

Later writers have fallen into this confusion but Hume was not thinking along those lines; he was arguing that a general diffusion of small amounts of extra purchasing power would not 'gather into sums' that would be available to provide finance to promote trade and industry. He was putting the question in its social setting, not supporting a mechanical theory of the relation of the stock of money to the level of prices.

(c) The last Mercantilist

Sir James Steuart (1712–80), a man of affairs rather than a philosopher, published in 1767 *An Enquiry into the Principles of Political OEconomy* which did not have much impact on the development of thought because it was overshadowed by Adam Smith's *Wealth of Nations* nine years later. On the subject of international trade, Steuart took a somewhat Mercantilist line, modified by hints of belief in the benefits of specialization which became fashionable after his time. One of the problems he examined was that of a country that finds itself undersold in some particular line of production.

> Trade having subsisted long in the nation we are now to keep in our eye, I shall suppose that, through length of time, her neighbours have learned to supply one article of their own and other people's wants cheaper than she can do. What is to be done? Nobody will buy from her, when they can be supplied from another quarter at a less price. I say, what is to be done? For if there be no check put upon trade, and if the statesmen do not interpose with the greatest care, it is certain, that merchants will import the produce, and even the manufactures of rival nations; the inhabitants will buy them preferably to their own; the wealth of the nation will be exported; and her industrious manufacturers will be brought to starve. We may therefore look upon this, as a problem in trade, to be resolved by the principles already established.[4]

In such a case, the last resort is to prohibit the import of the commodity in question and produce it at home, but it might be better to abandon production of that commodity

> if, upon examining how the hands employed in a manufacture may be disposed of, it be found, that they may easily be thrown into another branch of industry, in which the nation's natural advantages are as superior to her rivals, as their's are superior to her's in the branch she intends to abandon; and provided her neighbours will agree to open their ports to the free importation of the commodities in question. For though there may be little profit in a trade by exchange, I still

4. *Enquiry* (editor, A. S. Skinner), Oliver and Boyd, 1966, p. 284.   7

think it advisable to continue correspondence, and to avoid every occasion of cutting off commerce with other nations. A laborious, œconomical, and sagacious nation, such as I suppose our traders to be, will be able to profit of many circumstances, which would infallibly turn to the disadvantage of others less expert in commerce, with whom she trades; and in expectation of favourable revolutions, she ought not rashly, nor because of small inconveniences, to renounce trading with them; especially if luxury should appear there to be on the growing hand.[5]

James Steuart, like the Mercantilists, was concerned with the problem of effective demand. He observed that public expenditure, even on 'warlike stores', would create employment but he preferred to advocate peaceful construction:

The more a work is useful after it is done, so much the better; because it may then have the effect of giving bread to those who have not built it. But whether useful or not afterwards, it must be useful while it is going on; and many, who with pleasure will give a thousand pounds to adorn a church, would not give a shilling to build Westminster bridge, or the port of Rochefort; and the poor live equally by the execution of either. Expensive public works, are therefore a mean of giving bread to the poor, and of advancing industry, without hurting the simplicity of manners.[6]

This is a clearer view of the question than any that was to be seen until Keynes restated the case in the nineteen thirties.

2. The Physiocrats

Despite their often brilliant insights, the British philosophers did not formulate a coherent body of logical economic analysis. The first writers to do so were in France. The school that became known as the *Physiocrats* was the first to present the mechanism of an economy in terms of its system of social classes.

(a) Feudalism

France in the eighteenth century maintained the structure of a feudal economy. The rent of land, along with taxes levied from the cultivators, was the source of funds to support the court, the army, and all the arts of civilization. Rent was simply taken from the peasants as a share of the crop. The peasants had to provide their own subsistence and the necessary investment in seed and so forth, out of the rest. The Physiocrats based their doctrines on this picture; in their view the land, which yields rent, is the only source of net output.

François Quesnay (1694–1774), who was a physician at the court of Louis XIV, is sometimes acclaimed as the first modern economist, for he set out his analysis of the economic system in terms of an abstract model illustrating the flows of commodi-

5. ibid., pp. 284–5.
6. ibid., p. 387.

ties in the process of production and consumption. This model, which Quesnay based on the circulation of the blood, somewhat resembles an input–output table such as is nowadays used to show the structure of industrial production. There are three social classes: landlords, peasants, and artisans. If we simplify Quesnay's *Tableau Economique* somewhat, the relations between them are as follows.

At the beginning of each year, the peasants own a stock, the carry-over from last year's harvest. This feeds them and provides them with inputs of seed, etc., for a year; they cultivate the land and produce a crop which, in Quesnay's example, is twice the stock that they had to start with. With this, they replace the stock which has been consumed in the process of production; the surplus, or net output, they pay to the landlords. The landlords consume part directly—feeding their entourage—and the rest they use to buy the products of the artisans. The artisans own their productive equipment—a loom for the weaver, a forge for the blacksmith. The payments that they receive for their manufactures are their gross income, out of which they both replace raw materials and wear and tear of equipment, and feed themselves. What they receive is just the value of their output. They do not contribute to the surplus. The only surplus comes from land.

These views supported certain prescriptions for policy. Firstly, it was wrong to tax the peasants, for this would deplete the stock which is necessary for them to consume in the course of reproducing the surplus. Secondly, it was desirable to improve methods of cultivation to increase the ratio of surplus to stock and raise the share going to landlords, thus increasing the demand for the products of the artisans and the wealth of the nation in general. These were deductions from analysis concerned with the mechanism of the economy. But the main point of the argument was purely metaphysical. It provided a justification for the social system. Since only land produced a surplus, only the landowner had a right to enjoy it.

(b) Metaphysical argument

The hallmark of a metaphysical statement, in the sense that we are using that term, is that nothing would be different if it were not true. The statement that a peasant family pays rent out of the excess over their consumption of the crops produced on their holding is a statement of fact. The statement that rent is due to the productivity of the land has no meaning apart from the definition of the surplus of production over the peasants' consumption as that which is due to the productivity of the land. The metaphysical part of the argument has no function except to provide slogans favourable to the landlords.

Slogans favourable to the peasants could easily be drawn from the same picture of the economy. From a different political standpoint, it could be argued that there would be no produce without the work that the peasants do. Work, not land, produces the surplus—landlords consume without working only because they own the land and have the power of the state behind them to enable them to exact rent.

Similarly, we could produce slogans to show that the artisans are the ones who   **9** produce a surplus because the satisfaction which their artifacts give to the consumer greatly exceeds the price he has to pay. Nothing would be different in the analysis, in either case, except the propaganda it was being used to support.

The moral that the Physiocrats drew from their metaphysic was mere subservience to existing authority. But their economic analysis, however simple it may appear today, was penetrating and original. It bears a different moral at the present time in those countries which are emerging from feudalism in a struggle for modernization. If it is true that the surplus from agriculture is the basic requirement for developing industry, then it is by no means desirable to allow the landlords to consume it.

Chapter Two

Classical political economy

The growing importance of manufacturing industry made the Physiocrats' vision obsolete but their successors—who became known as the *Classical* school—took over the conception of an economic mechanism based on class, to provide an analysis of the dynamics of the new industrial society.

The prestige of Adam Smith (1723–90) put all former economic philosophy in the shade. The publication of *An Inquiry into the Nature and Causes of the Wealth of Nations* in 1776 heralded the dominance of a concept of economic affairs which was to last for almost a century. In that time, political economy became established as a distinct branch of social philosophy.

Smith's wide-ranging ideas were formalized, and developed within a tight analytical framework by David Ricardo (1772–1823), a retired London stockbroker who became a Member of Parliament and exercised an important influence on opinion about all contemporary problems of political economy.

In struggling to understand practical problems, Ricardo delved into theoretical analysis. Far more than Quesnay, he deserves the title of the father of modern economics, for he devised the method of analysis which we know as setting up a *model*. The method consists of extracting the bare essential elements of a problem, cutting out all irrelevant details, and examining the interaction between its parts. When the entities which have been chosen, and their modes of operation, correspond to reality in the broad, the relationships which can be deduced by manipulating the model are illuminating. But there is always a danger that some element that has been left out of the model may actually be important, so that the conclusions drawn from the model fail to apply to the real situation.

Ricardo had a remarkable natural gift for analysis and he was a pertinacious thinker. He took great trouble to submit his ideas to criticism, and revised them when he was convinced.

Ricardo's main critic was his friend T. R. Malthus (1766–1834). Malthus is most famous for his pessimistic *Essay on Population* (1798), according to which the human race tends to breed up to the limit set by the supply of food. But he later played an important role in the development of economic thought—most notably in his debates with Ricardo on all aspects of economic theory. A continual flow of letters between the two friends, from 1815 to 1823, contained sophisticated arguments on economic matters, comments on each other's published works, and criticism of the works of others—all written with remarkable candour and affection.

John Stuart Mill (1806–73), the son of another of Ricardo's friends, James Mill (1773–1836), besides making significant contributions to philosophy and ethics, was the last important liberal writer of the classical school. He added little of analytical substance. His *Principles of Political Economy* (1848), which was the basic textbook on political economy until the rise of the neoclassicals, reflects the increasing self-confidence of mid-nineteenth century Britain and, in the process, often obscures the clarity of Ricardian thought.

The conclusions that Mill drew from classical analysis were diametrically opposite to those drawn by Karl Marx (1818–83). Marx reformulated Ricardo's analysis in line with his own philosophy of history. The broad range of Marx's thought carried his work beyond the narrow bounds of classical economics, but important elements in his analysis were derived from classical conceptions.

Like all generalizations, labelling a diverse group of writers on economic affairs as a 'school' may be misleading. There were major divergences of viewpoint within the group: Ricardo's *Principles of Political Economy and Taxation* (1817) was regarded by contemporaries as the 'new economics' *vis-à-vis* Smith, and Marx was often virulent in his repudiation of the ideas of his predecessors. But there was an underlying framework of ideas common to all writers of the group, even though the direction and conclusions of their analysis often differed.

1. Fundamental ideas

(a) A class analysis

The basic concepts of classical analysis involve the economic characteristics of social classes. This framework, taken from Quesnay's original picture of peasants, landlords, and artisans, was transformed by Adam Smith into a structure composed of workers, capitalists, and landlords. The consumption of workers was near the subsistence level, the function of the capitalists was to accumulate, and the consumption of landlords was a deduction from the surplus available for accumulation. Since the three classes disposed of their incomes in different ways, the division of the total product between them governed the development of the economy.

Smith says of the 'three great orders' of society:

The whole annual produce of the land and labour of every country, or what comes to the same thing, the whole price of that annual produce, naturally divides itself, it has already been observed, into three parts: the rent of land, the wages of labour, and the profits of stock; and constitutes a revenue to three different orders of people. . . .

according to the different proportions in which [the whole annual produce] is annually divided between those . . . different orders of people, its ordinary or average value must either annually increase, or diminish or continue the same from one year to another.[1]

And Ricardo, after a similar statement, declares that

[t]o determine the laws which regulate this distribution, is the principal problem in Political Economy.[2]

Smith's definitions were less precise than Ricardo's, and his moral philosophy based on natural law led him to disapprove of the lack of humane relations between men which the Utilitarian Ricardo took for granted. Many of Adam Smith's observations would nowadays seem radical. On the position of landlords, he remarked:

As soon as the land of any country has all become private property, the landlords, like all other men, love to reap where they never sowed, and demand a rent even for its natural produce.[3]

And on the 'free competition' of master and man, he cast an equally candid eye:

Masters are always and every where in a sort of tacit, but constant and uniform combination, not to raise the wages of labour above their actual rate. To violate this combination is every where a most unpopular action, and a sort of reproach to a master among his neighbours and equals. We seldom, indeed, hear of this combination, because it is the usual, and one may say, the natural state of things which nobody hears of.[4]

But the main force of the argument is a defence of the rising power of industrial capitalism, and an appeal to release the play of self-interest from hampering restrictions:

[M]an has almost constant occasion for the help of his brethren, but it is in vain for him to expect it from their benevolence only. He will be more likely to prevail if he can interest their self-love in his favour, and show them that it is for their own advantage to do for him what he requires of them. Whoever offers to another a bargain of any kind, proposes to do this. Give me that which I want, and you shall have this which you want, is the meaning of every such offer; and it is in this manner that we obtain from one another the far greater part of those good

1. Adam Smith, *An Inquiry into the Nature and Causes of the Wealth of Nations*, Cannan edition, Methuen, London 1961, book 1, Ch. XI, p. 276 and Ch. VI, p. 61.
2. D. Ricardo, 'Principles of Political Economy', *Works and Correspondence of David Ricardo*, Sraffa edition, Cambridge University Press, Cambridge 1951–73, vol. 1, p. 5.
3. *Wealth of Nations*, book 1, Ch. VI, p. 56.
4. ibid., book I, Ch. VIII, p. 75.

offices which we stand in need of. It is not from the benevolence of the butcher, the brewer, or the baker, that we expect our dinner, but from their regard to their own interest. We address ourselves, not to their humanity but to their self-love, and never talk to them of our own necessities but of their advantages.[5]

But the self-interest to be released was that of the trader and the employer of labour. The self-interest of workers was not to be considered. Once the artisan has lost his tools and his market connections, he is reduced to dependence on wages. It is the employer who gets the benefit of the efficiency and discipline imposed by work in factories. For Adam Smith, wages were part of the cost of production, like the fodder for a plough horse. The wealth of nations did not include the consumption of the workers, only the surplus of production over costs, for the surplus could be reinvested to expand itself in an ever-widening spiral.

(b) Capital as an advance

To the classical economists, the only fundamental agent of production is labour, or more accurately, work. Thus, apart from the 'free gifts of nature', only human work creates wealth. The physical world is merely a set of conditions providing the environment in which human work is the active element.

The organization through time of the process of production requires *advances*, since wages have to be paid to the worker before completion of the product. By advancing wages for the creation of ever-more sophisticated tools, the productivity of labour is continually increased. Thus, *capital* is the command over resources which the capitalists use to gain command over labour. In a general sense, capital is, in the classical view, a *wage fund*, and a machine is the embodiment of past expenditure from the wage fund, carried forward to a further stage in production.

(c) The determination of 'surplus'

The *surplus* is the volume of commodities over and above that required to support the workers who produced it. Total production is technically determined, and the wage is a deduction from that production, a higher wage entailing a correspondingly smaller surplus. (As we shall see in the next chapter, this 'deduction' theory is quite different from the neoclassical theory of distribution formulated in the late nineteenth century, in which the wage and output per man are functionally related.)

The logic of Ricardo's argument required the level of the wage to settle at a subsistence minimum. This is not a perfectly satisfactory conception; the physical needs of subsistence are not precise—an insufficient diet produces a short expectation of life rather than an abrupt reduction of the population. Moreover, as Marx said, there is a 'historical and moral element' in the standard of life accepted as 'necessary' in a society.

14   5. ibid., book I, Ch. II, p. 18.

Ricardo (influenced by Malthus on population) supposed that if wages rose above the subsistence minimum, an increase in numbers would inexorably bring them down. Now, it is generally true for a labour force existing at a low standard of life that numbers are held in check by infant mortality. It may be that a rise of earnings will permit more babies to survive and increase the number of workers looking for employment. But this is obviously a slow response which could not act as a mechanism to keep wages exactly at subsistence, even if it were possible to detect a level of earnings at which the labour force would be constant in size.

However, all that Ricardo needed was the assumption that there would always be labour available to be employed at a constant wage rate, and this corresponded well enough to the contemporary situation that he was trying to analyse.

Marx rejected Malthusian population theory and the 'so-called law of diminishing returns' which predicted that output could not rise as rapidly as population. In his view, the existence of a 'reserve army' of unemployed labour forced the wages of those in employment down to the socially determined minimum.

Marx related the level of wages to the process by which surplus is created. Surplus is an historical phenomenon existing in all societies, except the most primitive, while the manner in which the surplus is extracted from production varies with the structure of society. It was this process with which Marx was concerned, in particular, with the form that it takes in capitalist society.

(d) Dynamic analysis

The classical economists were seeking to discover the 'laws of motion' of capitalist economies. Their analysis was necessarily dynamic, concerned with the accumulation of stock that would permit more labour to be employed, and with the production of machines which would, in turn, contribute to the production of more machines. They also considered the problems created in a growing economy by limitation on non-reproducible resources, in particular, land. Although the idea of a society attaining 'a full complement of riches', or a 'stationary state', figures in Smith, Ricardo, and Mill, this was always a condition to which the economy was tending, the natural outcome of a dynamic process.

2. The accumulation of wealth

Adam Smith was the prophet of the industrial revolution. The era of Mercantilism had left its legacy. The great fortunes made from trade and loot overseas supplied the funds that were now available to invest in building up industry. Channels of trade, and conquest and colonial settlement, had opened up markets where manufactures could undersell the local artisan products and, at the same time, provided supplies of raw materials to be manufactured. The narrow defensiveness of Mercantilist policies was now an impediment to growing wealth, and effective demand was no longer a matter of concern.

15

Adam Smith argued that the division of labour is the basis of technical advance, and he proclaimed that 'the division of labour depends on the extent of the market'. His attack on the Mercantilists was against restrictive policies which limited the growth of markets.

(a) The division of labour

The promotion of the division of labour, the division of work into ever-more minutely specialized tasks, was the main result—and, for Adam Smith, the main virtue—of the emerging factory system. The capitalists' surplus was necessary to promote specialization and facilitate access to the wider market necessary for the disposal of the increased output. As surplus expanded and stock was accumulated, output per man increased. Thus, to increase the surplus per man employed it was unnecessary to try to reduce the wage—far better to increase the productivity of the working time that a given wage could buy. Smith could thus claim that—through technological superiority—capitalistic production, which promoted the division of labour, eliminated craft and artisan production, and that the resultant increase in wealth would benefit the nation as a whole.

He advanced three arguments for the technical superiority of dividing tasks as finely as possible.

[The] great increase of the quantity of work which, in consequence of the division of labour, the same number of people are capable of performing, is owing to three different circumstances; first, to the increase of dexterity in every particular workman; secondly, to the saving of time which is commonly lost in passing from one species of work to another; and lastly, to the invention of a great number of machines which facilitate and abridge labour, and enable one man to do the work of many.[6]

Smith illustrated these arguments with his famous example of the pin factory in which:

One man draws out the wire, another straights it, a third cuts it, a fourth points it, a fifth grinds it at the top for receiving the head. . . .

and so on, so that

the important business of making a pin is, in this manner, divided into about 18 distinct operations.[7]

(b) The factory system

In the context of the pin factory, Smith's arguments are not convincing. To save 'the time that is commonly lost in passing from one species of work to another', it is

6. ibid., book I, Ch. I, p. 11.
7. ibid., book I, Ch. I, p. 8.

necessary only to persist in a particular activity for long enough to overcome time lost in arranging the materials required for the task. The solitary artisan pin maker could draw wire all one day, spend the next day straightening, the next cutting, and so on. Saving of time requires separation of tasks, and fixes the ideal duration of particular activities; it does not imply specialization by individuals.

Nor is the notion of increased dexterity tenable in circumstances in which the skills involved are not difficult to acquire. Most of the sectors in which the factory system first developed required skills which were relatively easy to learn, to the extent of being amenable to child labour. It was much later that technological sophistication created truly specialized tasks.

Finally, Smith's belief in an increased propensity to innovate was later contradicted by himself:

> The man whose life is spent in performing a few simple operations, of which the effects too are, perhaps, always the same, or very nearly the same, has no occasion to exert his understanding, or to exercise his invention in finding out expedients for removing difficulties which never occur.[8]

This is not to say that technical change has not accompanied the organization of labour in factories, but that the direction which technical change has taken was dictated by the method of organization of work required for the factory system.

Adam Smith was advocating the establishment of such a system, not looking back on its achievements. The original role of the division of labour was to discipline and control the manner in which work was performed and, by ensuring the necessity of an organizer, to guarantee a position for the capitalist in the production process. Before the introduction of expensive machinery, only specialization of workers created a need for detailed organization. But the capitalist must acquire a predominant role if accumulation is to proceed. Thus, in the first instance the social function of specialization of work and control of workers was to extract a surplus for accumulation.[9] The contribution to technical efficiency came later.

No other classical economist, apart from Marx, paid so much attention to problems of technical change as did Adam Smith. Instead, the technological effects of accumulation were taken for granted, and interest was focused on the main determinant of the rate of accumulation, the proportion of total product acquired by the capitalist class.

3. Distribution and prices

Adam Smith proclaimed the virtues of a capitalist economy but did not have a secure grasp of its mode of operation. Like all classical economists, he saw that the key to an understanding of economic behaviour lay in the forces determining the

8. ibid., book V, Ch. I, p. 303.
9. The argument of this section is based on S. Marglin, 'What do Bosses do? The origins and functions of hierarchy in capitalist production', Harvard Institute of Economic Research, discussion paper no. 222, November 1971.

distribution of income between the three classes of society—workers, landlords, and capitalists—but he was unable to offer a tenable theory of the distribution of the surplus between profits and rent. It was Ricardo who first formulated a complete theory.

(a) Ricardian distribution theory

Ricardo took it for granted that the share which the landlord took of the produce of the earth, in the form of rent, would all be consumed, while the greater part of profit would be saved and reinvested to increase employment and expand production. He needed to prove that rent was an incubus on a growing economy. But though he had a purpose, he was concerned to find the truth of the matter. His arguments were sometimes obscure but never deliberately fudged.

His model corresponded to the situation in English agriculture in his day. In eighteenth-century England, relations between the landowner and the cultivator were very different from those depicted by Quesnay. The enclosure movement had dispossessed the peasants and, at the same time, greatly increased production. Landowners *farmed out* their land; the farmer contracted to pay rent and employed labour at wages. The excess of net output over the wage bill covered the rent and some profit for himself.

In the first, and simplest, version of his analysis, Ricardo depicted the agricultural sector producing a single output—corn—requiring a year's work from harvest to harvest. This sector required only a single input, also corn, produced within the sector itself, to be invested in the form of seed and to pay the workers' wages.

A man must eat every day, but the harvest comes once a year. The farmer keeps enough corn from the last harvest to advance wages and seed over the year. The wage rate is set at a quantity of corn to be paid out week by week. It is because the worker has no other means to live by that he is obliged to take service with a farmer, unlike the peasant in the Physiocrats' world, who owned the 'advances' to be consumed over a year.

Ricardo's model exhibits the determination of the rate of profit on capital. Profit per man year is a quantity of corn, and the investment necessary to employ a man is a quantity of corn. The ratio of corn profit to the stock of corn is the rate of profit on the capital invested in producing corn.

Adapting Marxian notation, v is the wage bill in corn for a year for a particular amount of employment, c is the seed for the year's production and s is profit—the excess of output over rent minus the cost of production, $c + v$, all as quantities of corn. Since the capital invested to employ the workers is a year's bill for seed and wages, it is equal to $c + v$. The rate of profit on capital is

$$\frac{s}{c + v}$$

All other employers have to pay wages in corn, and the prices of the various commodities that they produce must be such as to earn the same rate of profit as that received by the farmers. If they earned a higher rate, some farmers would become manufacturers; if a lower rate, some manufacturers would become farmers. Thus, the rate of profit in agriculture, which produces the subsistence for the workers, determines the rate of profit throughout the whole economy.

The corn which is paid out as rent is merrily consumed in the landlords' mansions; the farmer is a capitalist who is ambitious to expand his business. From his share of the harvest, he retains not only enough to replace the advances that he made last year but an additional amount—net investment—with which he can employ more men next year. Since land is not all equally fertile, the differential advantage of better land grows as total employment expands and competition between farmers drives up rents. Output per man, net of rent, diminishes from year to year and, since the wage is at subsistence level and cannot be cut, the rate of profit falls.

This analysis led to a powerful attack on the Corn Laws which were protecting the interests of the landlords by preventing cheap imports of grain from Europe. Labour in England could produce manufactures to be exchanged for imported corn. The amount of corn per unit of labour, acquired in this way, would be greater than the amount that the same labour could produce on English farms which were extended on to relatively poor land. If imports were allowed, the corn cost of acquiring corn would be reduced. The less-good land would go out of cultivation. Rents would fall and the rate of profit would rise.

(b) Prices

Malthus pointed out that this argument had one important deficiency. There is no sector of the economy, including agriculture, in which all produced inputs and all outputs consist of the same commodity. Wages do not consist only of corn. Workers need to consume some manufactured and some imported goods. This means that the calculation of the rate of profit will involve comparing the heterogeneous bundles of commodities which comprise output, wages, and total investment. But to compare these bundles, they must be reduced to some single unit.

To meet this objection, Ricardo set out to find a unit of value which would enable him to measure, as a single quantity, the mass of heterogeneous commodities produced. His theory required a measure of value which would allow the heterogeneous bundles of commodities distributed between rent, wages, and profits to be reduced to a homogeneous measure, similar to the corn in his simple model.

Heterogeneous commodities may be reduced to a homogeneous measure in terms of their ratios of exchange in the market place—their relative prices. Moreover, since the problem is to determine the command over resources represented by the capitalists' profits, the relative exchange values of commodities with each other, and with labour, must form a part of any theory of value. But the total cost of produced inputs going into the production of each commodity includes the profit required by the capitalist as a return on his investment. Thus, the prices of particular

19

commodities depend on the rate of profit. The beauty of the corn model was to measure the magnitudes determining the rate of profit in physical terms, eliminating the complications caused by interdependence of prices and the rate of profit.

Faced with the same problem, Adam Smith had formulated a labour theory of value:

> In that early and rude state of society which precedes both the accumulation of stock and the appropriation of land, the proportion between the quantities of labour necessary for acquiring different objects seems to be the only circumstance which can afford any rule for exchanging them for one another. If among a nation of hunters, for example, it usually costs twice the labour to kill a beaver which it does to kill a deer, one beaver should naturally exchange for or be worth two deer. It is natural that what is usually the produce of two days' or two hours' labour, should be worth double of what is usually the produce of one day's or one hour's labour.
>
> If the one species of labour should be more severe than the other, some allowance will naturally be made for this superior hardship; and the produce of one hour's labour in the one way may frequently exchange for that of two hours' labour in the other.
>
> Or if the one species of labour requires an uncommon degree of dexterity and ingenuity, the esteem which men have for such talents will naturally give a value to their produce, superior to what would be due to the time employed about it. Such talents can seldom be acquired but in consequence of long application, and the superior value of their produce may frequently be no more than a reasonable compensation for the time and labour which must be spent in acquiring them. In the advanced state of society, allowances of this kind, for superior hardship and superior skill, are commonly made in the wages of labour; and something of the same kind must probably have taken place in its earliest and rudest period.
>
> In this state of things, the whole produce of labour belongs to the labourer; and the quantity of labour commonly employed in acquiring or producing any commodity, is the only circumstance which can regulate the quantity of labour which it ought commonly to purchase, command, or exchange for.[10]

This is not a theory of markets but, rather, a conception of the 'just price'.

When labour is the only cost, commodities *ought* to exchange at prices corresponding to the labour time embodied in them.

> As soon as stock has accumulated in the hands of particular persons, some of them will naturally employ it in setting to work industrious people, whom they will supply with materials and subsistence, in order to make a profit by the sale of their work, or by what their labour adds to the value of the materials. In exchanging the complete manufacture either for money, for labour, or for other goods, over and above what may be sufficient to pay the price of the materials,

10. *Wealth of Nations,* book I, Ch. VI, pp. 53–4.

and the wages of the workmen, something must be given for the profits of the undertaker of the work who hazards his stock in this adventure. The value which the workmen add to the materials, therefore, resolves itself in this case into two parts, of which the one pays their wages, the other the profits of their employer upon the whole stock of materials and wages which he advanced. He could have no interest to employ them, unless he expected from the sale of their work something more than what was sufficient to replace his stock to him; and he could have no interest to employ a great stock rather than a small one, unless his profits were to bear some proportion to the extent of his stock.[11]

But this leaves unsolved the problem of the relation of the rate of profit to prices, and the question of what the rate of profit may be:

In this state of things, the whole produce of labour does not always belong to the labourer. He must in most cases share it with the owner of the stock which employs him. Neither is the quantity of labour commonly employed in acquiring or producing any commodity, the only circumstance which can regulate the quantity which it ought commonly to purchase, command, or exchange for. An additional quantity, it is evident, must be due for the profits of the stock which advanced the wages and furnished the materials of that labour.[12]

(c) Produced commodities

Ricardo stated the problem much more clearly than Adam Smith had done. First, he divided all commodities into two groups, *produced commodities* and *scarce commodities*.

Possessing utility, commodities derive their exchangeable value from two sources: from their scarcity, and from the quantity of labour required to obtain them.

There are some commodities, the value of which is determined by their scarcity alone. No labour can increase the quantity of such goods, and therefore their value cannot be lowered by an increased supply. Some rare statues and pictures, scarce books and coins, wines of a peculiar quality, which can be made only from grapes grown on a particular soil, of which there is a very limited quantity, are all of this description. Their value is wholly independent of the quantity of labour originally necessary to produce them, and varies with the varying wealth and inclinations of those who are desirous to possess them.

These commodities, however, form a very small part of the mass of commodities daily exchanged in the market. By far the greatest part of those goods which are the objects of desire, are procured by labour; and they may be multiplied, not in one country alone, but in many, almost without any assignable limit, if we are disposed to bestow the labour necessary to obtain them.[13]

11. ibid., book I, Ch. VI, p. 54.
12. ibid., book I, Ch. VI, p. 55.
13. D. Ricardo, *Works*, vol. I, p. 12.

Thus, scarce commodities are those fixed in supply, or largely dependent for their production on resources which are fixed in supply. Produced commodities, on the other hand, being manufactured by labour with the use of other produced commodities (such as machines), are not limited in their supply by scarcity, but may be produced without a definite limit. The values of scarce commodities are determined simply by interaction of the fixed supply with demand, but the values of produced commodities, apart from short-run fluctuations, are not. This latter group comprises most commodities. In an industrial economy, the former group is of less importance.

It is the prices of produced commodities which are dependent on the rate of profit. The prices of produced commodities must pay both the wages expended on their production and the required profits on the stock.

Where do we go from here? Ricardo observed that, for technical reasons, different commodities require different proportions of materials and equipment to labour, and different lengths of time over which advances have to be made. Competition between capitalists tends to establish a uniform *rate* of profit on all lines of production. Thus, since the rate of profit per annum is simply the amount of profit earned per annum divided by the value of the investment required for production, the share of profit in the value of output of various commodities varies with the value of the investment necessary to employ a man in producing them. At a given uniform rate of profit, a commodity with a higher value of investment per man will have a higher share of profits. Thus, the pattern of relative prices depends on the rate of profit.

(d) An invariable standard

To generalize his simple corn model, Ricardo hoped to find an 'invariable standard of value' which would avoid the complications of the relation of the rate of profit to relative prices. He tried various ideas, such as a labour theory of value, but labour values do not accurately reflect relative prices; and an 'average' commodity standard, which he called 'gold', but which proved extremely difficult to define. Unable to find an invariable standard to measure distribution of a given volume of output, Ricardo patched up the argument as best he could, but he was never satisfied with it. At the time of his death, he was working on a paper which remained unknown till it was published in Piero Sraffa's edition of his works.

> The only qualities necessary to make a measure of value a perfect one are, that it should itself have value, and that that value should be itself invariable, in the same manner as in a perfect measure of length the measure should have length and that length should be neither liable to be increased or diminished; or in a measure of weight that it should have weight and that such weight should be constant.
>
> Altho' it is thus easy to say what a perfect measure of value should be it is not equally easy to find any one commodity that has the qualities required. When we want a measure of length we select a yard or a foot—which is some determined

definite length neither liable to increase or diminish, but when we want a measure of value what commodity that has value are we to select which shall itself not vary in value?[14]

This is based on a false analogy. The measure of length or of weight is only a convention but, once the convention has been accepted, it does not change from one continent or one age to another. It is, so to say, a relation between man and the physical world. But values arise within society. Weight and length were the same for Robinson Crusoe on his island as they had been at home, but value meant nothing to him; when he found a bag of gold, there was nothing to spend it on. Every society has its own requirements and its own technical possibilities, and both are continually changing through time. Nothing that has value has invariable value.

All the same, Ricardo's idea of using an 'average commodity' as a standard of value later bore fruit. Sraffa demonstrated how such a commodity might be formed as a composite commodity which can be used to analyse the distributive relations holding at a particular time in an economy of produced commodities.* By this means, he brought the essential meaning of Ricardo's theory of profits into a clear light.

4. Effective demand

Malthus raised a further objection to Ricardo's analysis of accumulation and distribution. In his study of population, he had laid great stress on diminishing returns from land—the fall in average output per head as the ratio of labour to land rises—but now, he would not accept the logical deduction that Ricardo drew from it. He was attached to the interests of the landed gentry and brought the problem of effective demand to their defence.

Malthus suggested that continual accumulation by the capitalists may prove to be self-defeating, in that it would lead to an excess of production which could not be sold because of a lack of demand. Would there not be a 'glut', a general over-production of goods with no money coming forward to pay for them? The only remedy was to maintain the income of the landlords who performed the socially desirable function of spending their rents on luxury consumption and, thus, keeping up the level of effective demand.

(a) Say's law

Ricardo denied Malthus' position on effective demand by invoking Say's law, according to which all that is produced can be sold at a reasonable price, including the customary profit, so that there can never be a general glut. Excess production of particular commodities can only be temporary, as demand is switched from one commodity to another.

14. ibid., vol. IV, p. 361.
* See **2** 6 §3(d).

Say's law derives from the discussion of problems of effective demand in the work of Jean-Baptiste Say (1767–1832), a French follower of Adam Smith, whose *Traité d'Economie Politique* was published in 1803. Two themes dominated Say's analysis. The first was an attack on the supposed confusion of the Mercantilists between money and wealth. The second was Physiocratic; in terms of the circular flow of production, it reiterated the idea that commodities exchange for commodities, and not for money. The combination of these two themes yields the statement:

> In reality we do not buy articles of consumption with money, the circulating medium with which we pay for them. We must in the first instance have bought this money itself by the sale of our produce.[15]

As commodities can only be bought with other commodities, it is implied that if the correct combination of commodities is produced, all will be sold, for all production is designed for purchase. 'Supply creates its own demand.' This view was reiterated by Ricardo:

> . . . there is no amount of capital which may not be employed in a country, because demand is only limited by production. No man produces, but with a view to consume or sell, and he never sells, but with an intention to purchase some other commodity. . . . By producing, then, he necessarily becomes either the consumer of his own goods, or the purchaser and consumer of the goods of some other person . . . .

> Productions are always bought by productions, or by services; money is only the medium by which the exchange is effected. Too much of a particular commodity may be produced, of which there may be a glut in the market, as not to repay the capital expended on it; but this cannot be the case with respect to all commodities; . . . .[16]

The same argument was repeated by J. S. Mill:

> What constitutes the means of payments for commodities is simply commodities. Each person's means of paying for the productions of other people consist of those which he himself possesses. All sellers are inevitably, and by the meaning of the word, buyers. Could we suddenly double the productive powers of the country, we should double the supply of commodities in every market; but we should, by the same stroke, double the purchasing power. Everybody would bring a double demand as well as supply; everybody would be able to buy twice as much because everyone would have twice as much to offer in exchange.[17]

Aggregate supply, for the economy as a whole, was considered identical to aggregate demand, and total output was limited only by the wage fund—the amount of capital available for the employment of workers. In its classical version, Say's law

15. J. B. Say, *Letters to Malthus*. Published in English 1821, p. 2.
16. D. Ricardo, *Works* vol. I, pp. 290–2.
17. J. S. Mill, *Principles of Political Economy*, Ashley edition, Kelley, 1965, pp. 557–8.

did not imply that there would be full employment of labour, only that there could not be a general excess of production. If there were a tendency for the supply of labour to adjust to the demand for it at the subsistence-wage rate, it was through a Malthusian process of population growth or famine.

A corollary to the concept that 'what constitutes the means of payment for commodities is simply commodities' is that 'saving is spending'. This is because commodities are produced to buy other commodities, either directly or indirectly, by being lent to others willing to pay interest to secure the benefits of borrowing. This idea was later summarized by Alfred Marshall, the great neoclassical economist:

> . . . it is a familiar economic axiom that a man purchases labour and commodities with that portion of his income which he saves just as much as he does with that he is said to spend. . . . He is said to save when he causes the labour and commodities which he purchases to be devoted to the production of wealth from which he expects to derive the means of enjoyment in the future.[18]

(b) Malthus' theory of 'gluts'

To defend the position of the landlords, Malthus attacked the proposition that all that is produced will be sold. He viewed the process of growth of productive capacity as analogous to that of population, and claimed that both increase in excess of the demand for their services.

> Though it may be allowed therefore that the laws which regulate the increase of capital are not quite so distinct as those which regulate the increase of population, yet they are certainly just of the same kind; and it is equally vain with a view to the permanent increase of wealth, to continue converting revenue into capital when there is no adequate demand for the products of such capital, as to continue encouraging marriage and the birth of children without a demand for labour and an increase of the funds for its maintenance.[19]

Malthus had two quite separate explanations of why there might not be 'adequate demand for the products of . . . capital'. The first was simply that mankind may display a preference for idleness over productive activity:

> It is an important error to take for granted that mankind will produce and consume all that they have the power to produce and consume

and account should be taken of

> the influence of so general and important a principle in human nature, as indolence or love of ease.[20]

18. A Marshall, *Pure Theory of Domestic Values*, L. S. E., 1949, p. 34.
19. Quoted in D. Ricardo, 'Notes on Malthus', *Works* vol. II, p. 331.
20. ibid., pp. 313–4.

Ricardo dismissed this argument without difficulty:

> Mr Malthus supposes the motive strong enough to produce the commodities and
> then contends there would be no market for them after they were produced, as
> there would be no demand for them.[21]

But Malthus' second argument was more weighty. It contains an important insight
into the determination of the share of profits. He pointed out that:

> the consumption and demand occasioned by the persons employed in productive
> labour can never alone furnish a motive to the accumulation and employment of
> capital.[22]

It is the demand for the products of 'productive labour' by those sections of the
labour force which are not productive (such as the servants in the landlords' mansions) which allows them to be sold at a price higher than their wage cost and thus
to earn a profit. This proposition is illustrated in the Figure. The productive workers
ab, produce consumption goods and spend all their wages on consumption goods.
The unproductive workers, *bc*, do not themselves produce the commodities that
they buy with their wages. Consumption goods may, therefore, be sold at a price
higher than their wage cost, that is, at a price which includes profit, the amount of
which depends on the expenditure of unproductive workers. (The shaded areas in
the figure are equal.)

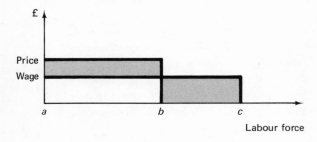

If savings by landlords and capitalists increased and consumption diminished, then,
claimed Malthus, the proportion of productive to unproductive workers would rise
as savings were used to employ productive workers.

> Under these circumstances . . . how is it possible to suppose that the increased
> quantity of commodities, obtained by the increased number of productive
> labourers, should find purchasers, without such a fall of price as would probably
> sink their value below the costs of production?[23]

21. ibid., p. 314.
22. ibid., p. 302.
23. ibid., p. 303.

This argument was all right so far as it went, but contained two fatal flaws, one of which Ricardo noticed immediately. He pointed out that Malthus' position implies that

vast powers of production are put into action and the result is unfavourable to the interests of mankind,

but what really happens is that

there may not be adequate motives for production and therefore things will not be produced,

in consequence of which

we see . . . vast powers of production which are *not* put into action.[24]

However, even Ricardo failed to notice the major error in the argument. It is not only unproductive workers who spend their wages on things they themselves do not produce, but also those productive workers who are engaged in producing investment goods, such as machines, or corn to be stored to pay additional wages next year. An increase in the rate of accumulation entails an increase in the latter group of workers and, consequently, in profits from the production of consumption goods.

The problem with Malthus' argument was that he held to the postulate that 'saving is spending' and did not realize that this was merely an alternative way of stating Say's law, which he wished to attack. It was not until Keynes in 1936 revealed the inconsistencies in this postulate, that Malthus' belief in the possibility of a 'general glut' was demonstrated to be well founded. In the meantime, the interests that he was defending were falling out of fashion. Ricardo and the capitalists won the argument.

5. Marx

After Ricardo, and up to the fourth quarter of the nineteenth century, the liberal tradition in classical political economy was dominated by John Stuart Mill. Mill's analysis derives from a prosperous age, in which the conflict between capitalist and landlord had diminished, and the growing antagonism of capitalist and worker was not emphasized in an analysis in which society was portrayed as tending towards a golden future. Mill confessed that he was

not charmed with the ideal of life held out by those who think that the normal state of human beings is that of trampling, crushing, elbowing and treading on each other's heels, which forms the existing type of life.[25]

He looked forward to the stationary state towards which society was progressing, in which the temperance of the working class would prevent excessive growth of their numbers:

24. D. Ricardo, Letter to Malthus, 9 July 1821, *Works* vol. IX, pp. 15–6.
25. J. S. Mill, *Principles.*, p. 748.

It is scarcely necessary to remark that a stationary condition of capital and population implies no stationary state of human improvement. There would be as much scope as ever for all kinds of mental culture and moral and social progress; as much room for improving the Art of Living, and much more likelihood of its being improved, when minds ceased to be engrossed by the art of getting on.[26]

But sometimes Mill was rather pessimistic, as when he commented that, despite the great wealth of America,

all these advantages seem to have done for them is that the life of the whole of one sex is devoted to dollar hunting, and of the other to breeding dollar hunters.[27]

At the same time that Mill was writing, his complacency was being challenged by an entirely new interpretation of classical economics, which emphasized the fundamental conflicts inherent in the capitalist economy. The new system, which combined many of Ricardo's ideas with a more general theory of history and society, was constructed by Karl Marx.

(a) Social relations and the creation of surplus

Marx accepted the basic tenor of many of Ricardo's ideas on income distribution but claimed that Ricardo had been analysing the wrong problem. The nature of capitalism could only be understood by an analysis of the origin of surplus, which is not to be found in technological relationships alone.

The distinctive nature of capitalism derives from the manner in which surplus is extracted during production. In a slave society, the manner in which the fruits of the work of the slave are appropriated by the slave owner is clear to all. Similarly, in an early feudal economy, the serfs worked part of the day for the landlord, and thus the landlord acquired directly the benefit of the surplus of their labour over what they required to feed themselves. But, in a capitalist economy, the manner in which surplus is extracted is concealed beneath the surface phenomena of wages and prices, which are set by bargains freely made in the market place.

To penetrate these surface phenomena, Marx took over the classical theory that commodities exchange at values determined by the labour time required to produce them, and interpreted it to mean that labour alone produces value. From this he deduced that, since all commodities exchange at their labour values, the commodity labour (which Marx called 'labour power') must also exchange at its labour value. The labour value of labour power is the labour time required to produce the commodities which provide the subsistence of the workers. Labour, then, has the unique quality of producing more than its own value. The workers are exploited by the capitalists, for the capitalists appropriate part of the value produced by labour. This is the origin of profit.

The proposition that only labour produces value is not intended to mean that a man can produce anything with his bare hands. Marx insisted that equipment and

---

26. ibid., p. 751.
27. ibid., p. 748n.

materials (which he called *constant capital*) must always be in existence before production begins and that a fund for subsistence (*variable capital*) is necessary to maintain the workers until the product emerges. Unlike Adam Smith, who had been confused about the distinction between net and gross output, Marx insisted that labour reproduces the value of the materials and wear and tear used up in production. Net output is the value added by labour to the constant capital.

Nor does the proposition mean that the worker has a right to the whole value that he produces. This was the contention of naive Utopian socialists, whom Marx despised. If wages absorbed the whole net output, there could be no accumulation.

The statement that only labour produces value is metaphysical. Its only logical content is a definition: labour produces value and value is what labour produces. But this metaphysic is powerful and has several times shaken the world.

The rate of exploitation, which is the basis of the Marxian system of analysis, is not metaphysical. It is the ratio of net profit to wages in the economy as a whole. Although there are some problems of measurement,* this is a matter of fact, not of definition.

Marx expressed the rate of exploitation as the ratio of the surplus labour performed by the workers to the labour embodied in their wages. The worker spends part of the working day producing for himself—producing goods to be consumed as wages —and the rest working for the capitalist. In a modern industrial economy, of course, production is interlinked; it can be represented only in an overall scheme of inputs and outputs. No one alone produces anything. The division of the working day is a way of presenting the division of the whole net output of industry between wages and profits.

This way of presenting things was appropriate to the concept of exploitation. The capitalist was obliged to pay a wage per week that would more or less permit the worker to support his family, but then he would squeeze as much work out of him as he could by exacting the longest possible hours of work. The struggle of the workers' organizations to limit hours was a struggle to reduce the rate of exploitation.

In modern conditions in the industrial capitalist world, the 'value of labour power' can no longer be identified with a subsistence wage, but the concept of the rate of exploitation as the relationship between capitalists and workers in the process of production is no less relevant. It leads to a consideration of problems such as conditions of work, the alienation of the worker from the object of his work, the nature of technical progress and its effect on employment and production. Furthermore, it reveals that the exchange of commodities is a social phenomenon which cannot be explained only in terms of technical relationships. All this is independent of a theory of prices corresponding to labour values.

(b) Value and prices

Marx took over from Ricardo the concept of labour time as the measure of value but he also accepted the view that competition between capitalists tends to establish a

* See appendix.

uniform rate of profit on capital throughout a national economy. Then, how is the statement that only labour produces value to be applied to the determination of prices in money terms?

The labour theory of value, as a theory of the relative prices of commodities, operates on two levels. On one level, it links up with labour value in the metaphysical sense. Many Marxists to this day maintain that it is impossible to make use of the concept of exploitation or to support the cause of revolution without believing that, *in some sense*, the prices of commodities are determined by their labour values.

On the other level, it is merely a tool of analysis. If the prices of commodities were proportional to their values, then the share of profits and wages in the money value of net output would be the same in every line of production—the ratio of net profit to the wage bill would be the same for all commodities. The rate of profit on capital could be uniform only if the techniques in use were such that the ratio of the money value of capital to labour employed was the same in all industries.

In general, Marx assumed that the rate of profit will be uniform and the prices of particular commodities greater or less in proportion to their labour values, according to whether the ratio of capital to labour is higher or lower than the average in industry as a whole. This pattern of prices Marx called *prices of production*. The rate of exploitation determines the total amount of profit, and the prices of production distribute the total profit in such a way that the rate of profit on capital is equalized. Thus, the prices of commodities are not exactly proportional to labour values, but related to them in a systematic way.

However, as we shall find,* it is not so simple to work out the exact relation linking prices proportional to labour values with prices of production, in any particular case, and Marx sometimes set up numerical examples in terms of labour values when prices of production would have been more appropriate.

There has been a great deal of confusion about the so-called problem of the 'transformation of values into prices', but, once it is freed from its metaphysical associations, it turns out to be merely an analytical puzzle which, like all puzzles, ceases to be of interest once it has been solved.

(c) The capitalist epoch

The manner in which surplus is extracted constitutes the essential characteristic of the capitalist system. Under capitalism, those who control the means of production do not own a specific resource, as the feudal landlord owned land. Rather, they control the operations of industry by virtue of their command of finance. The power of the capitalist derives from financial wealth. Money is no longer merely a medium which facilitates the exchange of commodities. The accumulation of financial wealth becomes an end in itself. The production and sale of commodities is merely the vehicle for accumulation.

Furthermore, the competitive nature of capitalism is such that each capitalist

* See **2** 6 §3(d).

must continually increase his financial power if he is not to be overtaken and eventually eliminated by his rivals. Thus, the sole aim of the system is accumulation, and this is its motive power.

In his 'schema of expanded reproduction', Marx laid the foundation for what is nowadays called the theory of development, in terms of the relation of investment to consumption in a process of capital accumulation. He considered the influence of technical progress both on production and on the share of wages in the distribution of the product. He discussed the problem of effective demand in terms of the necessity for the capitalists to *realize* by sales the profits extracted from production; he linked this conception with an examination of the periodic crises of the trade cycle. His analysis was illustrated by massive historical research, leading to a diagnosis of the inherent contradictions in the capitalist system which were leading it to self-destruction. At last, the expropriators will be expropriated, Marx foresaw, and the workers will take over all that has been accumulated and begin to run the system for their own benefit.

Meanwhile, economics was becoming an academic profession. More soothing doctrines were required. Marx was totally rejected by orthodoxy and, along with him, the whole classical system from which he had drawn such disagreeable conclusions.

Appendix: Marx's notation

The flow of production taking place over, say, a year in an industrial economy can be regarded as comprising a quantity of specific goods, as a sum of value in terms of money, or as a sum of value in terms of labour time, i.e., as a number of man hours of work. (Marx measures value in quantities of *abstract* labour. An hour of skilled work produces more *value* than an hour of ordinary labour. This is a complication that we can avoid by setting out the argument in terms of a model in which all workers are alike.)

Goods are divided into the following categories: means of production, consumption of workers, and consumption of capitalists—I + II + III. Money values consist of amortization, corresponding to stocks used up and wear and tear of plant, the money-wage bill and the total net profit—$A + W + P$.

Marx writes the flow of production in quantities of labour time as $c + v + s$. 'Constant capital', c, represents that part of the pre-existing stock of means of production used up during the year (the labour value corresponding to A, amortization); 'variable capital', v, represents wages; and surplus, s, represents profits. Since the labour value of 'constant capital' is added to the flow of value being produced by labour this year, then subtracted from gross income, it follows that net income in terms of labour time, $v + s$, is equal to the number of man hours of work performed during the year.

To represent net income, $v + s$ or $W + P$, in physical terms, we must divide the year's output of means of production into two parts, Ia, the replacement required to keep the pre-existing stock intact, and Ib, physical net investment. The workers consume all of category II; profits in physical terms consist of Ib + III—net investment and capitalists' consumption.

The question which we have to examine is the meaning of the rate of exploitation, which plays the main part in Marxian analysis. In terms of labour value, it is s/v. How is this related to P/W? We must first consider the meaning of wages. In some contexts the wage means what the workers get, the category II goods; in other contexts it means what the capitalists pay. From the worker's viewpoint, the real wage depends on the purchasing power of his money wage over the goods that he buys. From the capitalist's viewpoint, the real cost of labour is the money wage divided by the price of the goods that he sells.

Thus, there are two sources of discrepancy between s/v and P/W. Evidently, v means what the workers get as a quantity of labour value, and W means what the capitalists pay as a sum of money.

When the ratio of net profit to wages (at the prices ruling) is the same, on average, in the three categories of goods, money values are proportional to labour values, and what the capitalists as a whole pay is equivalent to what the workers get, so that the discrepancies do not appear: s/v and P/W are the same ratio.

Marx habitually reckoned in terms of labour value, even when it was inappropriate to his own argument to do so; in any case, such niggling points were unimportant in his grand design. Nowadays, however, when the Marxian apparatus is used in discussing modern problems, we must pay attention to them.

The ratios are purely descriptive. Causal relations must be specified in terms of how the economy operates. First, consider the case where the economy operates in such a way that the real wage per man hour is a specific quantity of goods of category II. Then v corresponds to the labour value of these goods, and s represents the purchasing power of profits over labour time, i.e., money profits divided by the money-wage rate, which is the money price of the goods which constitute the real wage.

In money terms, W corresponds to the wage goods valued at ruling prices, and P corresponds to the goods that the capitalists enjoy, categories Ib and III, valued at the prices appropriate to them. When prices are not proportional to labour values, W and P have to be deflated by two different price indices: P/W is then a rather awkward concept, but s/v still has a clear meaning.

But when the real wage is not a specific quantity of goods, then P/W is the operative relationship; the labour value of the particular goods that workers buy has no clear causal significance. Moreover, when the real wage is much higher than some basic standard bundle of goods, there may be a large overlap between categories II and III. In such a case, it seems natural to identify P/W with the rate of exploitation. At the same time, it is necessary to keep in mind the distinction between W deflated by prices in general, including those of category I—the real cost of labour to the capitalists—and W deflated by the prices of category II—the real wage that workers get. What is important is to consider how the economy operates, rather than to dispute about different ways of naming the same relationships.

There is another difficulty in Marx's notation, which arises even when prices are proportional to labour values. He writes $\dfrac{s}{c + v}$ for the rate of profit on capital. This is not correct except in such a simple case as Ricardo's corn economy.* In general, c is not the stock of 'constant capital' but the materials used up and the wear and tear of plant over a year. We should write C for the stock and c for the annual flow. Similarly, v, the wage bill, is not the same as V, capital committed to the wage fund. Marx followed Ricardo in taking a turnover period of a year, so that the amount of the wage fund necessary to employ a man for a year is equal to the wage bill for a man year of work. But even then, it is not the same thing. The wage fund is a quantity of 'corn' in the barn after harvest, and the wage bill is a flow of payments over the year.

Suppose that the stock of means of production is 10 times the amount used in a year's production, and that the period of turnover of working capital is six months. Then,

$$C = 10c \quad \text{and} \quad V = \tfrac{1}{2}v$$

The rate of exploitation is s/v, the rate of profit on capital is $\dfrac{s}{C + V}$: what is the 'organic composition of capital' which Marx writes as c/v? The meaning of this concept is roughly the ratio to the labour time currently employed of the stock of capital, measured as 'labour embodied', i.e., the sum of all the labour time used in producing capital in the past. The nearest to a representation of what this means in

Marxian notation seems to be $\dfrac{C + V}{v}$.

With these adjustments, the Marxian apparatus provides an invaluable instrument for analysing capitalist production, distribution and accumulation, and it provides the basis for a powerful critique of neoclassical theory. Without readjustment, however, it is a plentiful source of confusion.

---

* See **1** 2 §3(a)

Chapter Three

The neoclassical era

In 1871, W. S. Jevons (1835–82) published in England his *Theory of Political Economy*, and in Austria Carl Menger (1840–1921) his *Grundsätze der Volkswirtschaftslehre*. Three years later, the *Eléments d'Economie Politique Pure* of Léon Walras (1834–1910) appeared in Lausanne. At the same time Alfred Marshall (1842–1924) was propounding ideas similar to those of Jevons, which he had evolved independently, though the first volume of his great treatise, the *Principles of Economics*, was not published until 1890.

Many later contributions, too numerous to mention, were made to the development of economics between 1870 and 1914. Knut Wicksell (1851–1926) developed ideas derived from the Austrian school. Walras' system was elaborated by Vilfredo Pareto (1848–1923), his successor as the professor of economics at Lausanne, who also made significant contributions to statistical theory; and ideas derived from both Marshall and Walras were elaborated by the American, Irving Fisher (1867–1947).

It was Alfred Marshall who dominated the teaching of economics in the English-speaking world until the great slump of the 'thirties, or even until the outbreak of war in 1939, but the neo-neoclassical revival of orthodoxy in the mid-twentieth century was based largely on conceptions derived from Walras.

1. Victory of the new school

There were many diversities among the writers who came to the fore in the eighteen seventies, but they all had certain fundamental characteristics in common. Within a few years, what became known as *Neoclassical* economics had replaced the classical concept of accumulation with an analysis of the equilibrium of supply and demand in a stationary state.

34   The basic ideas of the new school were not, in fact, new in 1870. Auguste Cournot

(1801–77), in his *Recherches sur les Principes Mathématiques de la Théorie des Richesses* (1838), had developed a theory of market behaviour which was, if anything, superior to the analysis of the later writers; and Heinrich Gossen (1810–58) had, in 1854, derived all the principles of individual utility maximization which were to form the basis of neoclassical analysis. But these ideas had not occupied a central position in economic thinking.

The sudden increase in popularity of new statements of similar ideas, made simultaneously in different parts of Europe, and the remarkable academic dominance which they achieved, can be explained by two factors. First, the failure of classical political economy to offer solutions for a number of purely theoretical problems, and second, the change in the political and ideological climate which made classical ideas appear not so much irrelevant, as dangerous.

Classical economists had not been able to work out a general statement of the theory of distribution and prices; they were obliged to fall back on an incomplete theory of value derived from 'labour embodied' with attendant qualifications and obfuscations which destroyed the persuasive simplicity of Ricardo.

Moreover, they had left unsolved the old puzzle of the relation of value in use to value in exchange. Adam Smith had pointed out the difference between use values and exchange values by means of the paradox of water and diamonds. Water is undoubtedly very useful, but its exchange value is very low. On the other hand, diamonds are not necessary to life, but their exchange value is very high. Commodities clearly must be useful if they are exchanged at all, but usefulness clearly does not determine exchange value. Adam Smith even suggested that use values and exchange values are inversely related.

However, it was not so much a weakness in pure theory as a change in the political climate, that brought the reign of the classics to an end. Classical doctrines, even in their most liberal form, emphasize the economic role of social classes and the conflicts of interest between them. In the late nineteenth century, the focus of social conflict had shifted from the antagonism of capitalist and landlord to the opposition of the workers to capitalists. Fear and horror aroused by the work of Marx were exacerbated by the impact throughout Europe of the Paris Commune of 1870. Doctrines which suggested conflict were no longer desirable. Theories which diverted attention from the antagonism of social classes met a ready welcome.

2. Fundamental ideas

In the new economics, the existence of social classes could not be entirely ignored but the main argument was concentrated on the position of the individual, and standards of judgement were framed in terms of individualism. The labour theory of value and the concept of exploitation arose from considering the conditions of production. The neoclassics switched attention to exchange and based a theory of the relative prices of commodities on the concept of *utility*. The class origin of income then dropped into the background, and the analysis was conducted in terms of individuals meeting in the market place.

(a) Utility

As a metaphysical concept, utility has to be defined in terms of itself. Utility is the characteristic of commodities which makes individuals want to buy them, and individuals buy commodities to enjoy utility in consuming them.

An individual comes to market with his income and disposes of it in such a way as to maximize utility. A consumer, obviously, does not spend all his income on one kind of commodity. If he is rational, he allocates his purchases in such a way that he cannot get any benefit from transferring a dollar from one commodity to another, i.e., he maximizes his total utility by equalizing the *marginal* utility (the increment of utility to be expected from a small increase in the amount purchased) of a dollar spent on each kind of commodity and of the expected utility from saving a dollar. (The argument is quite foolproof, for an individual who does not behave in this way is not rational.)

This argument explained the common observation that a sudden increase of any commodity brought to market—say, tomatoes—will generally lead to a fall in its price; and it solved the old puzzle of water and diamonds. The price of a commodity is governed by its *marginal utility*, not by its usefulness. Where water is in plentiful supply, its marginal utility is low; the marginal utility of diamonds is kept high by their scarcity.

This conception led to an awkward conclusion. Since the marginal utility of each commodity falls as more is purchased, the marginal utility of income as a whole must fall as an individual has more to spend. It follows that, as Marshall put it:

> [A] stronger incentive will be required to induce a person to pay a given price for anything if he is poor than if he is rich. A shilling is the measure of less pleasure, or satisfaction of any kind, to a rich man than a poor man.[1]

The moral seems to be in favour of egalitarianism. Wicksell proclaimed that the very concept of political economy implies a 'thoroughly revolutionary programme'.[2] But the neoclassics had not come forward to advocate revolution. A way out of the difficulty was suggested by F. Y. Edgeworth (1845–1926):

> Capacity for pleasure is a property of evolution, an essential attribute of civilization. The grace of life, the charm of courtesy and courage, which once at least distinguished rank, rank not unreasonably received the means to enjoy and to transmit. To lower classes was assigned the works of which they seemed most capable; the work of the higher classes being different in kind was not to be equated in severity . . . The aristocracy of sex is similarly grounded upon the supposed superior capacity of the man for happiness.[3]

1. *Principles of Economics* 8th edition, p. 19.
2. *Lectures on Political Economy*, Routledge, 1934 vol. 1, p. 4.
3. *Mathematical Psychics*, L.S.E., 1932 p. 77–8.

A more thoroughgoing answer to the egalitarian moral of utility was later offered by Pareto. He denied that utilities of different individuals can be added up, so that there is no meaning in saying that a rich man gets less utility from spending a dollar than a poor man does. Since there is no scientific proof that it would increase total utility to take a dollar from the rich man and give it to the poor, we may as well let the rich man keep it. Pareto held that 'pure science' knows nothing of moral judgement, but he did not object to using it as a defence of the *status quo*.

(b) Equilibrium

The central concern of classical political economy was accumulation; the neo-classics substituted equilibrium in a stationary state.

For Walras, there is a list of specified commodities to be traded, and particular amounts—in existence at any moment—of specified means of production. Each individual has an endowment of capacity to work, or of ownership of some machines or stocks of raw materials, or an area of cultivable land. There are known methods of production for each commodity. Everyone meets, and by a process of higgling and haggling in the market, the outputs and prices of all commodities are arrived at, and a position is found in which no individual can do better for himself by changing the amount of any commodity that he buys or by changing the use to which he puts labour or means of production.

Walras himself realized that it is not practicable to reach the equilibrium position by trial and error, but he imagined that buyers and sellers could proceed by shouting out demands and offers, finding the equilibrium set of outputs and prices before production and trade took place.

His modern followers seem to have given up pretending that this is possible, and content themselves with finding the conditions necessary to ensure that at least one position of equilibrium exists.[4]

Marshall used demand and supply in a much more robust manner. He argued that, in any market, at any moment, the amount bought of a particular commodity will generally be greater at a lower price (because of falling marginal utility), and the amount offered less, so that there is some equilibrium price at which the amount offered is equal to the amount bought.* The Walrasians objected to treating commodities 'one at a time', on the ground that the demand for any commodity must depend on the availability and price of all others. Marshall, however, used his method to trace out particular relations between groups of commodities or workers, such as *joint supply* and *composite demand*, in a manner that appeals to common sense. For instance, a rise in the demand for wheat is likely to be followed by an increase in the supply of straw, or a sharp rise in bricklayers' wages may cause unemployment for building labourers. The Walrasians can only say that everything depends on everything else, so that common sense has no room for manoeuvre.

4. See G. Debreu, 'A Social Equilibrium Existence Theorem', *Cowles Commission Papers*, new series, no. 46.
* See **2** 5 §6(a).

(c) Factors of production

In the Walrasian scheme, *factors of production* are concrete items in existence at a moment of time. They consist of a list of workers with particular types of skill or training; machines of particular productive capacities; land of special characteristics, and so on. Walras seems deliberately to slur over the distinction between income from work and income from property. All factors are free and equal in the market. Each factor receives a hire price for its services—wages for workers, and rentals for machines. Although the physical factors are all quite specific, they must be supposed to be versatile, for the technical conditions allow various combinations to be used to produce any one commodity. The essential point is that there is *substitution* between factors of production on the supply side, as well as substitution by consumers between commodities on the demand side.

Marshall analysed particular specialized factors in certain contexts, but he also made use of the broad categories—derived from Ricardo—of wages, rent, interest, and profits. In doing so, he ran into trouble over the concept of the supply of capital, which he chose to call 'waiting'.

(d) 'The reward of waiting'

Marshall set himself to reconcile the classical cost of production theory with the new concept of utility, so that he could say that prices are determined both by supply and by demand, as a piece of paper is cut with both blades of a pair of scissors. In doing so, he gave the classical concept of surplus a violent twist. The *real costs* of production consist of human efforts and sacrifices; the only surplus is the rents which are due to the 'free gifts of nature'.

Wages are the 'reward' of the efforts of workers, necessary to overcome the *disutility* of labour; interest is a 'reward' for undergoing the sacrifice of waiting. But what does 'waiting' mean?

> It matters not for our immediate purpose whether the power over the enjoyment for which the person waits, was earned by him directly by labour, which is the original source of nearly all enjoyment; or was acquired by him from others, by exchange or by inheritance, by legitimate trade or by unscrupulous forms of speculation, by spoilation or by fraud: the only points with which we are just now concerned are that the growth of wealth involves in general a deliberate waiting for a pleasure which a person has (rightly or wrongly) the power of commanding in the immediate present, and that his willingness so to wait depends on his habit of vividly realizing the future and providing for it.[5]

Thus 'waiting' is linked in the reader's mind with the virtue of thriftiness and the prudence of the good householder who saves part of his income to secure the future of his family, yet obviously the 'reward' of saving is to own more wealth. Interest is

5. *Principles* pp. 233–4.

the 'reward' of the wealth that a man already owns. One of the advantages of owning wealth is to be able to lend it at interest. To get interest in the future may be one of the motives for saving, but in the present, an owner of wealth receives interest on the whole amount that he owns, provided that he chooses to lend it. Waiting means owning wealth and the 'sacrifice' is not consuming it.

Thus, Marshall sought to rescue Ricardo from the taint of association with the ideas that Marx had derived from him, by showing that not only labour, but also 'waiting', produces value.

As we have seen, the Mercantilists were the champions of the overseas trader; the Physiocrats supported the landlords' interest; Adam Smith and Ricardo put their faith in the capitalist who makes profits in order to reinvest them and expand production. Marx turned their argument round to defend the workers. Now, Marshall came forward as the champion of the rentier—the owner of wealth who lends to the businessman and draws his income from interest on loans. Profit, in this context, was identified with interest, and interest was justified as the 'reward of waiting'.

But, as we shall see, Marshall was not able to hold this position consistently, and his whole analysis, though richly suggestive in detail, is confused and ambiguous in its general outline.

3. Prices and distribution

There is an important difference between the conceptions of Walras and Marshall. Walras begins his story with a stock of means of production already in existence; substitution of one 'factor' for another, in response to changes in price, can come about only by altering the combinations of physical items with each other. In Marshall, there is a fund of 'waiting' that can be embodied in various forms in response to changes in demand.

(a) Scarcity

The central topic of Walrasian analysis is the free play of competition in the market allocating the given 'factors' between the production of different commodities under the influence of consumer demand. The scarcity of resources relative to demand is the essential determinant of prices.

In support of the general use of the concept of scarcity, Walras attacked the classical distinction between scarce and produced commodities.

There are no products that can be multiplied without limit. All things which form part of social wealth—land, social faculties, capital goods proper and income goods of every kind—exist only in limited quantities. Of these things, land and personal faculties are natural wealth, while capital goods proper and income goods are artificial wealth, because they are products by virtue of having passed through a productive process. In the production of some things, like fruit, wild animals, surface ores and mineral waters, land services play the predominant part. In the

39

production of other things like legal and medical services, professors' lectures, songs and dances, labour predominates. In the production of most things, however, land services, labour and capital services are found together. It follows therefore that all things constituting social wealth consist of land and personal faculties or the products of the services of land and personal faculties. Now Mill admits that land exists in limited quantities only. If that is also true of human faculties how can products be multiplied without limit?[6]

Walras, here, misinterprets the classical position. It is not commodities as a whole that may be produced without limit, but any one commodity. The composition of the stock of means of production may be adjusted to any flow of output so as to equalize the rate of profit accruing to the capitalists. The presence of scarce means of production, such as land, merely reduces the surplus available for distribution as profits.

Moreover, the concept of produced means of production implies a process going on through time, rather than a static situation in which the amount of each 'factor' is taken as fixed. Walras tried to introduce accumulation into his model, but equilibrium in the market can be maintained, while saving goes on, only on the absurd hypothesis that each individual has correct foresight, not of his own life alone, but of the behaviour of all prices, over an indefinite future. In fact, Walras' scheme of ideas can be used only (if at all) for timeless comparisons of positions of equilibrium.

Marshall's scheme also emphasizes scarcity, but it is scarcity at a moment in history. To him, time and change were always present, and he was continually perplexed in trying to reconcile historical processes with a concept of equilibrium based on the mechanical analogy of a position of rest, established by a balance of the contrary forces of supply and demand.

(b) 'Marginal productivity'

The neoclassical theory of distribution was derived from an adaptation of Ricardo's theory of rent. The *marginal product* of a given amount of labour, cultivating a given area of land of uniform quality, is the amount of output that would be lost if a unit of labour were withdrawn. Competition of farmers for land, and of landlords for tenants, establishes the level of rents that induces farmers to deploy labour in such a way that marginal productivity is equalized over the whole cultivated area.* As total employment increases and the intensity of cultivation rises, the marginal product of labour falls and rents rise.

In Ricardo's scheme, taking a man year of work as the unit, the marginal product of labour is equal to the wage per man year plus the profit on the capital necessary to employ a man for a year. The neoclassicals tried to apply the notion of marginal productivity to each factor separately.

6. *Elements of Pure Economics* (translator, W. Jaffé) Allen and Unwin, 1965, p. 399.
* See **2** 1 §4(c).

In Walras, there is no marginal productivity of labour in general. Each group of factors of a particular type—say, men of particular skill, or machines of particular specification—receives a rental per unit determined by the marginal product of that group. Here, the marginal product of a factor means the amount of output that would be lost if one unit of it were withdrawn and the rest of all the factors rearranged appropriately. The argument is that, if a unit of any factor could be had for a rental less than the marginal product, more of that factor would be demanded; if the rental were greater than the marginal product, less would be demanded. Thus, the higgling and haggling of the market establishes an equilibrium in which each factor gets a rental for its services equal to the marginal productivity of the group to which it belongs.

In Wicksell's theory of distribution, workers and means of production are separate factors but all on the same footing, without regard to the difference in their social relationships. He sets up a model in which the levels of wages and rents would be the same whether a landowner hires labourers for a wage, or labourers hire land for rent.[7] Some of his modern followers extend this to the argument that the income of workers who could borrow capital and produce for themselves would be the same, in equilibrium, as the wages that they are paid when they are employed by capitalists.

Marshall applied the concept of marginal productivity differently. He depicted the careful businessman choosing how many workers to employ at a given wage rate. This must depend on the price of the product he has to sell, the cost of means of production that he is planning to use, and the rate of interest on finance that he borrows. Marshall enunciated the rule that the marginal *net* product of labour will be equated to the wage. Net product is the value of the increment of product expected from employing a man minus the additional expenses that would be involved in employing him.

> This doctrine has sometimes been put forward as a theory of wages. But there is no valid ground for any such pretension. The doctrine that the earnings of a worker tend to be equal to the net product of his work, has by itself no real meaning; since in order to estimate net product, we have to take for granted all the expenses of production of the commodity on which he works, other than his own wages.
>
> But though this objection is valid against a claim that it contains a theory of wages; it is not valid against a claim that the doctrine throws into clear light the action of one of the causes that govern wages.[8]

This doctrine, of course, is purely circular. It states that, when a businessman maximizes his profits in a particular market situation, he is combining various factors of production in such a way that he could not make more profit by combining them differently.

7. *Lectures* vol. I, p. 109.
8. *Principles* p. 518.

At the same time, Marshall paid a great deal of attention to the moral element in economic life, and made many pronouncements on the subject. For instance:

There are many fine natures among domestic servants. But those who live in very rich houses are apt to get self-indulgent habits, to overestimate the importance of wealth, and generally to put the lower aims of life above the higher, in a way that is not common with independent working people. The company in which the children of some of our best houses spend much of their time, is less ennobling than that of the average cottage. Yet in these very houses, no servant who is not specially qualified, is allowed to take charge of a young retriever or a young horse.[9]

Reflections such as these help to distract attention from the thin places in the analysis.

John Bates Clark (1847–1938) in the United States had none of Marshall's hesitations and reservations. He proclaimed the 'law of final productivity' which, under free competition, 'tends to give to labour what labour creates, to the capitalists what capital creates, and to entrepreneurs [businessmen] what the coordinating function creates.'[10]

There are some difficulties about the marginal productivity of capital (let alone the 'coordinating function'). Capital is embodied in 'capital goods'—produced means of production such as machinery. Now, equipment embodies the technology which makes labour productive. How are we to find a separate productivity for capital goods? Moreover, interest is not paid to machinery but to owners of wealth who have lent money to businessmen. What is the relation between loans of money and the assumed 'productive function' of 'capital goods'? The analysis was not at all clear but the metaphysic was pleasantly soothing.

(c) Normal profits

Along with the analysis of equilibrium, there is a dynamic element in Marshall's view of the world. He introduced the invaluable distinction between short- and long-period effects of any change.* He can best be understood if we think of an economy rolling along through time with accumulation and technical progress going on. Here, the hero is no longer the thrifty rentier but the energetic businessman who makes innovations and takes risks. As accumulation proceeds, there is a steady mean level of profits in the growing economy, while short-period perturbations continually take place around the mean.

Investment plans are made in the light of expected future profits; as soon as finance is sunk in a particular piece of equipment, the returns that it actually receives depend on demand for the product to which it contributes. Gross profits are called *quasi-rents* because, once installed, a piece of equipment is fixed like an area of Ricardian land. When everything is working out *normally*, the quasi-rents received

9. ibid., p. 207, note 2.
10. *The Distribution of Wealth*, Macmillan, 1899. p. 3.
* See **2** 3 §1 and **2** 6 §1.

by a plant over its life are sufficient to recover the capital invested in it, along with a *normal rate* of net profit on the cost of the investment. Normality, however, is not guaranteed. In any particular case, net profits may be above or below the normal rate.

There is no explanation of what determines the normal rate of profit, though in some passages, it seems to be identified with the long-term rate of interest, which, in another context, is the 'reward of waiting'.

Marshall was anxious to bring an element of supply and demand into the story of a growing economy. He did so by dividing all commodities into two types: the first 'obeys the law of diminishing returns', for it requires some particular scarce factor of production so that, as for Ricardo's corn, 'cost at the margin' rises as output expands. The second type 'obeys the law of increasing returns'; capital accumulation, economies of large-scale operation, and technical progress bring about a fall in its costs, relative to the general level. As total output expands, prices of commodities of the first type rise, while those of the second type fall. Since the growth of demand determines how much the output of each commodity expands, there is work for both blades of the supply and demand scissors, but Marshall himself knew that he was fudging when he tried to squeeze these conceptions into the frame of equilibrium in a stationary state.[11]

4. Effective demand

The problem of effective demand was buried with Ricardo's victory over Malthus, and the neoclassicals saw no cause to resuscitate it.

In Walras, 'market-clearing prices' ensure that all that is produced is sold. When the supply of a particular commodity is in excess of demand, however low the price, its price falls to zero—it becomes a free good. This rule applies also to labour. In a position of equilibrium, enough workers must have died off, at any time in the past when wages were zero, to make the remainder sufficiently scarce today to command a living wage.

Marshall endorsed J. S. Mill's view of Say's law* but he also offered an explanation of equilibrium in terms of supply and demand, both for labour and for saving.

He seems to maintain—though it is all vague and hazy—that unemployment may be due to real wages being too high, and that a remedy could be found by cutting money–wage rates.[12] There is a still more hazy suggestion that the level of interest rates moves up and down in such a way as to equate the amount of saving, regarded as a supply of real investible resources, with the amount of investment that businessmen want to undertake.[13]

Marshall allows that a slump may be caused by a lack of confidence on the part

11. *Principles*, appendix H.
* See **1** 2 §4(a).
12. *Principles* p. 710.
13. ibid., p. 534.

of businessmen in the future profitability of investment,[14] but this suggestion is not allowed to disturb the general picture of equilibrium under the beneficent sway of Say's law.

The problem of the trade cycle was relegated to a separate volume and a separate course of lectures, under the title of 'money'. This compartment was dominated by the *Quantity Theory* which elaborated Hume's notion of how an increase in the stock of cash affects the price level. This was done by adding the concept of the *velocity of circulation*, that is, the average number of times that a piece of money enters into transactions during a year.

Marshall made many pronouncements on current problems, notably in the form of evidence before Royal Commissions, but he kept postponing his treatment of the problem of employment, perhaps because he could not reconcile his knowledge of the facts of economic life with his theory of equilibrium. His last volume, *Money, Credit and Commerce*, completed at the age of eighty, 'is merely pieced together from earlier fragments, some of them written fifty years before'.[15]

Wicksell was a very different character from Marshall. He eschewed fudging; when he came to questions that he could not answer, he frankly admitted that he was baffled. In trying to develop a coherent theory of the rate of interest, he abandoned 'marginal productivity' and prepared the way for the new wave now generally known as the Keynesian revolution.

5. Critics

During the reign of neoclassical orthodoxy, there was no lack of criticism from Marxists, socialists of various views, and dissidents within the fold. Here, we mention three outstanding critics whose views, in one way or another, are relevant to our central theme.

(a) A Marxist

Most Marxists, even today, are content to mock at academic economics without bothering to understand what it is trying to say. Nikolai Bukharin (1880–1938), writing in exile before the Russian Revolution, made a systematic study of the Austrian school in order to diagnose its social basis.

He called the work of this school *The Economic Theory of the Leisure Class* because it looks at all problems from the viewpoint of the rentier, who is not involved in production but merely in consuming the fruits of the labour of others.

The Marxian theory of value, Bukharin argued, is based on the objective facts of the process of production, while the bourgeois theory of value is derived from subjective 'utility' and consumer taste. The bourgeois economists lack a conception of history, they purport to find universal 'laws' that apply as much to Robinson

14. ibid., p. 711.
15. Keynes, *Essays in Biography. The Collected Writings of John Maynard Keynes* vol. X, p. 230.

Crusoe on his island as to modern monopolistic capitalism, and they begin from a study of consumption instead of the conditions of production.

> Everywhere we encounter the same motive: the theory of value is used as a theoretical starting point in order to justify the modern order of society; in this lies the 'social value' of the theory of marginal utility for those classes which have an interest in maintaining this social order. The weaker the logical foundations of this theory, the stronger is one's psychological attachment to it, since one does not wish to desert the narrow mental sphere defined by the static conception of capitalism.[16]

(b) A populist

In the United States, Thorstein Veblen (1857–1929) kept up a stream of criticism from within the academic fold. He attacked the ideology which reduces all human relations to commercial terms:

> The current economic situation is a price system. Economic institutions in the modern civilized scheme of life are (prevailingly) institutions of the price system. The accountancy to which all phenomena of modern economic life are amenable is an accountancy in terms of price; and by the current convention there is no other recognized scheme of accountancy, no other rating, either in law or in fact, to which the facts of modern life are held amenable. Indeed, so great and pervading a force has this habit (institution) of pecuniary accountancy become that it extends, often as a matter of course, to many facts which properly have no pecuniary bearing and no pecuniary magnitude, as, e.g., works of art, science, scholarship, and religion.[17]

Veblen many times exposed the shoddy logic with which the ideology was supported. The following is from a review of a book in which J. B. Clark further developed the theory referred to above.*

> Here, as elsewhere in Mr Clark's writings, much is made of the doctrine that the two facts of 'capital' and 'capital goods' are conceptually distinct, though substantially identical. The two terms cover virtually the same facts as would be covered by the terms 'pecuniary capital' and 'industrial equipment'. . . .
>
> This conception of capital, as a physically 'abiding entity' constituted by the succession of productive goods that make up the industrial equipment, breaks down in Mr Clark's own use of it when he comes to speak of the mobility of capital; that is to say, so soon as he makes use of it. . . .
>
> The continuum in which the 'abiding entity' of capital resides is a continuity of ownership, not a physical fact. The continuity, in fact, is of an immaterial nature,

16. *Economic Theory of the Leisure Class*, Martin Lawrence, 1927, p. 156.
17. *The Place of Science in Modern Civilization, and Other Essays*, Viking Press, 1919, p. 245.
* See **1** 3 §3(b).

a matter of legal rights, of contract, of purchase and sale. Just why this patent state of the case is overlooked, as it somewhat elaborately is, is not easily seen. But it is plain that, if the concept of capital were elaborated from observation of current business practice, it would be found that 'capital' is a pecuniary fact, not a mechanical one; that it is an outcome of a valuation, depending immediately on the state of mind of the valuers; and that the specific marks of capital, by which it is distinguishable from other facts, are of an immaterial character.[18]

Veblen could make no headway against neoclassical metaphysics, and his protest has been swept aside in the main stream of American economic teaching.

(c) Marx upside down

Joseph Schumpeter (1883–1950) was a critic of orthodoxy from a peculiar viewpoint of his own. He was much enamoured of capitalist enterprise, and maintained that orthodox static analysis does not bring out its true character.

His major work was devoted to an historical study of the trade cycle. In this field he made many penetrating observations but failed to provide a systematic analysis, such as that developed by Keynes, of the principle of effective demand.

As a student in Vienna, Schumpeter penetrated deeply into Marxist thought from an anti-Marxist standpoint. His picture of the turbulent, dynamic growth of capitalism, in which technical progress springs from the competitive struggle to accumulate, is very close to Marx's analysis though very far from his ideology.

Despite his contempt for static theory, Schumpeter had a high opinion of Walras and gave him the central place in his *History of Economic Analysis*.

He spent the greater part of his professional life in the United States but his erratic genius did not fit the requirements of neoclassical orthodoxy. Like Veblen, he has left little trace in modern teaching.

6. The Keynesian revolution

The flimsy intellectual structure of neoclassical theory could appear to stand up because little practical weight was put on it. The doctrine of the beneficent influence of competition in a free market meant, in effect: businessmen know best. Since any interference by government, however well meant, was held to do harm, theory led to no recommendations for action. It did not really matter whether theory made sense or not.

(a) Laissez-faire

For Adam Smith, *laissez-faire* was a programme—he predicted that if restrictive laws designed to protect particular interests were abolished, and private enterprise given

46   18. ibid., pp. 195–7.

free play, then the wealth of the nation would greatly increase. For the neoclassicals, *laissez-faire* became a dogma, and the benefits of free trade an article of faith. Economics was described as the study of the allocation of scarce resources between alternative uses, and the moral to be drawn from it was that free enterprise will allocate resources in the manner most beneficial to the whole society, provided that the government does not interfere with its operation.

Marshall's devoted disciple, A. C. Pigou (1877–1959), distilled from the *Principles* an apparently coherent logical system in terms of comparisons of positions of stationary equilibrium, eschewing the dynamic element in Marshall's thought. In *The Economics of Welfare*, Pigou described a number of cases in which *laissez-faire* is not necessarily beneficial, but he treated them as exceptions to a rule which, in general, could not be questioned.

In public policy, there were necessarily many departures from the pure doctrine of *laissez-faire*, notably the introduction of the principle of social insurance by the Liberal Government of 1906, from which was developed the payment of unemployment allowances. But, in the main, the teaching of orthodox economists and the beliefs that influenced policy were in line with each other.

Side by side with the equilibrium theory which purported to deal with real values, there was a theory of the price level in terms of money, regulated by the quantity of the medium of exchange created by government and the banking system.* There were discussions of the trade cycle, inflation, and financial crises which implied that these arose from faults in the monetary system. But this did not impinge on the main body of doctrine. In the great slump, when there was massive unemployment in all the industrial countries, economists were still maintaining that a free market tends to establish equilibrium and that interference with its delicate mechanism can only do harm.

In 1929, in Great Britain, Lloyd George's proposal to relieve unemployment by expenditure on public works was answered by the 'Treasury view' that there is a certain amount of saving that will be invested in any case, so that if the government borrows some for public works, other investment will be reduced to an equal extent.†

Unemployment allowances, contemptuously known as 'the dole', were widely held to be deleterious because they supported the foolish obstinacy of the trade unions in preventing wages from falling to the equilibrium level. If only wage rates could be cut, equilibrium would be restored.

During the British financial crisis of 1931, the hapless Labour Government was threatened by the Governor of the Bank of England, at the instigation of American financiers, that if unemployment allowances were not cut, overseas loans to maintain the gold value of sterling would not be forthcoming.[19] (The so-called National Government that was formed to save sterling was fortunately unable to do so.)

From the total bankruptcy of orthodox theory confronted with the slump, a new

* See **1** 3 §4.
† See **2** 3 §2(a)
19. See Henry Clay, *Lord Norman* p. 392.

wave emerged. Gunnar Myrdal in Sweden, who followed the lead of Wicksell, Michal Kalecki in Poland, and Maynard Keynes in England, working independently of each other, found a new diagnosis of the instability of capitalism.[20] This movement became known as the Keynesian Revolution, for Keynes was the most eloquent and famous of its expositors, though the version provided by Kalecki was, in some ways, more logically coherent than his.

(b) Time

The situation in which the private-enterprise system had evidently broken down was incompatible with the orthodox assumptions. The basic fallacy in the orthodox system was the belief that a market economy always tends to reach equilibrium, like a pendulum which, while swinging to and fro, always approaches a position of rest. The analogy is false. A movement in space may go to and fro, but a movement through time goes only one way, from the past into the future. Human life has to be conducted without 'correct foresight'; economic behaviour is governed either by guesswork about the future consequences of action taken today, by notions of proper behaviour derived from convention, or from the lessons of past experience, which may turn out to be deceptive.

In the slump, conventions had broken down, expectations had nothing to go on, and there was no prospect of an automatic recovery.

Myrdal had long since understood the ideological function of the concept of equilibrium.[21] Kalecki's analysis was founded on the dynamics of the Marxian scheme of reproduction.* But Keynes had a 'long struggle to escape' from the tradition in which he had been brought up.[22] For this very reason, he saw clearly that to recognize that the future is unknown brings down the whole structure of the orthodox theory based on the concept of timeless equilibrium.

In the controversy that broke out after the publication of the *General Theory*, Keynes restated what he thought to be the essential point of the innovation that he was making in economic analysis.

> [His contemporaries] like their predecessors, were still dealing with a system in which the amount of the factors employed was given and the other relevant facts were known more or less for certain. This does not mean that they were dealing with a system in which change was ruled out, or even one in which the disappointment of expectation was ruled out. But, at any given time, facts and expectations were assumed to be given in a definite and calculable form, and risks, of which,

---

20. Myrdal's *Monetary Equilibrium* was published in Swedish in 1931 (English edition, 1939). Translations of Kalecki's early Polish articles are reprinted in *Selected Essays in the Dynamics of the Capital Economy 1933–1970*. Keynes's *General Theory of Employment, Interest and Money* was published in 1936, though the ideas that went into it were developed from 1929 onwards.
21. See *The Political Element in the Development of Economic Theory*. Published in German, 1932, English translation, 1939.
* See **1** 2 §5(c).
22. See *General Theory of Employment, Interest and Money, Collected Writings* vol. VII, p. viii.

though admitted, not much notice was taken, were supposed to be capable of exact actuarial computation. The calculus of probability, though kept in the background, was supposed to be capable of reducing uncertainty to the same calculable status as that of certainty itself; just as in the Benthamite calculus of pains and pleasures or advantage and disadvantage, by which the Benthamite philosophy assumed men to be influenced in their general ethical behaviour.

Keynes observed that, since the future is uncertain, strictly rational behaviour is impossible. The conventions that guide decisions are

pretty, polite techniques, made for a well-panelled board room and a nicely regulated market. . . . I accuse the classical economic theory of being itself one of these pretty, polite techniques which tries to deal with the present by abstracting from the fact that we know very little about the future.[23]

Keynes called his orthodox contemporaries 'classical' for he drew no distinction between classics and neoclassics. To him, Ricardo was just as bad as Pigou, because he did not allow for the possibility of a deficiency of effective demand. Keynes tried to find predecessors among Malthus and the Mercantilists, but somehow overlooked James Steuart who would really have suited him better.*

(c) Prices

Keynes had been a pupil of Marshall. He was never in any way influenced by Walrasian static notions of general equilibrium. He broke up that fragile shell without noticing that he had done so. Inheriting from Marshall the conception of short-period equilibrium at a moment of time, he took it for granted that prices of particular commodities are determined by prime costs—wages, cost of materials, power, etc.—with some kind of allowance for overhead expenses. This theory was more precisely formulated by Kalecki in the concept of a mark-up over prime cost related to the 'degree of monopoly' in the market.†

Since wages are the main element in prime costs (including the costs of materials that one firm sells to another), it follows that changes in money–wage rates will bring about corresponding changes in the level of prices. This leaves no room for either 'marginal productivity' to determine real-wage rates or for the quantity of money to determine prices.

In some ways, the most important aspect of the Keynesian revolution was the recognition that, in a modern industrial economy, the general level of prices at any phase of technical development depends mainly on the level of money–wage rates. At the time, it showed that cutting wages is not a remedy for unemployment because it would cause prices to fall more or less in proportion to the reduction in costs.

23. 'The General Theory of Employment', *Quarterly Journal of Economics*, February 1937, reprinted in *Collected Writings* vol. XIV, pp. 112–113, and 115.
* See **1** 1 §1(c).
† See **2** 5 §4(c).

Nowadays, it provides the clue to the problem of inflation, though the authorities have taken a long time to grasp it.*

(d) Savings and investment

Orthodoxy was based on a version of Say's law according to which the volume of saving determines the rate of investment. Keynes pointed out that the amount of saving cannot be independent of the amount of investment (expenditure on adding to equipment and stocks). The level of saving varies with the level of income. When there is unemployment of labour and under-utilization of productive capacity, an increase in outlay on investment would increase income, and so increase both expenditure for consumption and saving. An increment of income that is not saved by its recipient is spent; spending increases incomes, therefore incomes go on increasing up to the point at which the addition to saving is equal to the addition that has taken place in investment.†

Uncertainty about the future provides the clue to fluctuations in activity in a private-enterprise economy. Expenditure out of income is for more or less immediate consumption but expenditure on investment depends on expectations of profits over a long future. A slump is a situation of self-fulfilling pessimism in which profits are low because investment is at a low level because profits are expected to be low.

The old puzzle of effective demand that preoccupied the Mercantilists and Malthus had been driven underground by Say's law; it now came to the surface in a violent eruption.

(e) The rate of interest

The analysis of the dependence of the level of income, given productive capacity, on expenditure for investment and consumption knocked out the theory that it was the function of the rate of interest to establish the equality of savings with investment. (Keynes did not deny that the level of the rate of interest may influence the amount of household saving out of a given income, but he considered this effect unimportant and left it out of his analysis to simplify exposition.)

Since the old theory had gone, it was necessary to offer an alternative. Keynes first cleared up the confusion in the old writings between interest and profits. Profit is what a firm is hoping to get from an investment, and interest is what it has to pay on a loan. Secondly, he observed that we must look for the determination of the level of interest rates, not to the flow of saving, but to the whole stock of wealth in existence at any moment and to the demand and supply of the stock of money.

Keynes divided the demand to hold money into two parts. There are balances required by individuals and institutions for convenience in carrying out transactions; in this sphere, the demand for money depends on much the same relationships as

---

* See **2** 7 §4(b).
† See **2** 3 §2(b).

in the quantity theory—the total volume of transactions in terms of money and the average interval between payments that determine the 'velocity of circulation' of money.*

There is also a demand for money as a form in which wealth can be held. Keynes asked why should anyone hold money in the form of cash or deposits that yield no interest, when he might be getting a return by holding securities? He found an answer in the concept of the desire for liquidity—the assurance that an individual needs of being able to 'touch his money' when he wants it. Interest is foregone for the sake of the liquidity provided by a holding of ready money.†

The need for liquidity, like the instability of investment, arises from the uncertainty of the future. Indeed, in a world of 'correct foresight', no one would have any need to hold money.

Keynes elaborated the theory of the rate of interest—and attached great import-ance to it—while Kalecki was content merely to take for granted that an increase in investment, income, and saving requires an increase in the quantity of money; if an adequate increase is not provided by the banking system, rates of interest will rise.

(f) Revolution and restoration

The change from the old orthodoxy brought about by the Keynesian revolution was, first and foremost, a descent from timeless equilibrium to the world in which we are living here and now. Secondly, the old dichotomy between 'money' and the real economy was broken down. The monetary system is seen as part of the operation of the whole economy. It has an important influence on the level of interest rates, but only a remote and roundabout relation to the level of prices.

There is nothing to guarantee continuous full employment when the private-enterprise system is left to itself, but it is possible by means of government policy to control or, at least, mitigate fluctuations in activity.

The experience of super-full employment in wartime converted public opinion to Keynes' views but, after the war, academic orthodoxy succeeded in re-establishing itself. The argument now was that the authorities have a duty to maintain the level of effective demand to provide full employment. Then there is nothing else that the authorities should do. *Laissez-faire* came into its own again. Economic theory returned to elaborating the properties of Walrasian equilibrium.

This new orthodoxy, in its turn, has now come to a crisis. Twenty-five years of near-full employment have left too many problems unsolved, and too many weak points in the neo-neoclassical logic have been exposed. It is time to go back to the beginning and start again.

---

* See **1** 3 §4.
† See **2** 8 §1(f).

Book Two

Analysis

Introduction

This text is called an introduction to modern economics because its aim is to draw from traditional and contemporary teaching of the subject those elements which may contribute to an understanding of modern problems. This is an ambitious and exacting task which lays demands on the reader no less than the authors. Moreover, it is a task that can never be completely accomplished because, especially in this age of rapid change, fresh problems are continually thrown up by history, and old conclusions questioned anew. All the same, we hope to show that the method of argument and the way of looking at the world that can be derived from a reinterpretation of economic teaching is useful, indeed indispensable, for understanding the world that we live in today.

1. Method
(a) Models

The doctrines, interpretations, and theories that make up the tradition of economic teaching are developed and expounded by a method of analysis peculiar to the subject. The method is to select from the flux of history (including the present as history) entitles such as commodities, prices, monetary units, cultivable land, productive equipment, employers, workers, and owners of wealth, specify the economic environment in which they are to interact, and set them up in a *model* in which their interactions are worked out by a kind of quasi-mathematical logic.

A model represents an hypothesis about reality. In the natural sciences, hypotheses can be tested by evidence drawn from experience. But an hypothesis about society cannot be tested, in the manner of the well-developed sciences, by controlled experiments in a laboratory, or by exact observation of unchanging regularities in nature. Economics has to rely on the experiments thrown up by events, and these experiments are not controlled; too many things are happening at once. If the predictions of a model turn out to be more or less correct, it may be by accident. The reasoning that led to the prediction is not necessarily vindicated by the result. If the predictions turn out to be wrong, it is hard to know in what respect the model was at fault, or concrete analysis based on it erroneous. The relations between a model and the reality it hopes to reflect are never clear-cut and are always subject to a variety of interpretations.

For this reason, economics as an academic subject lacks the intellectual discipline of the natural sciences; bad habits are difficult to eliminate from traditional teaching, and indeed, certain bad habits have displayed remarkable persistence. One such is to set up hypotheses that have no conceivable relation to reality and then to elaborate arguments in terms of them, to obtain 'results' and 'problems', all in a completely circular system of ideas. An example of this is to work out the behaviour of a market economy in which individuals have 'correct foresight' about an indefinitely long future, or to study the problems of international trade in a world in which imports and exports of each country are always in balance.

This is merely an idle amusement. More serious is the habit of making a model that pretends to represent reality, though in a highly simplified form, deducing conclusions from it and then using it to recommend policy, without first checking on how far the simplified assumptions correspond to the situation in which policy will operate. The most famous example of this was the neoclassical model of a perfectly competitive private-enterprise economy which operates in such a way as to secure full employment of the available labour force, provided that there is no interference with the free play of the market mechanism. From this, was derived the diagnosis that the massive unemployment of the 'thirties could be due only to wages being kept above the 'equilibrium level' by trade unions acting as monopolists. Then followed conclusions such as that unemployment insurance tended to increase unemployment and that government expenditure intended to create employment would actually reduce it.

Yet, we cannot get on without making models, and models must be simplified. A map at the scale of 1:1 is of no use to a traveller. The art of setting up models is to cut out all complications inessential to the point at issue, without eliminating the features necessary for safe guidance.

The most essential element to include in any piece of analysis is an indication of the nature of the social system to which it is applied. Economic relationships are relationships between people. Technical relationships—between mankind and the physical universe—set the conditions within which economic life is carried on, and while the level of technical development of a human society (or an animal society, for that matter) has an important influence on relationships within it, technical conditions do not determine them completely. For instance, at present, industries of much the same technology are operating in a variety of capitalist and socialist forms of organization.

At the same time, relations between people in an economy have an important influence on the kind of technology that it develops. For example, a society of independent peasant families would not adopt the methods of cultivation used by large-scale capitalist farmers employing wage labour.

The interaction between human and technological relationships is the subject matter of economic analysis.

The characteristics of a society which are relevant to its economic structure are reflected in legal rules and habits and in accepted notions of proper behaviour. They are concerned, that is to say, with who has power to do what, how power is to be exercised, and in what way the behaviour of one element in society reacts on others.

The following chapters are mainly devoted to modern industrial capitalism but the nature of that society is shown in contrast with other types of social organization.

We do not intend to offer a scheme of universal 'laws', but we hope to provide a first beginning of insight into the manner in which economic systems operate and the elements of analytical methods for discussing the problems to which they give rise.

(b) Simplifications

There is no aspect of economic life that is not extremely complicated and diverse. Insight into the technical or the human aspects of the operation of an economy cannot be gained through the thick fog of variegated detail which covers it in concrete reality. The method of analysis is to skin off all the details and expose the mechanism of the system in a simplified form. In what follows, we pursue this method in an extremely drastic manner. For instance, in the first three chapters we rule out all problems of relative prices and patterns of demand by working with a model in which there is only a single, uniform consumption good. When we are discussing agriculture, we abstract from variations in the weather. We assume that all workers are alike, and abstract from the difference between men and women. The object of the exercise is to display relationships that are important in reality, though in reality they are overlaid with intricate complications. Before any conclusion from such an argument can be applied to reality, the relevant details have to be put back. Here, we offer only the first stage of analysis. Much deeper study is needed before the reader will be able to judge what details he must take into account in applying the argument to particular cases.

Meanwhile, it is important that he should have proper warning as to what details have been left out. The requirements of fair play between authors and readers are that, as each model is displayed, the simplifications to be made are clearly set out, the entities entering into the argument are specified, and no quantities are referred to without indicating the units in which they are reckoned. The reader has every right to be on guard, to see that the rules of the game are not violated, but he must not demand ready-made conclusions. When he has mastered the art of analysis for himself, he can correct or elaborate any part of the argument which seems to him unsatisfactory.

55

The method that we shall pursue is to set up the simplest possible model and make use of it to illustrate all the relations that it is capable of showing, pointing out the problems that have been excluded as we go along. When we have got all we can out of the simplest model, we introduce another more complicated one and so build the argument from stage to stage.

The argument is illustrated by simple numerical examples and some diagrams. Numbers have been chosen in such a way that there is no possible danger of mistaking them for statistics of an actual economy. They are offered solely to help the reader to grasp some essential relationships in the simplest possible way. At the same time, the examples are not intended to carry him away from reality; no relationships are exhibited which are not important in principle in the operation of actual economies. The examples are imaginary, but they are simplifications of reality, not parables or fairy tales.

(c) Warnings

Our argument is in post-Keynesian terms. That is to say, we treat economic life as a process going on through time, in which the future is not known in advance. We also offer, in a section at the end of each chapter, a brief account of the corresponding pre-Keynesian equilibrium theory so that the reader can see in what respect our treatment of each topic differs from that which he may have met with elsewhere, and to warn him against some confusions of thought which are, unfortunately, prevalent in current teaching.

Some teachers, no doubt, will regard these sections as a caricature, and protest that this is not what they have ever believed. If so, so much the better.

2. Synopsis

Chapter 1, *Land and labour*, deals with those relationships that can be exhibited in terms of the simplest possible type of production. The technical relationships here involve, first, the effect on output per unit of work of the availability of cultivable land, and second, the necessity of stock for production that takes time. The social relationships are displayed in terms of various types of property in land.

We begin with an imaginary situation in which families are free to cultivate as much land as they please, then we discuss peasant proprietors with holdings of various sizes, and tenants of feudal landlords. Finally, we set out Ricardo's model of capitalist agriculture and explore its implications.

A section of diagrams introduces this method of exposition, showing its uses and limitations.

Chapter 2, *Men and machines*, sets up a model for industrial production. Here, the technical conditions are extremely simplified, preparing the way for a discussion of the social relations of a society consisting of capitalists and workers. An appendix deals with working capital.

Chapter 3, *Effective demand*, covers the ground of what is known as Keynes' theory, though we are following the version introduced by Michal Kalecki. The flows of production and income in the simple model are exhibited. Then, the structure of the system is examined by comparisons between situations which are alike except in one respect—say, a difference in the rate of investment or in the share of wages in the value of output. Finally, the effect of a process of change in a particular situation is examined and a preliminary sketch of the fluctuations of employment in a private-enterprise economy is set out. The appendix gives an example of fluctuations in output due to changing expectations of profit.

Chapter 4, *Technical change*, introduces innovations and accumulation in an industrial economy, still within the limitations of the simple model. We discuss the nature of so-called technological unemployment, the interaction between rising productivity and rising real wages, the meaning of obsolescence and amortization, and the relation of inventions to accumulation. Section 3, concerned with the meaning of neutral and biased accumulation, is somewhat formalistic and can be omitted at a first reading.

Chapter 5, *Commodities and prices*, departs from the simple model and introduces complex quantities such as output and consumption. This chapter covers a large part of what is usually called micro-economics. Markets for commodities are divided into two main types: those where supply and demand rules, and those where prices are formed by a mark-up on prime costs.

The first type is discussed in relation to dealings in primary commodities. Here, prices are usually fluctuating under the influence of changes in demand and supply and of the consequent reactions on expectations. Though the Marshallian analysis of markets is applicable in this context, there is no tendency for equilibrium to be established.

In the other type of market, prices are fairly stable in relation to changes in demand, while output varies. A brief discussion of the interaction between the two types follows. A section of diagrams shows the use and misuse of the familiar Marshallian picture of the equilibrium between supply and demand.

Chapter 6, *Rates of profit*, discusses prices from a long-period standpoint. Here, the argument is necessarily more difficult than what has gone before, because it cannot be made precise. 'The rate of profit on capital' is an important concept, both for economic theory and for business practice, but in reality there is no such thing as an exact ratio between net profit and value of capital.

Before an investment has been made, the cost of capital can be reckoned as a sum of money, but profit is then an uncertain and subjective expectation about the future. When finance has been committed to physical productive capacity, profit is accruing as sums of money but the capital has then ceased to be a sum of money, and there is no clear and unambiguous meaning to be given to its value. The rate of profit is the ratio between profit per annum and the value of capital, but the two elements in the ratio do not coexist at any one time.

In the first part of the chapter, we discuss the relation of prices to profits in a   **57** general way which, in the nature of the case, cannot be precise. We then set up an artificial model of a steady state, in which the rate of profit can be given a clear meaning, in order to discuss its role in economic theory. Having isolated some relationships with the aid of this model, we claim that they throw light on the operation of an industrial economy, though a great deal of work remains to be done in the gap between the conclusions of theory and the analysis of complicated and changing reality. Section 3, with the appendix, can be omitted at a first reading.

Chapter 7, *Incomes and demand*, turns from the earlier examination of prices and distribution from the viewpoint of the producer, to take up the standpoint of the consumer; it considers some aspects of the distribution of personal income and the subjective elements in demand. Unfortunately, the analysis of consumer demand has been so long trapped in a circular argument in terms of 'utility' and 'preferences' that economic theory has little to say about it.

The goods and services that households buy represent only part of their consumption. The rest is provided by public authorities empowered to levy taxes. The subject of 'public finance' has been an important part of political economy from the earliest times. In modern texbooks, public finance, like the 'theory of demand', is generally treated in highly conventional terms. Here, we suggest a point of view that brings it into the scope of post-Keynesian analysis. An appendix defines the relationship of accounting identities to causal equations.

Chapter 8, *Money and finance*, covers what is usually called monetary theory. This is a highly specialized branch of study. Here, we analyse the principles underlying modern monetary systems and policy, without going into all the intricacies of particular institutions and particular regulations, which vary from one country to another and in which some details are frequently altered.

We discuss the main principles of banking, the relations of the Stock Exchange to industry, the determination of interest rates (though this is treated only in outline) and the limitations of monetary policy as a means of controlling industrial activity.

Chapter 9, *Growth: firms, industries, and nations,* follows the suggestion made in earlier chapters that the mainspring of growth in a capitalist economy is the search for profits by business. From the seventeenth century or even before, growth of European economies was partly overseas. From one point of view, the whole world may be regarded as a market in which competitive expansion and accumulation can take place. From another viewpoint, the existence of nations, with more or less independent governments, commanding more or less loyalty from their citizens, has an important influence on the pace and direction of growth in the system as a whole.

We examine the concept of 'maximizing profits' in connection with the behaviour of firms. We discuss the worldwide growth of productive capacity and then examine the influence of national commercial policy on it.

Chapter 10, *International balances*, goes over the ground of international trade and payments from the viewpoint of the financial relationships between nations. We first set out an answer to the conundrum: Why is there a problem of the balance of payments of the UK but not of the county of Oxfordshire?

Having isolated the influence of national monetary systems, we discuss various types of relationships in international balances and the influence of the pattern of exchange rates on them. An appendix gives the formula for the income multiplier in an open system.

Chapter 11, *Socialist planning*, raises the question of the value of neoclassical and Marxist modes of analysis for dealing with planning problems. Since the Marxian theory of value was a diagnosis of exploitation under capitalism, it cannot be usefully applied to socialist pricing policy, but the Marxian analysis of accumulation is highly relevant.

The neoclassical slogan of 'market-clearing prices' is misleading but the concept of *efficiency* provides an approach to some of the problems of planning, though it could be followed only in a very rough and ready way. These exercises, in general, are more useful in giving insight into the meaning and limitations of theoretical propositions than in offering practical advice on methods of planning. Appendix 1 deals with the search for efficiency in Soviet planning, and appendix 2 constructs an example of the relations between sectors in a process of accumulation.

Chapter One

Land and labour

One of the basic elements in economic analysis is the relation of *inputs*, that is the ingredients or *means of production* required for a process of production, to *outputs* of commodities and of *produced inputs*. Natural resources are inputs required for production which cannot themselves be produced. In a modern industrial economy, the vast majority of inputs to any typical process of production are themselves produced—outputs of a previous process—though natural resources have entered into them in greater or lesser degree at an earlier stage. The distinction is not perfectly clear-cut. Even seemingly 'natural' inputs, such as the qualities of the soil, or the weather, have many characteristics which may be 'produced' by use of fertilizers, glasshouses, or air-conditioners. However, the most basic characteristic of land, its extent and location, is not reproducible, nor are some of the special qualities of particular pieces of land which permit the production of particular outputs (as Ricardo pointed out with respect to vineyards*). Mineral resources, also, are essentially non-reproducible.

The fundamental element in production, however, is work. No production can take place without human labour—even robots must have been made by men. Economics is a study conducted by human beings about human conditions. Mankind supporting life by labour is its central concern. Men cannot be treated merely as a 'factor of production' on the same level as natural resources and other inputs.

The manner in which work is organized, and the manner in which the product is distributed, depend partly on technical relationships and partly on the type of social system in which work takes place. Here, we shall first set up a model of very simple technological specifications and consider how it operates in various social settings.

To produce an output, a worker requires both space and time and some pre-

* See **1** 2 §3(c).

existing materials on which to operate. The particular characteristics of the spatial aspect of work—moving people and goods about—can be neglected at this stage in our argument, but we must pay attention to the fact that production takes time, and that it normally requires stocks of one kind or another for work to be effective.

Following our prescription of ruthless simplification, we will first consider an economy in which production takes place by means of work applied to one non-reproducible means of production, land, with inputs of a single homogeneous produced commodity, 'corn', which is also the only output of the system. In schematic terms,

$$\text{Work} + \text{Land} + \text{Corn} \rightarrow \text{Corn}$$

A long-established tradition is assumed to have determined methods of production; there is no technical change, but the tradition contains a knowledge of how different intensities of cultivation, i.e., different ratios of work to land, affect the level of output. We will observe the operations of this simple economy under different social systems. These technical conditions are such a severe simplification that we cannot pretend to give an account of actual historical situations, but it is intended to show the main principles underlying identifiable periods of economic evolution.

1. Conditions of production

(a) Units

We need to provide ourselves with units in which to reckon the means of production. We first consider the case in which land can be measured simply in terms of acres. Various qualities of land will be introduced later.

What is the unit of labour? We must first consider how to measure manpower. Traditionally, men, women, and children do different jobs, and their respective roles are different in various societies; this is an important aspect of an agricultural economy that we are leaving out of account. We consider a family as consisting of a number of standard 'men' (though in some communities the work is mainly done by women). Next we must specify work per 'man'. This is less simple. We need a unit in terms of man hours spread over a year. The seasonality of work in agriculture is a serious problem in reality; for instance, in a particular district there may be an acute shortage of labour at a rush season, and long periods of undesired idleness during the rest of the year. This is another matter which is too complicated for our simple model. We avoid it by supposing that the technique requires a particular succession of operations over a year. Our unit of work, then, is a number of man hours per year in a particular pattern over the year. This is not very neat, but it is necessary for the purpose of keeping the model as simple as possible.

(b) Stock

Production takes time, but a man must eat every day. The cycle of production must always begin with a carry-over from the past, to provide seed and to feed the family of the cultivator till the process of production yields an output. We have eliminated another set of complications by supposing that there are no produced physical inputs except seed—neither fertilizers nor ploughs—and that the quantity of seed per unit of output is fixed by technical conditions. The net output of a unit of work is the excess of the product over seed. We assume that seed per unit of output is fixed by technical requirements so that the proportion of net output to total product cannot vary.

Where the technique in use—the pattern of production—involves a single annual harvest, the stock required for production consists of a part of each harvest set aside to provide seed and to support life until next year. Just after the harvest, the stock exists as a heap of grain. As the year goes by, it exists as seed in the ground, and as a dwindling supply of food plus the gradually growing crop in which the work of the cultivators is embodied. Immediately before the next harvest, the stock consists of a small reserve plus the ripe corn in the fields. At the harvest, it reappears once more as a heap of grain.

Another pattern of production may be used where natural conditions permit continuous production instead of an annual harvest. When seed can be planted every day, and the ripe corn gathered every day from seed that was planted, say, a year earlier, the stock consists of plants of every age from zero to one year old. Once a balanced stock has been built up, output is a continuous stream of so much per day. The stock never exists all at once as a heap of grain; it takes the form of a stand of plants which always maintains the same age composition.

There are many more complicated time patterns of production, each technique requiring an appropriate stock to permit work to produce output.

(c) Social relations

The above patterns of production are technical relations which exist in every kind of society. But production is not merely a technical process, it involves social relations as well, in particular, legal rules and accepted conventions concerning claims to property. In all societies, the means of production are owned and controlled by someone, whether it be an individual, organization, or national state. Social systems may be differentiated by the patterns of ownership they have adopted. One type of feudal society, for example, is characterized by the exclusive ownership of the land and the stock of seed by the lord of the manor. The serf, who owns only his ability to work, pays his lord in labour services for the privilege of using some land and seed for himself.

The social relations inherent in the control of the means of production influence not only the manner by which the technical requirements of production are met, but also how much is produced and how the fruits of production are distributed.

An established system of social relations may be disrupted by changes in the pattern of technical possibilities. The discovery of new territory, for example, may make plentiful some means of production that once was scarce, thus reducing the influence of its owners. Similarly, technical progress may render a particular resource obsolete. The preservation of a social group's influence rests on its ability to adapt to, or control, the pattern of economic change—the adaptable British aristocracy has survived from feudal times to the present day.

In the light of these technical and social considerations, we shall now examine the manner in which production is organized and output distributed under differing social systems in our highly simplified model of an agrarian economy.*

2. Independent families

We first consider an economy consisting of independent peasant families living on a wide, uniformly fertile plain. Since there is no scarcity of land, each family can cultivate as much as it pleases. We neglect the cost and delay of breaking in new land for cultivation—all the area is ready to yield a crop—and we suppose that the technique in use preserves fertility indefinitely. Property in land is necessary so that a family can reap where it has sown, without fear of interference. In our imagined, fertile plain, each family enjoys property in the land it occupies, but there is no payment attached to the use of land, since there is more than enough for everybody. (Property is a more general notion than what we commonly think of as rent-bearing land owned by a landlord.)

(a) A stationary state

Output per unit of work depends on the amount of work per acre. If the available units of work were spread too thinly over the land, total output would be lower. It might be impossible to keep weeds in check, or too much time would be lost in walking. On the other hand, it would be a waste of effort to cultivate too little land too intensively. There is an optimum ratio of land to units of work provided by the family. The output that each family produces then depends simply on the amount of work that it puts in. Families which do more work cultivate a larger area, and enjoy a correspondingly higher income of corn. (Families differ in size and each individual may be less or more keen on working.)

Reality, of course, is never so simple, but we will suppose that each family operates in such a way that output per unit of work is at a maximum, i.e., at the highest level the known technique permits. If one family provides 10 units of work and cultivates 60 acres in order to maximize output per unit of work, then another family providing, say, 5 units of work, will cultivate 30 acres, each maintaining the optimum ratio of land to units of work.† Net output expands in a constant proportion to the amount of work performed and land in use. Output per acre and net output per unit of work do not vary with the total amount of work that a family does or with the area that it cultivates.

---

* The argument of the following sections is illustrated by diagrams in §5 of this chapter.
† See Fig. 1.1.

Income is shared within each family according to the traditions of the community. The distribution of total income between families is purely in accordance with the work that each family chooses to do.

With a constant population and a constant amount of work done, the economy is in a *stationary state*; conditions of production and consumption are unchanging through time. Each family has the same output of corn from year to year (we neglect differences in the weather). In the case of an annual harvest, each year they consume last year's harvest, after providing for seed, while working to produce next year's.

In the case of continuous production, each family maintains a constant stock in the form of growing plants and continuously consumes and plants the ripe corn that it harvests day by day.

(b) Growth

Now, suppose that the population is growing. Each family provides for new members so that they can support themselves at the standard that the family is accustomed to. When the number of young men reaching maturity is greater than the number of old men who die, a typical family finds itself able and willing to do more work one year than the last. When a family has grown by one 'man', one of them sets out to cultivate new land. The family provides him with the stock that he needs.

In the expansion of output from the level of the stationary state, the time pattern of different techniques of production is important. As we have seen, each time pattern has associated with it a particular stock of means of production which is necessary for production to proceed.

In the case of an annual harvest, the family must hand over to the man setting out on his own enough to provide seed, all of which is planted at once, and they must provide for a year's consumption. In the case of continuous production, they can hand over the seed, which is planted daily, as well as the food that he needs, day by day. In either case, their own consumption for the year has to be cut accordingly. (Since total numbers are growing, the total amount of work that those left behind are doing, and the output they produce, is still the same as it was before one moved away.)

With both techniques, crops take a fixed time—say, a year—to grow. In one case, the young man gets a harvest a year after he left home and lives on it over the next year; in the other, he begins to get a yield at the end of the first year and goes on getting it in a steady flow thereafter. In either case, he becomes self-supporting from the end of the first year. The corn on which the young man lives for the first year, and his seed corn, is an investment that a family makes to enable the son to live. He does not pay them any interest, or even repay the advance, but accepts a moral obligation to play his part in providing for the growth in the next generation when his turn comes. Even in the ideal world where land ready to cultivate is freely available, a growth in numbers imposes a burden on the community, for the investment needed to equip younger sons as cultivators has to come out of the consumption of their elders.

65

Since economic theory was first developed in high latitudes, an annual harvest was taken for granted, both by the Physiocrats and by Ricardo. We shall follow the same tradition in these exercises. Continuous production will come up again when we are discussing industry. Meanwhile, we assume that our 'corn' is produced at a harvest once a year.

(c) Diminishing returns

Now, suppose that the population has spread over the whole cultivable area. There is no more land available. Each family has possession of a particular holding. Net output per unit of work for a family now depends on the size of their holding, and none has a holding large enough to permit it to get a living with the same amount of work as when land was free. Output per unit of work can no longer be kept at a maximum by maintaining the optimum ratio of land to work (in our example, 6 acres to 1 unit of work). Now, they have to work the land more intensively, with finer cultivation, more weeding, quicker harvesting, and so on. The smaller the area of land, the more the work required to get a given income. Conditions of *diminishing returns* prevail in the sense that, for a given acreage, output increases with work in a smaller proportion than work increases. Thus net output per unit of work falls as the labour to land ratio rises.*

Suppose that conditions are as in Table 1.1. We compare a number of families, each doing 10 units of work per year, which have different sizes of holdings. Conditions for a number of families, each with a holding of 60 acres, doing different amounts of work, are shown in Table 1.2. These numbers are quite arbitrary; they are chosen to illustrate the nature of diminishing returns in the simplest way. The point is that, at successively greater ratios of work to land, output per acre is higher and output per unit of work is less. At some ratio, total output from a given area of land ceases to rise as more work is applied to it. Beyond this, more work with more seed is wasted. A family may have great need for more output than they are getting, and be willing to work for it, but with the only technique that they understand they are unable to make good use of all their potential labour with the little land that they have. They must perforce spend much of their time in undesired idleness.

Table 1.1

Holding of land in acres	Total net output of corn	Acres per unit of work	Net output of corn per acre
60	480	6	8
50	450	5	9
40	400	4	10
30	300	3	10

* See Fig. 1.2 (a–c).

		Table 1.2		
Units of work	Total net output of corn	Work per acre	Net output of corn per unit of work
10	480	$\frac{1}{6}$	48
12	540	$\frac{1}{5}$	45
15	600	$\frac{1}{4}$	40
20	600	$\frac{1}{3}$	30

A technology which yields diminishing returns gives rise to the concept of *marginal productivity*, that is, the relationship of differences in the level of output to differences in the ratio of work to land. This is most easily seen if we consider the effect of a change in the ratio taking place in given conditions. In the above example, we were *comparing* different families with different ratios of work to land. We now suppose that the same relations hold when one family *changes* the amount of work done on a given holding. Diminishing returns means that a proportional increase in work done on an area of land, with appropriate seed, leads to a less than proportional increase in output. This means that average output per unit of work falls as the total of work increases, and the increment of output due to an increase in work by one unit is less than the average. Reinterpreting our example to show the effect of changes instead of comparisons of ratios, an addition of 3 units of work, from 12 to 15, leads to an addition to output of 60, from 540 to 600, and a fall in average net output per unit of work from 45 to 40. To make a finer division (see Table 1.3), let us fill in the figures between 540 and 600. Again, the numbers are quite arbitrary and merely illustrate a principle which we shall find useful in the argument which follows.

		Table 1.3	
Units of work		Net output of corn	
	Total	Average per unit of work	Increment for one unit of work
12	540	45	—
13	565	43·5	25
14	588	42	23
15	600	40	12

We have already seen that beyond the ratio of 15 units of work to 60 acres there is no further increase in output. Beyond this point, average output per unit of work

67

falls in the same proportion as the amount of work increases; total output does not increase and the marginal productivity of work is zero.

(d) Overhead labour

In some conditions, a substantial amount of work is required to get any output at all. Every year there is a certain 'overhead' operation without which extra work would not yield any return. (Say, the irrigation ditch has to be cleared out in the spring. This is not to be confused with investment in improving land. It is part of the requirements of the given traditional technology.) The output is nil at very low ratios of work to land; when the necessary minimum ratio is passed, average output jumps up and the marginal product of further work is much above the average.*

If a family found itself unable to do enough work to provide the annual overhead labour, it would be to its advantage to join forces with other families who had smaller holdings, pool their land and manpower, and work cooperatively. The problem would then be the principle on which the joint product should be distributed. They might agree on a payment of so much per acre put into the pool, and so much per unit of work, or they might operate joint ownership in the land and pay only for work. Or they might operate on the same principle as the family, in which rights and duties are based on traditional notions of what is proper. Or they might fall into disputes and fail to agree to work together at all.

(e) Income and effort

It is to be observed that there are diminishing returns per unit of work rather than per man. For a family of a certain number of 'men' the amount of work done depends on circumstances. When output per acre ceases to rise at a certain level of intensity of cultivation, as in our simple numerical example, it is of no use for a family with a limited holding to do more than a certain amount of work. Another type of case is possible in which—because of the nature of the soil and the technology in use— output per acre does not abruptly cease to rise at a particular level of intensity of cultivation: marginal productivity never falls actually to zero, but at high ratios of work to land it tails off gradually at a low level. In such a case, a family with a relatively small holding need not be reduced to unwanted idleness by lack of land on which to work.† Then a different limit comes into play, i.e., the amount of work that it finds worthwhile to do.

The family may have to do the maximum amount of work physically possible, merely to keep alive. Then, with a larger holding giving a higher return per unit of work, a bigger income can be had with less effort. With more land available, it would be unnecessary to work so desperately hard. The amount of work per man is successively less, over a certain range, with a higher return per unit of work. Over another

* See Fig. 1.4.
† See Fig. 1.3.

range, with still more land available, habits of high consumption may have developed, and it may seem more worthwhile to work more if the return is greater. But, at very high levels of consumption, a bit more income does not seem to be worth an extra effort.* From this, it appears that members of a family with a larger holding of land may not only have a higher income but also do less work to get it.

(f) Large and small holdings

Returning to the case in which output per acre reaches a definite limit at a certain level of intensity of cultivation, we may compare the situation of two families composed of an equal number of 'men' with different-sized holdings. A typical kulak family has a large holding, a typical poor peasant a very small one. We must now take account, also, of differences in the quality of land. The kulak's holding may have better soil, be better placed for irrigation, and so on.

The kulak family, depending only on its own work, can make a relatively comfortable living while the most that the peasant family can get is a meagre income perhaps insufficient to provide a diet that enables them to work well. On the poor peasant's small plot, total output is narrowly limited. The poor peasant family is willing to work more than the kulaks, but its holding is so small that the amount of work at which they are getting all they can out of it is less than the amount they are willing to do. It would not be worthwhile to work harder. Thus, they may be even more idle than the kulaks, though from compulsion not choice.†

A kulak family can offer a wage for the labour of poor peasants, and gain a larger income by employing workers on its own land. The wage rate is set at a conventional level around the average income of the poorest peasants. They are driven to accept the offer by their need to live. Given the wage rate, in principle it pays the kulak to apply units of work up to the amount at which marginal productivity on his land is equal to the wage. (In our example above‡ taking a man year to represent a unit of work, when the wage per man year is 23, we find that a kulak owning 60 acres will not employ more than 14 men, even when the kulak family is doing no work.) To apply a larger amount of work would add more to the wage bill than to the product. To apply less would be foregoing a potential gain. Thus, if the kulaks are efficient, and keen on getting all they can from the land, they apply work (with appropriate seed) according to this rule. If so, they are being led by native cunning to act according to the principles laid down in economic theory.

(To make use of our simple assumption we have to reckon in terms of work per year. In reality, a kulak would usually hire the labour of poor peasants at so much per day during the rush season only.)

On the labour that they employ, the kulaks enjoy a surplus equal to the excess of the net output from the extra work over the wage bill in corn that they pay. From

* See Fig. 1.3 and 1.5.
† See Fig. 1.6.
‡ See table 1.2.

this, they can live comfortably. If the holding is large enough, they need do no work at all beyond organizing the wage labourer's tasks and keeping them up to the mark.

3. Landlords and peasants

We now consider an economy, such as that described by Quesnay, in which the land is all owned by feudal lords who regard it simply as a source of income.

(a) Conflicting interests

The important feature of these feudal institutions is that property in land is separated from work on it. This brings about an organization of production that is unlikely to be very efficient. In order to have no trouble with cultivation, the landlords let out the land to tenants, the rent being a traditional proportion, say, half, of the gross output of the land. The landlord has no direct control over the work that the share croppers do. Tenants have neither the means nor the motive to maintain the productivity of the land, while the landlord can get his income without bothering about it. In these conditions, the greater the number of workers on his estate, the larger is the landlord's return. The landlord gains most when the holdings are so small and the level of intensity of cultivation so high as to maximize output per acre, i.e., at the level at which more work would bring no appreciable increase in output (the marginal product from an additional tenant would be zero). This is the exact opposite of the interests of the peasants, who, as we have seen, are best off when holdings are large enough to maximize net output per unit of work.

From the landlord's point of view, the smaller the holding per tenant the better, provided that it is not so small that the tenant families are unable to live. The area of the minimum size of holding depends on the fertility of the soil: on more-fertile land, the number of families that a landlord can crowd into his estate is greater. With a larger size of holdings (a smaller number of tenants on a particular estate) output per acre is lower; the landlord's income is less and the income per share cropper's family greater.

When there are not enough tenants to cultivate the whole area, the landlords will not let out such large holdings that output per acre falls very low; they prefer to keep a part of the land unlet (in any case, they reserve a good part in forests, for sport) to prevent the peasants from becoming prosperous and independent. But if they keep too much land empty they may run into political trouble, for their control of land rests, in the last resort, on force.

In these conditions, growth of population is in the interest of the landlords and against the interest of the peasants, though an individual may regard his sons as providing security for his old age. Growing numbers reduce income and may lead to extreme misery, not mainly (as Malthus maintained) because of diminishing returns to labour but because of the weak bargaining power of tenants *vis-à-vis* landlords. True Malthusian misery is not reached until the density of population is so great that the *whole* produce of the maximum amount of work that a family can perform is insufficient to support life. Malthus' fondness for the landed gentry blinded him to the mechanism by which population pressure produces misery. (Though, as we have seen, growth of numbers may be a burden even when land is not limited.*)

(b) Moneylenders

To produce corn by means of labour applied to land takes time; at any moment, there is a stock of 'work in progress' which allows an annual flow of output to be produced. The tenants are obliged to maintain the stock, providing seed out of their half of the annual gross product. (Here variations in the weather, which we have left out of the model, are a serious menace in actual feudal conditions.)

A share cropper who cannot provide the stock for himself (because his share of one harvest is not enough to feed his family till the next) is obliged to borrow. This provides a source of income for anyone who owns a stock of corn that he does not need for his own use. For the peasant, it is a matter of life and death. He is in a weak bargaining position and must agree to any rate of interest which lenders demand. The interest is more than he can pay; at the next harvest he has to renew the loan with arrears of interest added; once in debt he can never escape. The return which a moneylender gets on his loans is less than the nominal rate of interest, for he cannot squeeze out of the share croppers more than the difference between their net income and the consumption necessary for bare subsistence. The point of the high nominal interest is to make it impossible to repay the debt so that the debtor is in perpetual servitude.

In the story of the poor peasant and the kulak the situation is similar. A peasant who has a title to his holding of land may borrow by pledging it as security. The interest may then be lower than when there is no security but, if all the same he cannot repay, the lender can take the land over. The kulaks enlarge their holdings in this way, by lending to their poor neighbours.

Extravagant sons of the landlords may also borrow, to spend on luxury more than their share of the rent. It was because borrowing accompanied both misery and vice that lending at usury was condemned by religion.

(c) Improving landlords

As the Physiocrats pointed out, it is to the interest of a landlord to make improvements in cultivation on his estate. The share croppers have little motive and no means to invest in fertilizers, or to experiment with new seeds or methods. In England, in the eighteenth century, landlords took an interest in agriculture, partly as a hobby and partly as a means of increasing the income from their estates. They financed experiments and made investments that brought about a revolution in techniques of

* 2 1 §2(b).

cultivation. To carry this through, it was necessary to throw tenants off their holdings, enclose common land, and recruit dispossessed peasants as wage labourers.

The owner of a great estate might keep some home fields in which he could take a direct interest, but the greater part of the land was *farmed out* in units of convenient size. The farmer undertook to pay rent to the landlord and employed labour on the farm to produce crops for sale. If all went well, the proceeds of sales enabled him to pay wages, pay rent, and take a profit for himself. This was the setting in which Ricardo developed the analysis of capitalistic production. However, his analysis can be best understood if we ignore problems of marketing and money prices and continue to argue in terms of a homogeneous product, 'corn', in which both wages and rents are paid.

4. Capitalist farmers

The capitalist farmer described by Ricardo owns no land but provides the stock required for production—supplying seed and paying wages in advance of the harvest. Since the farmer owns the stock of corn from which wages are paid, he is in control and can organize the way in which work is carried out on the land that he rents. With the same, or even a higher, labour to land ratio than under peasant cultivation, he gets a higher output per man by economies of specialization of both land and labour, and by organizing the 'overhead' work which increases productivity.

Labourers have long since lost their rights in land; they are obliged to work for wages in order to live. The wage rate—a quantity of corn per man year, to be paid weekly—is set at a conventional level, determined by social and historical influences, which just about permits the labourer to work and to raise a family. There are generally more workers available than the farmers employ. The men are eager to get employment; competition for jobs keeps the wage down to the conventional level. The farmer exacts a regular amount of work for the wage that he pays. For this reason, we now take a man year of employment as the unit of work.

The landlords are subject to commercial motives in the sense that each wants to get as much rent as he can on his estate, but they do not take any interest in management, or invest in improvements. They leave all that to the farmers, and their rents are all consumed in supporting their great households. In this sense, they retain the traditions of feudalism.

Differences in the fertility of different areas of land play an important part in Ricardo's argument. (In reality, convenience of situation—say, proximity to a market —is also of great importance, but here, to keep the analysis simple, we consider only one kind of variation in the economic quality of land.) We have to take account of the fact that each area has its own response to work applied to it. We cannot now reckon merely in terms of acres. In each particular district, the land must be specified in a list, a 'Who's Who', giving the fertility, convenience for working, etc., of each area. The measure of the quality of a piece of land is expressed by output per man employed on it.

Looking at the matter from the farmer's viewpoint, the wage per man is everywhere the same, while net output per man is higher on the better land. The profit, which he keeps for himself, is equal to the excess of net output over wages minus what he pays for rent. The excess of output over wages is greater when men are employed on better land. Therefore the farmer is willing to pay, and the landlord is able to exact, more rent for better land than for less-good land. When commercial principles apply strictly and there is general competition by landlords for tenants and by farmers for land, differences in rent for different farms will settle at the level which just offsets differences in the quality of land. Some land yields a larger excess of net output over wages, and costs a correspondingly higher rent per acre, and some land yields less and costs less, so that the farmer keeps for himself the same profit per man employed no matter what the quality of land of his farm may be. (To be realistic, there are many complications which would have to be brought into the picture, but this is the general underlying principle of commercial relations between landlords and farmers.)

The number of men that a farmer employs depends on the stock of corn that he can invest. As well as providing seed, he has to command a *wage fund* consisting of enough corn to pay the conventional wage per man, over a year, from harvest to harvest. (To simplify the argument, we have assumed that seed is a fixed proportion of total output, and we leave out of account investment in other inputs. Any implements a man needs he makes in the winter out of materials gathered on the farm.) The stock of seed and the corn in the wage fund constitute the farmer's *capital*, on the use of which he will make his profit. From the point of view of the farmer, profit per man employed is equivalent to profit per unit of corn invested. If the farmer is behaving as a capitalist trying to maximize the profit on the quantity of corn capital that he commands, he aims to maximize profit per man employed. Since the wage per man is fixed, this means taking on the area and quality of land that maximizes output per man after payment of rent.

The profit per annum that a farmer gets is the total output of the men he employs after replacing seed minus the rent and the wages that he pays.

The rate of profit on capital, expressed as a percentage per annum, is profit per man divided by the wage fund necessary to employ a man plus the seed that he handles. This rate is the same for all farmers, since differences in output per man are offset by differential payments of rent.

These relationships, of course, depend on our assumption that corn is the only output and that there is no investment of capital except the seed and the wage fund. A complex of outputs and inputs cannot be dealt with so simply. These assumptions serve to bring out the main point of Ricardo's argument, though he himself was perplexed by complications that he could not reduce to these simple terms.*

---

* See **1** 2 §3(b).

(a) The extensive margin

To see how the principle of differential rent works, let us first take a simplified case in which technical conditions are such that the number of men per acre required to cultivate the land is everywhere the same, while output per man year varies with the quality of the land. The total amount of employment organized by the farmers (and the total amount of corn produced per annum) depends on the stock of corn invested. When this employment is spread over the cultivated area, there is some quality of land—the least fertile—which is yielding the lowest net output per head. Net output per head on the least-fertile land cultivated thus depends on technical conditions and the total amount of employment. Provided that there is some vacant land of the same quality as the poorest land being cultivated, competition between landlords for tenants drives its rent to zero, while competition between farmers for better land ensures that the level of rent on each quality of land takes up the excess of the output of the team of men cultivating it over the output on the no-rent land.

In any year, the total of employment (governed by the total stock of corn capital) determines the amount of land cultivated, and so determines which quality of land is *at the margin*, paying no rent. This lowest quality of land in use is said to be at the *extensive margin* of cultivation, since it is the margin which defines the extent of cultivation of the available land area. Net output per head on this land (the wage being given) determines profit per man employed, and the level of rents is such as to make profit per man employed over the whole area equal to that on the no-rent land.

When employment, relative to available land, is so great that there is no potentially cultivable land unused, landlords will exact rent for even the least-good land; the differential rent of better land must then be expressed as its superiority over the lowest-rent land, rather than over no-rent land.

(b) The intensive margin

The analysis of the extensive margin has been based on the provisional assumption that an equal number of men are used per acre, whatever the quality of the land. We must now bring into the model of capitalistic production the principle of diminishing returns with intensity of cultivation, which we have already discussed in connection with self-employed peasants. Here, we are no longer dealing with a geographical fact, like the line between the desert and the sown, but rather with a matter of calculation. Moreover, the analysis is concerned with calculations that the economist assumes that producers make, rather than with what he observes them to do. Applied in other contexts, the notion of marginal productivity may be treacherous, but in the setting of Ricardo's model it is a useful exercise to work out how the farmers would behave if they were strictly maximizing the profit obtainable on an investment of corn.

On each area of land, the larger the number of men employed on it, the lower the average product per man; and marginal product at each ratio of labour to land is less than average product per man, as we saw above. Each farmer can regulate the intensity of cultivation of the land that he rents. The number of men he employs in any year is fixed by the amount of the stock of corn that he invests and he has to choose how much land to employ them on. He adjusts the intensity of cultivation of each acre that he rents so that the marginal product of an additional man year of work on any piece of land is not less than the average product minus rent of an additional piece of land. Thus, the farmers will not push the intensity of cultivation on a piece of land to the point at which the marginal product of an extra man year of work on that land is less than the product per man on some other piece of land minus the rent for it. There is an *intensive margin* of cultivation corresponding to the extensive margin; over the area as a whole, the marginal product of labour is everywhere equal to the average product of the poorest land in use minus its rent.* Of course, things never actually work out so neatly, but the principle is broadly correct.

(c) Equalizing margins

It is a striking theoretical proposition that the equalization of marginal products brings about the distribution of a given labour force over the cultivable area so as to maximize total output. (This proposition was not specifically stated by Ricardo but is entailed by his argument.)

It is obvious that, if labour were employed in such a way as to make marginal productivity greater on some farms than on others, then output could be increased by moving labour from the lower-marginal-product area to the higher.

In terms of our simple example (with land all alike), suppose that the overall ratio of labour to land is 14 men to 60 acres. Then, if one farmer employs 13 men on 60 acres, he produces a net output of 565 units of corn per annum. Another employs 15 men and produces 600 units. The two together produce 1165. But with 14 men, 60 acres yield 588 units. The two farms together could produce 1176 units. The increment due to adding one more man where 13 are employed is 23 units, and the reduction in output due to taking a man away where 15 are employed is 12 units. Thus, 11 units is being lost by the wrong distribution of men to land. The same principle applies where land varies in quality. The total output is at a maximum when employment is adjusted to fertility in such a way that the loss of output due to withdrawing one man from employment for a year would be the same on all farms.†

From the farmer's viewpoint, in Ricardo's system, it is the productivity of land that the farmer has to calculate, and the rent to be paid for it. Each farmer employs the number of men that his wage fund permits, and hires the amount of land to employ them on that will maximize net output minus rent. The competition between farmers for land then leads them to find the ratio of land to labour that maximizes

* See Fig. 1.7.
† See table 1.3.

total net output. The relation of productivity to the intensity of cultivation of different qualities of land is purely technical, with no variations due to the human element (for we assume that all farmers are equally good managers and that all workers are obliged to work in the same way). The equalization of marginal products and the maximization of total net output comes about through the mechanism of the commercial relations between farmers and landlords and the pursuit of profit by the farmers.

Again, nothing in economic life is so simple, but the principle that charging differential rent helps to enforce the economical use of scarce resources is important in reality.*

(d) Saving and borrowing

In Ricardo's scheme, the amount of employment in any year depends on the stock of corn that the farmers control. It is natural for a capitalist to be ambitious and to want to expand his operations to increase the flow of his profits. The farmers are saving a large part of their profits and increasing the employment that they organize from year to year.

A farmer is not necessarily confined to investing only his own savings. Because he has a secure prospect of profit, he may enlarge his investment faster than his own saving by borrowing at interest. When a farmer wants to invest more corn than he possesses, he can borrow from anyone who has a stock that he does not use to employ labour himself. The lender cannot get more interest than it pays the farmer to offer. The upper limit to the rate of interest is somewhat below the rate of profit on corn, which, as we have seen, is determined by technical conditions and the wage rate; it would not be worthwhile for the farmer to borrow if he had to part with the whole additional profit.

Interest of this kind is very different from the usury exacted by moneylenders from miserable peasants. It represents a way in which an owner of wealth can get a share in the profits due to production.

(e) Growth and income distribution

Ricardo devised the analysis of capitalist agriculture in order to show that rising rents were setting a drag on accumulation. Agriculture plays the central part in his argument because agriculture produces the subsistence of the workers. It is the relation of net output per head in agriculture to the level of wages which determines the rate of profit that can be got by employing labour, not only in agriculture but in industry as a whole. (In a modern economy, in which the acceptable level of workers' consumption includes much more than 'corn', this is not accurate, but the general principle that profits depend on the relation of productivity to real wages is still a basic characteristic of capitalism.)

* See **2** 11 §2(c).

The output of corn in any year (given technical conditions, including the quality of land) depends on the investment of corn that the capitalist farmers as a whole can make. Each year they add to their stock (from their own savings or from loans) and increase employment next year. As they do so, the margin of cultivation is extended and the level of rents rises. If things were to go on like this for some time, the level of profits would fall to the point at which it was not worth saving any more and impossible to borrow any more, so that stagnation would set in.

This argument turns on the view that accumulation will always be halted by diminishing returns on land, and the consequent inability to support a growing population. Once it is recognized that investment in land (evolving new techniques of production) can push back the margin more or less indefinitely, so that the constraint that land places on growth is removed, the sharp difference between agriculture and industry is blurred. Moreover, when landlords no longer spend their rents on maintaining their retainers and enjoying a luxurious life, but begin to save and invest, the position of the landlord becomes analogous to that of the capitalist. With the spread of capitalism, the clear distinction between landlords and capitalists, as classes of the community, was lost. Instead, the capitalist class became divided into *rentiers*, who receive income from property, and *entrepreneurs*, who organize production. Thus, the division of the community into idle consumers and active producers becomes a division between rentiers of all kinds (including landowners), on the one hand, and managers and workers on the other.

5. Diagrams

Exposition in terms of diagrams is widely used in theoretical economics. These diagrams are of a special kind. They do not convey factual information nor can they be used to prove propositions. They are merely a way of describing relationships that are complicated when expressed in words, and oversimplified when expressed in algebra. Many of the arguments of this chapter are easier to grasp if they are set out in diagrams, and the habit of sketching diagrams for oneself is an aid to thought. They must be used, however, with due regard to their limitations. Both diagrams and formulae appear much more definite and precise than any economic relationship ever is in reality. They should be used only as a means to follow an argument, not as the argument itself.

A diagram is used to express a relationship, say, between work per acre and output, with the two variables shown by distances along the axes and the relation between them shown by a curve. There are three absolute rules that must be observed in constructing diagrams of this kind. The first is that the quantities to be measured must each be homogeneous so that it can be expressed as a number of units: in this case, physical units of corn and units of work. The second is that when the diagram illustrates flows, say, of inputs and outputs, the rate per unit of time must be stated. Here, our unit of work is spread over a year and our unit of output is corn at the harvest. Thus, all our quantities are flows per annum. The third rule is that a plane diagram can show only relationships between the quantities represented on the axes, not the effect of changes. It shows for instance, the difference between output per acre with a greater or lesser intensity of cultivation. It cannot show the effect of *increasing* the intensity of cultivation. A change is an event which takes place at a moment of time and its consequences run forward through time. To express changes we need a third dimension. However, for the present, we can manage well enough with two dimensions, provided we keep the rules in mind.

(a) Labour to land ratio and output

The relationship we want to illustrate links three quantities: work, land, and corn. The simplest way to set it out is that used in the numerical examples above, i.e., we express output of corn per acre with a given quantity of labour, or output per unit of work with a given area of land.

To illustrate the first story, in which peasant families are free to take in as much land as they like, we take units of work performed by a particular family as given. The y-axis represents quantities of corn per unit of work, and the x-axis, areas of land. The curve then shows how output produced by the family for which it is drawn would vary with the area that they might cultivate.

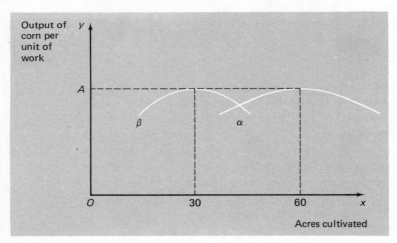

FIG. 1.1

Figure 1.1 shows the production of two families: one, β, is doing 5 units of work, and the other, α, 10 units. Each produces a net output of OA per acre, with a ratio of 6 acres per unit of work.

We now take the area of land as given. In Fig. 1.2a, the **A** curve shows how net output varies with work per acre. The y-axis represents units of corn produced per unit of work, and the x-axis, units of work. At low ratios of work to land, net output per unit of work is at the maximum possible, OA. After a certain point, diminishing

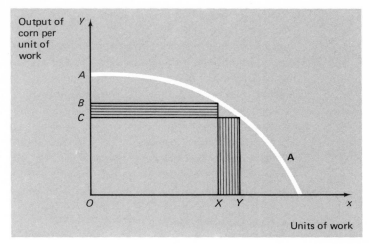

FIG. 1.2a

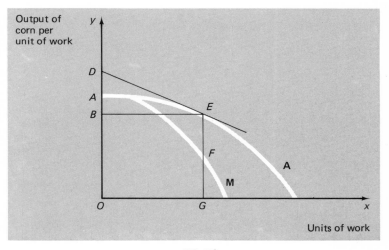

FIG. 1.2b

returns set in, and thereafter, net output per unit of work is lower at a higher ratio of labour to land. When OX units of work are being done in the given area, total net output of corn, i.e., net output per unit multiplied by the number of units of work, is shown by the area $OB \cdot OX$. With OY units of work, net output is $OC \cdot OY$. The increment of net output due to the increment of work shown by XY is $OC \cdot XY - OX \cdot BC$. At the point at which these two areas are equal, total output has reached the limit. Beyond this point, more work fails to produce more output. We cannot use the diagram directly to describe a *change* in employment from OX to OY, or from OY to OX, but we may use it, as in our arithmetical example, to see what the effect of a change would be provided that all conditions remain the same over the interval of time in which the change takes place.

For a very small difference in work, points X and Y are close together, as are points B and C. In the limit, for an indefinitely small difference, the ratio of the difference in net output per unit of work to the difference in the amount of work is shown by the slope of the curve. Of course, in economic relationships there can never be an indefinitely small difference; to have any effect, a difference must be of a perceptible size. However, the mathematical properties of a continuous curve may be used to illustrate an argument, provided that its limitations are kept in mind.

In Fig. 1.2b, curve **M** shows the marginal net output at successive amounts of work on the given area of land. At point E, the ratio of the reduction in net output per head to the small increment in work to which it is due is shown by the slope of the

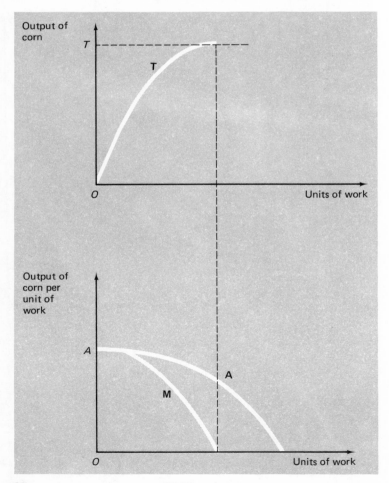

FIG. 1.2c

tangent to the curve at *E*, i.e., *BD/BE*. The amount of loss due to the lower average output per head is *BD/BE* times *BE*, i.e., *BD*. Average net output at this point is *EG*. The *marginal net output* is average net output minus the loss, i.e., *EG* − *BD*. If we take *EF* to equal *BD*, the marginal net output is shown by *FG*. At the point at which output reaches its maximum, marginal productivity is zero, and the marginal curve cuts the *x*-axis.

The same relationships can be shown by a curve relating total net output to work in the given area. In Fig. 1.2c, the upper part of the diagram shows the total net output of corn, from the given area of land, rising with units of work done. The total net output curve, **T**, is at first a straight line whose slope corresponds to average net output, *OA*, for the range over which it is constant. As diminishing returns set in, the slope of the curve slews round, until it is horizontal where output reaches the limit, *OT*, at which marginal output is zero.

The lower half of Fig. 1.2c shows the relation of the marginal curve to the total net output curve. At the point corresponding to the amount of work that produces *OT*, the marginal output is zero and the marginal curve cuts the *x*-axis.

Figure 1.3 illustrates a different set of technical conditions, in which total product

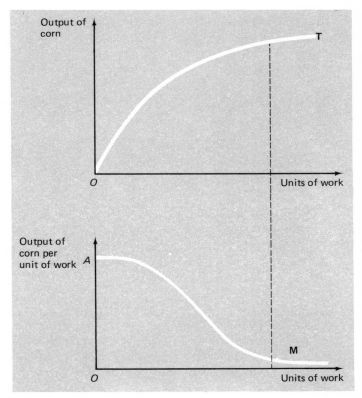

FIG. 1.3

reaches no limit but rises indefinitely, though very slowly at high ratios, as the ratio of work to land rises.

Figure 1.4 illustrates a case in which a particular amount of work, OX, is necessary to make a year's production possible on a holding of 60 acres. For the first units of work in addition to OX, the increment of net output is XA per unit. This is the marginal product of work at this point. The overhead work, OX, is now averaged out with the additional work, so that average output per unit of work is rising over the range XZ. Beyond this point, diminishing returns set in. The marginal curve lies above the average over the range where it is rising, and cuts it at its highest point.

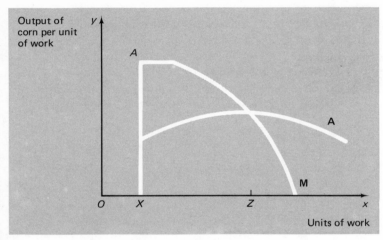

FIG. 1.4

(b) Income and effort

Figure 1.5 represents a plausible case of the response of work to return per unit work for an individual. An income $OB.OY$ is the necessary minimum for efficiency. At rates of return below OB, his work is less than OY because he has not enough to eat. Over the range of rates of return per unit work OB to OC, he does less work. From OC to OD, he begins to respond the other way. Above OD, his work falls off again as the rate of return rises.

(c) Size of holdings

In Fig. 1.6, two pairs of curves are drawn in the same axes to represent the relation of work to net output on two different pieces of land owned by two families comprising an equal number of 'men'. A_k and M_k are the curves of average and marginal net output on the kulak's land, and A_p and M_p, on the poor peasant's land.

The maximum output that the poor peasant can get from his holding is $OA.OX$.

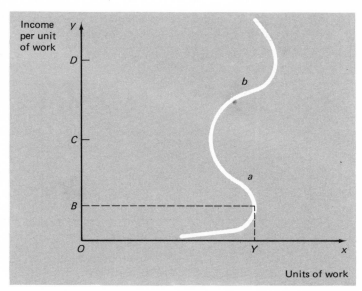

FIG. 1.5

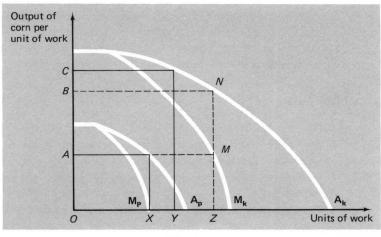

FIG. 1.6

The kulak family, when working its own land, puts in OY units of work and gets an income OC.OY. The peasant family is doing less work than the kulaks, though their need and willingness to work is much greater.

   When the kulaks hire wage labour, we suppose that the wage rate is equal to the income of a typical poor peasant. (This is not a commercial relationship, but an accepted idea of what is reasonable.) When the wage rate is OA per unit of work, the kulaks arrange for OZ of work on their land, at which the marginal productivity of work, *ZM*, is equal to the wage rate. In the case illustrated, the kulaks do no work themselves when they hire labour. They then enjoy the income represented by *AB . OZ*.

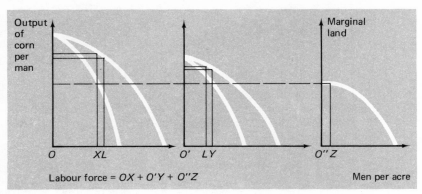

FIG. 1.7

Figure 1.7 shows the relation of average and marginal product to labour employed on three different areas of land. When the labour force, which is equal to *OX* + *O'Y* + *O"Z*, is deployed in such a way as to make marginal productivity on the better land equal to the average product on marginal land, total output is maximized. It can be seen that if a small amount of labour, *LY*, equal to *XL*, were transferred from the middling land to the best land the loss of product would be greater than the gain.

6. A false trail

The 'marginal' element in Ricardo's theory of rent was taken over by the neo-classicals, but they gave it a peculiar twist. They maintained that, in a market economy, the real-wage rate tends to be equal to, or, as some say, measures or sometimes is determined by, the marginal product of labour in the economy as a whole.

In our simplified version of Ricardo's model, in which the only elements are corn, land, labour and a corn-wage fund, the marginal product of labour, as a quantity of corn per annum, at a given ratio of work to land, is determined by the technical conditions prevailing, while the wage rate is fixed at some conventional level and does not change as the ratio alters.

In Fig. 1.8, curve **A** represents output per man over the whole cultivable area. **M** is the corresponding marginal curve. When *OX* represents the total amount of labour employed, *OB* is the marginal product of labour. The corn-wage rate is *OC*. Total net output per man is *OA*. Subtracting *BA*, the rent per man paid to landlords, we are left with *OB*. That is to say, the marginal product of labour is equal to the wage per man plus profit per man. This was the essential point of Ricardo's argument.

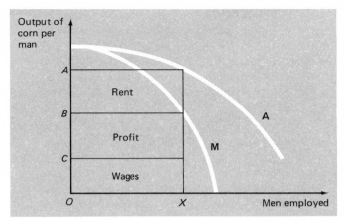

FIG. 1.8

Let us see if we can devise a set of property relations, in the same technical conditions, that would suit the neoclassics.

(a) The free market: workers hire land

First, suppose that cultivators hire land for themselves, without the mediation of capitalists, by promising to pay rent out of the harvest. To make the analysis work, we must suppose that they have such a psychology and such an income per unit of work that they are in the situation depicted in Fig. 1.5 between *OC* and *OD*, i.e., they are willing to do more work for a higher return per unit work. This was put into the picture only to give the neoclassical argument a chance, because there is no reason to suppose that it is a common case in real life. We must also suppose that the cultivators own an appropriate stock of seed.

Allowing the above conditions, we can draw a *supply curve* of work for a given group of cultivators, showing the return per unit of work required to induce each quantity of work to be done. This return represents the *supply price* of work—the quantity of corn per unit of work that must be earned to make it worthwhile to do a particular amount of work. (This supply price is sometimes said to represent the *marginal disutility* of work, but this is illogical, for it is measured by corn per unit work, not by the utility of corn.*)

The supply curve of work, from a given labour force, is confronted with the average and marginal return per unit of work from the available land. The cultivators are willing to hire such an amount of land that the marginal return per unit of work is equal to the supply price of that amount of work. Competition for land requires the cultivators to pay an amount of rent that absorbs the difference between the average and marginal return per unit of work.

* See **1** 3 §2(a).

Figure 1.9 shows the supply curve of work, curve **S**, for a given number of culti-vators, and the average and marginal products per unit of work. The cultivators hire such an area that the marginal product of the work done is equal to the supply price of the amount of work.

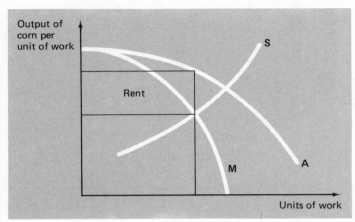

FIG. 1.9

(b) The free market: landlords hire workers

Now, suppose that landlords hire workers to cultivate their land, promising to pay wages each year out of the harvest. There must then be a standard amount of work required from each man per year. There is a certain labour force available to be hired. Competition between landlords for hands, and between men for employment, ensures that the wage rate is equal to the marginal product of the total number of men working the whole area, and each landowner employs men on his own holding so that marginal productivity for him is equal to the wage.

We can reduce these two 'free-market' cases to the same if we suppose that work per man year is fixed and that all land is alike. Then, in both cases, the wage or income per man year is equal to the marginal productivity of the total labour force, and rent per acre is equal to the marginal productivity of the amount of land being cultivated.

(c) A 'fair' distribution of income

The marginal product of land is the quantity of corn that would be lost if one less acre were cultivated. When one less acre is cultivated with a given amount of labour, there is so much the more labour to work on the remaining space. The labour released adds to the product of the rest of the land; this is a partial compensation for the loss of product of the acre of land withdrawn from cultivation. The product of the men transferred is equal to the marginal product of labour multiplied by the

number of men employed per acre; it is, therefore, equal to the wages paid for the labour released from the acre that has been withdrawn. Thus, the marginal product of land is net output per acre minus wages paid per acre. Similarly, the marginal product of labour is output per man minus the rent paid for land cultivated per man. Total output is equal to the marginal product of land multiplied by the area of land in use plus the marginal product of labour multiplied by the number of men employed, and this is equal to the total of rents plus the total of wages. This means, it is sometimes said, that total output is fairly distributed according to the productivity of each 'factor of production', land and labour.* (The product of work, of course, goes to the man who does it, while the product of the land goes to its owners in proportion to the area that each owns.)

(d) Some confusions

There are several points to be observed about this argument. Firstly, it can survive only in the strictly limited model in which the product is homogeneous with the only produced means of production, the seed corn, and in which the ratio of labour to land can be varied continuously in small steps so that the marginal physical productivity of each can always be distinguished, made up of a physical unit like our 'corn', or of bundles of goods in completely fixed proportions, so that a bundle can be treated as a physical unit. The assumptions made in our model, merely for simplicity, are essential for the neoclassical argument, which would collapse if they were removed.

When equipment and other inputs are brought into the picture, it would be highly artificial to suppose that the proportions in which they can be combined are sufficiently flexible for the marginal physical productivity of each to be distinguished. Where inputs require work in technically given proportions, we might be able to distinguish the productivity of, say, work plus fertilizers plus seed applied to the land, but we could not distinguish the products of work, seed, and fertilizers separately. In such a case, our model would have to be made more complicated, but the neoclassical model would become inapplicable.

Secondly, in the neoclassical model, there are no capitalists or moneylenders. The workers, as well as the landowners, are living each year out of last year's income. Wages are paid in arrears, so that the worker is, in effect, lending a year's work to the landowner. The wage, which is equal to the marginal net product of labour, must include the payment for this loan. Even when there are no other inputs, it is necessary to take account of investment in the wage fund over the year from harvest to harvest.

Thirdly, the argument requires complete equality of bargaining power between the parties, and free competition within each group. If the landowners agreed among themselves to keep rents up, they could force the workers down to a level of income at which they would work just as hard for a smaller return (as from point b to point a, in Fig. 1.5). If the workers had sufficient reserves to last out, they could reduce rents,

* See **1** 3 §3(b).

and share out a bonus over and above the income corresponding to the marginal product of labour.

Finally, we must observe that, even within the terms of the argument itself, it is not true that a system in which each 'factor' receives an income equal to its marginal product corresponds to some kind of natural justice according to which, what each 'factor' gets is what it contributes to total output. On the contrary, if land were more fertile, so that each acre contributed more to total output, it is the marginal productivity of a given labour force that would be greater; the level of rents might well be lower. Similarly, if workers would work harder for the same wage, rents would be higher. It is not its productivity but its scarcity relative to the other 'factors' that determines the marginal productivity of each.

We have spelled out this argument to disentangle some elements in economic teaching that have caused a great deal of confusion. The notion that wages tend to equal the marginal product of labour belongs to the metaphysic of neoclassical economics; we have hard work to make sense of it even in this simple analytical system. When we include a variety of produced means of production it makes no sense at all.*

* See **2** 6 §3(d).

Chapter Two
Men and machines

The foregoing analysis was designed to illustrate the importance of social relations in the process of production. Even in the simple agrarian economy, social relations were seen to dominate the way in which production was carried on and the product distributed. For the next few chapters we will be concentrating on a simplified version of an advanced *capitalist* economy, an economy in which the means of production are owned by one particular social group—the capitalists—each of whom attempts to earn profits with the stock of means of production that he owns.

In this model, the only inputs, apart from labour, are produced means of production. In even the most advanced industrial economies, land and natural resources are indispensable, but the greater part of the means of production used in industry are industrial products. In order to concentrate on one thing at a time, we now leave non-produced means of production out of the story.

We begin by examining a simple economy in which men work with machines to produce a single consumption good and to produce new machines. For the time being, we assume that there is only one type of machine, and that production of the consumption good requires a stock of machines but no other stock.

For this purpose, it is impossible to make a lifelike model, since in real life, many sorts of stock—previously produced means of production—are required for any output. However, there are some relationships which are easy to grasp in a model with one kind of stock that become excessively complicated with several. (In the appendix to this chapter, we discuss the relation between equipment, such as our 'machines', and a stock of materials which is used up and renewed during production.)

1. Conditions of production

We are concerned in this chapter with the operation of the economy as a whole; we need not yet open up the problem of markets for particular commodities. We can, therefore, still make use of a single homogeneous consumption good, which we shall continue to call 'corn'. Corn is now produced by men with the aid of machines.

(a) Technical relations

Production of corn entails a man operating a machine, the actions of which produce corn. To eliminate the need for a stock of corn, we have to assume that the period of throughput is very short so that, for the purpose of our model, work in progress in corn can be neglected and a man can eat every day the product of that day's work. Schematically, our production process is:

$$\text{Machine hours} + \text{Work} \rightarrow \text{Corn}$$

in one time period.

Machines are also produced by men operating machines, without requiring raw materials, but the time that it takes to build a complete machine, its *gestation period*, is rather long, so that a continuous flow of output of new machines involves a considerable stock of part-made machines at any moment. Thus:

$$\text{Machine hours} + \text{Work} \rightarrow \text{A machine}$$

over several time periods.

Obviously, the first machine was not made by a machine. We shall not, however, deal here with the history of how one technology emerges from another, but break into the story when a particular technique is in use and a stock of machines already in existence.

In our model, there is only one type of machine: machines to produce corn and to produce machines are alike; they are all produced in exactly the same way but, to avoid an unnecessary degree of unreality, we assume that corn-making machines and machine-making machines are not interchangeable. Thus, when a machine has been set up to produce corn, it cannot be switched to producing machines.

We assume that workers are all alike; they require no special training for any operation. They can operate machines to produce the homogeneous consumption good, corn, and machines to produce machines.

Thus, the technical relations of our model consist of one technique for producing corn, and one for producing machines. These govern the relation of work to machines and to output in each sector. In this model, there is no problem of limitations on space. Land commands no rent, and since it enters into the process of production in no way other than as a site for machines, its role in production may be ignored.

(b) Productive capacity

The *productive capacity* of a set of machines must be specified in terms of two dimensions. It depends, firstly, on output per man hour of a team of men working machines, and secondly, the hours per day and days per year that the machines can be worked. The length of the working day for a team of men involves problems of great social and political importance; the possibility of multiple-shift working involves economic and technical considerations. These questions we leave on one side; we assume that there is a standard length of a single shift both in the sector producing corn and the sector producing machines.

A stock of machines can be worked more or less intensively, to produce a higher or lower rate of output. We assume that full-capacity output of a stock of machines requires a particular number of men working for the standard time. Under-capacity working can be organized in various ways, say, by keeping the full complement of workers on short time, working full time for some days and shutting down for some days, and so on. The simplest case for our purposes is where utilization of a stock of machines varies with the number of men employed. Say, 100 machines at full capacity are operated by 100 men for the standard working week. When 75 per cent of capacity is utilized, 25 machines are idle and 75 men work for the standard week. In making these assumptions, we gain a clear definition of capacity utilization in terms of the number of men employed.

We suppose, moreover, that output per man employed is not affected by the level of utilization of machines. If 75 per cent of the full-capacity labour force is working, production is 75 per cent of full-capacity output.

The relation of labour to machines is quite different from the relation of labour to land. Land is given by nature; it is essentially non-reproducible and has to be used by man as best he can. The technique of cultivation has to be adapted to the ratio of land to labour, whatever it may be. But a set of machines embodies a particular chosen technology and is designed to be used in a particular way. There is no presumption that output per man will be higher when the utilization of the stock of machines is below capacity, as in the case of a land and labour economy in which diminishing returns prevail. (Indeed, in reality it may be the other way about; output per man is often found to be highest when a plant is running with the full complement of workers for which it designed, efficiency being less when it is running at a lower level.) In our model, technique is such that, in each sector, output per head is constant up to the capacity of the stock of machines in existence. Beyond full capacity, output cannot be increased.

(c) A private-enterprise economy

If the economy were controlled by a rational plan, the allocation of men and machines between the machine-producing sector and the corn-producing sector would have been decided by some central authority. There, the net output of the corn sector would be distributed to the population on some accepted principle—say, to each

91

according to his work. If accumulation were considered to be particularly urgent, a large proportion of resources would be in the machine sector, and average income per head in terms of corn would be kept low. The higher the rate of accumulation, the lower the output of corn at any moment of time, but faster accumulation in-creases the potential output of corn more rapidly through time, by providing more workers with productive capacity.

In a planned economy of this type, there are formidable problems of organization but no problems of *effective demand*, i.e., of ensuring that all that can be produced is sold, for productive resources are directed to meet requirements that have been decided on by the planners. In a private-enterprise economy, the individual producer has to find a market for his output to get any benefit from it. The capitalist has to take decisions today about operations which will yield a benefit to him in the future; in the case of investment in machines, over a long future. He dwells in a world of uncertainty, and each capitalist operates in more or less active competition with others. There is no reason to expect the overall result of their individual decisions to conform to any rational scheme.

(d) Classes and incomes

We shall use our model to analyse a pure capitalist economy, in which there is no government activity. We are concerned with a *closed system*, so that there is no scope for international trade. For the time being, we are ruling out important features of a modern economy in order to concentrate on a single aspect of our problem.

The classes in the economy are somewhat different from those in Ricardo's story. There are now no landlords. Production is controlled by *firms* which own machines, employ labour, and make profits. Consumption takes place in *households*, which receive income from the firms. There are two kinds of households, those of workers, who receive wages, and those of *rentiers*, who have a claim on a share of profits.

At this stage in the analysis, the size of individual firms—that is, in our model, the number of machines controlled by an individual capitalist—is unimportant. We may suppose there are a large number of more or less equal size in the corn sector and a smaller number in the machine-making sector. Firms in the machine sector may produce machines for their own use as well as those which they sell to the corn sector.

Workers consume all their wages, week by week. Unemployed workers are supported by those who are earning.

The rentiers are identified with the households of the capitalists. We do not allow the rentiers any income except what the capitalists choose to give them. This, in the main, was the case with the old family firms described by Marshall. The head of the business gave an allowance to his wife. Although legally very different, the situation of a modern corporation is in essence the same—interest and dividends are paid out of profits. These matters will be discussed later. Meanwhile, we assume that the firms pass over a certain share of profits to their households, and that all rentier income is consumed, year by year. The firms regard it as prudent not to distribute profits before they have accrued. Thus, the part of the current output of corn consumed by rentier households is in respect of profits that have been earned in the past.

Since neither workers nor rentiers save, all the savings required for accumulation are made within the firms.

These assumptions have been made deliberately to play down the importance of the rentier element in capitalism, which was flattered by Marshall's treatment of the 'reward of waiting'. Marshall's concept implies that accumulation is for future consumption. But in a capitalist economy firms take on a life of their own. They do not exist merely to earn profits for rentiers. It is normally regarded as necessary and right for a business to reinvest a substantial part of its profits in expanding its operations. Thus, accumulation becomes the purpose of making profits, rather than consumption being the purpose of accumulation. Although our simple model leaves out many complications, it corresponds broadly to the character of modern capitalist industry.

2. Wages and profits
(a) Money wages and real wages

The wage rate in our model is a certain quantity of corn per man per week. The profit per man employed in the corn sector is, thus, output per man minus the wage. This simple treatment of profits per man might appear to put too much weight on our assumption of a single consumption good, but for our purposes it can be justified. In reality, of course, firms specialize in a narrow range of commodities, and no one can pay its workers simply by handing over part of its own product. A hosiery firm cannot pay its wage bill in stockings, or a match firm in boxes of matches. Wages must be paid in money, that is, in general purchasing power, so that workers can buy the products of many firms. The *real wage* from the workers' viewpoint—the amount of commodities that the money wage will buy—depends on the prices of the goods that they want to purchase. The cost of labour to the employer depends on the relation of the prices of his products to the money-wage rate. Thus, there is a 'stocking' cost of labour—the number of stockings that must be sold to pay the wage bill, a matchbox cost, and so on. In terms of our corn, which represents consumer goods in general, the real-wage rate from the workers' point of view and the cost of labour for corn-sector firms are identical.

In capitalist industry, prices of goods sold to the public are formed by adding a *mark-up* to *prime cost*. Prime cost is the direct cost of producing a batch of goods—the costs that would be saved if that batch were not produced—wages, cost of materials, etc. The mark-up constitutes the *gross margin* in the selling value of commodities. This is represented in our model by the ratio of profit per man in the corn sector to output per man. By assuming uniform prime costs throughout the economy, a single homogeneous consumption good, and a uniform wage rate in

93

terms of it, we represent an economy in which the ratio of gross margins to prime cost is uniform throughout all the industries producing consumption goods. This is a simplification but not an essential misrepresentation of the character of a modern industrial economy.

In reality, the excess of receipts over prime costs is partly required to cover *overhead costs*, the general expenses of keeping a business going. Gross profits (which Marshall called quasi-rents*) are receipts minus both prime and overhead costs. Moreover, gross profits include an allowance for amortization to provide for replacement of machines when necessary. Net profit is what remains after these deductions are made from gross profits. Payments to rentiers are normally made out of net profits.

In our highly simplified model, wages are the only prime cost. There are no overhead costs in our firms and, for the time being, we shall assume that a machine, once installed, can be employed indefinitely without loss of efficiency, so that we shall not be concerned with amortization (this will be discussed after we have introduced technical change†). Thus, in our model, the gross margin is all net profit.

We assume that the corn-wage rate is the same in both the machine-producing and corn-producing sectors, but the explanation of the level of profit margins in the machine sector involves a number of complications that we are not ready to discuss. (It involves determination of the relative prices of different products, in this case corn and machines, which we take up in Book 2, chapter 5.) For the time being, we shall work on the simple hypothesis that the mark-up of profits on wages is the same in both sectors.

(b) The share of profits

The total output of the economy is divided in the form of wages and profits between workers and capitalists. Since profits bear a constant ratio to wages, profit to a firm per annum depends on average employment over the year. Profit per machine depends on the average utilization of a stock of machines over a year.

The constant ratio of profits to output is reflected in constant shares of total income going to wages and profits. Suppose that in the corn sector the wage is $\frac{3}{4}$ of a unit per year, and one man produces 1 unit of corn per year. Then in the corn sector, the ratio of profits to wages is $\frac{1}{4}:\frac{3}{4}$, or 1:3. Since we assume that the mark-up is the same in both corn and machine sectors, the ratio of wages to profits is the same; and so the ratio of profits to wages in the economy as a whole is 1:3. In other words, when the mark-up on prime cost is $33\frac{1}{3}$ per cent the share of profits in output is 25 per cent.

(c) The determination of profits

Total profit per annum is a share of total income per annum: in our example, $\frac{1}{4}$ of income. For the economy as a whole, we can look at national income in two ways

---

* See **1** 3 §3(c).

† See **2** 4 §1(d).

(i) as the flow of income, and (ii) as the value of expenditure. Thus:

Income	Expenditure
Profits	Investment in machines
Wages	Rentier consumption of corn
	Workers' consumption of corn

Since workers consume all their wages, it follows that:

Profits = Investment + Rentier consumption

What is the significance of this equation? Does it mean that profits in a given period determine capitalists' consumption and investment, or the reverse of this? The answer to this question depends on which of these items is directly subject to the decisions of capitalists. Now, it is clear that capitalists may decide to consume and to invest more in a given period than in the preceding one, but they cannot decide to earn more. It is, therefore, their investment and consumption decisions which determine profits, and not vice versa.[1]

Furthermore, from our assumption that there are no savings out of household income, the excess of profits over distribution to rentiers, i.e., saving, is equal to the value of investment. A year's investment is defined as the value of the work done in the machine sector during the year, not as the value of the machines completed and installed in that year. The two would be equal only if employment in the machine sector has been constant for a sufficiently long time.*

(d) Notation

To set out these relationships in terms of our model, we use the following notation, in which each symbol represents value for a year in terms of corn.

Corn sector	Machine sector
C = Total output (consumption)	I = Value of work done (investment)
W_c = Wages	W_m = Wages
P_c = Profits	P_m = Profits
P_c^e = Profits consumed (eaten)	P_m^e = Profits consumed (eaten)
P_c^s = Profits saved	P_m^s = Profits saved

Taking the two sectors together, we write:

Y = Total income P = Total profits = $P^s + P^e$

W = Total wages $Y = C + I = P + W$

1. M. Kalecki, *Selected Essays on the Dynamics of the Capitalist Economy* pp. 78–9.
* Cf. appendix.

In real terms, a year's income is the output of corn plus the contribution made to the production of machines. In terms of corn values, it can be set out thus:

$$C = W_c + P_c^e + P_c^s$$
$$I = W_m + P_m^e + P_m^s$$
$$\overline{\qquad\qquad\qquad\qquad\qquad}$$
$$Y = W + P^e + P^s$$

and

$$C = W_c + W_m + P_c^e + P_m^e$$

If we subtract the fourth line from the third, i.e., subtract consumption from income (since wages and distributed profits are all consumed), the remainder is P^s that is to say, that saving is equal to the value of investment.

Writing s for the proportion of saving in income, we find:

$$sY = I \quad \text{or,} \quad Y = \frac{1}{s} I$$

Writing s_p for the proportion of saving in profits:

$$s_p P = I \qquad P = \frac{1}{s_p} I \qquad s = s_p \frac{P}{Y}$$

Our model enables us to see these relations in physical terms, as flows of corn wages and profits and corn value of investment. The same principle is at work in an actual capitalist economy, in a greatly complicated form. There is some saving out of household income; net profit is not equal to gross margins; foreign trade and the operations of government enter into the relations of income, savings, and investment. But the main principle is not affected. The purpose of our model is to enable us to see the basic relationships in a clear and definite way while obliging us to recognize the complications which we leave out of the story at each stage.

We have set out our table of total income in terms of corn values but have not yet considered how payments are made. This we must now do, before using the model to analyse problems of effective demand.

3. Credit

The economic system in which corn was the only product, and the only stock needed for production, could be described without introducing money. We could conceive of all transactions being conducted in terms of corn. In a model of any degree of complexity, with more than one commodity and with transactions spread through time, it is necessary to introduce some kind of financial system. A large part of Keynes's argument was concerned with the monetary and financial system of an advanced economy. Some of this will be discussed later. Here, we introduce only the minimum assumptions required to make the model work.

First, we must consider the relations between the two sectors. Payments to workers and households can be made directly in corn, so that it partly fulfils the function of money, but purchases of machines cannot be made so. A machine is a large indivisible unit which cannot be sold piecemeal week by week. Furthermore, the machine-sector firms need corn to pay wages before having a machine ready for delivery; in short, they need credit. We assume, therefore, that machine-making capitalists can issue *bills* against themselves. A bill is a promise to pay a specified sum at a specified date, for example, a promise to pay the bearer (whoever he may be) 100 units of corn, one year after the date of issue. Bills are used to buy corn to pay the wages of workers building machines and the share of profits to rentiers.

A machine-sector capitalist issues bills step by step as he requires corn to make payments to workers and rentiers. When a completed machine is delivered to the corn sector, bills equal to its value are cancelled, while the firm that produced it is again building up debt for the next round of production. In this way, a stock of bills remains in existence equal, at any one time, to the total outstanding indebtedness of the machine sector.

Bills may be dealt with at second hand. A lender may decide that, before the bill is due for payment, he needs the corn he has lent. He can obtain his corn by selling the bill to another lender who is willing to hold the debt for some time. Thus, bills provide a currency in which transactions can take place between one firm and another.

We have now introduced a special kind of money into the model. Corn is money in respect to payments of wages and payments to rentiers, while bills represent purchasing power over machines, since machine-sector capitalists redeem their own bills by delivering a machine. Receipt of a bill cancels the debt. Effectively, they pay off bills in machines instead of in corn.

Saving for the individual corn-sector capitalist is the part of corn profit which he does not distribute to his household. But savings cannot be held in corn; it is perishable and costly to store. Savings have to be *placed* in bills which represent future purchasing power over machines. Bills are a kind of *placement* or security, which provide a financial form in which wealth can be held.

Bills play an intermediary role in the process of saving and investment. Savings are placed in bills, and bills are then used to buy machines. As we shall see, it is this divorce between saving and investing, or between getting income and spending, which gives rise to instability in effective demand. This does not mean that the problem is somehow to be blamed on the monetary system. A private-enterprise economy could not operate without money in some form or other but, as we shall see, it is the private enterprise, not the money, which gives rise to instability. We have introduced only the bare minimum of 'monetariness' into our model in order not to distract attention from the basic problem.

(b) Lending and borrowing

The purchase of bills represents lending by corn-sector capitalists to finance the machine sector. A machine ready to start work is more valuable than one to be delivered later, as a result of the profit that is expected to be made over the period of delay. Correspondingly, a bill is issued with a *discount*, depending on the date of maturity—the day it falls due to be redeemed. That is to say, the face value of a bill, showing what it will be worth at maturity, is greater than the corn price paid for it by an amount corresponding to the discount. For example, a promise to pay 100 units of corn in one year's time may raise only 90 units of corn now, the discount being equal to 10 per cent per annum. The discount corresponds to interest on the loan for the purchaser of the bill, who is providing finance in the form of corn to the issuer. Thus, the corn value of a completed machine is greater than the amount of corn actually paid for the bills issued against it, by the amount of the interest on the bills.

There may also be borrowing in respect of the finance of investment in machines. A firm which is planning to add to its stock of machines expects to increase its flow of profits and its saving in the future. It is worthwhile to pay something to begin getting the profits sooner than if savings had to be accumulated in advance. A firm may therefore borrow *mature bills*, i.e., bills due for immediate repayment, which may be used to purchase a machine, and promise to repay the bills at a later date. To pay for the privilege of borrowing, the borrower repays with a premium—with bills of a higher value. The premium represents interest on the loan.

The firms that buy immature bills in effect get machines cheaper, by paying in advance, and those that borrow mature bills pay extra because they are paying in arrears.

A firm which is postponing the use of its savings for its own investment may get a return on them, meanwhile, in either of two ways. It may hold immature bills to maturity, enjoying the discount, and then exchange them for immature bills, the face value of these bills being greater than that of the matured bills by the amount of the discount. The firm is thus continuously getting a rate of interest corresponding to the rate of discount on the original sum placed in bills. For example, a sum of 100 units is lent at the start of year one, and 110 received at the end. This 110 is re-lent and 121 received at the end of the next year; 10 per cent per year is being received on the original loan of 100 units. Alternatively, this firm can lend mature bills to another which is investing ahead of its own savings, getting interest in the form of the premium.

There is some risk attached to lending, for the possibility exists that the borrower might get into trouble and fail to repay. This risk might be somewhat greater in lending mature bills to corn-sector capitalists for a fairly long term than in holding short-dated bills of the machine sector but, in either case, the risk is much less than in investing finance in long-lived machines whose future earnings cannot be relied on with perfect confidence. The level of interest rates therefore has to be low compared with the expectation of profit that induces investment to be undertaken. It will vary, as we shall see, with the level of expected profits.

The rate of interest plays a minor role in our model. The importance of the bill market is that it allows individual firms to save without immediately investing, and to invest ahead of saving, as they please.

A financial mechanism that provides firms with a command over resources beyond what they own is a basic characteristic of a modern capitalistic economy. It derives from the ability of capitalists to inspire confidence of future gain in those who lend to them. The less confidence they inspire, the higher the premium they must pay on borrowed funds. But if capitalists as a whole ceased to inspire any confidence at all, this would entail a collapse of the financial system, and indeed, of the whole economic system.

In this chapter, we have outlined the elements of a simple model of industrial capitalism. In the next chapter, we analyse how these elements relate to each other and what the consequences of their interactions may be.

4. A different model

The model of capitalist industry which we have set up is very different from that which underlies the teaching of many contemporary textbooks.

The so-called micro-theory of the present orthodoxy is an elaboration of the equilibrium system developed by Walras. The economy consists of a number of individuals. Each is a producer, a consumer, and a trader in one. Each individual has an endowment of some 'factor of production': the ability to perform a particular kind of work, an area of land suitable for a range of crops, or a stock of machines useful for various kinds of production. There is a specific list of known commodities which individuals want to consume, and which these factors are able to produce.

Individuals meet and exchange commodities and the services of factors among themselves. Bargaining in the market place is supposed to produce a pattern of supply and demand which determines the composition of output and the relative prices of commodities. From the demand for commodities is derived the payments for the services of factors that can be combined in various proportions to make them. From the payments for the factors is derived the incomes of their owners, and the expenditure of incomes constitutes the demand for commodities. An equilibrium of the market is thus established by a circular system of simultaneous relationships. The law of supply and demand declares that a market will be brought into equilibrium if, when a commodity is in excess supply, its price is lowered, and when there is excess demand for it, its price is raised. The same rule applies to work and its price (wages). Thus, in this system, involuntary unemployment of labour is impossible, since if a man were unemployed for a moment, he could secure employment by accepting a lower wage.

The most important differences between our model and this are, first, that we stress, instead of slurring over, the distinction between income from work and income from property, and second, that our model is set up to analyse processes going on through time, while this model can describe only the equilibrium corresponding to arbitrarily given initial conditions.

Our model will be used to exhibit both the influence of an unknown future on current decisions, and the interdependence of the wage level and price level in a system of produced commodities. Our model, with only two products and rigid technical conditions, is adequate for a discussion of the problems of effective demand, even though it leaves out all the complicated details of a multiproduct economy. As the argument develops, we shall discuss the manner in which many details can be introduced.

Appendix: Working capital

The model exhibited above portrays a process of production which uses only one kind of stock—'machines'. Our machines are characterized by durability: they last longer than a single round of production, indeed, in the model they are indefinitely durable. Stock of this kind is known as *fixed capital*. Production generally also requires inputs such as raw materials which are used up in the process of production and must be replaced if production is to continue. Furthermore, wages have to be paid before selling the product; to employ labour, a firm must command a *wage fund* (which Marx called 'variable capital') to bridge the period between starting to pay the workers and disposing of the output. These two elements constitute *working capital*.

When there is an increase in employment, raising the level of utilization of fixed equipment, an addition is made to the stock of working capital. Each week, the wage bill for the addition to the labour force and the bill for materials, power, etc., is paid, adding to the value of the firm's investment (and to its debt if it is working with borrowed finance). At the end of the *period of throughput*, the additional product emerges and from then on (if all goes according to plan), the value of a week's output pays the bill for wages, materials, etc., for a week, with a mark-up which covers a due share of the total cost of the business, and a contribution to its annual gross profit. After this, there is no further investment in working capital in respect of the initial increment of employment.

We have already met this principle in the story of the peasant's son who built up a stock of corn (of the continuous production variety) by planting some seed every day for a year, living on a daily allowance from his family until he became self-supporting at the beginning of the second year.*

When the finance invested in working capital has been borrowed, the loan (excluding accrued interest) for a period of throughput of, say, 20 weeks, is one week's debt outstanding for 19 weeks, one week's debt outstanding for 18 weeks, and so on. The total debt (not counting interest) is, thus, the weekly bill paid for a continuing flow of output multiplied by roughly half the period of throughput.

When a decision to reduce output has been taken, and employment begins to

* See **2** 1 §2(b).

fall, the fixed capital remains intact for the time being, while working capital is *dis-invested*. In the first instance, the weekly output of finished product remains unchanged, being the result of work begun and materials fed into production 20 weeks ago. As each batch of output is completed, the men who began the work on it are dismissed and the materials that went into it are not replaced. Over the period of throughput, the wage fund and the stock of materials are run down until they settle at the size corresponding to a new steady rate of output at a lower level.

In our simple model, we continue to make use only of fixed capital (our machines). In a model in **2** 6§3(d), we use working capital only. In the same chapter,§2, we make some general remarks about the relation between the two kinds of stock. There is no difficulty, in principle, in setting up a model with several kinds of stock, but it would be complicated and hard to follow. For this reason, we deal with one kind at a time, but it is important to remember that reality is less simple.

Chapter Three

Effective demand

In the picture of capitalism derived from Ricardo's model, there is no room for the problem which concerned the Mercantilists and Malthus: the problem of effective demand, i.e., of finding an adequate overall market to ensure the sale of goods produced. This problem cannot be exhibited in terms of the assumptions of Chapter 1 of Book 2. Whether corn belonged to the cultivator, or was paid to the landlord or a money-lender, or whether it was owned by a capitalist employer, any that was not consumed over a year was added to stock. There was no distinction between saving —refraining from eating corn—and investment, increasing the stock of corn. We set up a more complicated model in the last chapter in order to discuss the problems of effective demand, fluctuations in the level of employment, and the relation of saving by individuals to the accumulation of productive capacity by an economy. For this purpose, we included in the model an embryonic financial system (the bill market) but, of course, the reason for fluctuations in employment is not the existence of credit. It arises because industrial workers, unlike peasants, do not have access to means of production (in the model, machines) which they could use to meet their own needs, but have to wait until it suits the requirements of profit-seeking firms to employ them.

The orthodoxy that was still prevalent at the onset of the great world slump in 1930 was based on what Marshall called the 'familiar economic axiom', that saving is the same thing as an accumulation of stock, so that a 'man purchases labour and commodities with that portion of his income that he saves just as much as he does with that which he is said to spend'.* On this view, overall expenditure on goods and services would necessarily be sufficient to purchase the total supply of them; there could never be a general excess of production, or underutilization of productive capacity,

102   * See **1** 2 §4(a).

Furthermore, since it was assumed that the operation of the 'labour market', so long as it was not interfered with by trade unions, would always lead to an 'equilibrium wage' at which all seeking employment were employed, general unemployment could be due only to wages being too high. This might be true in a particular abstract model, but in the situation of the great slump, it was evidently absurd. Keynes carried out a wide-ranging attack on this orthodoxy, and developed suggestions for a totally different approach to the analysis of a modern economy.

Keynes took for granted the institutions of capitalist industry but did not always specify exactly what he had in mind. Michal Kalecki (who discovered independently the main points of what became famous as Keynes' General Theory) gave a narrower but more precise analysis of the operations of the capitalist economy. It is his formulation that we developed in the last chapter and that we follow here.

1. The short-period situation

Marshall's distinction between long-period and short-period changes in production is based on the fact that industrial firms own equipment which is long-lasting (the machines in our story) and that, once they have got it, they have to make the best use of it that they can. They can take on more or less workers and produce more or less output as sales rise or fall, but they do not commit themselves to creating new plant unless they expect that it can earn profits over a long future. Thus, decisions about the utilization of plant involve short-period considerations and decisions about creating new plant involve long-period considerations.

Here, we are concerned with a short-period situation. We use our model to examine the condition of a capitalist economy at a moment of time. There is a given number of machines in existence. No technical change is taking place. New machines are being produced; the stock of machines is slowly changing through time but, at a particular moment, there is simply a given amount in existence. The population has been increasing at least as fast as the stock of machines has been growing; there is no problem of scarcity of labour to man the machines in existence. The maximum amount of employment that can be offered at a particular moment is set by the capacity of the machines, but they are not necessarily being operated at full capacity. The amount of employment at any moment depends on the level at which the machines are utilized, which, in turn, depends on the effective demand for industrial output.

(a) Total income

At a particular moment, there is a certain level of employment in the corn sector, and a certain rate of output of corn.

Part of the profits currently accruing to corn-sector capitalists is distributed to rentiers as a share of profits received earlier. What is left of the current profits is saved and used to purchase bills in the bill market, which an individual capitalist

103

may hold temporarily with a view to future purchases of machines or merely as a placement to earn interest.

The machine-sector capitalists issue bills to obtain corn, because they have orders on hand which will enable them to make a profit on the machines that they are constructing. The bills are to be redeemed by selling finished machines to corn-sector firms. The machines are valued at corn prices which will include a margin of profit over and above the corn cost (in wages) of constructing them. (As we saw in the last chapter, the share of profit in the price of a machine is somewhat arbitrary in the short-period situation. We merely assume that the mark-up, the ratio of profits to wages, is the same in the two sectors.)

With the corn that they receive in exchange for bills, the firms in the machine sector pay wages to workers engaged in producing machines, and pay a share of their profits to their rentier households, who also receive payments in corn, which they consume. To avoid complicating our simple financial system, it is convenient to assume that the machine sector does not borrow to finance an increase in its own productive capacity. We suppose that firms in the machine sector pay the costs of any machines that they are making for their own use, directly out of their corn profits. They value a machine made for their own use at the same corn price as one sold to the corn sector and pay rentiers the usual share, but the element of profit in its cost is only a matter of bookkeeping. It accrues directly to the machine-making firm which produced it. The excess of the bookkeeping profit over what is paid to rentiers is reckoned as the share of saving out of that profit. These relationships are consonant with the pattern set out in terms of symbols in the last chapter.

The payment of interest redistributes some of the value of the output of machines between sectors and between individual capitalists.

(b) Accounts

Let us suppose that the mark-up is $\frac{1}{3}$, so that the ratio of wages to value of output is $\frac{3}{4}$ (i.e., 0·75) in both sectors, and that the proportion of current profits consumed by rentiers works out at $\frac{3}{5}$ (0·6). Then, starting from any convenient number, say, 3600 men employed in the corn sector, producing an output of 3600 units of corn per year, we can set out the accounts for the two sectors in terms of annual flows as units of corn. The consolidated accounts of the corn-sector firms taken together, on the basis of the above assumptions, is shown in Table 3.1.

The machine sector receives 360 units of corn per annum in return for new bills drawn against itself. We assume that the ratio of wages to profits and of rentier consumption to profits is the same in the two sectors. Thus, of 360 units of corn flowing to the machine sector, 270 are used to employ workers to build machines to be sold to the corn sector, and 90 accrue as profits (neglecting the discount). From these profits, 54 units are paid to rentiers. Of the remaining 36 units, 30 units are used to employ workers to build machines for use in the machine sector. The value of the work on these machines is $(1 + \frac{1}{3})30$, i.e., 40 units. The value of the bookkeeping

Table 3.1

Corn sector

	Units of corn produced	Expenditure of corn	
C	3600		
W_c		2700	
P_c		900	
P_c^e			540
$P_c^s = B^*$			360
			———
			900
	———	———	
	3600	3600	

* Net purchase of bills by the sector as a whole.

profit is 10. Of this, 6 units are paid to rentiers. The consolidated accounts of the machine sector are shown in Table 3.2.

Table 3.2

Machine sector

Receipts from bills sold 360 units of corn.

	Wages	Profit	Payment to rentiers	Value of output
Machines to sell	270	90	54	360
Machines to keep	30	10	6	40
	300	100	60	400

Ultimate recipients of corn

Workers	300
Rentiers	60
	———
	360

In general, the division of the machine output between machines for the corn sector and machines to keep will be influenced by the discount at which bills are sold by machine sector capitalists. This influence has been neglected in the numerical example.

Total employment in the machine sector (including workers who are adding to the stock of machines for use in the machine sector) is the wage bill, 300, divided by the wage rate, 0·75, i.e., 400. In each sector, profits equal $(1/s_p)I$. In the corn sector, investment is 360 and profits are $\frac{5}{2}(360)$, i.e., 900. In the machine sector, investment is 40 and profits are $\frac{5}{2}(40)$, i.e., 100.

The two sectors can now be put together in the overall accounts, as in Table 3.3. The value of output of the two sectors together is 3600 + 400 = 4000. The value of new bills sold to the corn sector, B, is 360.

Table 3.3

C	3600			
W_c	2700			
P_c	900			
P_c^e		540		
P_c^s		360 = B = 360		
			270 + 30	W_m
			90 + 10	P_m
			54 + 6	P_m^e
			36 + 4	P_m^s

For the two sectors together, investment has a value of 400 units of corn, and total profits are 1000 units. Total employment in the two sectors is 4000 men a year.

(c) Investment and saving

Table 3.3 shows relationships ex-post, looking back over the past year; it records what happened. But what happens depends on decisions taken ex-ante, looking forward. The relationships shown in the table were brought into existence by decisions that had already been taken.

Evidently, the sales of corn to the machine sector are due to plans for investment that had already been made. They may have been the result of orders for new machines placed by the corn sector, or of production of machines started by machine-sector firms in the expectation of sales. The machine-sector firms, also, have decided what part of their profits to devote to making machines for themselves. Furthermore, rentier expenditure comes out of profits after they have accrued. The level of profits in the economy as a whole—the level of output and employment—is determined by the level of investment.

The central point of the theory of effective demand is that the sales value of goods that are *available* to be sold to the public (our corn) is determined by expenditure out of the incomes earned in producing them plus expenditure out of incomes earned in producing *non-available* output (our machines). Since less than the whole income (including profits) derived from available goods is spent on those goods, expenditure from other incomes is necessary to maintain profitable sales. (This was the point that Malthus almost, but not quite, succeeded in formulating.*)

As well as investment, government expenditure and export earnings generate income from non-available sources, partly offset by taxation and by expenditure on imports. As we shall see, a budget deficit and a surplus of foreign earnings contribute to maintaining effective demand in the home country. We have so far excluded these elements and confined the argument to what is generally the main source of non-available output, investment.

Translated into terms of our model, the central point of Keynesian theory is that the key to the level of employment (and utilization of the stock of machines) lies in the orders placed for new machines to be produced for the corn sector, which, in turn, stimulate the production of machine-sector machines. The determining factor is the decisions that govern the volume of investment.

As we have seen, a particular firm in the corn sector is not confined to investing only its own savings, for it can borrow. Nor is it obliged to invest all that it saves, for it can buy second-hand bills. Each firm can invest ahead of saving, or save ahead of investing, as it pleases. Yet, for all together, saving cannot be greater or less than investment. The excess of the production of the corn sector, as a whole, over its own consumption, i.e., its savings, is determined by the demand for corn from the machine sector.

In Ricardo's view, savings are made in order to be invested. In this view, investment is causing savings to be made.

In one sense, for any society taken as a whole, savings and investment made over a period must be equal, if the accounting definitions are correct, for savings and investment ex-post are two ways of looking at the same thing—the total addition to wealth made over that period. The peculiarity of the private-enterprise system is that investments planned by firms, in the light of their own particular interests and expectations, decide for society as a whole how much it is to save.

(d) Investment and income

To explore these relationships further, let us see the effect of differences in the level of investment. Suppose that orders have been placed by the corn sector for 450 units' worth of machines, in the course of a year, instead of 360, and suppose the same proportions of current profits are consumed and saved as in the former example. The corn sector now produces 90 more units of corn with which it buys bills from the machine sector. In the machine sector, this is used to pay wages and rentier incomes. To produce that 90 extra units, the corn sector requires 67·5 more units of corn to pay wages, and this will be accompanied by 13·5 more units of rentier consumption. To produce this extra 81 units of corn involves 60·75 more of wages and 12·15 more of rentier consumption, and so on. In short, every unit of corn produced in the corn

* See **1** 2 §4(b).

sector involves 0·9 units of corn consumed (as wages and rentiers consumption) within the corn sector and 0·1 units of corn are available to pass to the machine sector. Saving is 10 per cent of total corn-sector income. Similarly, when machine-sector receipts are higher by 90 units, investment in machines for their own use is higher by 10 units, including the bookkeeping profit.

The effect of corn-sector investment being higher by 60 units is as follows:

ΔY	ΔC	ΔI	ΔW_c	ΔW_m	ΔP_c^e	ΔP_m^e	ΔP_c^s	ΔP_m^s
1000	900	100	675	75	135	15	90	10

Δ signifies an increment in the quantity concerned; δ would signify an indefinitely small increment.

With a higher level of investment in both sectors, worth 100 units, total value of income is 1000 units higher, when the customary proportions of profits consumed and saved, and the customary mark-up, are ruling.

The point of this argument is to show how the overall rate of saving is determined by expenditure on investment. If corn-sector firms try to save more by distributing less of their profits to rentiers, without placing more orders for machines, the level of output and employment in the corn sector is less. If they simply produce more corn without waiting to see what would become of it, extra wages and rentier consumption can absorb part, but part of the extra output would be unsold.

For example, suppose corn-sector firms save half their profits, but together still spend only 360 on bills. Their total profits are equal to what they invest plus their rentier consumption, i.e., 360 + 360. Since profits are still one-quarter of output, the output of corn would be only 2880 units instead of 3600. An attempt to save more by consuming less would be frustrated by the fall in spending out of profits, and the consequent fall in production.

Keynes' doctrine was at first felt to be extremely shocking; he seemed to be saying that saving is deleterious because it causes unemployment, whereas, for the neoclassics, thriftiness was the greatest of all economic virtues. Keynes, of course, did not deny that saving is necessary to make an increase in productive capacity possible (if households consumed the whole product of industry, there could be no investment). He was merely pointing out that, when there is under-capacity utilization of plant and unemployed labour, it is decisions to invest that determine the level of saving, and not saving that sets a limit to the level of investment.

(e) Consumption and investment

Keynes discussed the relation of the amount of consumption to the level of income in terms of the 'propensity to consume'. He based this on the view that everyone is likely to consume more per annum if his income is higher, so that a higher total income, in the economy as a whole, is accompanied by a higher level of consumption. Our argument follows Kalecki's version of Keynes' theory, which lays the main stress on the distribution of income between wages and profits.

Kalecki's analysis is summed up in the saying: The workers spend what they get and the capitalists get what they spend. Workers' households spend their pay-packets individually; the capitalists as a class receive collectively as profits what, taken together, they spend on investment and consumption.

In terms of our simple model, a higher level of profits (whether due to more invest-ment or a higher share of profits distributed to rentiers) is associated with propor-tionately more employment and a higher wage bill, since the mark-up does not vary. Conversely, a lower rate of investment, or a vain attempt to save more by distributing less to rentiers, is associated with an amount of employment lower in the same proportion as profits.

The model works in this simple way because we have so far confined the argument to situations in which there is always some surplus capacity, and in which the share of wages is a fixed proportion of the value of output.

Consider the effect of a difference in the mark-up in the corn sector, all other features of the model being unchanged. With the same amount of investment per annum in terms of corn, and the same proportion of profits consumed by rentiers, the total of profits is the same whatever the mark-up may be. With a lower mark-up, there is a higher ratio of wages to profits, and a correspondingly larger wage bill. The lower profit per man is compensated by a higher level of employment, in such a way as to keep the total of profits unchanged. Contrariwise, if capitalists attempt to get more profits by means of a greater mark-up, without a higher level of investment, the only result will be less employment. The capitalists may be able to increase the *share* of profits by reducing real wages, but they cannot increase the *amount* of profit per annum except by increasing expenditure out of profits.

Table 3.4a

Corn sector

	Units of corn produced	Expenditure of corn		
C	4500			
W_c		3600		
P_c		900		
P_c^e			540	
$P_c^s = B$			360	
			——	
			900	
	——	——		
	4500	4500		

Table 3.4a shows the position in our numerical example, otherwise the same, with a ratio of profits to wages of 1:4 instead of 1:3, while Table 3.4b shows the equivalent

position for a mark-up of 1:2. In both cases, 60 per cent of profits are distributed to rentiers. Only the corn sector is shown in the tables. Expenditure on the machine sector remains at 360 units.

In the first case, the lower mark-up entails a wage rate of $\frac{4}{5}$ of a unit of corn instead of $\frac{3}{4}$. The wage bill is 3600 instead of 2700, associated with employment of 4500 men, instead of 3600.

Table 3.4b

Corn sector

	Units of corn produced	Expenditure of corn	
C	2700		
W_c		1800	
P_c		900	
P_c^e			540
$P_c^s = B$			360
			___
			900
	___	___	
	2700	2700	

In the second case, the higher mark-up leads to a wage rate of only $\frac{2}{3}$ of a unit of corn, and employment of only 2700 men.

2. Changes in activity

The numerical examples in this chapter are not intended to be realistic (the specification of our model was much too narrow to make an approach to reality). They are set out merely to illustrate the basic relationships; they show how it is that the level of investment determines the level of saving and the overall level of employment, how it is that profits in the corn sector equal the wage bill of the investment sector plus the rentier expenditure of both sectors, and how the share of wages in the value of output influences the level of employment.

These relationships illustrate the main points of Kalecki's formulation of the theory of employment but are only preliminary to the important part of the argument, for they are set out purely in terms of static comparisons.

(a) Comparisons and changes

To see the structure of a model it is useful to make comparisons, as above, showing how it would look if only one thing were different (the level of investment, the share

110

of saving in profits, or the share of wages in output). But such comparisons are necessarily artificial. Two different situations in an economy must occur at different points of time. A movement from one to another involves events taking place through time; this requires different analysis from the comparison of two positions, each of which is at a moment on a particular path that has been arrived at from its own particular past history.

In the above exercises, we compared different levels of employment when the same stock of machines existed. In each position, we supposed that rentier consumption, in both sectors, was a given share of the profits currently received. This is not the same thing as considering the effect of a change in the level of employment, which involves a time lag between the firms receiving more profits and the rentiers consuming their share.

The original argument about the relation of total income to the level of investment came up in the context of changes rather than comparisons. In a time of heavy unemployment in Britain, a policy was advocated of government expenditure on public works (not covered by extra taxation), with the object of increasing the number of jobs. Official orthodoxy objected to this policy, using the argument (which, nowadays, seems absurd) that there is a certain volume of saving that is bound to be invested in any case, and that when the government borrows part of it to pay for public works, some other investment necessarily falls off. Keynes met this objection by pointing out that, if investment is increased, total income will increase and, consequently, saving will increase.[1] From this, R. F. Kahn worked out the theory of the *multiplier*, that is, the relation of the total increase in employment to the primary increase in employment in the investment sector by which it is caused.[2] This was incorporated by Keynes in his *General Theory* as a key element in his analysis. In relation to policy, clearly, the effect of a change is what matters, but in an account of the behaviour of the economy as a whole, the overall relation of the sectors to each other, shown in static comparisons, is also important. These two aspects of the argument often get mixed up; this has caused a great deal of unnecessary confusion. Not only here, but in every department of economic theory, it is necessary to keep a firm grip on the distinction between comparisons of specified positions and the analysis of the effects of an event taking place at a moment of time.

(b) Changes in investment

Suppose that, after the sale of corn to the machine sector has been at a steady level for some time, there is a sudden rise in the value of orders placed for machines, which then remain constant at the higher rate. At first, there is only an increase in orders, which does not involve immediate payment to the machine sector. But the

1. J. M. Keynes and H. D. Henderson, *Can Lloyd George Do It?* 1929.
2. 'The Relation of Home Investment to Unemployment', *Economic Journal* June 1931. Reprinted in *Selected Essays on Employment and Growth*, 1972.

machine-sector capitalists begin to issue more bills to obtain the extra command over resources—the corn and, thus, the men—that they need to increase their rate of production. The additional issue of bills creates a demand for more corn to be produced, and corn-sector capitalists increase their output accordingly, earn greater profits, and use these partly to buy bills, that is, to increase their rate of saving. (While the rate of investment is rising from year to year as more part-made machines are passing through the production pipeline, the stock of bills outstanding is growing in corn value. It will become stabilized at a higher total value when the output of finished machines has again become constant at the higher level.)

Initially, as employment and the output of corn rise, there is an increase in corn-sector profits, but not yet any addition to rentier receipts, for profits are paid out some time after they accrue. Additional employment and additional profits will follow when rentier consumption begins to increase.

The investment of machine-sector firms for their own use may also increase, but not necessarily in the former ratio to their issue of bills. We now throw together the two elements in employment in the machine sector—production for the corn sector and for their own use—and consider the effect of a change in its total amount.

Starting from the position in Table 3.3, we suppose that there is an addition to machine-making employment, at a particular moment, of 180 men, and that employment in the machine sector remains constant at the new level thereafter. This requires an increase in the wage bill of 135 units of corn, which requires an addition to employment in the corn sector of 135 men. These additional 135 men require wages of 101·25 units, and so on. The total addition to employment in the corn sector is

$$135 + \tfrac{3}{4}(135) + \tfrac{3}{4} \cdot \tfrac{3}{4}(135) + \cdots$$

which finally adds up to 540 men.

The increase in employment in the economy as a whole, at this stage of the expansion, is 540 men in the corn sector and 180 men in the machine sector. Thus, the total increase in employment is four times the increase in employment in the machine sector brought about by the decision to increase investment—the employment multiplier is equal to 4.

The full story of this initial effect on income and employment is shown in Table 3.5. (E_m is employment in the machine sector, E_c employment in the corn sector.)

(c) Further expansion

The increase in profits is 45 in the machine sector, and 135 in the corn sector. In our numerical examples of a situation with a steady rate of investment, saving was 40 per cent of profits. Now, saving, 495 + 85, i.e., 580, is made out of profits of 1035 + 145, i.e., 1180. Saving is now approximately 49 per cent of profits.

Our model, of course, is extremely primitive. There are no raw materials and no wage fund in the corn sector. Therefore, no secondary investment in increasing the

Table 3.5

Corn sector

Stage	C	W_c	P_c	P_c^e	$P_c^s = B$	E_c
0	3600	2700	900	540	360	3600
1	4140	3105	1035	540	495	4140
Δ at initial stage	540	405	135	0	135	540

Machine sector

Stage	B	W_m	P_m	P_m^e	P_m^s	E_m
0	360	300	100	60	40	400
1	495	435	145	60	85	580
Δ at initial stage	135	135	45	0	45	180

wage fund is required to make an increase in employment possible. We have left out both taxation and social security payments to unemployed workers, which played an important part in the original argument about the value of the multiplier. All the same, the point illustrated here is important in reality. An increase in investment and profits is accompanied, in the first instance, by a sharp increase in the ratio of saving to profits, for profits accrue in the first instance to firms, and none is distributed to rentiers till perhaps six months or a year later.

The rise in activity continues. Some time after an increase in investment has started and profits have risen, rentier expenditure in both sectors begins to increase, as profits begin to be paid out. Rentier consumption begins to rise towards its previous ratio to total profits. This increase will involve a further increase in employment and thus in total output and profits, and so a further rise in rentier consumption. We set out the rest of the story in Table 3.6.

The full increase in employment when all the effects of the once-for-all rise in the level of investment have worked through, is $1620E_c + 180E_m = 1800$ men overall. The multiplier effect of the initial increase of employment in the machine sector is 1800:180 or 10:1.

Thus, the multiplier is equal to $1/s$, where s is the proportion of saving in income. The size of the multiplier in our model depends on the proportion of profits in the value of output and the proportion of saving in profits: the greater the proportion of saving, the less the multiplication of consumption due to an increase in profits. In our example, the proportion of profits in the value of output is $\frac{1}{4}$, and the proportion of saving in profits $\frac{4}{10}$. The proportion of saving in the value of output is $\frac{1}{10}$. For any given increase in investment, output must increase by 10 times before the proportion of saving in output returns to its customary level. Thus, the multiplier equals 1/0·1, i.e., 10.

Table 3.6

Corn sector

Stage	C	W_c	P_c	P_c^e	$P_c^s = B$	E_c
0	3600	2700	900	540	360	3600
1	4140	3105	1035	540	495	4140
2	4572	3429	1143	621	522	4572
3	4831·2	3623·4	1207·8	685·8	522	4831·2
4	4986·72	3740·04	1246·68	724·68	522	4986·72
	5220	3915	1305	783	522	5220
Δ when all effects have worked out	1620	1215	405	243	162	1620

Machine sector

Stage	B	W_m	P_m	P_m^e	P_m^s	E_m
0	360	300	100	60	40	400
1	495	435	145	60	85	580
2	522	435	145	87	58	522
3	522	435	145	87	58	522
	522	435	145	87	58	522
Δ when all effects have worked out	162	135	45	27	18	180

The effect of a once-for-all fall in the level of investment can similarly be spelt out in terms of our model. When new orders for machines are insufficient to replace those which are being completed, machine-sector firms dismiss some workers and reduce their purchases of corn. Sales of corn to the machine sector fall off, so that men are dismissed from the corn sector. (The workers who are still employed share their wages with the unemployed; total workers' consumption falls with the total wage bill.) The fall in demand is scattered over the corn sector. The level of utilization of machines has fallen all round. Finding profits reduced, firms reduce the payments to the rentiers, which reduces the output of corn still further, which reduces the wage bill further, and so on down. At the same time, the machine-sector capitalists—receiving less profits—reduce payments to rentiers, and employment in producing machines for themselves.

3. Instability

So far, we have considered the consequences of differences or of changes in the level of investment, but have said nothing about what determines them. This raises the most difficult and disputed question in the theory of the behaviour of a private-enterprise economy. Here we can give only a provisional account of it.

(a) Expectations

We assume that corn-sector firms were planning to increase their productive capacity when they found that a high proportion of their existing capacity was being utilized. Profits on their existing machines were then high and this caused them to believe that, if they had more capital, they would be able to make still more profits. We suppose, that is to say, that their expectations about the future are strongly affected by present experience.

The financial system (the bill market) allows them to translate their expectations into command over resources, and thus increased production. Expectations may be self-generating. Variations in optimism or pessimism may cause investment expenditure, and thus total output and employment, to rise or fall, and so appear to some extent to justify themselves.

It is the dependence of expectations on current experience that introduces fluctuations in activity into the model. It gives rise to the phenomenon generally called the *trade cycle*. On this view, instability arises from the interaction between the multiplier and the 'accelerator', i.e., between the rise in income due to a rise in investment and the increase in investment plans that follows from a rise in income. When the current levels of utilization and profits have recently risen, investment is encouraged and utilization rises still higher. There is never likely to be a once-for-all step from a lower to a higher rate of investment, such as we analysed above, or the reverse. The relation of consumption to one level of investment may never catch up before the rate of investment changes. The economy then never settles down into a steady position such as is shown in Table 3.6; the level of employment is constantly rising or falling relatively to the stock of productive capacity in existence.*

* See appendix.

(b) The rate of interest

Changes in expectations of profits, which lead to changes in the rate of investment, also react on the rate of interest. When a larger profit per annum is expected from a machine, corn-sector firms are more anxious to install new machines as soon as possible. The premium on mature bills is therefore bid up. The more optimistic firms borrow mature bills from the less optimistic ones, confidently expecting to pay the premium out of the extra profits that they will make from the new machines as soon as they are installed.

The increase in the premium means that the return to be got by an individual firm postponing the investment of its saving has gone up and, correspondingly, the cost of borrowing has risen. Similarly, when expectations of profits are damped and the rate of investment falls, the rate of interest is bid down—borrowing becomes cheaper. Thus, movements of interest rates tell in the direction of offsetting the influence of changes in expectations on investment, but when expectations are held with some conviction this cannot have much effect. (These matters are discussed further below.)*

(c) A boom

Since a rise in investment causes a rise in investment, what stops an upswing from going on indefinitely? In terms of our model, when the rate of investment has recently risen relative to productive capacity in existence, there has been a rise in the level of utilization of machines in both sectors. The level of profits is now higher than it was when the investment being carried out was planned. When an increase in output has been sharp, it may run up to the capacity output of corn-sector machines, so that the rate of investment in machines, i.e., the flow of purchases of corn by the machine sector, has to be held up till more machines have been installed and manned in the corn sector. Then, after a time, the upward movement can continue.

The consequences are different when the machine sector reaches full capacity. Then, for a time, the rate of investment cannot grow further. The demand for corn reaches a peak and remains at an upper limit for a time. But meanwhile, machines have been coming out of the pipeline of production. As the stock of corn-sector machines grows, it overtakes the growth of output. Once capacity has increased relative to the rate of investment, average utilization of plant is reduced and the prospect of profit on further new investment sinks. The boom breaks and a decline sets in.

If investment fails to recover from a slump, output, employment and profits remain at a low level. Low profits are discouraging to investment. Firms may remain indefinitely in a state of self-fulfilling pessimism.

4. Long-period demand

The foregoing argument is entirely in short-period terms. We have been discussing the level of employment in relation to the productive capacity in existence at a

* See **2** 8 §3.

moment of time. We have not discussed the relation of productive capacity to the total number of workers looking for jobs. We assumed that there was at least enough labour available to man equipment at full capacity but we did not assume that there was enough equipment to employ all the labour force. There might be any number of workers unemployed even when existing capacity was fully utilized.

Unemployment that results from a deficiency of effective demand is sometimes called Keynesian; unemployment that is due to a deficiency of equipment provided by profit-seeking firms is sometimes called Marxian because of the emphasis which Marx laid on the phenomenon known as the 'reserve army of labour'. We may use the terms *unemployment* for the first and *non-employment* for the second. The amount of non-employment in an economy is the number of workers who would not find jobs even when all existing capacity was fully manned. (In a modern industrial economy, it is sometimes claimed that the non-employed are individuals who are unemployable because of inefficiency, indiscipline, or other bad habits. This is because it is taken for granted in a private-enterprise economy that it is the business of workers to adapt themselves to the requirements of profit-seeking firms, rather than the other way round.)

This distinction enables us to see how Malthus and Ricardo were at cross-purposes.* Malthus argued that expenditure out of rent would maintain effective demand just as, in our model, rentier expenditure helps to maintain employment in the short-period sense, while Ricardo argued that higher profits would increase the rate of growth of the stock of capital and so promote a growth of employment in the long-period sense. Malthus failed to take in Ricardo's point, that long-run accumulation of productive capacity requires saving, and Ricardo would not admit Malthus' point, that short-run profitability requires expenditure. Similar confusions are not unknown today.

5. Pre-Keynesian theory

The orthodox opinion attacked by Keynes was based on the notion that there is a natural tendency to equilibrium in a private-enterprise economy and that the operation of a free market will ensure full employment of available labour, unless trade unions interfere to keep wages too high.

We noticed above that a free market in land and labour (if such can be conceived) would lead to an efficient use of resources since the marginal productivity of labour would be equalized over the whole cultivable area.† If this argument is applied to our model of men and machines, it produces an awkward result. Suppose that there are a certain number of machines in existence, and a certain number of workers. When they are brought together in a free market, the wage and the hire price of machines is settled by supply and demand. When there are more men than the machines could accommodate at full-capacity utilization, the wage is bid down to

* See **1** 2 §4(b).
† See **2** 1 §4(c) and Fig. 1.7.

zero, and the whole of the corn produced accrues to the owners of machines. When there are too few workers, the hire price of machines is bid down to zero, and the entire proceeds go to wages. If there happened, by chance, to be just enough men to utilize the machines in existence, the share of wages and profits in proceeds would be indeterminate.

To avoid this awkwardness, the model has to be set up differently. Substitutability between labour and 'capital' has to be assumed. Formerly, this concept was rather vague, but in the modern revival of pre-Keynesian theory, it has been precisely specified.

The stock of equipment is created directly from saving out of output, as though a 'machine' in our story consisted of a quantity of 'corn'. In one way, this resembles the Ricardian corn economy, for there, the whole stock of capital was a quantity of corn. But in another respect, this story is quite different. For Ricardo, the amount of employment that a stock of corn could offer was fixed by technical conditions and the conventional wage rate. The point of the corn capital in the pre-Keynesian full-employment model is that it can be remoulded into such a form as to employ any amount of labour. This does away with the distinction between long- and short-period demand for labour, for it means that the concept of productive capacity has no existence independent of the level of employment.

For this story, technology is such that output per head rises at a decreasing rate as the stock of 'corn capital' per man employed rises. That is, there are diminishing returns from stocks of corn applied to labour, a concept borrowed from the traditional notion of diminishing returns from labour applied to land. Given the quantity of 'corn capital' in existence, workers offer themselves for corn wages. Owners of 'corn capital' employ the amount of labour that makes the marginal product of labour equal to the wage, thus maximizing corn profit per unit of the stock of corn. If any labour is unemployed in this scheme, the wage rate is reduced; if there is a scarcity of labour, it is raised. Thus, there is always some wage rate at which full employment is guaranteed.

This reproduces the position which we discussed above in terms of landlords employing wage labour (when all land is alike and wages are paid in arrears), except that 'corn capital' with its 'marginal productivity' takes the place of land. There is no need to go over it again.

This model slips past the problem of effective demand. Equipment is just a stock of corn; savings of corn are simply added to the stock. When the available labour force grows at the same rate that corn is accumulating, the wage rate remains constant. If it grows less quickly, the wage rate is rising (the marginal productivity of corn capital is falling), and vice versa.

More elaborate forms of this model have been proposed. For instance, 'corn capital' may be owned by employers who distribute their profits entirely to households. Rentier households and wage earners save part of corn income and hand it over to employers to add to their stock.

118 Our model differs from this in two important respects. First, the amount of employment at any moment depends on the number of machines in existence and their level of utilization, which is governed by the state of effective demand, not by bargaining over real wages. Indeed, in our model, the relationship between wages and employment is reversed, for if the corn-wage rate were cut, there would be a reduction of employment in producing corn.

Second, the rate of accumulation depends on the investment decisions of the firms, not on the savings of households. A form of finance has been introduced into our model to permit these basic characteristics to be displayed.

Minor differences are that we allow no saving at all out of household incomes, and that we have made a number of drastic simplifications about the nature of technology which are at the opposite extreme from those represented by continuous substitutability between 'corn capital' and labour. The minor differences will be modified as our argument proceeds. We shall allow for saving out of household income and for less rigid technical conditions. The major differences constitute the gulf which divides pre-Keynesian from post-Keynesian analysis.

Appendix: Instability

The instability of a private-enterprise economy is connected with the two-sided relation between investment and income. An increase in the rate of investment, at any moment, leads to a rise in the level of income and the rise in the level of income is likely to give a further stimulus to investment. These relationships are extremely complicated in any actual situation and in any economy vary from time to time with general circumstances. The essence of the matter, however, can be understood in terms of our simple model.

(a) The multiplier

In §2 above, we set out the effect of a once-for-all rise in the rate of investment, starting from a position at which it had been steady for some time before. Such a movement is not likely to happen in a continuously fluctuating economy but, for purposes of our example, we shall make use of the same numerical relations as are shown there. Dividing time into discrete periods for the sake of convenience, we can say that the multiplier in respect to an increase in investment, in the first period, is 4. An increase of employment and the wage bill in the machine sector leads immediately to an increase in total employment and in the output of corn four times as great. The effect continues to expand over subsequent periods as profits begin to be paid out to rentiers. Thus, when the rate of investment changes from period to period, the ratio of consumption to investment in any period is partly the result of investment made in earlier periods.

119

(b) The accelerator

The effect of a rise in income on the level of investment is not so easy to reduce to simple terms. It is sometimes expressed as an 'accelerator', relating investment in one period to the change in output in the previous period.

$$I_t = v(Y_{t-1} - Y_{t-2}) = v \Delta Y_{t-1}$$

where I_t is the investment in the current time period, ΔY_{t-1} the increment in output in the preceding time period, and v the *accelerator coefficient*. For example, if the increase in output during the past time period was 100 units of corn, and the accelerator coefficient is 0·25, the value of investment in the current period would be 25. This form of the accelerator seems to embody a mixture of two ideas: (i) that there is some technical relation between output and the stock of equipment needed to produce it, so that an increased output requires investment to make an appropriate addition to productive capacity; (ii) that the rise in output stimulates confidence about future prospects and thus encourages investment.

The first element in this argument cannot be separated from the second. When equipment is being used to capacity, in conditions of a seller's market—more than capacity output could be sold at a satisfactory price—there is an incentive to increase the stock of equipment only if the situation is expected to last long enough to make it worthwhile to do so. And when a decision to increase productive capacity has been taken, it remains to say at what rate the investment in it will be carried out. A purely technical accelerator is a misleading conception.

Since investment is guided by prospects of profit, it seems more plausible to connect changes in the rate of investment with changes in the level of profits, and to suppose that in conditions of uncertainty, expectations are strongly influenced by what has happened in the recent past. We make use of a formula for the accelerator as follows. First, we introduce the idea of a threshold. There is a certain level of increase in profits below which investment will not increase. Since the stock of machines has been growing for some time, an increase in total profits from period to period is necessary even to keep investment constant. Starting from our former numerical example, in which corn-sector profits are 900 units, we assume that the threshold is 120 units. Furthermore, we assume that the change in investment in any period is $\frac{1}{3}$ of the excess of the increase in corn-sector profits above the threshold. Thus,

$$\Delta I_t = \tfrac{1}{3}(\Delta P_{c,\, t-1} - 120)$$

The meaning of this formula is that—as activity changes—if the increase in profits from one period to the next is greater than 120, corn-sector capitalists think it worthwhile to order new machines from the machine sector at a greater rate than before. If the increase in profits is less than 120, their optimism is not sufficiently maintained and they tend to cut back investment below previous levels.

The choice of a relatively large threshold enables us to show rapid reactions in the model, so as to make our story extremely dramatic.

120

The use of discrete periods of time is a device to enable us to give a definite time sequence to our story. A change in investment today relates to the change in profits one period ago, i.e., the reaction of investment is *lagged* by one period. Similarly, the pay-outs to rentiers are based on the profits of the previous period, and thus, any increase in pay-out is delayed for one period beyond that in which the increase in profits took place.

It is the lagged reactions of investment to changes in circumstances which endow the system with instability. If investment decisions were taken in the light of correct foresight, the economy could move smoothly from one balanced position to another, without a tendency to overshoot or wobble. But future conditions must be guessed, they cannot be known. Decisions to invest are necessarily based on information that is to some extent out of date, or will be rendered out of date by changes that investment itself induces.

(d) A boom

We may trace the effects of an increase in investment, starting from the position in Table 3.3, showing the reciprocal interaction of the increase in corn-sector profits with the value of orders placed for machines. We now see how these relations work out when investment increases. We assume that in the initial position there are 5400 machines in the corn sector which could give employment to 5400 men at full capacity. In the initial position, employment in the corn sector is 3600 men. In the machine sector, there are only 600 machine-making machines and those which are in the pipeline will not be available for use until after five time periods. In the initial position, employment in the machine sector is 400 men.

Our story begins with an increase of employment in the machine sector from 400 to 600 men, which takes it to full-capacity output. The path that the economy then follows is shown in Table 3.7. The initial increase of employment in the machine sector requires an increase of wages of 150 units of corn, which leads to an increase in the output of corn of 600 units. The increase in employment is accompanied by increased profits, but pay-outs to rentiers have not yet increased. The demand for corn from the machine sector has risen by the 150 units needed for wages, which entails an increase in corn output by 600 units.

As we know:

$$\Delta P_c = \Delta P_c^e + \Delta P_m^e + \Delta W_m = 0 + 0 + 150 = 150$$

In period 2, the increase in corn-sector profits stimulates a desire for further growth of productive capacity. The rate of investment should rise:

$$\Delta I_2 = \tfrac{1}{3}(150 - 120) = 10$$

But this increase in investment is not possible since machine-sector capacity is

121

Table 3.7

Corn sector

Stage	C	W_c	P_c	P_c^e	$P_c^s = B$
0	3600	2700	900	540	360
1	4200	3150	1050	540	510
2	4680	3510	1170	630	540
3	4968	3726	1242	702	540
4	5092·8	3819·6	1273·2	745·2	528
5	5069·28	3801·96	1267·32	763·92	503.4
6	4293·29	3692·47	1230·82	760·40	470·42

Machine sector

Stage	B	W_m	P_m	P_m^e	P_m^s	I
0	360	300	100	60	40	400
1	510	450	150	60	90	600
2	540	450	150	90	60	600
3	540	450	150	90	60	600
4	528	438	146	90	56	584
5	503·4	415·8	138·6	87·6	51	554·4
6	470·43	387·27	129·09	83·16	45·93	516·36

limited for the time being to 600 machines, and these 600 are now fully utilized $(450/0·75 = 600)$. Investment must remain at 600, and machine-sector wages at 450. The demand for corn continues to rise, however, as the consumption of corn-sector rentiers is increased by 90 units of corn, and that of machine-sector rentiers by 30 units. So that

$$\Delta P_{c2} = 90 + 30 + 0 = 120$$

and output is increased by 480 units of corn. But now,

$$\Delta I_3 = \tfrac{1}{3}(120 - 120) = 0$$

Consequently, wages in the machine sector do not rise after period 2. However, payments to corn-sector rentiers are increased by 72 units, and thus $\Delta P_{c3} = 72$. This is a relatively modest increase. At the same time, the stock of machines in the pipeline has been growing relatively to the total profits. These influences together precipitate a cut in investment in the fourth period:

$$\Delta I_4 = \tfrac{1}{3}(72 - 120) = -16$$

122   and $$\Delta W_{m4} = \tfrac{1}{4}(72 - 120) = -12$$

Rentier payments in the corn sector are still rising, however, so

$$\Delta P_{c4} = 43{\cdot}2 - 12 = 31{\cdot}2$$

At the next stage:

$$\Delta I_5 = \tfrac{1}{3}(31{\cdot}2 - 120) = -29{\cdot}60$$

and

$$\Delta W_{m5} = \tfrac{1}{4}(31{\cdot}2 - 120) = -23{\cdot}2$$

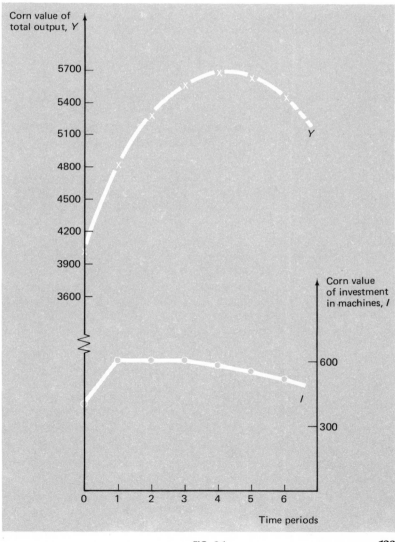

FIG. 3.1

Rentier consumption in the machine sector is also cut, and despite a small rise in corn-sector consumption,

$$\Delta P_{c5} = 18\cdot72 - 2\cdot4 - 22\cdot2 = -5\cdot88$$

and total corn output is cut by 23·52. Additional capacity for the machine sector is now at last available, but it is no longer required; falling profits precipitate falling investment and output. The decline will continue until the rate of investment ceases to fall, which may not be until $I = 0$.

The process is illustrated in Fig. 3.1. Note that, while investment ceases to rise after period 1, the lagged effect of rising rentier consumption maintains a rising demand for corn output for some time after the period when investment begins to fall. But profits and rentier consumption cannot be maintained in the face of falling investment and, eventually, output begins to decline.

(e) A slump

The path of a decline into a slump is described in Table 3.8. In this case, also, we tell a more dramatic story than could occur in a more complex economy. The slump is

Table 3.8

Corn sector

Stage	C	W_c	P_c	P_c^e	$P_c^s = B$
0	3600	2700	900	540	360
1	2952	2214	738	540	198
2	2191·2	1643·4	547·8	442·8	165
3	1314·72	986·04	328·68	328·68	0
4	1200	900	300	300	0

Machine sector

Stage	B	W_m	P_m	P_m^e	P_m^s	I
0	360	300	100	60	40	450
1	198	150	50	48	2	200
2	165	79·5	26·5	25·5	1	106
3	0	0	0	0	0	0
4	0	0	0	0	0	0

the consequence of a reduction in machine-sector employment by 200. Investment is related to the change in profits in the preceding period in the same way as for the boom. By period 4, pessimism is so great that no further orders are placed for machines.

In our former examples, profits were equal to investment, plus rentier consumption, which was a regular proportion of profits when income was at a steady level. Now, investment has fallen to zero and the machine sector provides neither employment nor profits. But the corn-sector firms do not let their own families starve. At the worst, they continue to pay out 300 units and so continue to make profits of that amount. Thus, as the total profit falls, the proportion consumed rises until it reaches 100 per cent.

From period 4 on, profits are maintained only to the extent of rentier consumption;

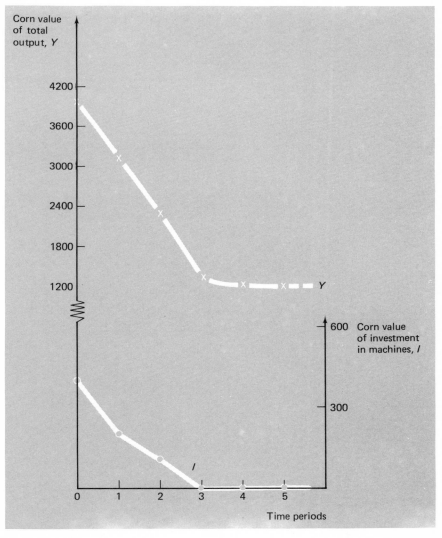

FIG. 3.2

there is no tendency for output to increase and the slump may continue indefinitely. The story is illustrated in Fig. 3.2.

To apply analysis on these lines to an actual case, it would have to be elaborated to incorporate more complex lag structures, the influences of investment in working capital, different forms of capacity constraint, and the effects of unexpected events. However, our simple examples exhibit the main point: the destabilizing influence of uncertainty concerning the future, which is at the centre of any analysis of the dynamics of a capitalist economy.

Chapter Four

Technical change

A model of a capitalist economy with a single technique of production does not correspond to any actual history. From the first, capitalism developed and flourished through continuous innovations in methods of production, organization, transport, trade, finance, and in means of controlling the labour force. This has been the essence of the capitalist process and the source of its success. In any economy that has reached a certain level of industrial development, inventions and discoveries are continually being made, providing the basis for new methods of production.

Inventions may be the result of purposive research or chance bright ideas, or they may be thrown up as a by-product of scientific discoveries. *Innovations* are made when inventions are put into practice. There is always a backlog of potentially serviceable inventions that have not yet been put into use. Technical change comes about through innovations embodying new designs of plant, new materials, new processes, or new types of commodities.

1. Accumulation

Investment to enlarge productive capacity is rarely made in the same form as equipment which is already in operation. Investment is continually embodying new technical knowledge, and from time to time, major changes—for instance in the source of power—require the whole stock of equipment to be transmogrified into new forms.

Technical change affects the nature of the commodities being produced, as well as the methods of producing them. New methods of production influence the character of products, and new products are invented to take advantage of new methods.

An investment is never immortal, for even if equipment is physically durable, the profitability of various products and methods of production is constantly changing. To continue in being, an industrial firm has to maintain its capacity to earn profits by replacing old equipment with new, and moving from one line of production to another.

Technical innovations also affect the character of the labour force. As technology grows more sophisticated, a higher general level of education is required for workers to adapt themselves to the special skills required. Every industrial nation finds it necessary to provide a system of state schooling. (The purpose of education is no longer to enrich the life of a gentleman but, rather, to provide a necessary factor of production for industrial firms to employ.) There is a great deal of investment embodied in the special skill of a worker; frequently, changes in technology may make special skills obsolete so that investment in human capital is at risk no less than investment in machines, and it is not so easy for a worker to 'maintain his capital intact'.

All this opens up important questions which affect every aspect of economic and social life. Here, we discuss only some general principles that can be exhibited in terms of our simple model.

We shall continue to take 'corn' as the single consumption good and to assume that all 'men' are alike, but there is no longer one uniform type of equipment. Technical change takes place in the design of 'machines'. The machine-making sector continually provides the corn sector with new types of machines and readapts its own plant so as to be able to do so. We can get some way within these restrictions, but it is important always to remember how limited they are.

(a) Employment

Technical progress almost always has the effect of raising output per man employed. How does this influence the demand for labour in private-enterprise industry? When the labour force is growing so that there is always a 'reserve army' of workers anxious to take a job, the real-wage rate may remain constant, so that profit per man employed is rising. For instance, if we compare Table 3.1 with the situation which would exist with a different type of machine in use, giving an output per man of, say, 1·2 units instead of 1, while the corn-wage rate remains at 0·75, profit per man is 0·45 instead of 0·25. Then, 3600 men produce 4320 units of corn. If the share of profits consumed by rentiers is 0·6, as before, we have the relations shown in Table 4.1. It now needs investment by the corn sector of 648 units, instead of 360, to sustain a level of employment of 3600 men in the corn sector.

Will an increase in profit per man employed lead to an increase in the rate of investment? It is not necessary that it should. Just as a higher return per unit of work is as likely to reduce as to increase the amount of work that a man is willing to do, so easier profits may make a group of capitalists feel that there is no need to struggle so hard to expand.

128   To take the simplest case, suppose that after equipment for a new technique has been installed, investment remains the same as when the old technique was in use. Profits are passed to rentier households only after they have accrued, and rentier consumption is assumed to be in an unchanged ratio to profits. It follows that, if investment remains the same as before, total profit remains the same as before, just as in the case of a lower real-wage rate which we discussed above.* The same total of profits is now earned with less employment. The wage bill is reduced. The share of profits has risen while the total of profits per annum remains the same.

Table 4.1

Technique	Output	Wages	Profits Consumed	Saved
(i)	3600	2700	540	360
(ii)	4320	2700	972	648

In the above example, if investment remains at 360 units, profits remain at 900; employment in the corn sector is reduced to 2000 men, and the wage bill to 1500.

These numbers, of course, are quite arbitrary but the phenomenon which they illustrate—employment falling when output per head is rising faster than total output—is a serious problem in the capitalist world.

The fall in employment in a case of this kind is sometimes described as 'technological unemployment'. Improvements in technique are then blamed for the result. In a rationally planned economy, an increase of output per unit of work obviously ought to be an advantage to all concerned. How can it be a misfortune for the workers in a capitalist economy? The answer is that, in a rational economy, the improvements would be used according to a conscious policy. If the situation was one in which accumulation was considered by the authorities to be the top priority, consumption would not be increased; the labour released by the rise in output per head from the consumption sector would be drafted into the investment sector to speed up accumulation. If investment was considered adequate before, consumption could be increased by raising the payment to workers per unit of work, by distributing a bonus to all, or by raising the level of pensions, scholarships, etc., which are not payments in respect of current work. If the level of consumption was considered adequate before, the amount of work could be reduced by shortening the working day, lengthening holidays, or allowing earlier retirement and longer education. The benefit from increased output per head might be taken out in these ways in any proportion that the authorities decreed, or public opinion approved. The trouble in a private-enterprise economy, with rising output per worker employed and constant real wages, is that potential output and potential profit have increased but are not being realized because investment does not increase fast enough. (In the industrial revolutions of England in the early nineteenth century and Japan in the early twentieth,

* See **2** 3 §1(e).

there was rapid technical progress without rising wages. The reason why this did not lead to stagnation was that, in both cases, the reduction of costs led to a great expansion of exports so that neither economy had to rely solely on increasing consumption to maintain effective demand.)

(b) Real wages

The situation in a highly developed modern economy is not so bleak as the above argument suggests. For more than a hundred years, the overall average of real wages per man hour of work has been rising. This may have been partly at the expense of low incomes in the rest of the world, associated with low prices of imported materials,* but it has been largely the effect of technological development.

In the simple model with one technique, we assumed that the workers meekly accepted the wage that they were offered. In fact, the wage bargain has been a constant battleground. The balance of forces is highly unequal because, in the nature of the case, employers are fewer than workers and they are financially much more secure; they obey the convention that Adam Smith noticed,† of backing each other up, and in most situations they can appeal to the apparatus of the state to defend their interests. But workers have considerable power if they can combine to wield it.

It is not easy for trade unions to force a rise of wages at the expense of profits. Even if an increase in money-wage rates is granted, when output per head is constant, employers can keep proportionate profit margins constant by raising prices. But when innovations in the production of a certain range of commodities have reduced costs of production (at the old wage rate) relative to the sales value of output, the workers are in a strong position to demand a share in the increase in profits. Employers then buy off the threat of a strike by conceding a rise in wages, leaving themselves, at worst, with the same expected level of profits as before.

At the same time, many innovations are bound up with economies of large-scale operation. New plant may require a large indivisible investment which is profitable only at a high rate of output. Then prices are cut dramatically to tap a mass market. Either way, there is a strong tendency for real wages to rise with rising productivity. We shall return to this question after we have introduced a variety of consumption goods into the model.

Meanwhile, we can see how rising real-wage rates help to mitigate the tendency for increasing productivity to cause so-called 'technological unemployment'. We have seen that if real wages remained constant as output per head rose, profit per man employed would increase so that to keep even a constant labour force employed, with unchanged share of saving in profits, it would be necessary to bring about a continuously increasing share of investment in output. An increased share

---

* See **2** 5 §5(b).
† See **1** 2 § 1(a).

of consumption out of profits would help to maintain employment, but a growing disparity in standards of life might cause other troubles.

When investment fails to expand fast enough to maintain the level of employment, as the ratio of saving to income rises, potential profits are not realized and techno-logical improvements run to waste in unemployment.

When real wages rise in step with output per head, the problem of absorbing growing savings is much less acute. The share of profits in the value of output is then more or less constant, and a constant ratio of investment to income is sufficient to allow profits to be realized, and the level of employment to be maintained.

In our example, if an increase in output per head of 20 per cent were accompanied by a proportional increase in the corn-wage rate, the position would be as shown in Table 4.2.

	Output	Wages	Profits	
Technique			Consumed	Saved
(i)	3600	2700	540	360
(ii)	4320	3240	648	432

Table 4.2

Now, an increase in investment per annum in the same proportion as output, i.e., 20 per cent (from 360 to 432 units of corn), is sufficient to maintain employment of 3600 men in the corn sector.

The constancy of the share of wages, of course, does not guarantee adequate effective demand, but it makes it less difficult to attain than it would be if the share of wages in the value of output were falling. Again, the numbers are chosen only to make arithmetic easy, but the principle that they illustrate is important in reality.

The possibility of maintaining a constant share of wages in the face of growing productivity depends not only on the power of trade unions but also on the growth of productive capacity relative to the growth of the labour force. When population is increasing faster than the demand for labour in capitalist industry, there is likely to be a growing reserve of labour in non-employment, which both weakens the bargaining position of those in work and reduces average consumption per head. When available labour is growing no faster than employment, there is a better chance that real-wage rates will rise with productivity; moreover, then consumption per family rises with wages.

A rising level of consumption per family has an important consequence. The workers become, to some extent, attached to the capitalist system. Our one-technique model was very unreal; in such a case, if the workers band together to demand higher real wages, the capitalists would have to resort to force to maintain their position. But, with technical progress and rising wages, the workers have a stake in the system. At the same time, they are overawed by technical complexities which they fear that they might not be able to master. Thus, rising wages are an advantage to the capitalists. Each individual capitalist resents a rise in his costs but, for the capitalists as a whole, rising wages are essential to the successful operation of the system.

(c) Innovators and followers

Every firm which takes the risk of installing a new method of production knows that, sooner or later, profit on the investment will be eroded by competition from later improvements. Why, therefore, does anyone introduce new methods? The answer is that each fears that if it does not take advantage of a new method, some other firm will. In any particular phase of technology, there are some firms in each line of production who are ahead of the rest. When some have installed a new method, others have to follow or go out of business, for their old techniques would not be profitable with the level of real wages that the new technique makes possible. The leading firms are not confined to adopting inventions that happen to be made. They employ their own research departments to devise improvements, and adapt to their own line of production discoveries made by pure science or in the course of the space race. They also take over successful experiments made by adventurous innovators who do not have sufficient command of finance to exploit their ideas on a large scale.

The firms that are most progressive from a technological point of view keep a jump ahead of the rest, and enjoy a higher mark-up over wages. The leaders protect themselves by patents and by secrecy as far as possible. By the time that followers have caught up with them in one line of production, they have embarked on something new. The pace of technical progress depends to a large extent on the energy with which firms play the competitive game. The faster the leading firms raise productivity, the faster real wages rise and the sooner, therefore, followers are obliged to discard old methods in order to follow. The process of accumulation of productive capacity takes place, as Schumpeter put it, in 'a gale of creative destruction'.[1]

Our model, in which consumption goods consist of 'corn', the character of which remains unchanged, does not permit us to discuss innovations in products, but we can represent technical change in terms of innovations in the design of machines for the corn sector. The firms employ engineers to improve the performance of machines; from time to time, one firm or another installs a machine, with the same corn cost as an earlier model, which gives a higher output per man employed. (The salaries of the engineers may be added to payments to rentiers. This makes no difference to the model, provided that engineers' households consume all that they receive.) When one firm is doing better than before, others copy and some produce new designs that are still better. Then, as investment is going on, only the best machines known at the time are produced at each round of investment.

In the model, a particular corn-sector machine maintains the same physical

1. *Capitalism, Socialism and Democracy* part I, vii.

efficiency so long as it is in use, that is to say, output per man employed with a machine of a certain design remains constant while better machines are being invented. As the corn-wage rate rises from year to year, the profit per man employed with a particular machine falls. Over the lifetime of a machine, gross profit —the excess of receipts over prime cost and overhead expenses when utilization is constant—is lower each year than in the year before. Moreover, when there is slack in the level of effective demand, output from old machines is likely to be reduced more than from newer machines, so that spells of under-utilization become more frequent as the machine grows older. Finally, the corn-wage rate reaches a level at which, even with full-capacity operation, costs would absorb the whole output. Gross profit falls to zero. The machine is no longer worth using and is scrapped.

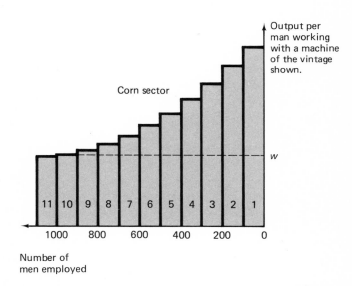

FIG. 4.1 In the case illustrated, the stock of machines is increased by 100 every year. Each new addition has a higher productive capacity than additions in the previous period. Column height indicates output per man from a machine of the vintage shown on the column. The thickness of each column indicates the number of men employed on each vintage in existence. In this case, since one man works with one machine, the columns are all the same width, and represent 100 men. The wage is set at w units of corn. It is not worthwhile to use machines of any vintage earlier than 10 periods, since machines of 11 periods old cannot cover their wage costs.

When the level of activity is sufficient to maintain near-full employment, the workers who were formerly employed with the now-obsolete machine will be transferred to plant of the latest design, whether they remain with the same firm or are recruited into firms with newer plant. In slack times, the workers dismissed from operating the machines which have ceased to be profitable remain unemployed for the time being.

(d) Amortization

A firm which acquires a machine does not want the value of the invested capital to wither away with its lifetime. The firm must recover enough from the returns that a machine provides, over its earning lifetime, to be able to invest in another machine, of at least equal value, when the profitable life of the old one comes to an end. Thus, the firm makes an allowance for amortization which is intended to provide a sufficient sum to re-create the value of the investment over the life of the machine. When a business is successful, the finance invested is continually recovered and reinvested in fresh types of physical capital. Thus, the value of an investment may be maintained in perpetuity while the earnings of each successive set of machines fall during its lifetime.

In our model with perfectly durable machines and no new inventions, a machine always had an indefinitely long, potentially profitable life in front of it, however long it had already been in use. The whole gross profit was then net profit. Now we have to distinguish between gross and net profit from an investment. Gross profit is the excess of receipts over costs. (In our model, the wage bill was the only cost. Overheads will be discussed later.*) To arrive at net profit, a sufficient obsolescence allowance has to be subtracted from gross profit to maintain the value of the investment permanently.

In reality, the meaning of a constant real value of investment over time is by no means a simple matter. In general, what is important for a business is value in terms of purchasing power over resources; thus, when prices are expected to be fairly constant, amortization is reckoned in terms of money. When inflation is going on, it should be reckoned in terms of the current reproduction cost of equipment equivalent to that which is being scrapped, but this concept can never be precise.

Within the terms of our model, we avoid discussing these difficulties by continuing to reckon all values in terms of corn, but even so, other problems remain.

In an uncertain world, the calculation of an appropriate amortization allowance for an investment is partly a matter of convention. When a set of machines is first installed, its earnings lie in the future. The length of its profitable lifetime cannot be known for certain (it depends on the rate at which it will be rendered obsolete by innovations that have not yet been made), and the level of its gross earnings will depend on what kind of period it is going to live through. The proper allowance for amortization cannot be known exactly in advance. If it is set too low and a large part of the calculated net profit is distributed to rentiers, the firm is allowing the value of its capital to be eroded. But if it is set too high, the only consequence is that net profit is counted too low. Part of what the firm calculates as amortization of past investments is properly part of net saving. This is a fault on the right side. Prudent firms adopt a convention that tends to underestimate net profit. Since successful firms are, in any case, normally carrying out net savings to finance new investments, it does not make much difference where the line is drawn, provided that it is not so

* See **2** 6 §2(d).

low as to allow capital to be lost inadvertently by failing to take account of obsolescence.

In what follows, when we discuss accumulation, we assume that the distinction between gross and net profit has been correctly drawn. Then, in the same way as in the short-period case, we can treat corn-sector investment of any period as the total amount of corn passed to the machine sector. This covers the wages and profits of the machine sector; as before, we suppose that the machine sector looks after investment in its own plant from its own savings. Again, total profits of the corn sector consist of corn investment plus consumption by corn-sector rentiers.

The only difference is that this investment is now gross. The cost of new machines for any period exceeds the growth of the corn value of the stock of machines by the loss of value due to obsolescence over the period.

Once again, we must remember that we have chosen a model that makes the argument easy for ourselves. A study of technical change in actual industry is not so simple.

2. Instability

There is a two-sided relationship between technical change and fluctuations in the level of effective demand. Inventions and discoveries are being made all the time, within industry or resulting from purely scientific research or from space or military developments, but they do not come forward at an even rate. At some times, the prospect of profits being opened up by new inventions is greater than at others, and the amount of investment required to install a new technique is greater for some innovations than for others. Equally, when the rate of investment is high, for whatever reason, the rate at which innovations are made will also be high, simply because new investments will always be made in plant of the latest and most-approved design.

Schumpeter argued that variations in the rate of technical change are sufficient to explain the historically observed fluctuations in the activity of capitalist industry, known as the trade cycle. From time to time, an invention is made, in some line of production, that promises a great increase in profits to firms that adopt it. (In terms of our model, the engineers design a machine which, with more or less the same corn cost of investment, promises a much greater output of corn per man than any machine known before; but our model is too narrow to represent the full scope of Schumpeter's vision.) Go-ahead firms jump to invest in the new process, and others follow. During the period of high investment, there is high employment, high consumption, and high profits all round. Consequently, there is a rise in investment in industries not affected by the first innovation; these investments draw upon a backlog of ideas not yet exploited, and so increase their productivity for the future. High investment continues until equipment for the original invention has been installed (say, railways have been built); then investment in that line tails off; soon profits begin to fall, the general level of investment relapses and a depression sets in. New inventions and discoveries go on being made but, with a low rate of investment, few are put into use, so that a backlog of unexploited ideas accumulates again until one or other of them is sufficiently exciting to start a new boom.

A story of fluctuations on these lines seems more convincing than a mechanical trade-cycle theory. A mechanical theory in terms of the multiplier and the accelerator can provide a picture of the development of a boom and its breakdown,* but it has never been shown to provide a mechanism which will necessarily ensure a recovery from a slump. However that may be, any theory of effective demand in a purely private-enterprise economy is obsolete, for nowadays governments always take a hand in the game.

3. Neutral and biased accumulation

One of the topics that has been most discussed in the economic theory of technical change is the relation between inventions and the amount of accumulation required to absorb them into productive capacity. Innovations may be *neutral* in the sense that a constant proportion of investment in the value of output is required to implement them, or they may be biased in the direction of requiring a lower or a higher proportion than those that have gone before. In general, new technology may tilt demand in favour of current labour or in favour of equipment, compared with the technology that is being displaced. When innovations are neutral they do not alter the relation between labour producing the flow of current output and labour embodied in equipment with an unchanged time-pattern of production.†

In the flux of technical change in an industrial economy, it is not easy to fit actual innovations into these categories; we can interpret the argument in terms of our simple model, in which investment consists only in making 'machines' and final output consists only of 'corn'. In terms of our model, innovations are neutral when the man years of labour required to equip a man with the latest technique remain constant as technical progress goes on. With a constant labour force employed, the improvements in technology show themselves in an increase in output per man employed in the corn sector, while requiring a constant amount of employment in the machine sector to carry them out.

The machine-sector workers are assumed to be provided with a stock of equipment which they maintain and adapt to new technology at the same time as they are producing a flow of output of corn-sector machines. When the ratio of profits to wages in the machine sector remains constant through time, the corn price of a new machine varies with the corn cost of current labour time, but when innovations are biased, or accumulation fluctuating, relations between the sectors are subject to short-period disturbances. The ratio of profits to wages in the machine sector may then no longer always remain constant. For this reason, we conduct the argument in terms of the division of a constant labour force between sectors, rather than in terms of the corn cost of investment.

* See **2** 3 appendix.
† See (b) below.

Suppose that there is a steady flow of innovations. The machine-making sector is continuously producing newly designed machines for the corn sector and keeping its own equipment up to date. If we take a year to represent the period of gestation of machines, the type of machine produced each year provides for a higher output per man in the corn sector than the type produced the year before.

Now, if investment is going on in such a way that a constant proportion of corn-sector labour is re-equipped every year with the latest type of machine, then, when innovations are neutral in the above sense, the ratio of employment in the two sectors does not vary as time goes by.

When employment in the corn sector remains constant, there is also constant employment in producing machines for the corn sector and constant employment in keeping the machine-sector machines up to date.

Suppose that improvements are going on at such a rate that the output per head on a machine of the latest design, at each round of investment, is 2 per cent higher than that of the year before, and that 10 per cent of corn-sector labour is re-equipped every year, so that the length of profitable life of a machine is 10 years. Then, when 1000 men are continuously employed in the corn sector, 100 are taken each year from the oldest machines just going out of use, and transferred to machines of the latest type. Since each type of machine is 2 per cent better than the last, the output of these men is raised by something more than 20 per cent, i.e., by 21·9 per cent. If this continues from year to year, the output of corn is growing at the rate of technical progress—2 per cent per annum.

When the corn wage is rising at the same rate, the wage bill of the machine sector is rising at that rate (since employment there is constant). In this case, and only in this case, the ratio of profits to wages in that sector remains constant through time so that a constant share of corn investment in the value of output of corn maintains a steady rate of growth.

The neutrality of innovations is not sufficient in itself to guarantee a constant ratio of employment in the two sectors. This result requires not only that the inventions are neutral in their technical nature but also that the wage rate rises in proportion to output per head, and that investment is maintained in a steady proportion to income. If wages rose in a smaller proportion, total output would rise less than output per head; the conditions for steady growth would be upset even though technical change was neutral from a technological viewpoint.

When technology develops in such a way that there is a reduction, from one round to the next, in the labour required to equip a man, innovations have a *capital-saving* bias, and in the opposite case, a *capital-using* bias. (The terminology of this subject is various and confusing. Earlier writers called capital-using innovations 'labour-saving', and many, nowadays, call neutral progress 'labour-augmenting'. To translate into our system, it is necessary to look at the definitions and see what the various terms are intended to mean.)

(b) Capital-saving bias—a digression

To be able to keep track of the analysis, which is sufficiently complicated at best, we have restricted production in our model to a rigid time pattern. In the corn sector, production is practically instantaneous, so that there is no need to invest in an increase in the wage fund or other working capital when employment increases; in the machine sector, there is a constant gestation period, called a year. This does not allow discussion of capital saving of the type which consists in saving time. In reality, the most important source of capital-saving bias is the possibility of speeding up productive processes and so reducing the amount of investment required to support a given rate of output. There may be a saving in the length of throughput, which reduces the wage fund and working capital per man employed (even railways, which appear highly capital using at first glance, must have led to a great reduction in working capital by speeding the delivery of goods to market); alternatively there may be a reduction in the gestation period of plant. However, to remain within the terms of our model, we can discuss only the kind of capital saving which occurs when the engineers present the firms with a type of machine that requires less machine-sector labour to equip a man in the corn sector than the types hitherto in use.

From a technological point of view, a capital-saving innovation of this kind is a greater improvement than a neutral one which brings the same increase in output per head of corn-sector labour, for it saves labour also in the machine sector. But its effect on employment depends on how the rate of investment in terms of corn is influenced by it.

(c) Capital-using bias

When the best machine on offer requires a higher investment per man employed in the corn sector than machines invented earlier, technology has taken on a capital-using bias. Now a round of investment that keeps machine-sector employment unchanged will provide equipment for fewer corn-sector workers. Either there will be a fall in corn-sector employment, or the rise in wages will be checked sufficiently to keep older machines in service, so that no more labour is released by scrapping machines than can be employed on new ones. In either case, the share of wages in the value of output will have fallen.

Ricardo considered a special case of capital-using innovations, and had to admit that it would be unfavourable for the workers.[2] He was reluctant to do so because he was generally strongly in favour of accumulation and technical progress but he was sufficiently candid to accept the logic of the analysis. (In the neoclassical era the point was hushed up; conflicts of interest were rarely mentioned.) Ricardo put the case in terms of his concept of capital as a wage fund. When a constant corn-wage fund is reinvested every year, employment is constant. If new machines are introduced, the capitalists can raise their profits by converting part of the wage

2. See *Works*, vol. I, p. lviii.

fund into fixed capital by employing labour to produce machines. When the machines are in use, output per man is higher. But now, the corn wage fund has been depleted and there is a reduction in employment. A smaller labour force provides a larger total of profits. Either there is a reduction in employment or a fall in the corn-wage rate. This comes to the same thing as capital-using innovations with a constant rate of investment.

Marx took a different line. It is not clear how his concept of rising *organic composition* should be interpreted* but it seems to correspond to a rise in the ratio of labour embodied in capital equipment to labour currently employed—in our terms, to a rise in the labour cost of a machine to be operated by a worker in the corn sector. Marx maintained that there is a general presumption that technical progress raises organic composition—i.e., that it has a continuous capital-using bias—and that over the long run it is impossible to reduce the share of wages (raise the rate of exploitation) sufficiently to prevent the rate of profit on capital from falling.

This seems to be one of his predictions that has not been fulfilled, so far as modern industrial capitalism is concerned. Advanced technology can be just as much capital saving as capital using. Moreover, when it *is* capital using, Ricardo's view that it causes a fall in the share of wages seems more plausible than Marx's view that it causes a fall in the rate of profit.

(d) Widening, superior, and deepening investments

Techniques that offer neutral or capital-saving innovations are *superior* to those that they displace, in the sense that they raise output both per unit of employment and per unit of cost of investment.

Capital-using techniques are superior when the rise in the cost of investment required to install them (compared with the best technique already in use) is not more than proportional to the rise in output per head that they make possible. Thus, in our example, when output per head is increased by 2 per cent at each round of innovations, a new technique is superior if it increases the machine-sector labour time required to equip a man in the corn sector by less than 2 per cent, assuming a constant ratio of profits to wages in the machine sector.

When the best technique that the engineers can offer would raise the cost of investment per unit of output of corn, the firms see no advantage in it. They would prefer to go on installing the type of machine that is already in use. If no new superior techniques are offered after a certain date, then, when all the old machines have been replaced with the best available type, investment can continue only if there is a reserve of labour to take into service (for output per head has ceased to rise), or if the population is growing at a sufficient rate. To increase the number of machines in use, all of the same type, is known as *widening* the stock of equipment.

When the labour force is not growing, no 'reserve army' is available and no superior techniques are being invented, the firms may still be anxious to increase their pro-

* See **2** 2 appendix.   **139**

ductive capacity; they may be willing to accept innovations that raise the cost of investment per unit of output because they see no other way to increase output with a constant labour force. This is known as *deepening* the stock of equipment, or increasing the *degree of mechanization.*

In the most-advanced industries, increasing mechanization requires new inventions just as much as installing superior techniques. Deepening means adopting very capital-using innovations when superior ones are not available. (For so-called developing countries which are trying to industrialize themselves by copying techniques from developed countries, other considerations are involved which will be discussed later.*)

(e) Lifetime of plant

A special kind of deepening is to increase the proportion of the labour force re-equipped every year, so that the service life of plant is shortened and the proportion of it, at any moment, which is of a later, more productive kind, is being increased.

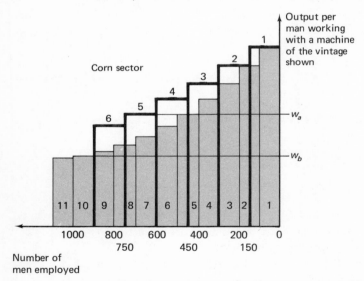

FIG. 4.2   Two economies *A* and *B* with the same labour force have wage rates w_a and w_b. The higher wage rate in *A* means that the oldest machine used is only five periods old compared with the 10-period-old machine used in *B*. In *A*, more men are employed in the investment sector than in *B*—and consequently fewer men in the corn sector—and 150 machines are replaced every year; in *B*, 100 machines are replaced every year. Average output per man is higher in *A* than *B*. The greater the number of machines replaced every year, the higher the average output per man and the higher the gross profits. With no rentier consumption and no workers' saving, gross profits in the corn sector are equal to investment sector wages. The structure of vintages for the wage level appropriate to this amount of investment sector employment is that which gives maximum consumption. A higher amount of investment sector employment is possible only if there is some saving out of wages in addition to the saving of the whole profit.

The point can be seen, first, in terms of a comparison of two cases in which the same rate of technical progress and accumulation is going on, one with a shorter life of plant than the other.

In the above example of a steady state, we supposed that 10 per cent of corn-sector labour was re-equipped every year. Compare this with a case passing through exactly the same series of innovations, where, say, 20 per cent is being re-equipped. Then, the oldest plant in use at any moment is only five years old, instead of ten. The average of output per head is higher because the proportion of workers equipped with better, more recent machines is higher, as in fig. 4.2.

However, more men must be re-equipped every year in the 20 per cent case; this requires a larger proportion of the labour force to be in the machine sector. The total output of corn would be higher than in the 10 per cent case in a somewhat smaller proportion than output per head. But the wage is higher in the same proportion as output per head for the oldest plant (if it were not so, the six-year-old plant would still be yielding profit; it would not yet be scrapped, so that the 20 per cent of re-equipment would not be taking place). Thus, the share of profit in the output of corn is less in the 20 per cent case, and the share of investment is greater. This is possible only if the distribution of profits to rentiers is less.

It follows that, comparing one case with another where the consumption of rentiers is less, the life of plant is shorter, wages are higher and the output of corn is greater, at any phase of technical development.

In a case in which all profits are used for investment, rentiers are consuming nothing; the share of consumption in output (which all goes to the workers) is at the highest level for which the given rate of growth can be consistently maintained. (If the life of plant were shorter, workers would have to be consuming less and financing part of investment.) In this case, a further reduction in the length of life of plant would reduce the output of corn.

The proposition that, within the terms of these assumptions, the highest level of consumption (at each point in the process of growth) is attained when all wages are consumed and all profits saved, is sometimes called the *golden rule* of saving. But capitalists can please themselves. There is no rule to tell them that they *ought* to give their rentiers less, and set about scrapping equipment sooner.

Moreover, the argument is conducted only in terms of comparisons of stocks of capital of different 'depths'. A process of deepening by shortening the life of plant is a different matter. This kind of deepening is not likely to be carried out under the influence of the golden rule, but it may often occur in conjunction with a spurt of technical progress which leads to more rapid replacement of plant, so that the level of wages rises by more, and the share of profit by less, than would otherwise be the case.

(f) Rough and tumble

In terms of our model, we can draw a distinction between pure deepening, that is adopting innovations that raise output per man in a smaller proportion than investment per man, and superior, though capital-using, innovations. In any actual case, it would not be easy to do so. Indeed, in the rough and tumble of actual accumulation, going on at a fluctuating rate, with technical progress taking place here and there throughout a diverse and complex structure of industry, all these distinctions would be difficult to make out.

Looking back over the statistics for industry over a run of fairly prosperous years, it is possible to iron out fluctuations and derive an annual rate of growth in the value of output in terms of some unit of account. Then it is often found that no marked change has occurred in either the ratio of the value of the stock of equipment in existence (as represented by the estimated capital of industrial firms) to the value of total output, or in the share of wages in the value of net output, all in the same units. This seems to indicate that, looked at ex-post, technical change over the period has been more or less neutral for industry as a whole. However, this gives only the vaguest indication of what choices particular firms had to make, ex-ante, when particular investments were being planned.

(g) Pollution

Capitalists install innovations that reduce their costs, that is, the costs that they have to pay. They have no hesitation in using up free goods—air, water, and space—increasing the output of things that they can sell while robbing society of resources which it would much rather have. The most technically progressive economy may pay the highest wages in terms of commodities but it by no means provides the most agreeable life.*

4. A false trail

We have seen that pre-Keynesian theory can be rationalized if the stock of productive capacity—equipment and working capital—is treated as though it were made of the same stuff as the flow of output, like corn in our story, and that an important feature of that system of ideas is 'substitution between labour and capital'.† There, capital in the sense of finance commanded by an industrial firm is identified with the stock of means of production in existence. The conception is that, 'in a given state of technical knowledge', an increase in 'corn capital' per man employed is subject to diminishing returns—it raises output per man while reducing output per unit of 'corn capital'. That is, without technical progress, accumulation is confined to pure *deepening* in the sense distinguished above.

How can this be translated into terms of a world in which capital goods are not made of a homogeneous material identical with consumption goods? Wicksell, following the Austrian tradition, tried to measure a quantity of physical capital in terms of the 'average length of the period of production'. He took an example in

* See **3** 1 §4(e).
142   † See **2** 3 §5.

which stock is accumulated merely by allowing time to pass. A man plants a tree every year. After 20 years, he cuts down a 20-year-old tree. He can continue indefinitely, cutting down and planting one tree every year for ever after. If, in the first instance, he had waited for 25 years before felling the first tree, he would get a larger annual output per unit of work thereafter, since a 25-year-old tree contains more timber but does not take appreciably more work to fell. Then, the 25-year-old stand of timber is a 'deeper' stock of capital than the 20-year-old stand. This is all very well as far as it goes, but it is obviously a special case. Moreover, Wicksell found that, even in this case, it is impossible to identify a physical quantity of capital with the cost of investment that has gone into it.

When we discussed the debt incurred by borrowing finance for an investment in working capital, we excluded accrued interest from the debt.* What worried Wicksell was that, properly, interest cannot be excluded. Compound interest over the period of production is part of the cost of the investment. For a 20-year-old stand of timber, interest on the sum borrowed in the first year is added to the debt. Then interest on the whole debt outstanding (including the first year's interest) is incurred in the second year, and so on over the 20 years. The amount of the total debt corresponds to the value of the capital invested. Thus, Wicksell realized that, even in such an apparently simple case as a set of trees of a constant age composition, it is impossible to calculate the value of a physically specified stock of means of production without knowing the rate of interest (which, for him, was identified with the rate of profit on capital).

When a 'given state of technical knowledge' is represented by a book of blueprints, specifying the equipment required for each technique that might be chosen as the most profitable at some level of real wages, two further difficulties appear. Firstly, what is a larger or smaller 'quantity of capital' when the equipment required for each technique may consist of quite different items? (The concept of 'corn capital' was invented precisely to dodge this question.)

Secondly, a move from one technique to another cannot be represented as adding some capital to a pre-existing stock (like adding corn to a heap in the barn). To change from one technique to another would require the whole stock of equipment for one technique to be transmogrified into a different form. Here, accumulation as pure deepening makes no sense.

In any case, all the controversies that have been going on about the concept of a 'given state of technical knowledge' represented by a book of blueprints belong to the sphere of economic doctrines rather than to the analysis of an actual economy. Obviously, in industry in real life, a great number of alternative blueprints for different techniques do not coexist in time. In real life, techniques are continually being invented, and each is blueprinted only when it seems likely to be used.

Certainly, there may have been moments in history when deepening was the only form of investment available, but even this requires new techniques to be adopted to make use of capital-using inventions. The whole concept of 'substitution between

* See **2** 2 appendix

labour and capital' in 'a given state of technical knowledge' is an inextricable confusion between comparisons of stationary positions and the analysis of events taking
place in time, compounded with the confusion of a 'quantity of capital' as a sum of
finance and a stock of means of production specified in physical terms.

Chapter Five

Commodities and prices

So far, we have ruled out a great range of complications by our assumption of a single, uniform consumption good. Now we must come out from this shelter and begin to approach the problems presented by the complexity of flows of output made up of a variety of commodities.

1. Complex quantities

Many economic categories, such as national income, output per man employed, or the available labour force, are habitually discussed as though each were a simple quantity, consisting of a number of some well-defined unit. This may be legitimate in some contexts but it is liable to be misleading. In economics, mechanical analogies are deceptive. When an engineer is making a calculation in terms of 'heat' or 'stress', he knows within what limits meter readings indicate the quantities that he has to take into account. In economics, such meter readings as there are—published statistics—represent extremely complex entities which cannot be precisely specified. Moreover, any change in a total shown in overall statistics is usually accompanied by changes in its composition.

For instance, in a situation of unemployment and under-capacity utilization of plant, an increase in expenditure on investment usually leads to an increase in employment, consumption, and income. But each of these changes is made up of particular elements—particular workers, particular commodities, and the incomes of particular families. Movements that would be represented in statistics as being of the same overall amount may be made up of quite different elements and affect different people in different ways. The change is not always in the same direction for everybody; some workers may lose their jobs when total employment is increasing, demand for some commodities may fall and some firms get lower profits when total sales are increasing.

The representation of any overall movement is always crude. To discuss a movement properly would involve a specification of the manner in which it is measured, and this raises some of the most intricate and confusing questions in economic theory. All the same, some form of statistical compromise is usually possible, and there are some broad features of many types of movement which would show up whatever measure was used. To bring out such features, without getting lost in a fog of complexities, we set up our simple model in which all quantities were numbers of specified physical units—man hours of work, 'corn', and 'machines'. We used these simplifications to discuss how a stream of output is distributed, so to speak, horizontally, between the broad categories of income—wages, rents, profits, and interest. We must not forget how broad those categories are. By emphasizing the extreme simplification of the model, we have tried to avoid the temptation to make inadmissible generalizations. In particular, our 'corn' was a reminder that there are more problems waiting to be discussed. We must now say goodbye to 'corn', and consider a stream of production that is divided, so to speak, vertically, between the outputs of particular commodities. The problem of determining the relative prices of different products then comes into the story.

2. Categories of prices

A variety of commodities is necessary to meet the requirements of human life but this does not give rise to a problem of prices so long as everything is produced within a family, say, the household of an independent peasant. Different members of a family perform different tasks but they do not exchange their products or services with each other on commercial principles. The economists who describe Robinson Crusoe reckoning the marginal values of coconuts and fish are reading commercial notions into an economy in which they had no place.

In a market economy, calculations of relative values arise from exchange, and exchange arises from specialization. When individuals are engaged in producing a narrow range of commodities, they must be involved, directly or indirectly, in exchange, for they need to consume a wider range of goods than they produce. They must then be concerned with the purchasing power of their own product over the other commodities.

Specialization in production may arise from differences in natural resources, such as mineral deposits, the type of soil, or a climate propitious to certain crops, or from the skill and lore of particular trades handed down from generation to generation. In an industrial economy, specialization derives from investment in plant for particular manufactures and from the technical requirements for the investment that it is profitable to make in any one line. Each group of workers is specialized in that they have only their own labour to sell.

(a) Commodities

The classical economists drew a sharp distinction between scarce goods, the prices of which depend on demand, and produced goods, of which prices depend on costs, primarily in terms of labour time.* The distinction corresponds, in the main, to the distinction between products requiring specific natural resources and those for which man-made equipment can be provided as required. Where supply depends on natural resources, the price the sellers can get depends on the demand for their product, while man-made equipment is directed to meet demand that promises to be profitable and (apart from mistakes) does not come into being unless proceeds from sale of the product will be such as to yield a profit. As we have seen, the gross profit that the capital of a firm yields when embodied in one kind of equipment can be used, over time, to create equipment in some other line, or for some other technique that promises to yield more. The firm is not tied down to a particular line of production but can go wherever prospects of profits lead.

The classical distinction between scarce goods, for which demand determines price, and produced goods, for which cost determines price, broadly corresponds to the distinction between specialization based on natural resources and specialization based on equipment or training of labour. The technological distinctions which create the two categories of prices are related to the manner in which commodities are brought to market.

(b) Markets

A market constitutes a meeting of buyers and sellers, whether at a village fair or in a centralized produce exchange where worldwide transactions take place in a city office. Market dealings give rise to the use of money. In a market, there is no need to confine transactions to swaps of goods, in which each exchange requires a double coincidence of wants and supplies: you offer cheese and require beer just at the moment when I have beer to offer and require cheese. The essence of a commercial transaction is that the seller is acquiring general purchasing power which he may use later—minutes later, hours later, or years later—as he pleases.

Any durable commodity that is expected to continue to be in general demand can serve as a means of carrying purchasing power into the future, and so can serve as a medium of exchange. Equally, an acknowledgement of debt by a reliable business (like the bills in our simple model) can be used for transactions between third parties. Official currency, such as treasury notes, is endowed with acceptability by the status of *legal tender* for settling debts within the jurisdiction of an established government. The political organization of a state, with established law and order that guarantees recovery of debts, makes its paper money a reliable vehicle for carrying purchasing power. If the state collapses, its money ceases to be acceptable. In such a case, a market economy evolves some form of money for itself, such as the cigarette currency that circulated in Germany for many months after the defeat of Hitler. A market

* See **1** 2 §3(c).

could not function without a medium of exchange to permit three-cornered trans-actions and a unit of account to facilitate calculations. Money is a social institution that necessarily arises out of specialization and exchange. A non-monetary market economy is an unnatural conception which sometimes appears in economic theory but never in real life.

Except in rare cases (as when a housewife buys from a farmer), market transactions are not made directly between an original producer and a final buyer. Markets are formed by groups of intermediaries who buy and sell, intending to make a profit out of the difference between buying and selling prices. The function of a market is to collect products from scattered sources and channel them to scattered outlets. Intermediaries function at several stages, dealing in raw materials or components for industry, or passing products down from the manufacturer to the household pur-chaser. From the point of view of a seller, dealers focus demand for his product, while from a buyer's point of view they bring supplies to his reach. (In the USSR, the lack of intermediaries causes difficulties which are partly overcome by the activities of illegal but useful 'fixers'.)

There are two broad categories of markets in which the relations of supply and demand for particular commodities operate differently. Although, in a complex economy, many borderline cases and overlapping relationships exist, the two prin-ciples can be clearly distinguished. In the first type, the producer offers his goods to a dealer and takes whatever price they will fetch; in the second, the producer sets his price and sells as much as the market will take. These two types of market are linked to the two categories of commodities distinguished above.

3. Primary products

The first type of market is found among primary products, those which depend on animal, vegetable, and mineral resources. By no means all trade in primary products is of this type—oil and some metals are controlled by large and powerful concerns operating on more or less industrial principles—but we can find many examples of this type of market where agriculture or animal husbandry is conducted by small-scale competitive producers spread over a large area. Final purchasers are also scattered and centres of consumption are distant from regions of production. Dealers (often at several stages) are therefore indispensable. The dealer provides finance to carry stocks, collecting produce as it becomes available and feeding it out as required. Dealers are in more or less close competition with each other but, collectively, they are in a generally stronger economic position than producers. This is especially so when the producer is a peasant who lacks both commercial know-ledge, and finance to hold stocks for himself, and is obliged to sell as soon as the harvest comes in. The capitalist planter in a colonial or ex-colonial territory, who produces an exotic product for sale in the home market, or the Australian pastoralist with a large capital invested in his flocks, are less helpless than a peasant, but they also depend on dealers and have, in general, to accept the price that the market offers.

(a) Supply and demand

In the above kind of business, we can make use of something like the notion of an equilibrium between supply and demand that came into fashion with the neo-classical economists. Marshall's 'one at a time' partial equilibrium method is not inappropriate when the source of supply is sharply demarcated from the rest of the economy.* We can then look at the relations of demand and supply in one market, ignoring (at least at the first stage of the argument) repercussions on the rest of the economy.†

Without going into the metaphysical notion of 'utility' that was so important for the neoclassics, we can agree that, given the incomes, habits, and tastes of the final buyers to whom a commodity will be sold, and the availability and prices of substi-tutes—i.e., given the *conditions of demand*—the amount of a commodity purchased varies with the price ruling, a lower price leading generally to a larger flow of pur-chases.

In given conditions of demand, when a relatively small amount of the particular commodity is coming on to the market, the price is relatively high. Buyers are those who have a larger disposable income, a stronger taste for the commodity, or less access to substitutes than those who are going without, while, under the same conditions of demand, a larger supply would lead to a lower price and purchases by poorer or less eager buyers.

The market is in balance at a moment when the flow of output available for sale equals the flow of purchases, so that dealers' stocks are neither silting up nor running down. In such a situation, when a reduction occurs in supplies coming on to the market, stocks are initially depleted. This drives prices up towards the level at which demand is cut back to equality with the lower level of supplies. An increase in supply drives prices down towards the level at which purchases are sufficiently increased to prevent stocks from silting up.

Similarly, starting from a position of balance, a change in the conditions of demand drives prices up or down as the case may be. A change in price cannot have much effect on the amount offered, for the essence of the situation is that supply is governed, at any moment, by natural conditions which set a more or less rigid limit to produc-tion. Sellers are generally in a weak position relative to buyers. When prices fall, producers are unable to withhold their supplies. Indeed, in some cases they may be so anxious to get money that they actually try to increase the amount that they sell when the price is lower. On the other tack, they are unable to increase supply quickly to take advantage of a high price.

Thus, in markets of this kind, changes in conditions of supply relative to demand

* See **1** 3 §2(b).
† This analysis is illustrated by diagrams in §6 below.

and in conditions of demand relative to supply bring about sharp changes in prices. But this does not mean that there is a general tendency for markets to get into equilibrium, i.e., into a self-sustaining position of balance. Firstly, the reaction of the market to any change depends very much on expectations of what will happen next. When expectations about the future are influenced by the changes taking place today, the relations between supply and demand may become perverse; when a rise in price creates expectations that it will rise further, it is a signal for a rise, not a fall, in purchases, for dealers are buying in stocks to sell later at a higher price; and vice versa.

Secondly, even when expectations go the right way, so that balance tends to be established from moment to moment, conditions in the market never remain stationary for long.

Demand for primary products in general is subject to large swings with the state of trade, and, for particular commodities, there are erratic movements due to changes in tastes (as when the British began to drink coffee instead of tea) or changes in techniques of manufacture (as when plastics replaced jute). Such events shift the conditions of demand in an unpredictable fashion. Supplies are subject to natural variations through weather conditions, pests, and so forth, and big swings take place with changes in technique and the opening up of new sources of supply or the exhaustion of old ones; even when supply is rigid at any moment, it is liable to shift violently from time to time.

When conditions of demand and supply are continually shifting, the market can never catch up with one potential position of balance before the position has changed. In these markets, under a regime of unregulated competition, there are continuous fluctuations in prices and in the volume of business. Dealers may mitigate this to some extent, holding up stocks when demand is low relative to supply and releasing them when it is high. But this depends on the dealers having a clear view of where the future balanced position will be. A dealer is necessarily a speculator. He has to guess how the market is going. Each wants to be the first to sell off his stock when demand seems to be falling and the last when it seems to be rising, so that movements in stocks often exaggerate swings in prices instead of smoothing them out.

(b) Markets and incomes

For the sellers, the reaction of the price of their commodity to changes in the amount offered on the market is a matter of great importance for it governs their income. Here, a concept developed in the neoclassical theory of markets is useful, namely the concept of *price elasticity of demand*. This represents the response of the amount bought to a change in price in the opposite direction, measured by the proportional change in quantity divided by the proportional change in price. Writing P for price and Q for quantity purchased, we see that elasticity is $\dfrac{\Delta Q/Q}{\Delta P/P}$.* The inverse of this

150   * See §6(d) below and Fig. 5.8 for the explanation of the calculation of elasticity.

ratio measures the response of price to a change in quantity offered under given conditions of demand.

Conditions of demand in a particular market are represented by Table 5.1. Between $5 and $4, when price is lower by $\frac{1}{5}$, associated purchases are up by $\frac{1}{3}$ of the new total. (Note that to avoid ambiguity, proportional changes must always be measured in the same direction, i.e., in both cases from the lower figure to the higher, or contrariwise.) The price elasticity over this range is $1\frac{2}{3}$. Between $4 and $3, when price is lower by $\frac{1}{4}$ associated sales show an increase of $\frac{1}{4}$. Here, price elasticity is equal to unity. From $3 to $2, a price lower by $\frac{1}{3}$, has associated sales increased by $\frac{1}{5}$. The price elasticity is $\frac{3}{5}$.

Table 5.1

Price per ton ($)	Purchases (tons)	Value of sales ($)	Elasticity
5	1000	5000	$1\frac{2}{3}$
4	1500	6000	1
3	2000	6000	$\frac{3}{5}$
2	2500	5000	

Over the higher range of prices, elasticity is greater than unity. Here, larger sales are associated with greater receipts. But when elasticity is unity, more tons are sold for the same total amount of money, and where elasticity is less than unity, a lower price is associated with lower receipts for more tons sold.

When a group of competitive sellers is faced with inelastic demand for their product (with elasticity less than unity), they find that the more they sell, the less their receipts. This is the normal situation for primary producers. Even when the demand for the final product sold to consumers is highly elastic, the demand for the primary product is unlikely to have an elasticity greater than unity, for the final price contains the dealers' profits at various stages, transport and packaging charges, and the retail margin of the final seller. Still more, when the commodity is a raw material, it may play a very small part in the cost of the manufactures in which it is embodied. Thus, a large cut in the price to the original producer would be only a small percentage reduction in the price to the final buyer, and would, at best, bring only a small increase in sales.

(c) Attempted remedies

When demand is inelastic, it benefits sellers to restrict their offer and get a larger return for smaller sales. Restrictions are not easy to organize in this kind of market, and when they are set up, they are always in danger of breaking down. There are strong conflicts of interest, each group of producers wanting *others* to restrict sales

151

so that they can sell as much as they like at the higher price. Even when the main producers succeed in getting the price up, outsiders are able to gain the advantage without restraining their own production; they are liable to spoil the game. When there is a natural reduction of supply through a bad harvest or the spread of a disease, those producers whose crop has been devastated suffer a loss, while the rest gain from higher prices.

The benefit of either an arranged or a natural reduction in sales rarely lasts long. On the one hand, fresh sources of supply may be opened up, attracted by the higher price. On the other, demand may be eroded by speeding up the introduction of substitutes by manufacturers, or by a switch of tastes to a substitute by consumers. A competitive market, for the unfortunate seller, operates under the rule: Heads you win and tails I lose.

The important feature of this situation is that it arises out of the very fact that producers are specialized. (They have often been lured into giving up food production for themselves to devote all their land to a cash crop.) When income from one source fails, they have no means of shifting to something else. Thus, their livelihood is at the mercy of the market. This is true both for the peasant producer (say, of cocoa beans in West Africa) or of the employees of a capitalist plantation (say, tea in Ceylon), for when the price of the product falls, the planter is bound to cut wages to remain in business. The wealthy pastoralist or rancher also suffers swings of income with the state of world activity, though he is in a better position to put up with them.

In this sphere, the vertical division of output, into specialized production of particular commodities, is superimposed on the horizontal division between classes. The distribution of income between whole communities is affected by the situation in the market that they depend on, while within each community, distribution depends on the relations between workers and capitalists, tenants and landlords, or rich and poor peasants.

(d) Conflicting interests

The neoclassicals sought to represent a competitive market as a scene of social harmony in which the forces of supply and demand operate to the benefit of all, but the very nature of a market is to present a conflict between the interest of the seller, who wants a high price (a high purchasing power for his commodity over others), and the buyer, who wants a high purchasing power for his income, whatever its source (low prices and plentiful supplies).

Where an agricultural community is part of an industrial economy, it often has sufficient political influence to secure protection from the devastating effects of the laws of supply and demand. Prices are regulated by various support schemes, protective devices, or methods of limiting production. Such prices are settled by political means, not by the market.

The marketing of oil and some metals is controlled by large international corporations who regulate prices on more or less monopolistic principles.

For commodities produced in competitive conditions (mainly the legacy of colonial development when sources of supply were brought into being for the benefit of industry), there has been a good deal of talk about regulation, but few schemes have come into being, and fewer have survived for long. The producers, who have the most to gain by regulation, are weak and hard to organize, while the buyers —dealers and manufacturers—are powerful but have little interest in changing a system which, on the whole, works to their advantage.

4. Manufactures

In industry, the means of production are man made, not given by nature, and designed to contribute to the production of particular commodities by means of particular techniques. Markets for industrial goods operate quite differently from those for the general run of natural commodities.

(a) Conditions of supply

The prices of manufactures are set by the producer. Industrial firms do not throw output on the market to see what it will fetch, but announce prices at which they are willing to sell. Commodities are never completely standardized, for each business has its own style, reputation, and location. Even small businesses that depend on the services of dealers have the final say in what prices they will accept. Powerful firms glamorize their products in the eyes of the public and make it a favour to allow retailers to handle them, at prices which are set to suit the manufacturers' policies.

In a modern industrial economy, under-utilized capacity normally exists for almost every commodity, and stocks are held at several points along the line as goods pass through the stages of production and sale, so that supply can respond readily to changes in demand. Output is limited by capacity only if there has been a large, sudden, and unforeseen rise in purchases. When this occurs, a group of firms may find themselves in the situation of a *seller's market*, with buyers ready to take, at a price profitable to the sellers, more than the total output that they can produce.

When this is believed to be a temporary spurt that will not last, sellers may prefer to lengthen delivery dates and ration supplies to customers, rather than raise prices to a level which chokes back demand to equality with capacity output. Future sales are thus assured. When the situation of a seller's market is expected to last, it will not do so. Whether prices are raised or kept constant, profits are high when full-capacity outputs are being sold; this attracts new investment, enlarges capacity, and brings the seller's market to an end. (If the bottleneck setting a limit to capacity were the supply of skilled workers, investment would take the form of mechanization, to reduce dependence on them in the future.)

Thus, a seller's market is a rare and ephemeral phenomenon. In a short-period situation, plant of all kinds is running below full capacity and there is less than full employment, at least in the sense that much more output could be produced by

153

the same labour force. Somewhat of a *buyer's market* is normal everywhere, in the sense that it is impossible to sell the whole of capacity output at a price which the seller considers reasonable. This situation renews itself as time goes by; capacity increases in step with the growth of sales, or ahead of it. We therefore have to discuss how prices are determined when output is below capacity.

(b) Prime costs and gross margins

In this chapter, we are considering the prices of manufactured goods from a short-period point of view. (There are also long-period aspects of price formation which will be discussed in Chapter 6.) An economy is never 'in the long period'. Every Tuesday or Wednesday, when the manager goes down to his office, he has to decide to leave prices the same, or change them, in that short-period situation. And trade union leaders decide whether to leave wage rates the same or to demand a rise. Everything that happens, happens in a short-period situation, under the influence of current conditions and expectations about the future. Today is a moment in historical time, between an irrecoverable past and an uncertain future. Decisions must be taken today, things must be done; it is not possible to wait for certainty.

At any moment, there are a number of firms operating various types of plant, producing various kinds of commodities. They are incurring a flow of prime costs— for wages, power, materials bought from other industrial firms or from markets for primary products, and so forth—and they are selling goods at prices which include a gross margin, over and above prime cost.

The prime costs per unit of a particular commodity depend on output per man in terms of that unit, the wage rate, and the prices of the various ingredients used up in making the commodity. The prices of these ingredients, in turn, depend on wage rates, output per head, and the prices of ingredients used in making them. These prices include gross margins, so that the gross margin at one stage of production enters into prime costs at others. Before going further, we must discuss the determination of gross margins.

(c) The degree of monopoly

The level of margins that each firm can establish for its own products is usually only remotely related to the conditions of demand for the total output of the commodities concerned. The structure of the market differs very much from one commodity to another. For some, there is an *oligopoly* of two or three powerful firms selling different brands of the same article. For others, a large number of firms sell a more or less standardized product or sell a range of varieties of a particular commodity. In every case, the prices that any seller can charge are mainly determined by the prices that other sellers charge for similar products or for commodities that, from the buyer's point of view, are close substitutes for them.

154   Kalecki called the ratio of gross margins to the value of output the *degree of* *monopoly*. It is better to use this term to mean, not the ratio itself, but the conditions in a market which permit a particular level of the ratio of gross margins to be realized. (In our story of the corn sector, where wages were the only prime cost, the ratio of margins to value of output was the ratio of profit per man to output per man. This might be taken as representing the outcome of the degree of monopoly obtaining in the market for corn.)

'Monopoly', in this sense, has a narrow meaning; it is essentially the opposite of competition in prices. A high degree of monopoly means a weak state of competitiveness in terms of price: the keener the price competition within a group of firms serving the same market, the lower the degree of monopoly.

When various techniques are operated side by side, and firms serving the same market differ in efficiency, there may be a wide spread of prime costs for a commodity sold at more or less the same price. High-cost producers have to accept lower gross margins than low-cost producers. The low-cost producers are free to choose the price policy that suits them, and high-cost producers have to accept it or go out of business. A strong firm is often acknowledged as *price leader* for the group. The level of margins for the group is then governed by the judgement of the price leader as to the degree of monopoly in that market.

Competition is not confined to price. Advertisement of a brand name, credit to the buyer, service such as deliveries, convenience of location, difference in the appearance or real usefulness of the commodities, are all means of attaching buyers to particular sellers, and various combinations of these factors are attractive to various customers. There is never *perfect competition* in the sense that the smallest possible difference in price will switch demand from one source to another. A difference in price (with advertisement to draw attention to it) has to be appreciable to have an effect. Generally, other forms of competition are preferred to price cutting. A cut in price is an obvious challenge by one firm to its rivals, which they may meet by an equal cut, so that the challenger gains nothing, and all lose. Apart from occasional price wars when leadership is in dispute, the level of margins maintained by a group of competitors is very stable.

In a deep slump (an acute buyer's market), the situation is different. Then, the more competitive markets served by small firms have something of the character of the markets for primary products; there is often price cutting. But this is liable to lead to some kind of defensive agreement to check it. (Many price-fixing rings formed in a depression hold together when trade improves and continue into good times to regulate prices to the advantage of their members.) Conversely, strong firms may raise prices when demand falls, arguing that the margin that gave a remunerative level of returns at a higher level of output is too low when output has fallen.

(d) A single seller

In the ordinary sense, monopoly means that a single seller controls the whole supply of a particular commodity. The difference between monopoly and imperfect competition is that a monopolist has to consider the market demand for the commodity as such, rather than the behaviour of his competitors. The distinction is not clear-cut; on the one hand, there is no commodity that does not have substitutes, near or remote; on the other, the price leader of a group of competing firms has to pay some attention to the effect of price on demand for the group as a whole. However, there are cases of a well-recognized commodity—sewing thread, for example—supplied by a single seller, where price policy has to be conceived in terms of demand for the commodity in the market as a whole.*

A monopolist controls all the plants which can produce his commodity; they will generally differ as to efficiency so that average prime cost per unit of output varies from one plant to another. Then there is an internal and external margin, as in Ricardo's theory of rent. If the monopolist is sufficiently keen on producing at minimum cost, he will allocate output over plants in such a way that marginal cost is everywhere equal. Low-cost plants are used to capacity, and average prime cost of the marginal plant represents marginal cost for the whole output.†

However, it is unnecessary for a monopolist to minimize costs in this way. His position is strong enough to allow him to indulge in some inefficiency. He may allocate output between plants so as to give each a 'fair share', or in any way he pleases.

According to traditional theory, the monopolist chooses the price for his commodity which gives him the maximum excess of proceeds over costs. Here, the concept of price elasticity of demand comes into the argument.‡ If the monopolist behaved according to the rule of maximizing gross profits, he would never choose a price at which demand has an elasticity less than unity, for at such a price, larger sales bring less revenue (as well as more costs); he could gain more at a higher price. However, when a monopolist is supplying the whole demand for a well-defined commodity, the market is more or less saturated, and price elasticity of demand is very low. To charge the full profit-maximizing price would produce an enormously high ratio of gross margin to receipts. Generally, price is much less than this, though high enough to give the monopolist a comfortable excess of receipts over total overhead costs.¶

To reconcile the principle of profit maximization with inelastic demand it is sometimes argued that demand in the long run is much more elastic than it is immediately, either because new entry of rivals into the market could not be prevented if profits were very high or because substitutes would be invented to take away demand from the monopolized commodity. This may be true, but a more usual explanation of price being below the profit maximizing level is likely to be that the monopolist is enjoying a comfortable life, with no need to exert himself to squeeze the last drop of profits out of the market.

* The following analysis is illustrated by diagrams in §6 below.
† See Fig. 5.14.
‡ See Fig. 5.10.
¶ See Fig. 5.11.

The above applies to the type of monopoly in which a single firm has productive capacity to supply a whole market (there may be outsiders nibbling at the edge but, by fair means or foul, he can keep them under control). A different type of monopoly exists in the formation of a ring in which a number of formerly competing firms agree to regulate prices. Rings may be of the defensive type referred to above. When the normal degree of monopoly has crumbled under the impact of an overall fall in demand for a group of producers, they get together and cement an artificial degree of monopoly by agreement. To restrict output and keep up prices, they have to have some way of allocating demand among themselves. This may lead to conflicts of interest within the ring, some demanding a higher share of total sales than the others are willing to grant. This kind of monopoly does not often set prices at less than what is believed to be the profit-maximizing point, for this may be quite low. Indeed, rings have been known to misjudge the market and charge more than what proves to be the full monopoly price (taking into account the supply of substitutes) so that they are cutting off their nose to spite their face.

Another kind of ring is aggressive rather than defensive. A commodity which has low costs and a highly inelastic demand (because it represents a small part in customary household expenditure or is a small component in some larger product) is a tempting object for monopoly. Matches were a case in point: monopolies in various countries were set up by the great Swedish financier, Kreuger. (He came to a bad end, but his monopolies persist.)

Another well-known example is that of electric light bulbs. High profits can be made by regulating prices in such a situation, and they are well worth the trouble of policing the ring, keeping outsiders out, and devising an apparatus for dealing with disputes about the distribution of the benefits inside.

Many countries have legislation against *restrictive practices* of this kind. This is sometimes useful to energetic outsiders who are trying to break into the preserves of a ring but there does not seem to be much evidence of any benefit that it brings to the public (apart from the legal profession).

(e) Charging what the traffic will bear

A monopolistic firm usually produces a range of commodities which may have overhead costs in common, but which sell in different markets subject to different conditions of demand. In such a case, when margins are adjusted to the conditions of demand in the various markets, total profits are higher than if a single proportional margin were set for the whole output.*

Although monopolists do not necessarily find the profit-maximizing price in each market, the principle of taking the relative strengths of sectors of demand into account is widely diffused throughout industrial production. (Among broadly competitive firms, the practice is followed by price leaders, or just observed by common consent as being obviously right and natural.)

Wherever possible, markets for consumer goods are split up (often by the snob

* See Fig. 5.12.

appeal of a 'better-class article') so that a higher price can be charged to wealthier customers without having to sacrifice mass sales at a lower, but still remunerative, price. In dealings between firms, many considerations come into bargaining. A powerful firm is often anxious to keep the prices charged to various buyers secret, so that those who are paying more will not know that others are better treated.

5. Wages and profits

(a) Real wages and labour costs

The relations of prices to money-wage rates in the various lines of production determine the real cost of labour to employers and the real-wage rates that workers receive. In our simple model, in which corn was the money in which wages were paid, the corn cost of labour and the real wage were identical. Now we must distinguish between them. The real cost of labour to a particular employer is the wage cost per unit of output divided by the price of the commodity he sells. (When his labour force produces a range of commodities, the overall price of a unit of output represents the various items in the proportions that they enter into sales.) This is the inverse of 'labour commanded' by the output of one unit of labour. Given the ratio of other elements in prime cost to the wage bill, we find that the real cost of labour is less (labour commanded greater) the higher is the ratio of the gross margin to prime costs.

Suppose, for example, a worker who is paid $20 per week is employed in the production of saucepans, of which output per man is 100 a week. Furthermore, suppose that the cost of other inputs per unit of output is 20 cents. Then variations of gross margin will affect the real cost of labour to the employer as in Table 5.2.

Table 5.2

Output of 100 saucepans per man per week

Wage ($)	Other costs ($)	Mark-up (%)	Value of output ($)	Wage/value of output
20	20	10	44	0·45
20	20	20	48	0·42
20	20	50	60	0·33

This principle applies to the sellers of each commodity, including those selling inputs for further production to other firms. Thus, the higher the degree of monopoly throughout the system, the lower the real cost of labour to employers as a whole.

When physical output per head is rising as time goes by, then, if the degree of monopoly (and so the proportionate level of gross margins) is more or less constant throughout industry, the real cost of labour is constant on average, taking one commodity with another. Then, if money-wage rates are rising on the whole less fast than output per head, some prices must be falling. If money wages are rising faster than output per head, the general level of prices is rising.

Prices falling by less than the excess of the rise in output per head over the rise of wages—or rising by more than the excess of the rise in wages over the rise in output per head—indicate an increase in the degree of monopoly (with higher gross margins) in some or all markets, and a fall in the real cost of labour to employers.

The real-wage rate, from the workers' viewpoint, does not necessarily correspond to the general cost of labour. It depends on the purchasing power of the money wage over those things that the workers want to buy. (In our simple model, they were interested in wages in terms of corn, not in the price of machines.)

Ricardo thought of the necessary wage as fixed in terms of the means of subsistence. If the money price of corn were reduced (by allowing imports) the corn wage would remain the same; the real cost of labour to employers in manufacturing industry would be lower and profits would be higher. (He did not worry about low wages causing a deficiency of demand because he took it for granted that more profits would mean more investment.)

In a modern economy, workers buy the output of many industries (though the price of food is still of great importance). Real wages are influenced by the degree of monopoly in those markets in which they are customers. When luxury goods are sold at inflated prices, capitalists are swelling profits and reducing the purchasing power of rentier income at the same time. The interests of the workers are not affected.

However, as real wages rise, more and more types of commodities and services come into the customary standard of life, and provide a sphere of profitable sales for mass production. Here, we see again the paradox of modern capitalism. Each employer dislikes a rise in the real cost of labour in his own line, but he likes real wages in general to be rising, so that he can find a growing outlet for his sales.

(b) The terms of trade

The two kinds of markets that we have distinguished—those governed by supply and demand and those governed by the degree of monopoly—are connected through the purchase of primary products as raw materials for manufactures.

In our simple model, we discussed movements of effective demand with constant prices. We must now observe that fluctuations in the level of employment in industry are generally accompanied by sharp changes in the relative prices of manufactures and primary products. An upswing in industrial activity means an increase in demand for raw materials, and where supply is inelastic, their prices rise sharply. Similarly, a fall in activity may send prices—and the incomes of producers—down to ruinous levels. This is true of movements of markets as a whole. There may also be erratic changes in prices of particular products which enter into particular manufactures.

159

The mechanism by which prices are formed sets up a conflict of interest between industrial workers and the producers of primary products. When there is scarcity relative to demand, the price of a primary product is high. This is good for those of its producers who have some to sell (though, of course, the purchase price contains dealers' margins, transport costs, and other elements). At the same time, the situation tends to depress real wages in industry.

When proportional profit margins remain the same while prime costs change, the ratio of prices to money wages is raised by a rise in prices of raw materials. In terms of our example above, if other costs are higher, the ratio of wages to value of output is lower.

Table 5.3

Wage ($)	Other costs ($)	Mark-up (%)	Value of output ($)	Wage/value of output
20	20	10	44	0·45
20	30	10	55	0·36
20	40	10	66	0·30
20	50	10	77	0·26

In industry as a whole, when raw material prices are rising, a rise in price at one stage is multiplied through the chain of production, margins being added to prime cost at each stage at which goods change hands. Conversely, low primary-product prices help to keep up industrial wages.

The effect on real wages is most marked when the raw material goes into a commodity of general consumption, in particular, foodstuffs. Whether associated with low incomes in underdeveloped countries producing foodstuffs, or with high productivity in the agricultural sectors of advanced economies, low agricultural prices have made an important contribution to high real wages in industrial countries.

The case is more complicated when a backward agricultural sector is under the same political roof as industry. Ricardo objected to protecting home agriculture from cheap imports because the benefit went to the landlords. Nowadays, protection is often used as a means of subsidizing cultivators whom a free market would reduce to misery. Many wealthy countries which passed from feudalism to democracy without going through the painful process of developing efficient capitalist agriculture, now have a great mass of peasant families to consider. When they look after them by keeping prices at a level at which inefficient small-scale producers can more or less make a living, the burden falls directly on the industrial labour force (including the unemployed, pensioners, etc.) while at the same time depriving ex-colonial producers, outside, of a market. In the defence of such policies, there is usually a good deal of mystification about 'fair prices' to disguise their effects on the interests of various sections of the community.

(c) **The share of profits**

The foregoing has touched on only some of the points to be seen in the varied and shifting scene of industrial production. Yet the main lines of the argument were shown in our simple model of production of 'corn' and 'machines'. We saw that, in the simple model in which all household income is consumed, profit earned in any period equals the total investment of the period plus the total consumption out of profits. Elaborating the model to allow for government activity and foreign trade, and to allow for saving out of household income, does not alter the argument. The total of gross profits, accruing to all sellers taken together, is determined by the general level of activity in the economy, and varies with the level of effective demand. The share that goes to the sellers of each commodity depends on how demand is distributed among them, which determines the level of utilization of plant that they are enjoying—and on the level of margins that each has set.

This is all very well, but out of their gross profits, the firms must meet their overhead costs and provide for amortization to keep the value of their capital intact. These long-period costs must enter into the determination of prices, as we shall see in Chapter 6.

6. Diagrams

To explain the relations between supply and demand for a particular commodity, Marshall used a diagram which, unfortunately, has often been misused. We must take trouble to set it out correctly.

(a) **Marshall's cross**

The first step is to depict the conditions of demand for a particular commodity, say, peanuts, in a particular market in which conditions can be supposed to remain unchanged for a certain length of time. The conditions of demand are shown as a relation between prices and amounts purchased (Fig. 5.1). Lengths on the x-axis represent quantities, say, in tons of peanuts bought in this market per month; lengths on the y-axis represent prices per ton.

The demand curve shows that if OQ_1 tons were sold per month, OP_1 would be the price, or if OP_1 were the price, OQ_1 would be bought per month; if OQ_2 were being sold, OP_2 would be the price; and so on.

Then the supply curve is drawn showing the quantities of the commodity offered per month at each price (Fig. 5.2a). At price OP_1, OQ_1 is offered for sale, and at price OP_2, OQ_2 is offered. As we have seen, the supply curve may contain a range over which a lower price leads to a greater output, as in Fig. 5.2b. Now the two curves are

161

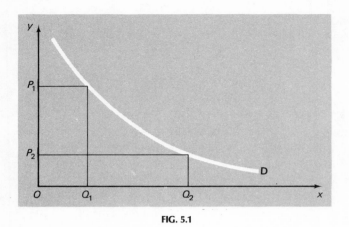

FIG. 5.1

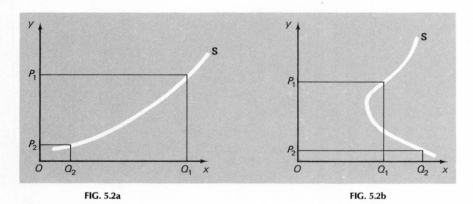

FIG. 5.2a   **FIG. 5.2b**

superimposed on each other in the same axes (Fig. 5.3). This depicts the situation in which OP is the equilibrium price in this market. At that price, sellers offer OQ tons per month and buyers purchase OQ tons. What meaning is to be attached to other points? Suppose that price were OF. At this price, purchasers would buy OJ, presumably if they expect this price to continue to rule for some time. Similarly, if sellers expect OF to be the price, they are willing to offer OK. Neither set of expectations can be correct, since OF is not a possible equilibrium price. So what is the picture intended to mean? This has never been explained.

(b) A false analogy

In would-be elementary textbooks, a diagram such as Fig. 5.4 is often used in an inadmissible way. It is said that, when price is at OP_1, supply exceeds demand and the price is falling. When it is at OP_2, demand exceeds supply and it is rising. Price may never actually settle at the equilibrium point, but it is always tending to move

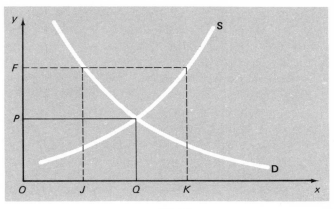

FIG. 5.3

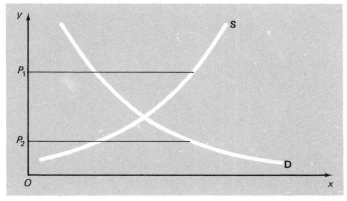

FIG. 5.4

towards it. The obvious objection to this way of thinking is that the diagram has only two axes. It shows only one set of relations: between prices and quantities. Any movement that takes place must take place at a particular moment in time and there is no history in the picture.

Here, no events can happen. To discuss events, we must use a third dimension. Time may be conceived as lying at right-angles to the page, with the known past behind it and the expected future in front. But if time comes into the argument, what do the curves mean? When price is OP_1 today, the quantity bought would not be the same if the buyers know that price is expected to fall, as it would be if they had had a long experience of its remaining constant, or again, if they had recent experience of its rising continuously.

Moreover, the idea of *tending* towards a position that is never actually reached is not easy to grasp. How long are the conditions depicted in the curves supposed to remain in force while the market is wobbling about? Will not movements themselves

163

affect the position towards which they are going? The methodological error is a symptom of a deep-seated confusion in the argument.

The equilibrium of supply and demand was originally conceived in terms of a mechanical analogy, as of weights in a pair of scales. Walras took over the idea of general equilibrium from an engineer.[1] Marshall often resorted to biological analogies when discussing a process going on through time, but his supply and demand was expressed in mechanical terms, as two blades of a pair of scissors or as a number of balls resting against each other in a bowl.

Now, if we move weights from one pan to another on a pair of scales, the balance will wobble for a little, then settle in a new position. It does not tend to get into equilibrium, it actually gets there. Moreover, we can move the weights back and restore the first position if we want to. This is quite unlike a movement through time. In time, we go only one way, from the past into the future, and whatever happens once, affects what will happen next.

The notion of equilibrium—whether in the market for peanuts or in the level of employment in a private-enterprise economy—is part of the wishful thinking of neoclassical economists, which betrayed itself, in the large, in their inability to understand the great slump and, in the small, in fudging the argument about supply and demand.

(c) A diagram as a map

With due caution, it is possible to use Marshall's diagram in a different way, as one plane in a three-dimensional map showing the possible positions in a market that are compatible with the conditions shown in the curves. We must then take account of movements in stocks which permit differences between purchases and sales to occur.

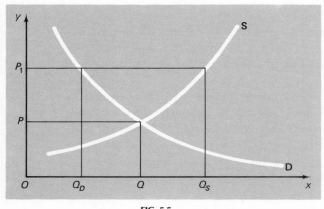

FIG. 5.5

1. See W. Jaffé, 'A. N. Isnard, Progenitor of the Walrasian General Equilibrium Model', *History of Political Economy* 1, 1970.

The diagram then represents a slice of time 'today' with the past behind it. We are comparing possible positions, not representing changes. It is impossible to move from one point to another by changing past history. Any movement must be in the dimension of future time. In Fig. 5.5, when price is OP_1 the rate of sales per month is OQ_D to final buyers, while purchases from suppliers are at the rate of OQ_S per month. Stocks are then rising at the rate of Q_DQ_S per month. This might be because dealers expect a future rise in price or because they have been mistaken about the strength of demand and price is shortly going to fall. When price is OP, stocks are running level. The situation in the immediate future may then be expected to remain the same unless something happens to alter the conditions shown in the curves. When price is below OP, stocks are falling.

Read in this way, the use of diagrams can assist thought instead of confusing it. Marshall himself used the diagram to compare situations in which the conditions of demand could be taken to be the same but the conditions of supply different, or vice versa.

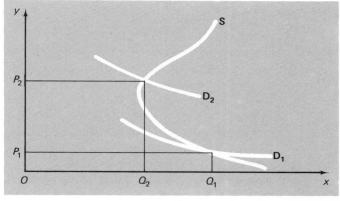

FIG. 5.6

Thus, we might consider the conditions of supply shown in Fig. 5.2b with two different levels of demand as in Fig. 5.6. With the high level of demand shown by D_2 the amount bought is less than with D_1 and sellers are a great deal better off.

This way of using diagrams merely illustrates an argument. The diagram is not intended to prove anything, but merely to save words. Even so, it must be used with care. It is important to remember that two different states of demand cannot coexist' in time. We must imagine the curve showing the later state of demand painted on glass in front of the page, at a distance representing the appropriate interval of time, and then projected back on to the page on which the earlier curve is drawn. The picture can be used in this way only if we have good reason to believe that the conditions of supply shown in the curve are based on some solid relationships that do not easily change and which are independent of alterations in the conditions of demand.

(d) Price elasticity of demand

The notion of price elasticity of demand involves an attempt to summarize in simple numerical form the relations of price and amount bought in given conditions of demand. It is defined simply as the proportionate difference in the amount bought divided by the proportionate difference in price. In the case which is taken to be normal, a higher price is associated with a smaller amount bought, under given conditions of demand, and thus the price elasticity is, strictly speaking, a negative number. It is, however, customarily expressed simply as a number, say, $1\frac{2}{3}$ or $\frac{3}{5}$, the minus sign being omitted. We followed this convention in the numerical example above.*

As we have seen, a demand curve cannot exhibit a change taking place at a moment of time but, as in the case of a curve exhibiting the relation of output to work,† we can use it to show the effect of a change, provided that the conditions it represents can be taken to remain unchanged.

Price elasticity of demand represents the effect of a change in price on the amount bought under unchanged conditions of demand. A price elasticity of unity forms an important dividing line. When it obtains, a proportionate increase in price is exactly matched by the proportionate fall in the amount sold, so that the total revenue from sales remains the same. If the price elasticity of demand is less than one, a given proportionate increase in price is associated with a smaller proportionate decrease in sales, and total revenue is higher. If the price elasticity of demand is greater than one, the resultant proportionate decrease in sales is the greater, and total revenue is lower.

A simple way of illustrating the magnitude of the price elasticity of demand was devised by Marshall and improved by A. P. Lerner.[2]

In Fig. 5.7, we show the effect on the quantity demanded, of an increase in price from OP_1 to OP_2, which results in the quantity demanded being OQ_2 instead of OQ_1. The chord between the two points on the curve, B and C, is extended to cut the y-axis at A and the x-axis at D. The elasticity of demand over the stretch of the demand curve from B to C is measured by the proportionate decrease in sales measured from the final quantity $(Q_1Q_2)/(OQ_2)$, divided by the proportionate increase in price, $(P_1P_2)/(OP_1)$.

The fall in output must be measured as $(Q_1Q_2)/(OQ_2)$ rather than $(Q_1Q_2)/(OQ_1)$, for though proportions are always the same in whatever way they are expressed; $4:3$ and $3:4$ are exactly equivalent, percentages vary with the direction of measurement; $(4-3)/4$ is not equal to $(4-3)/3$. Both change in price and change in sales must be measured in the same direction (from lower to higher, or contrariwise) to avoid ambiguity. In this case, the lower sales and the lower price are taken as the bases of measurement.

---

* See **2** 5 §3(b).
† See **2** 1 §5(a).
2. 'The Diagrammatic Representation of Elasticity of Demand', *Review of Economic Studies* Vol. 1, 1, 1933.

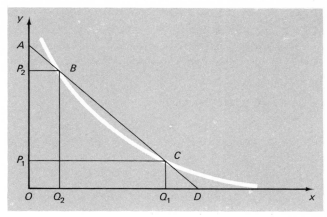

FIG. 5.7

Now
$$\frac{Q_1Q_2}{OQ_2} = \frac{BC}{AB} \quad \text{and} \quad \frac{P_1P_2}{OP_1} = \frac{BC}{CD}$$

therefore the price elasticity of demand

$$e = \frac{BC}{AB} \div \frac{BC}{CD} = \frac{CD}{AB}$$

It is a simple exercise in geometry to show that, when total revenue is the same at both prices, i.e.,

$$OP_2OQ_2 = OP_1OQ_1, \qquad CD = AB$$

and thus $e = 1$.

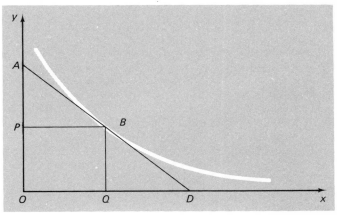

FIG. 5.8

For smaller differences in price, B and C are closer together, until in the limit, the difference in price is indefinitely small and the chord becomes a tangent, as in Fig. 5.8.

Elasticity is then shown by the ratio *BD/AB* (or *OP/AP*). This is the elasticity corresponding to the price *OP*. In real life, of course, there is no such thing as an indefinitely small difference in price, and the notion of arc elasticity (Fig. 5.7) is more useful than that of point elasticity (Fig. 5.8).

(e) Prime costs and gross margins

This analysis involves long-period, as well as short-period considerations. It is explained further in **2** 6 §2(d). In industry, prices have to be chosen in advance of sales. An investment will not be made unless there are reasonably confident expectations of a volume of sales that will yield a sufficient gross profit for a sufficient run of years to repay the investment and yield a net profit.

As we have seen, the gross margin (the mark-up on prime cost) which is expected to cover costs and yield a net profit, is generally fairly stable in face of changes in demand. Variations in demand lead to variations of output rather than price. This suggests that the mark-up must be calculated on the basis of some normal level of output. In Fig. 5.9, total costs consist of prime costs, which vary with output, and

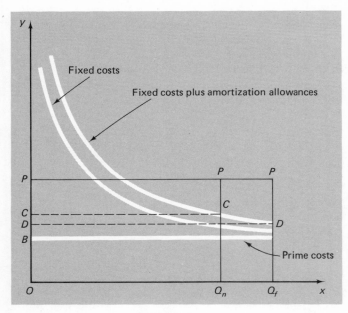

FIG. 5.9

fixed costs (including amortization allowances) to which the firm is committed whatever the level of output. Average prime cost, *OB*, does not vary with the level of output. Average fixed cost is in inverse proportion to the level of output.

When OQ_n is the 'standard' level of utilization of plant, the price is set at *OP* to yield the gross margin BP and a net profit of $CP.OQ_n$, the size of which is dictated by the degree of monopoly in the industry concerned.

At lower levels of demand, output is reduced below OQ_n. The price is not cut so long as price competition can be avoided, i.e., so long as the degree of monopoly is not weakened. A seller will not cut his gross margin, unless he is obliged to, at a time when his net profit has fallen. Some sellers in this situation actually raise prices. In the case illustrated, price is independent of the level of sales.

When demand is higher, output is greater, up to the limit of capacity shown by OQ_f. The concept of full capacity is rather a hazy one. If the level of demand is sufficiently high, production can usually be reorganized in one way or another to increase output, say, by employing workers at overtime rates. (A change to shift working is to be regarded as a long-period increase in productive capacity.)

Prices are generally not increased even when marginal costs are higher. In any case, profits are high near full-capacity working. In the diagram, at output OQ_f net profit per unit of output is DP, and total net profit is $DP.OQ_f$ which exceeds the 'normal' level, $CP.OQ_n$.

(f) Monopoly

When a monopolist commands the whole supply of some well-defined commodity, the conditions of demand can be represented by a demand curve, which is taken to be stable through time. To the monopolist, this is an *average-revenue* curve showing the receipts from sales at each price; from this, is derived the *marginal-revenue* curve.

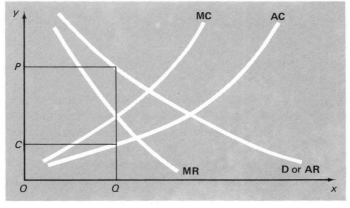

FIG. 5.10

The traditional argument is that, to keep up the price, the monopolist deliberately restricts the output that he sells. He maximizes profits by producing the output at which marginal revenue is equal to marginal cost. In the diagram, the output OQ is being sold at price OP, and net profit is equal to $CP.OQ$. At a higher price, marginal

169

revenue would be greater than marginal cost; the loss of receipts would be greater than the saving in cost. At a greater output, marginal cost would exceed marginal revenue; the addition to revenue from greater sales would be less than the addition to costs.

The case of the lazy monopolist discussed above, in **2** 5 §4(d), is illustrated in Fig. 5.11. The output that he can sell is limited by the situation of the market, and demand is very inelastic at the price at which he is selling. Marginal revenue is negative, but he does not dare, or want, to raise price to a level at which it would be positive.

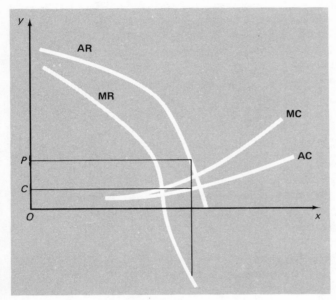

FIG. 5.11

(g) Charging what the traffic will bear

The principle of price discrimination—charging what the traffic will bear—is depicted in Fig. 5.12. The conditions of demand are represented by **AR₁** in a limited market, and **AR₂** in a mass market for the same commodity. To keep the argument simple, we show a constant marginal cost and assume that there are no special separate costs for each part of the output.

The price is OP_1 for OQ_1 in the snob market, and OP_2 for OQ_2 in the mass market. At any intermediate uniform price, there would be lower profits from sales in both markets.

7. Other formulations

The aim of neoclassical theory was to demonstrate that the uninhibited operation of the market can be relied on to produce equilibrium between supply and demand

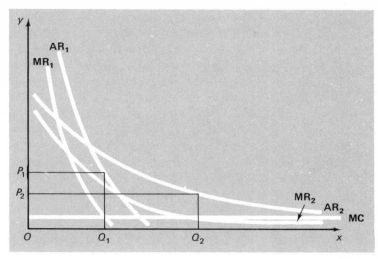

FIG. 5.12

for commodities and thus harmony among producers and consumers. The neo-classics treated free competition as both right and normal; any kind of price fixing was wrong and unnatural.

For Marshall, the theory of prices operated at two levels. At the metaphysical level, he maintained that the money prices of commodities measure or correspond to the 'real cost' of the 'efforts and sacrifices' involved in producing them. The 'efforts' are made by workers and managers; the 'sacrifices' are undergone by rentiers who are refraining from consuming wealth in order to get interest on it.

At the realistic level, he observed how family businesses behave (the great corporations do not fit well into his scheme). His conception of competition was vague and general; he admitted, and even approved, the imperfection of the market that permits profit margins to be maintained in face of a fall in demand.

Pigou worked Marshall's account of the behaviour of firms into a logical scheme, without reference to reality. He defined *perfect competition* as a situation in which each firm faces a perfectly elastic demand for its product at the ruling market price. Each firm can sell as much or as little as it pleases at that price. Therefore, the amount of output produced by a firm is always limited by rising marginal costs. (At any output at which marginal cost is less than price, it pays the firm to produce and sell more.) This is illustrated by Fig. 5.13.

On this view, profit margins depend on the difference between marginal and average prime cost. This is easiest to visualize if a firm is identified with a single plant. When low- and high-cost producers are serving the same market, the supply price for any quantity of the commodity is governed by the marginal cost of the highest-cost plant for which price exceeds average prime cost. Prime costs may be supposed to include a quasi-fixed element of expenses which have to be undertaken to make output possible, but which do not vary with the level of utilization of plant.

171

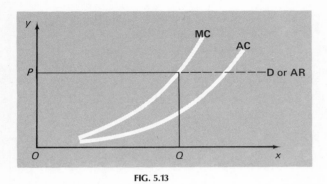

FIG. 5.13

Figure 5.14 shows three one-plant firms out of a perfectly competitive group. When price is *OA*, all three are producing. When price is *OB*, the third is knocked out, because this price does not cover its average prime cost. (The best it could do would involve negative gross profits.) The other two continue to produce up to the limit set by marginal cost. The profit margins of those that remain are now lower than when the price was high enough to keep the third in business. (This corresponds to the allocation of output between plants that we attributed to a cost minimizing monopolist.*)

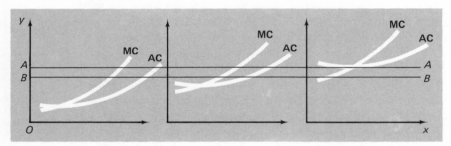

FIG. 5.14

A world of perfect competition would mean that total industrial output is divided into sharply demarcated commodities, each homogeneous within itself, each produced by a large number of small one-plant, one-good firms. Then, for each commodity separately, output and price are determined by the intersection of demand and supply curves, shown in the type of diagram which we borrowed for a discussion of commodity markets.

During the slump in the 'thirties, it was sufficiently obvious that not all the plants that were working at all, were working to capacity, or that prices were driven down to equality with prime costs for marginal producers. More or less all firms were suffering from under-utilization of plant, and yet gross profit margins were almost everywhere appreciably above zero.

* See §4(d).

Two explanations were invented to account for this. One, derived from Piero Sraffa[3] and elaborated by R. F. Harrod,[4] Joan Robinson,[5] and others, was that competition is never perfect. Each firm has a monopoly of its own product, and each is faced with a sloping average-revenue curve (as in Fig. 5.10). Profits are maximized by selling the output at which marginal revenue is equal to marginal cost. At this point, price exceeds average prime cost, so that the gross margin is not competed away.

The other explanation was offered by Keynes.[6] There is a *user cost* of working plant, due to wear and tear, etc., which is over and above prime cost in the ordinary sense. Prices, even under near-perfect competition, must be sufficient to cover this cost, otherwise production is not worthwhile. User cost is the loss incurred by depleting productive capacity so that it will not be available to use later. The estimate of user cost thus depends on views about what the value of productive capacity will be in the future. In pessimistic conditions, user cost is lower than when the market is buoyant. This helps to account for a reduction in gross margins in the slump.

Each suggestion, imperfect competition and user cost, may apply to some particular special cases but neither provides a plausible general hypothesis about the behaviour of gross margins, such as is expressed by Kalecki's degree of monopoly. E. H. Chamberlin's *Monopolistic Competition* offered a much more interesting suggestion than either. Firms do not inevitably *have* a monopoly of their own products; they are continually striving to *create* monopoly by differentiating their products and manipulating demand for them by advertisement and salesmanship of all kinds. This dynamic concept of market behaviour was a break with traditional theory and opened up a new approach to the meaning of competition, which we have followed in this book. Professor Chamberlin himself did not develop the idea of artificial product differentiation far, but devoted his subsequent work to arguing that it was in no way incompatible with the doctrine that the free play of market forces produces beneficial effects for consumers and producers alike.

All these ideas follow the Marshallian tradition, which distinguished between households as consumers and firms as producers. The concept of competition in the general equilibrium system of Walras is quite different. In that scheme, the economy consists of a number of individuals each of whom has, on the one hand, an 'endowment' of labour power or property in some means of production and, on the other, tastes for particular commodities. Then technical conditions, the endowments, and the tastes determine an equilibrium in which the prices and the amounts produced of commodities, the hire prices of the services of labour and means of production, and the incomes of the individuals, are all consistent with each other. This notion of equilibrium is completely timeless. The theory only pretends to take account of a process of adjustment to change, and leaves no room for decisions taken in a situation of uncertainty about the future.

3. 'The Laws of Returns under Competitive Conditions', *Economic Journal,* December 1926.
4. 'The Law of Decreasing Costs', *Economic Journal,* December 1931.
5. *The Economics of Imperfect Competition* 1933.
6. *General Theory,* Ch. 6.

The essence of the Keynesian revolution was to place analysis in historical time and to emphasize the all-pervading influence of uncertainty. In the revival of orthodoxy after Keynes, the textbooks seem to have fallen back on the concept of perfect competition but they do not often make a sufficiently clear distinction between the Walrasian concept of equilibrium, in which physically given 'factors of production' can be combined in various proportions to produce physically specified commodities, and the Pigovian concept of perfect competition, in which each firm calculates in terms of money costs of production in relation to the money price of the commodity that it produces.

In traditional teaching, a monopoly was a special case. The analysis of the profit-maximizing position for a monopolist faced with a stable and known demand curve was worked out by Cournot. He also attempted to work out the case of a *duopoly*—two firms selling an identical commodity, each taking account of the influence of his own behaviour on that of the other. The argument was extended, along with the theory of imperfect competition, to the case of *oligopoly*—a few firms in one market each trying to maximize profits while considering how the others will react to its behaviour. This led to the application to economic analysis of a new branch of mathematics, the *theory of games*,[7] which sets the whole subject in a fresh light, though there is an essential difference between a game with known, accepted rules, and the struggle for survival and growth in the complex and variable conditions of a private-enterprise economy.

7. J. von Neumann and O. Morgenstern, *Theory of Games and Economic Behaviour* 1944.

Chapter Six
Rates of profit

So far, we have considered the short-run aspects of the behaviour of markets and the price policy of firms. We have discussed the *share* of *gross* profits in the value of output. We must now consider costs from a long-period point of view, the determination of *net* profits and the ratio of net profit to the value of capital, i.e., the *rate of profit on capital*. The ex-ante, forward-looking rate of profit expresses expectations of returns to be obtained from the finance invested in business; the ex-post rate of profit is a calculation of the returns actually realized.

1. Long and short periods

Marshall's conception of the short and long period was connected with the idea of the length of time that it would take to restore 'normality' after a change in circumstances. A rise in demand for a particular commodity at a moment of time leads immediately to an increase in output, a higher level of utilization of existing plant and, for the time being, a higher level of profits. Profits above the 'normal' level attract new investment so that, over a certain period, productive capacity is expanded to meet the increased demand. Marshall assumed that expansion goes just far enough to bring the level of profits back to 'normal'.

These concepts arise from the nature of capitalist industry. At any moment, capacity is limited by buildings, equipment, and know-how already in existence. An industrial firm has committed finance to more or less long-lived installations on which it expects to recover a net profit over some years of operation. It is committed, also, to employing professional staff through contracts which cannot easily be terminated. But ordinary labour can be employed week by week, or even day by day, and running expenses for power, raw materials, etc., vary with weekly output.

Firms can change the level of utilization almost instantaneously if they find it profitable to do so, but changing the productive capacity in existence takes time.

We can make use of the distinction between the long- and short-period concepts without being committed to Marshall's faith in 'normal' profits being established 'in the long period'. Indeed, it is absurd to talk of 'being in the long period', or 'reaching the long period', as though it were a date in history. It is better to use the expressions 'short period' and 'long period' as adjectives, not substantives. 'Short period' does not refer to a length of time but to a state of affairs—the situation at a particular moment when productive capacity, and all that goes with it, is whatever past history has brought into being. Every event that occurs, occurs in a short-period situation; it has short-run and long-run consequences.

Short-period decisions concern the use of plant already in existence. They are taken in the light of expectations about the immediate future (say, of rates of sales) which are held with fair confidence (though in the outcome they may not be exactly fulfilled). Long-period decisions are those which produce consequences that will be spread over a much greater stretch of future time, in particular, decisions that lead to changes in productive capacity. When we discussed technical change, we were discussing long-period problems but we did so within the shelter of our simple model. We must now open up the analysis of long-period aspects of complex production.

2. Investment decisions

A capitalist business is normally trying to expand its operations. This is in the nature of the case. A business, once set up, does not want to lose its capital, and if it stands still, it is in danger of being pushed back. (An individual family may look forward to selling its assets at some time and retiring from business to become rentiers, but they have all the more reason to want to have something to sell.) When a business is running successfully, in an uncertain world, it would obviously be imprudent to distribute the whole net profit (let alone part of the capital) to be consumed as household income. A successful business is saving part of its net profits along with its amortization allowances. A secure and lazy monopolist, such as we discussed above, may amass large sums of idle finance, but generally, saving out of profits is expended on investment intended to yield further profits. As we have seen, the expenditure is not necessarily made immediately, but when a favourable opportunity turns up.* Thus, successful firms—either piecemeal or in occasional bursts—are expanding their operations, carrying out, over a run of years, gross investment that is more than enough to keep capital intact.† The question may be raised: is it rational to act in this manner? Keynes maintained:

> Most, probably, of our decisions to do something positive, the full consequences of which will be drawn out over many days to come, can only be taken as a result

---

* See **2** 2 §3(b).

† See **2** 4 §1(d).

of animal spirits—of a spontaneous urge to action rather than inaction, and not as the outcome of a weighted average of quantitative benefits multiplied by quantitative probabilities. Enterprise only pretends to itself to be mainly actuated by the statements in its own prospectus, however candid and sincere. Only a little more than an expedition to the South Pole, is it based on an exact calculation of benefits to come.[1]

But, rational or not, the urge to expand does exist in capitalist business; indeed, this is a fundamental characteristic of capitalism. It is the constant competitive struggle of rival firms to survive and grow that brings about accumulation for the economy as a whole.

In our simple model, firms were all alike and we considered their behaviour as a whole. We must now look at investment from the viewpoint of an individual firm and see what influences play upon the particular plans that it makes.

(a) Gross and net profit

A firm that is planning to expand its productive capacity and increase its flow of sales is making a selection of possible investment projects. To be eligible, a scheme of investment must promise a flow of gross profits that are enough, not merely to amortize the investment over the expected profitable life of its first incarnation in plant, but are enough, also, to promise net profit, for it is net profit which permits payments to be made to rentiers and savings to be accumulated for further expansion. The eligibility of a scheme of investment in conditions of fairly confident expectation can be calculated as the rate of net profit on the cost of the investment, allowing for amortization over its earning life. (This is sometimes called the expected *internal rate of return*, or the *marginal efficiency of capital*.)

Since, in general, prospects are uncertain, it is impossible to estimate rates of return precisely. A crude standard for choice between projects may be used, such as the *pay-off period*—the time that it would take for gross profit to cover the total initial cost of the investment. When schemes are compared, that with a shorter expected pay-off is preferred. Another policy that a firm may adopt is to make it a rule not to go in for any scheme that has a longer pay-off than, say, three years. This does not mean, of course, that it expects to scrap a plant after three years. A scheme which merely covered the cost of the investment would yield no net profit at all. The firm is hoping to operate the plant for many years beyond the pay-off period, when profit will be all net gain. The pay-off rule is a means whereby the firm tries to prevent itself from going in for schemes which might lead to actual losses. The choice of a short pay-off period may represent a high degree of uncertainty, or great caution and aversion to risk.

In any case, profits lie in the future. The way in which the signs are read depends very much on what Keynes called the state of 'animal spirits'. An optimistic or pessi-

1. *General Theory* pp. 161–2.

mistic interpretation of similar situations may be made by one firm at various times or at one time by various firms.

All this concerns the forward-looking rate of return on a sum of finance to be invested today. Later, it will be possible to look back and calculate what the outcome has been. At the moment when the finance to be invested exists as a sum of money, the profits are only an estimate. When profits have accrued as sums of money, the finance has been sunk in plant (or in expenses of research and development or in advertising to create goodwill), and the value of the investment on which actual profits are to be expressed as a rate is largely a matter of accounting conventions. The value of machines may, for instance, be estimated at their original cost, or at the cost of replacing them today, or by various complicated formulae which attempt to measure depreciation accurately. Thus, the forward-looking rate of profit expected on an investment, and the rate of profit actually achieved, are rarely in line with each other.

All the same, experience teaches. In an on-going industrial economy, except in a period of great upheaval, the convention of behaving as though the future will be like the past is not too far wrong. There is likely to be sufficient information to assess the risks attached to different types of investment, and a broad general correspondence between ex-ante and ex-post rates of profits.

(b) Risks of investment

The riskiness of an investment contains two elements. One is the element of gambling. Some investments offer an estimated chance of high profits along with a chance of loss, while others show a fairly secure prospect of moderate gains. The other element in riskiness depends on the inflexibility of the commitment involved, that is, on the difficulty of recovering the finance if the scheme turns out to be disappointing. To discuss this element in risk, we must bring together the two kinds of investment which we separated in our simple models—working capital (our stock of 'corn') and plant ('machines').*

To employ labour, a firm must command a wage fund to bridge the time involved in the period of throughput between starting to pay the workers and selling the product. Thus, if wages are paid at the end of each week, while the period of throughput of the product in question is, say, 15 weeks, the employer must command finance equal to 14 weeks of his wage bill, while workers 'lend' him one week's work. Similarly, he or his suppliers must finance materials and other elements of prime cost over the period of throughput. Once the build-up of working capital has been completed, each week's bills are paid out of the week's receipts. The fund of working capital appropriate to a constant rate of output is kept intact without further investment.

* See **2** 2 appendix.

Now, if the market fails, or if a preferable line of production comes into view, the working capital can be disinvested simply by dismissing workers, taking one week's, perhaps rather disappointing, receipts and refraining from paying out next week's costs. Then the finance can be held in the form of money, waiting for better times, or it can be transferred to another investment which seems more promising. Here, there is some risk in committing finance, but it is much less than that involved in long-lived equipment.

Finance that has been sunk in plant has to be recovered out of the gross profits over a fairly long period of operation. The risk of losing it, if expectations are failing to materialize, is greater the greater the size of the minimum capacity necessary for efficient operation with the technique involved, and the greater the cost of the investment per unit of capacity. An investment of this kind will not be made unless they promise a high probability of a sufficiently high level of gross profits for a long enough period to justify the commitment of finance. The two elements of risk often go together. New commodities or new techniques that involve risk in the gambling sense often require large and inflexible commitments of finance.

Here, we have the clue to the relation between gross margins and long-period costs—overheads and amortization. Where entry of new competitors is easy, so that the degree of monopoly is low, risky investments which involve a high cost per unit of capacity will not be made. But the high cost keeps out competition. Thus, the degree of monopoly has a tendency to adjust itself at least to the level required to make it possible to cover overhead costs and make profits in each line, i.e., the degree of monopoly rises with the gambling risk and with the cost of investment per unit of capacity. Thus, there is no inconsistency in saying that the levels of gross margins in the prices of particular commodities depend on the degree of monopoly in the markets where they are sold, and that gross margins are affected by long-period costs in the industries in which they are produced.

Schumpeter pointed out that, although textbook morality approves of competition and regards monopoly as an evil, every industrial country supports a system of patents.[2] A patent provides an artificial monopoly for a term of years and is justified on the ground that it is intended to encourage investment in novel forms. This is an acknowledgement of the necessity of an element of monopoly to overcome risk.

Patents, secrecy, and the power of large firms to strangle small would-be competitors are required, in a private-enterprise economy, to attract investment into risky fields; but there is nothing in the system to ensure that barriers to the entry of competition will be no higher than is just necessary to offset risk and costs of investment. There is, rather, a presumption that a high degree of monopoly in the short-period sense, which permits high gross profits, will be associated with monopolistic profits in the long-period sense, that is, with a high rate of ex-post net profit on capital for the firms concerned or (as in the case of our lazy monopolist) slack control over costs.

2. See *Capitalism, Socialism and Democracy* p. 88.

179

(c) Oligopoly

Since profits feed growth, and growth feeds profits, the output of successful firms expands faster than the total output of industry, and they eat up or knock out unsuccessful competitors. Heavy investments can be undertaken only by a strong firm, commanding large sums of finance, and covering many ventures so that the failure of one or two would not be fatal.

Nowadays, in many markets, there are only two or three such firms in operation—an oligopoly*—and these firms are not interested in cutting prices in such a way as to destroy each other's gross profits. Moreover, a barrage of advertisement, exclusive deals with retailers, and so forth, make it extremely hard for an outsider to break into their preserves.

The tolerance by one oligopolist of the other's prices is not absolute. When the level of prices that one oligopolist is setting is at a level that would seem to another to provide extravagantly large margins, the second will attack, either by price cutting or sales pressure, to get business from it. But, generally they are obliged to allow each other a more or less regular share in the markets in which they are rivals, and each allows others a level of margins that it would consider adequate for itself. Thus, in those lines to which heavy investment is devoted, there is a sufficient degree of monopoly, not only to permit costs to be covered but to secure a higher rate of return on capital than can be extracted by competitive firms from lines of production that can be started on a small scale.

It is sometimes said that the higher rates of net profit enjoyed on heavy investments, particularly those embodying revolutionary techniques or radically new types of product, are the *reward of risk bearing*. Now, it is true that such investments are more risky than those that small firms can make, but risk in the gambling sense does not account for high ex-post profits. Riskiness means high chances, ex-ante, both of large gains and large losses. If risk were the only factor, ex-post profits would average out. The way in which riskiness keeps up profitability is by limiting investment, and so keeping up a sufficiently high degree of monopoly to provide a high ex-post rate of return for those who can secure themselves well enough to undertake the venture.

(d) Full-cost prices

Price policy is, in one sense, concerned with the short-period aspect of production, but from the point of view of the firms it has a quasi-long-period aspect. Prices of a firm's products are set in relation to costs. The prime cost of a batch of output is known (more or less); average total cost depends on the amount of output that can be expected from the plant, that is, on its average level of utilization, month by month and year by year over its life. Prices have to be chosen in advance. The price setter estimates what he regards as a normal or reasonably satisfactory average

* See **2** 5 §4(c).

utilization, or the average that the firm has learned to expect from past experience. He calculates an allowance for average cost, such that, if the notional level of utilization were actually realized, this allowance would cover overheads and amortization. Then he adds a further allowance which, if notional utilization were realized, would yield a level of net profit which is the best that it seems to be prudent to go for. This level depends on the degree of monopoly in the markets in which the firm's products are sold, for this determines how much its competitors (direct and remote, actual and potential) are willing to let it get away with. These calculations then determine the mark-up that the firm adds to prime cost to determine the price of its output.*

Businessmen describe this as full-cost pricing. The term is somewhat misleading, for the costs are notional, not actual—actual average cost can only be known after the actual level of utilization has been realized; and the allowance for net profit is not the same thing as a cost, in the normal meaning of that word. Moreover, there is a considerable element of charging what the traffic will bear. Each oligopolist is producing a variety of goods and selling in many markets: one may have a monopoly in some speciality or, by common consent, they may all set a high price on some commodity that obviously has an inelastic demand over the relevant range of prices. (This practice may be reconciled with the 'full-cost' principle by allocating different shares in total overhead cost to different commodities, the largest share being set on the product sold in the strongest market.)

'Full cost' is rather in the nature of a euphemism. It seems to be better to call the prices arrived at in this way, *subjective-normal* prices.[3] Then, when actual utilization is above the notional level, the firm is enjoying more than subjective-normal profits, and conversely, when utilization is below. Over a run of years, the average level of utilization experienced determines the actual ex-post net profit that the business yields.

At any moment, in an industrial economy, we should expect to observe a hierarchy of realized rates of return—high for the great oligopolistic firms and low for the small firms in competitive markets. But, within the hierarchy, there are great variations between individual firms, due to variations in their luck or business acumen. And, for industry as a whole, we expect to see fluctuations over time in the overall level of net profits with fluctuations in effective demand.

3. Normal profits

So far, we have been discussing prices and rates of profit in a modern industrial economy. We must now consider the role of profits in economic theory. The first question that came up in the classical theory of value was how to find the pattern of prices that corresponds to a uniform rate of profit on all the capital involved in production. Ricardo wanted to find a unit of value in which to measure total product

* See **2** 5 §6 Fig. 5.9.
3. See Joan Robinson, *Exercises in Economic Analyses* part 4, p. 87.   **181**

in order to discuss its distribution; Marx sought to explain the relation between labour value and the 'prices of production' that would obtain when competition between capitalists equalized the rate of profit; Marshall wanted to present the *normal* rate of profit as part of the costs of production of particular commodities.

There are a number of puzzles and difficulties in the concept of a rate of profit uniform throughout industry. First, there is the problem, which we have already met, of the relation between ex-ante and ex-post profit. It is possible to think of a world in which there is free entry, on not too large a scale, to all markets, so that competitive conditions prevail in a broad sense, and profits cannot be maintained for long at a higher level in one line than in another. But the mechanism by which competition tends to equalize the rate of profit is the influence of the expected profit on investment, as Marshall very well understood. The ex-post rate of return corresponds exactly to ex-ante calculations only when expectations are exactly fulfilled. When we discuss decisions and motives, we are talking about future expectations; when we discuss the distribution of the product, we are talking about past experience. The concept of a uniform rate of profit is not at all precise when expectations and experience are out of line with each other. The argument, therefore, has to be conducted in the artificial setting of some kind of steady state, such as we used above to discuss the neutrality of technical progress.*

(a) Land and equipment

The next difficulty is to deal with the distinction between land, in the sense of the 'free gifts of nature', and man-made capital. The notion that *normal prices* correspond to a normal rate of profit obviously excludes primary products. The capital value of a tea garden or of a tin mine has nothing to do with the cost of the investment that went into opening each of them up. It is derived from their earnings, which depend on the demand for the commodities that they supply.†

In an industrial country in which agriculture is part of the capitalist economy, it is not possible to distinguish the 'free gifts of nature' from the effects of investment; this is still more obvious in the case of urban development.

Marshall tried to distinguish between rent of land and the interest received by rentiers, which he treated as the 'reward of waiting', for 'waiting' was a 'real cost' while rent was a pure surplus,‡ but, in fact, property in land, which does not require any 'waiting', is one of the most important forms of rentier wealth.¶

Whether as means of production or as a source of income, land is inextricably mixed up with the total stock of man-made means of production.

---

* See **2** 4 §3(a).
† See **2** 5 §3(a).
‡ See **1** 3 §2(d).
¶ See **2** 7 §1(a).

(b) Amortization and replacement

Leaving these problems aside and looking only at a stock of man-made equipment, we come upon the next problem. The rate of profit that is to be equalized is the rate of net profit, after allowing for all ingredients used up in the course of production. How can this principle be applied to long-lived plant? In a world of changing techniques and a changing pattern of consumption, what is the proper equivalent to allow for the replacement of equipment which is going out of use? Does the accountant's reckoning of net profit give the true meaning of profit required by the economist's philosophy? These questions have never been clearly answered, and perhaps in the nature of the case they never can be.

(c) Input–output

Now, leaving all these puzzles aside, let us analyse a case in which they do not arise. Imagine a cycle of production repeating itself exactly from year to year so that the physical stock of means of production is kept intact. In such a case, if we had absolutely complete information about the processes of production, we could distinguish net output in physical terms.

A certain number of specific man hours of work are applied to specified physical inputs—measured in tons, pints, or yards—and produce, over a year, a stream of physical output, measured in the same units. From the output (including all part-worn equipment handed on to the next year), subtract the physical equivalent of everything that was in existence at the beginning of the year; then we have net output as a list of quantities of specified products.

The input–output tables used in some forms of national accounting are made from the statistics of actual industrial output. They represent an important contribution to understanding the structure of production and they are useful in many contexts, but they cannot help us to find a physical meaning for net output. Industrial production is finely graded. The output, say, of steel, cannot be presented adequately as a number of tons. The statistics for an input–output table are collected in the first instance in terms of, say, dollars: all the items that make up the use of an input such as steel are entered in terms of the dollar prices ruling at some base date. Then the element of gross profit entering into the prices of inputs is in the figures. The statistics do not represent purely physical quantities; they are, so to say, contaminated with values that depend on the level of gross margins in the markets in which goods are sold.

(d) 'Production of commodities by means of commodities'

All these difficulties must be borne in mind when we study the problems of profits in actual economies but it is worthwhile to examine an abstract system in which the difficulties are eliminated, in order to understand the central problem of economic philosophy—the nature of profits. Piero Sraffa devised a model for this purpose **183** in the 'twenties, even before he began to work on editing Ricardo, though it was not published until 1960.[4]

In this model (in its simplest form), the production of each commodity in a period of time (say, seven months) requires a particular amount of labour time (all workers being alike) and particular inputs of other commodities. At the beginning of each period, there are stocks in existence of the inputs required for a particular rate of output. The stocks are entirely used up in the process of production (there are no 'machines'). When the system is viable and can continue to produce, the stocks are re-created in the process of production. The excess of the product over the replacement of the necessary inputs is the net output of the period. Thus, suppose we have the following technical conditions:

> 12 men with 1 ton of steel produce 4 tons of iron
> 32 men with 4 tons of iron produce 4 tons of steel
> 10 men with 3 tons of steel produce 100 tons of bread

This means that 44 men, with an initial stock of 4 tons of iron and 1 ton of steel, can replace the stocks and produce a net output of 3 tons of steel in seven months. With 3 tons of steel, 10 more men produce 100 tons of bread in seven months.

Steel is required to produce itself, for steel is needed to produce iron, and iron is needed to produce steel, but bread is a pure consumption good, it does not enter into its own production either directly, or indirectly through iron or steel, though, of course, it is necessary to support life.

When the economy is in a stationary state, reproducing itself from period to period, there is no net investment, and all net profits as well as all wages are consumed. Then, 54 men with 4 tons of iron and 4 tons of steel produce a net output of 100 tons of bread, every seven months; at the same time, they are reproducing the iron and steel used up in production so that the whole process can repeat itself from period to period.

The stocks of iron and steel are owned by capitalists who employ the workers for wages, and take part of the bread as net profit. (The wage is paid out of the product; there is no wage fund which the capitalists advance. This is a simplifying assumption that is not necessary to the argument.)

The physical data cannot tell us how the net output is divided between wages and profits. We may postulate that the rate of profit is uniform, so that there is the same percentage return on the value of the stock of means of production (quantities of iron and of steel) required for each product, but then all we know is that the prices of the commodities must be such that each yields the same rate of profit.

The point of Sraffa's argument was to show that the 'value of a stock of capital', in general, has no meaning independently of the distribution of net product between wages and profits; so that there is no meaning in the idea that the rate of profit is determined by the 'marginal product of capital'.[5]

4. See *Production of Commodities by Means of Commodities.*
5. Cf. M. H. Dobb, *Theories of Value and Distribution Since Adam Smith,* Ch. 9.

When the rate of profit is given, then we can work out the pattern of prices that it entails. Prices are such that the output of each commodity yields profits at the given rate on the value, at the corresponding prices, of the stock of inputs required to produce it. When we know the pattern of prices, we can value the net output and the initial stock in terms of a unit of commodity, or in terms of labour time. (Sraffa himself used a composite unit, the *standard commodity*; this was designed for a special purpose in doctrinal debate which need not concern us here.)

The simplest way of setting out prices is in terms of the cost of labour time. Then we can operate with a money-wage rate per unit of labour time so that the cost of labour in terms of each commodity depends on the money price of that commodity. Suppose that the wage is $10 per man for seven months' employment. There will be corresponding dollar prices of iron, steel and bread, appropriate to the given rate of profit. Suppose the rate of profit is 50 per cent per period, then the price of iron is such that:

$$12 \text{ men} \times \$10 + (1 \text{ ton steel} \times \text{price of steel}) \left(1 + \frac{50}{100}\right)$$
$$= 4 \text{ tons of iron} \times \text{price of iron per ton}$$

The price of four tons of iron is equal to the wage paid for its production, plus the value of the steel input, plus a 50 per cent profit mark-up on the value of the steel. Similarly, the price of steel is such that:

$$32 \text{ men} \times \$10 + (4 \text{ tons of iron} \times \text{price of iron}) \left(1 + \frac{50}{100}\right)$$
$$= 4 \text{ tons of steel} \times \text{price of steel per ton}$$

and of bread, such that:

$$10 \text{ men} \times \$10 + (3 \text{ tons of steel} \times \text{price of steel}) \left(1 + \frac{50}{100}\right)$$
$$= 100 \text{ tons of bread} \times \text{price of bread per ton}$$

Sraffa demonstrated that only one set of prices could be found that satisfied all these relations at the same time. The algebra involved in working them out can be quite complicated*. Here, we merely give the results for our example. Sets of prices appropriate to different rates of profit are shown in Table 6.1, for a money wage of $10 per man. When the rate of profit is zero, all the bread goes to the 54 workers. Since the workers have $10 each, all of which they spend, and 100 tons of bread are available, the price of bread per ton must be $5·40.

We can now calculate the value of the inputs to the production process (4 tons of iron and 4 tons of steel) and the value of net output (100 tons of bread) at different rates of profit (as in Table 6.2) and the share of wages in the value of net output, the money-wage rate being set at $10 per man for the period of production. The value of the capital that has been invested (the value of produced inputs) and the value

* See appendix.

of output are both functions of the profit rate, and have no meaning independent of it.

Table 6.1

Profit rate (% per period)	One ton of steel ($)	Prices of One ton of iron ($)	One ton of bread ($)
75	565·3	277·3	30·68
50	285·7	137·1	13·86
25	192·8	90·3	8·23
0	146·7	66·7	5·40

Table 6.2

Profit rate (% per period)	Value of produced inputs ($)	Value of net output ($)	Share of wages in net output (Total wage bill $540)
75	3370·4	3068	0·18
50	1691·2	1386	0·39
25	1132·4	823	0·66
0	853·6	540	1·00

Our example also illustrates the distinction between the wage as the real cost of labour to the capitalist and the real wage from the viewpoint of the worker who wishes to buy bread. When the rate of profit is 50 per cent, the steel-sector capitalist must pay a worker the equivalent of 0·035 of a ton of steel $(10/285·7) per period, with which the worker may buy about three-quarters of a ton of bread $(10/13·86).

Just as for a particular flow of inputs and outputs there is a pattern of prices and of shares of profits and wages in net output corresponding to a given rate of profit, so there is a rate of profit corresponding to given shares of profits and wages. Besides the technical data, it is necessary to know one of three relationships—the rate of profit, the share of profit in net output or the real wage in terms of one commodity or bundle of commodities. The value given to any of these entails the value of the other two and settles the pattern of prices.

In the special case in which the ratio of profits to wages is the same for each commodity, labour-value prices prevail. There is then a pattern of prices given by the technical input–output relations which is independent of the rate of profit.* In all other cases, the pattern of prices and value of the stock of means of production vary with the rate of profit, as in the above example.

In every case, a higher rate of profit means a higher share of profit in the value of net output and a lower share of wages in the sense of the cost of labour, for with given money wages, a higher rate of profit entails higher money prices. Generally (except in some special conditions), the real-wage rate is lower where the cost of labour is lower, though not necessarily in the same proportion.

4. Theories of distribution

The setting of Sraffa's argument was highly abstract. It was offered as a challenge to received ideas, such as the notion of 'marginal productivity of capital'; for this purpose, his narrow and strict assumptions are appropriate. If the textbook writers who propagate these ideas cannot answer him on those assumptions, they can do no better with more complicated and looser assumptions. For a discussion of actual prices in an actual industrial economy, the difficulties mentioned above—about the concept of a uniform rate of profit—have to be taken into account. All the same, Sraffa's analysis of the distribution of the product of industry between wages and profits in given technical conditions provides the indispensable framework for an understanding of the problem of distribution in a private-enterprise economy.

(a) The share of wages and the rate of profit

Looking at a near-enough self-contained industrial economy, the flow of output at current prices and the wage bill in terms of money are aggregate figures which reflect actual transactions taking place between the individuals, firms, and households that the economy comprises. The aggregate value of the capital controlled by firms and aggregate net profit do not correspond to precise financial relationships. They are influenced by subjective estimates and by the accounting conventions adopted by firms. However, with a given overall rate of profit ruling, in a very rough, general way, these values reflect the underlying realities. Taking the conventional figures at their face value, we find that the wage bill plus net profit for, say, a year, represents the money value of net income:

$$Y = W + P$$

The value of the stock of means of production, K, is taken to represent the total capital invested and maintained by all firms together.

Then, in general, the share of wages in net income, W/Y, the ratio of wages to profits, W/P, the capital to income ratio, K/Y, and the overall rate of profit on capital, P/K, correspond to the underlying physical and social relationships in the economy,

* See **1** 2, appendix.

though these magnitudes observed solely in statistics of overall money values can be only a rough guide to what is really happening.

(b) Classical theory

In these terms, we can see how the theory of distribution developed, stage by stage, along with the development of the capitalist economy. In the main, the classics thought of real wages as being fixed by the needs of subsistence defined in some physical terms. Marx pointed out that there is an historical and moral element in the minimum level of real wages, depending on the standard of life to which peasants and artisans were accustomed in the pre-capitalist period. In Volume 1 of *Capital*, he foresaw real-wage rates fluctuating around a level that would be more or less constant over future time.

When real wages are given, the share of profits in net output is determined, as Ricardo saw, by technical conditions in the production of wage goods. The surplus of the net output of 'corn' over the corn-wage bill for the production of 'corn' pays the wages for all other industries. When 'corn' is consumed only by workers, the physical counterpart of net profits is the net output of goods produced by the labour employed in the other industries, to be used for investment and rentier consumption.

This view of the matter was relevant when England was an underdeveloped economy; it is still important in the so-called developing countries today. The stark fact, that the limit to investment and luxury consumption is set by the difference between what a peasant produces and what his family eats, is at the base of their problems.

(c) The share of wages

In Volume III of *Capital*, Marx seems to have been thinking in terms of a process of development in which the rate of exploitation would be more or less constant; in our notation, P/W would not vary much over time, so that there would be a more or less constant share of wages in the value of net output.

If the share of wages is constant while technical progress and capital accumulation are raising total output, the real-wage rate must be rising. It might be said that Volume I of *Capital* reflects the ferocious conditions of the eighteen forties, when the *Communist Manifesto* challenged the world, and that Volume III reflects the milder situation at the end of the eighteen fifties, when real-wage rates had begun to rise, and Engels remarked that 'the English proletariat is becoming more and more bourgeois, so that this most bourgeois of all nations is apparently aiming ultimately at the possession of a bourgeois aristocracy and a bourgeois proletariat *as well as* a bourgeoisie.'[6]

6. *Marx–Engels Correspondence* pp. 115–16.

Volume III was not completed by Marx; it is unfair to complain of lack of coherence in a work which is not a statement of the final and considered views of the author, but it is also wrong to treat incompatible statements as all being equally correct. Marx did not deal with the relation between Volume I, in which the rate of exploitation is expected to rise (technical progress being accompanied by more or less constant real wages) and Volume III, in which the rate of exploitation may be constant. Nor did he give a clear and specific account of what determines the rate of exploitation when real wages are not constant. The spirit of his analysis, however, suggests that the rate of exploitation is the outcome of the struggles of the 'class war'.

This view certainly seems to be cogent. The share of wages in the value of output varies, from one country and one period to another, with the strength and militancy of trade unions and the help which they get from social arrangements such as unemployment insurance. It is noticeable that the share of wages is very low (and the rate of profit on capital very high) where branches of modern capitalist firms have been set up in countries where massive non-employment deprives the workers of bargaining power; while among the developed economies, the share of wages is highest in countries, such as Australia and Sweden, where legislation and public opinion are favourable to labour.

(d) The post-Keynesian theory

The third theory of distribution is that the overall rate of profit, rather than the level of wages, is determined by the operation of the economy. The share of wages then becomes the residual, dependent on technical conditions. This theory can be exhibited in terms of the imaginary steady-growth path which we have used to give an unambiguous meaning to the rate of profit. With a rate of profit constant through time, technical progress neutral, and money-wage rates rising with output per head so that money value of output per man is rising at the same rate, the growth of the value of capital, K, corresponds to the growth in physical productive capacity. The level of utilization of plant is assumed to be constant. As we have seen, when the rate of profit, P/K, is determined, Y/K is determined.* Then:

$$\frac{P}{K}\cdot\frac{K}{Y} = \frac{P}{Y} \quad \text{and} \quad \frac{Y-P}{Y} = \frac{W}{Y}$$

Thus, in the conditions of a steady state with a constant rate of profit, the share of wages in the value of output is constant.

Assuming there is no saving out of wages, and aggregating the experience of all firms, we know that the total net profit of a year is equal to the value of net investment expenditure plus rentier expenditure. This can be summed up in the formula:

$$P = \frac{1}{1 - c_p}\cdot I$$

* See table 6.2.

P is net profit for, say, a year; *I*, net investment, is the growth over the year of the value of capital; and c_p is the proportion of profits consumed, so that $1 - c_p$ is the proportion of net saving in net profits, s_p.[*]

We can now set out the long-period version of Kalecki's saying: the workers spend what they get and the capitalists get what they spend. From Sraffa's argument (which can be adapted to a steady-growth path), given the technique of production, there is a rate of profit appropriate to *P*, which determines the set of normal prices and the value of the stock of capital, *K*.[†] Then, if technique develops in such a way that the ratio of the value of capital to the value of output remains constant through time, and the uniform rate of profit is constant, *I/K* is the rate of growth, *g*, of the economy, and *P/K* is the rate of profit, π; the long-run formula can be written:

$$\pi = \frac{g}{s_p}$$

Thus, when there is no saving out of earned income, the rate of profit is determined by the rate of accumulation and the capitalists' propensity to save.

We have already seen this theory at work. The share of wages and the subjective-normal rate of profit for each group of firms are determined together in the formation of prices by the addition of a mark-up on prime costs. The allowance for net profit which enters into gross margins over and above long-period costs, is, so to say, a 'tax' which the firms levy from the public to provide for savings to finance net investment and the distribution of profit to rentiers. Each firm levies the 'tax' at the rate that it thinks best, given the conditions of its own particular market, and the yield that the 'taxes' bring to all taken together depends on the investment and rentier consumption that all bring about.

The model of steady growth is merely a convenient way of presenting the argument in a simple form. In reality, growth is never steady, the rate of profit is not uniform, and the relation of gross to net income is never precise. But, as a first approximation to a long-period theory of distribution, this seems to be a useful starting place.

(e) The inflation barrier

The theory that the relative shares of wages and profits are determined by bargaining power and the theory that they are governed by the overall rate of profit are not incompatible. The rate of profit that can be enjoyed by the firms depends on the share of wages that the workers are willing to accept. In a modern economy in which trade unions are strong, an attempt by firms to raise the rate of profit in such a way as to depress the overall share of wages—particularly, if it leads to an actual fall in real-wage rates—is strongly resisted. Strikes are bought off by raising money-wage rates; then, if money prices are raised correspondingly, so that the level of real wages is not restored, the situation repeats itself—prices and wages go on indefinitely

[*] See **2** 2 §2(c).
[†] See **2** 6 §3(d).

chasing each other upwards. This is known as the *inflation barrier* to raising profits.

At the same time, to maintain the rate of profit it is necessary for effective demand to keep up, i.e., for accumulation to go on. When, for whatever reason it may be, 'animal spirits' fail and a capitalist economy falls into stagnation, it cannot raise profits, to get out of it, by trying to depress the level of real wages.*

(f) Profits and exploitation

The neoclassical critics of Marx misunderstood the labour theory of value. They took it to mean that, since labour alone creates value, the worker has a right to the whole product; if profit arises from exploitation, then profit is wrong. A great part of their polemic was directed against this view. But this was not the theory propounded by Marx. True, exploitation is an opprobrious word; Marx's language is saturated with moral indignation, but the logic of his analysis shows that profits are the source of investment—so long as accumulation is desirable, exploitation is necessary. The revolution should not come until capitalism has fulfilled its historic task of raising the productivity of labour to the highest possible level, so that when the workers take over they can enjoy the fruits of the exploitation that past generations have suffered.

Schumpeter understood this well; he produced a far more effective defence of capitalism than the neoclassics by following Marx's analysis and altering the adjectives.†

The function of profit is to provide for accumulation. But the element in net profit which provides what Marshall called 'the reward of waiting' for rentiers can properly be regarded as a burden on the workers. If all profits were saved and used to finance investment ($s_p = 1$), annual net investment, I, would be the same thing as annual profits, P; then, the rate of profit would be equal to the rate of growth, $P/K = I/K$, or $\pi = g$.

Keynes shocked the orthodox by pointing out that, in a slump, thriftiness is a cause of unemployment. In this long-run version of Keynes' theory, saving is once more a virtue. It is a virtue because, given the rate of accumulation, the level of real wages is the higher the smaller is the amount of consumption out of profits. Despite the highly simplified, abstract nature of the above argument, it seems that there may be an important truth in this conclusion.

The device of an imaginary steady-growth path is useful for exhibiting the roles of accumulation and of consumption out of profits in the distribution of income but, in other ways, it may be misleading. It might be taken to suggest that there is only one path and one way of organizing production available to the economy. From a worker's viewpoint, the power that capitalists have over his manner of life is more important than the share that they take in consumption, while from the viewpoint of society as a whole, the destruction of land, air, and water in the process of accumulation is an important cost of the growth in productive capacity for the commodities

* See **2** 3 §1(e).
† See **1** 3 §5(c).

that capitalists find it profitable to produce. Steady growth is just an analytical device, not the specification of an ideal state of affairs.

5. Neoclassical theory

The theory of profits in the neo-neoclassical scheme is not easy to make out. It seems to be derived from a combination of two strands in neoclassical thought: the Austrian notion (elaborated by Wicksell) of the greater productivity of more 'roundabout methods' involving a 'longer period of production'* and the Marshallian notion of interest as a necessary cost of saving.†

We have seen what far-fetched assumptions are required to identify the rate of profit with the 'marginal product of capital',‡ but there is a deeper concept: the notion of a private-enterprise economy as a harmonious society.

Imagine a co-operative such as a kibbutz—a group of individuals who collectively own an area of land and all the means of production so far accumulated, and who are able and willing to do a particular amount of work. They have to decide (by the will of a leader or by some democratic process) how much of their resources to put into production for current consumption and how much to use to increase productive capacity for the future (say, by draining a swamp in their territory). They must also decide how much time to give to education, whether as investment in human capital by training younger members of the group for skilled work, or as a valuable consumption good. In deciding how to allocate resources, they may be supposed to take into account the additional product in the future to be expected from an increase in resources (say, new cultivable land) and to set it against the loss of leisure and consumption foregone in carrying out investment. The neoclassical argument presents this choice in terms of 'discounting the future'—what rate of future return over present cost makes a scheme eligible? In some cases, the calculation can be expressed as a rate; for instance, if current consumption and the extra output to be expected in the future are made up of identical 'baskets' of goods. Then, a return in terms of the increase, in perpetuity, of future consumption could be expressed as a percentage on the quantity of present consumption foregone.

Even when the choice cannot be expressed as a rate of return, it still has a genuine, though vague, meaning. It is this real meaning of present sacrifice for future gain which underlies the neoclassical concept of the cost of 'abstinence'. We met it when the peasant family was equipping a younger generation with the same means of production per head as the older generation enjoyed. This is a real and important element in economic life. Here, there is a meaning to be given to the cost and the benefit to society of investment, that is of adding an increment to the stock of means of production.

But it has nothing whatever to do with the rate of profit on the stock of capital

* See **2** 4 §4.
† Cf. **1** 3 §2(d).
‡ See **2** 3 §5.

already in existence in a private-enterprise economy. In the kibbutz, there is current real income and future real wealth, for the group as a whole. There is no division between wages and profits. The rate of profit has no meaning for them.

Certainly, under capitalism, with given technology, a higher rate of accumulation involves lower consumption. But 'abstinence' from consumption falls on the workers through lower real-wage rates. The capitalists get *more* consumption as a result of a higher rate of investment because they are gaining a higher rate of profit. Moreover, the choice of schemes of investment is made by individual firms in the light of their individual prospects. The productivity of investment from the standpoint of society as a whole has nothing to do with the case.

Appendix: The wage–profit line

The relationship between the wage rate, the rate of profit, uniform throughout the system, and the appropriate prices, may be set out in algebraic terms.

The first step in the argument is the specification of the technology in terms of *input coefficients*. An input coefficient measures the amount of an input required directly to produce one unit of output with the technique in use, inputs being consumed within each period.

The technology of the iron-producing sector of our example was:

12 men with 1 ton of steel produce 4 tons of iron

Thus, for the production of 1 ton of iron the steel input coefficient is equal to 0·25 tons of steel, and the labour input coefficient is 3 men.

We will denote the input coefficients a_{ij}, which specifies the amount of commodity i required to produce one unit of commodity j. Thus if i is steel and j iron, $a_{ij} = 0\cdot25$. The input of work into the production of commodity j is defined by the coefficient a_{0j}, which in the case of iron production is equal to 3.

The input coefficient a_{ii} measures the amount of commodity i required directly per unit of its own production (iron used in iron making). The size of the coefficient must clearly be less than 1. Indeed, the sum of the direct *and* indirect input requirements of commodity i in its own production must be less than 1 if the technology is to be viable.

The price of a commodity corresponding to a given rate of profit is equal to the total value (at the corresponding prices) of the inputs required to produce it, plus the profit on that value calculated at the going rate, plus the wage rate times the labour input coefficient. Thus for commodity i

$$(a_{1i}p_1 + a_{2i}p_2 + a_{3i}p_3 + \cdots)(1 + \pi) + a_{0i}w = p_i$$

The price equations for all the commodities produced in the economy form a set of simultaneous equations which may be solved for the unknowns: the wage rate, the profit rate, and the prices.

To see how this works we will return to our example and label iron, commodity 1,   **193** steel, commodity 2, and bread, commodity 3. From the specification of the technology we know that a_{11} and a_{22} are equal to zero, and that bread is not used as an input at all.

The price system is thus defined by the equations:

$$(a_{21}p_2)(1 + \pi) + a_{01}w = p_1$$
$$(a_{12}p_1)(1 + \pi) + a_{02}w = p_2$$
$$(a_{23}p_2)(1 + \pi) + a_{03}w = p_3$$

We have three equations to find five unknowns, π, w, p_1, p_2, and p_3.

We may first notice that although the equations for the prices of iron and steel are interrelated—the price of iron depends on that of steel and contrariwise—neither is dependent on the price of bread. Commodities with the characteristic of bread in our example—that enter neither directly nor indirectly into the production of other commodities—are called *non-basics* by Sraffa, as opposed to *basics* which enter directly or indirectly into the production of the whole output. Non-basics are eliminated from the determination of the relationship between the wage rate and the rate of profit.

Commodity 1 is chosen as the numeraire, $p_1 = 1$, and the wage rate and the price of steel expressed in terms of their exchange ratio with iron. The equation system is now:

$$(a_{21}p_2)(1 + \pi) + a_{01}w = 1$$
$$(a_{12})(1 + \pi) + a_{02}w = p_2$$

a system of two equations and three unknowns. To solve for the relationship between π and w, p_2 may be eliminated to give:

$$\frac{1 - a_{21}a_{12}(1 + \pi)^2}{a_{01} + a_{21}a_{02}(1 + \pi)} = w$$

a quadratic equation.

We may now insert the values of the coefficients from our example.

$$a_{21} = 0 \cdot 25 \qquad a_{01} = 3$$
$$a_{12} = 1 \qquad a_{02} = 8$$
$$\frac{1 - 0 \cdot 25(1 + \pi)^2}{3 + 2(1 + \pi)} = w$$

The relationship between the wage rate and the profit may be seen to have two characteristics:

1. A higher rate of profit entails a lower wage rate.
2. There is a maximum rate of profit, when $w = 0$, equal, in this case to 100 per cent, and a maximum wage rate in terms of the numeraire, iron, when $\pi = 0$.

The various combinations of profit rate and wage rate may be traced out to form the wage–profit line, along which we may compare the possible wage rate–profit rate combinations of the technology.

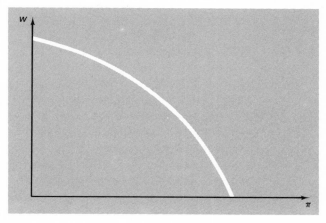

FIG. 6.1 **The wage–profit line may be concave or convex to the origin, or alternately concave and convex, depending on the conditions of production. The shape shown is that of our example.**

Now, as in our example above, take as numeraire, $w = 1$, then

$$p_1 = \frac{a_{01} + a_{21}a_{02}(1 + \pi)}{1 - a_{21}a_{12}(1 + \pi)^2}$$

and

$$p_2 = \frac{a_{02} + a_{12}a_{01}(1 + \pi)}{1 - a_{21}a_{12}(1 + \pi)^2}$$

Once p_2 is known, p_3, the price of bread, follows immediately from the third price equation.

Chapter Seven

Incomes and demand

Thus far, we have looked at incomes and prices in an industrial economy from the side of production. Households have been treated as completely dependent on firms for their incomes. They were of only two kinds: those of workers and those of rentiers (the engineers responsible for technical progress have been included with rentiers). We have regarded consumers' expenditure purely as making a market—providing pasture, so to speak, on which profit-seeking firms can feed, that they fertilize for their own benefit. Now we must look at the economy from the point of view of households, and expenditure on commodities from the point of view of consumers. To do so, we have to bring many complications into the picture. We will first discuss the multiplicity of types of income derived from the market, and the causes and the effects of unequal distribution of purchasing power among the population of a modern industrial economy. We then open up the subject of public expenditure and taxation, which is no less important than the market in its influence on incomes. (We are not yet dealing with foreign trade.) Finally, we discuss the relation of money incomes to the level of prices.

1. Earned and unearned income

The philosophy of the British tax system is based on the distinction between earned and unearned income, that is, between income from work and income from property. As we shall see, there are borderline cases, and often definitions framed in legal terms fail to fit exactly to economic categories. Nevertheless, the distinction provides a useful starting point for the discussion of various types of income.

(a) Income from property

Some rentier households fit the specification of our simple model: they are the families of individual businessmen, whose expenditure is an allowance paid directly out of profits. In general, however, rentier families have an independent claim to property, acquired by inheritance, saving within the current generation, speculation and luck, or as Marshall put it, 'by any other means, whether moral or immoral, legal or illegal'.[1] Many large private fortunes go back originally to property in land, such as wealth inherited from feudal times or the result of an oil strike. Others have been built up in industry and commerce or in the business of supplying finance, which we shall discuss in Chapter 8. Here, we are concerned with wealth from the viewpoint of the distribution of purchasing power among consumers.

In every country for which statistics are available, wealth is unevenly distributed. The concept of wealth is difficult to define statistically—how does one value an old master against a lathe? Nonetheless, most assets have some form of conventional valuation, and though comparisons over time and between countries may be un-reliable in detail, the overall picture is so clear that it cannot be misunderstood. Here, we use statistics derived from official sources. Table 7.1 shows the proportion of wealth in the U.K. owned by the top 1 per cent, 5 per cent, and 10 per cent of the population over the age of 25, and the share of all personal income from property accruing to the top percentiles. Perhaps the most striking figures are those that show that, in 1960, 75 per cent of personal property was owned by the wealthiest 5 per cent of the population and that the same group received 92 per cent of all personal income derived from property.

Table 7.1

Distribution of personal wealth in the UK[a]

Percentage of population over 25	Percentage of total personal wealth			Percentages of personal income from property
	1911–13	1936–38	1960	1958–1959
1	69	56	42	60
5	87	79	75	92
10	92	88	83	99

[a] See Jack Revell, *Changes in the Social Distribution of Property in Britain during the Twentieth Century* Department of Applied Economics, Cambridge, reprint no. 295, 1969.

1. *Principles* first edition, 1890, p. 614.

(b) Mixed incomes

In the nature of the case, the few families of great wealth are not an important part of the market for food and manufactures. Their expenditure is mainly on personal services, custom-made products, and on living space. In the next range, incomes are partly unearned and partly earned. Middle-class and professional families generally own some property, and their level of earnings is partly a return on investment in human capital in lengthy education. (The high earnings of a few in show business might better be regarded as prizes in a lottery.) The salaries of the higher executives in business of all kinds are a special case. They count as an element in overhead costs, but are partly in the nature of a share in net profits. The larger and more successful the company, the higher the level of executives' salaries and bonuses, and the more lavish the amenities provided for them.

(c) Household saving

The assumption of our simple model, that all rentier income is spent on consumption, now has to be modified. From the point of view of individual families, saving is important. It is largely a means of distributing purchasing power through time; for instance, refraining from spending the whole income in earning years in order to have more after retirement. In studying habits of saving of different communities, it is not of much use to propose a universal *a priori* theory of rational behaviour, independent of particular social conditions. Natural-history investigations of how people actually behave are more to the point.

The relation of household saving to the finance of industry will be discussed later. Meanwhile, we must glance at its relation to fluctuations in effective demand. Keynes expressed his theory of how short-period movements in employment depend on movements of investment in terms of the *propensity to consume*. He believed in a fundamental psychological law 'that men are disposed, as a rule and on the average, to increase their consumption as their income increases, but not by as much as the increase in their income'.[2] This treatment of generalized 'men', with generalized incomes not distinguished as to source or amount, is at the opposite extreme from Kalecki's sharp distinction (followed in our simple model) between wages and profits, and from our assumption that all household income is consumed so that saving comes only out of undistributed profits.

When we bring household saving into the story, we must make some concessions to Keynes' point of view. An overall increase in household income, accompanying a rise in employment, does increase both household consumption and household saving. The multiplier, relating an increase in total employment to an increase in investment, is more complicated than it appears in our simple model. In the simple model, an increase in household incomes was all consumed, so that the level of consumption depended solely on the sums being paid out by firms as wages and

2. *General Theory* p. 96.

rentier income. In fact, there are other sources of income, and households have more discretion in expenditure. The principle of effective demand can be seen in the simple model, but, in an actual situation, there are many complications to take into account.

Keynes was writing in a deep and persistent slump, looking forward to the effects to be expected from a revival of investment. His hypothesis was that the increment in total saving, when income increases, would be proportionately much greater than the overall ratio of saving to income. Thus, to begin with, saving may be 10 per cent of total net income, and expenditure on consumption 90 per cent, while a sudden rise in income, due to the upswing of a boom, would be accompanied by an increase in consumption of only three-quarters of the increase in net income, as in our example of the immediate and long-run values of the multiplier.*

It is necessary to distinguish between the kinds of increase in income that come about as a consequence of an upswing of effective demand and of growth in the long-period sense. There seems to be no clear evidence that the ratio of household saving to total net income rises through time with the general level of real income.

The existence of middle-class mixed incomes, and the possibility of saving out of earnings, impairs the simplicity of our model and spoils the neatness of Kalecki's epigram that the workers spend what they get and the capitalists get what they spend, but it requires only minor modifications of the main argument.

The formula for the rate of profit in steady growth, $\pi = g/s_p$, is derived from the concept of a clear-cut division between earned and unearned income, with saving coming only from unearned income. To include middle-class mixed income, the formula has to be modified, though, again, the main principle of the analysis is not affected.

It is important to grasp the main argument in terms of the simple model; it is also important to remember that there is a great deal more to be learned before its conclusions can be applied to actual cases.

(d) Earned incomes

Adam Smith argued that the earnings of various occupations should be such as to equalize their net advantages so that all appear equally eligible to potential recruits. But the opposite is the case—boring and disagreeable work carries the lowest wages, and the highest salaries are accompanied by comfortable conditions and social prestige. The explanation of this paradox lies in the conditions of entry into various occupations.

How far are occupations related to natural ability? Obviously, there is a genetic element in the distribution of ability of various kinds among individuals. This has led some investigators to classify the population by some biological criteria, such as sex or colour, and to generalize as to the relative ability of the groups on the basis of scores in intelligence tests. There is some dispute over what intelligence tests

* See **2** 3 §2(c).

measure apart from ability to score in intelligence tests, and there are great difficulties in separating the element of nurture, such as diet and the attitude of parents to education, from natural, innate capabilities. Moreover, though the investigators claim to be purely scientific, their observations are bound to feed prejudice. Anglo-Saxon males in the USA evidently prefer to dwell on the 'inferiority' of blacks and women, rather than on the higher scores of children from families of Japanese origin.

But, at the very best, biology is not going to be much help in the study of economic inequality. It has been found that the statistics of the score indicating any human characteristic tend to follow a *normal distribution* within each group, i.e., the peak numbers of individuals are at the average score, with a symmetrical spread on either side. When it is found, as between two groups of equal numbers, that the individuals from families of Japanese origin have a slightly higher average score than those from families of Anglo-Saxons, this would only mean that slightly less than half the latter group do better than half of the individuals among the former, and that correspondingly slightly more than half the former group do better than half of the individuals among the latter.

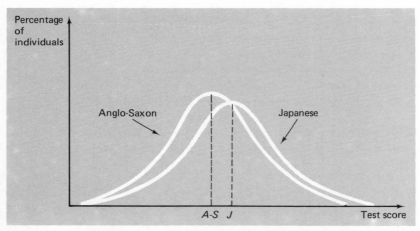

FIG. 7.1 Distribution of test scores of children of Anglo-Saxon racial origin and children of Japanese racial origin. The numbers attaining particular scores are spread symmetrically around the mean score of each group. Since the distributions are symmetrical, the mean score is also that score attained by the largest number of the children in each group (A-S = mean Anglo-Saxon score, J = mean Japanese score).

Comparisons of such statistical averages do not throw much light on the relative economic positions of so-called racial groups, still less on such vague and indistinct groupings as social classes.

There is considerable inertia in traditional views, formed over a long past, as to the proper status of various occupations, and status carries a corollary of the proper level of relative income. However, the main factor determining different levels of earnings is that a chance to compete for the best jobs requires either property, or an expensive education which poor families cannot provide. An unequal distribution of wealth and income tends to perpetuate itself. Some professions limit recruitment by taking advantage of the educational qualifications that they need, so that they can always enjoy the benefits of scarce supply relative to demand, and charge for their services accordingly. Within the class of workers who have no property, privileges are defended on the basis of skill, length of membership of a trade union, sex, colour, language, or whatever can be used to mark off one group from another. Those with the weakest bargaining power are obliged to take whatever jobs they can get; conditions are then often such as to reduce the relative net advantages of the work further below the level shown by relative pay.

Low-wage labour provides a sphere for small-scale, inefficient or ill-equipped capitalists. The workers are then trapped, for if they did exact higher pay, their employers would be ruined and they would be worse off than ever.

In recent years, in the successful industrial economies, there have been important changes in the requirements of industry for different types of work. With the growth of mechanization, less muscle is needed and more capacity to follow written in-structions. This has led to an increase in the supply of education, which reduces the privileges attached to it. Nowadays, automation is reducing the requirement for simple clerical work, while increasing the demand for higher qualifications. Such changes are apt to upset established ideas of the acceptable hierarchy of rates of pay.

Once the question is thrown open—what are the relative values of various kinds of work?—each group feels itself to be worth more than its members are getting. There is no generally accepted social philosophy to provide criteria for settling the question, and bargaining power becomes all the more important. (The 'marginal productivity' theory* does not throw light on the matter, for there is no independent measure of relative 'marginal productivities' except the relative wage rates themselves.)

2. Demand for commodities

The neoclassical writers seized with enthusiasm on Adam Smith's claims for the benefits of a free market. This was, indeed, the central message of their system. The examples that Adam Smith used—getting a dinner from the butcher, the brewer, and the baker—show that he was thinking of a market supplied by artisans and small traders.† The neoclassicals overstrained his case when they tried to include modern industry in the same framework.

Moreover, they formalized Adam Smith's commonsense observations in a way which has turned out to be unhelpful. The concept of *utility* was introduced to account for the behaviour of consumers. The central idea was expressed in the picture of a housewife doing her week's shopping, maximizing the utility from her expendi-ture by choosing to fill her basket with such amounts of each item as to make their

* See **1** 3 §3(b).
† See **1** 2 §1(a).

relative marginal utilities proportional to their prices. An enormous structure of *a priori* analysis was built up on this basis, elaborating the conceptions of substitution, complementarity, joint demand, and so on.* This was 'pure theory' at its purest. Only Thorstein Veblen introduced reality into the debate with his sarcastic description of 'conspicuous consumption' in *The Theory of the Leisure Class*.

In the neo-neoclassical era, it was recognized that utility is not an operational concept, and *revealed preference* was substituted in an attempt to find an empirical basis for the theory of consumers' demand. It was argued that the preferences of individuals are revealed by the purchases that they make at various prices. But this concept expresses no more than the notion that consumers can be observed to buy what they can be observed to buy.

(a) Consumer's choice

It is true that there are great advantages in the system of allowing individuals to spend their money as they please on the various goods offered to them at particular prices. The buyers have a sense of freedom; each can fit his purchases to his individual requirements. For many, shopping is a kind of sport that gives pleasure for its own sake. When alternatives within the broad categories of food, clothing, etc., are available at various prices, consumers at the same income level can choose various combinations to suit their fancy. Above all, the market regulates itself without need for an administrative apparatus. Except for a few highly idealistic experiments, which have never lasted in a pure form, no better way of distributing goods to the civilian population has been found than providing them with purchasing power in terms of money, and letting them decide for themselves how to spend it. (In Britain, during the Second World War, to overcome the inequality of distribution of purchasing power in terms of money, a special currency for purchasing scarce goods was introduced, over and above specific rationing of basic foodstuffs. Coupons, worth a certain number of ration 'points', were distributed to families, and prices in terms of points, as well as their money prices, were attached to various goods. This system combined the principle of rationing in a siege economy with the advantages of free consumer's choice.)

However, whatever the practical advantages of a retail market, to say, as a theoretical explanation, that households buy goods to enjoy utility in consuming them does not add anything to saying that households buy goods. The concentration of the so-called theory of demand on the tastes of isolated individuals has led to neglect of social influences on consumption. Obviously, there are some strong individual idiosyncrasies, but, for the most part, habits are influenced by the group in which a family lives, and the propaganda to which it is subjected.

A great deal of detailed sociological research on consumers' habits has been conducted by the sales departments of manufacturing firms and by advertising agencies. This is largely devoted to the problem of manipulating demand in particular directions, often on a long-term strategy, rather than to giving a rounded survey of

* See **1** 3 §2(b).

the whole field. Still, we can learn a good deal about the motives of consumers from studying advertisements. These show what advertisers believe consumers' motives to be, and advertisers have studied the subject more closely than economists. To judge by advertisements, snobbery, anxiety and sexual associations play a major part in influencing consumers' choice.

(b) Rationing by the purse

In a country in which there is a hierarchy of incomes, there is a hierarchy of patterns of consumption. At the bottom end, there has been a good deal of research on poverty, and calculations are made as to what proportion of a given population is living below the minimum standard of human needs. There are official sample surveys of income and expenditure, and there have been academic investigations, mainly of the consumption habits of working-class families, with a few of the middle class.

General observation shows that, as we ascend the hierarchy of income levels, there are some commodities of which a representative family buys more at a higher level of income. Such cases conform to the notion of properly behaved conditions of demand—either at a lower price relative to income, or at a higher income relative to price, more of the commodity is bought.*

There are a great number of items of which less is bought at a higher income. These are *inferior goods*, or inferior methods of supplying a general need, such as for food or entertainment. A particular case of this kind has long been known as the *Giffen paradox*, because Sir R. Giffen pointed out that a rise in the price of bread (relative to given money income) made it impossible for working-class families to afford meat, so that they had to eat more, not less, bread. The effect of the rise in price in reducing real income more than offset its effect in directing expenditure to substitutes. Marshall regarded inferior goods as an exception to the general rule and maintained that 'such cases are rare'.[3] But this seems to be special pleading. Generally, a comparison of consumption at different income levels within the same broad culture will show many examples of commodities of which less is bought at the higher income. In general, a higher level of consumption means a greater variety of items and greater emphasis on quality, rather than greater quantities of the same assortment.

The neoclassicals, though laying great emphasis on demand, were not keen on discussing problems connected with the distribution of purchasing power between families; discussing tastes and ignoring distribution is looking after the pence and forgetting the pounds.

(c) Supply creates demand

Consumers choose (for whatever motives) from among the commodities offered. They have a power of veto—they need not buy what they do not like—but none of

* See **2** 5 §3(a).
3. *Principles* p. 132.

initiative. The pattern of demand for particular commodities in a society is strongly influenced by the supply of what is available. Everyone requires food, clothing, and amusement but the particular form in which these needs are met depends on what is produced. There is a marked preference for a diet of rice in the countries where rice is grown; the habit of eating mutton in England presumably goes back to the mediaeval wool trade. Industrial production is continually modified by technical developments and as soon as some new commodity is seen in use, the 'demonstration effect' rapidly spreads the desire to own it among the whole population. Thus supply creates demand. The enormous revolution in attitudes and behaviour brought about by the motor car (for good or ill) is the leading example.

The great productiveness of modern industry raises a problem for the capitalist firms. It would be technically possible to satisfy the demand for manufactures now known, at an acceptable standard, for the whole population of the industrial countries in a few years, but then how would the system continue to function? The problem has so far been solved by the *creation of wants*.

A producer of consumption goods has power to influence the demand for his product. In the market for intermediate goods, materials, equipment, etc., buyers and sellers are equally professionals; the seller has limited opportunities to persuade the buyer except by appropriate design and service and genuine information. In the market for consumption goods, the buyer is an amateur. He may be an expert in the line in which he earns his living but he—or more often, she—must buy goods over a wide range of lines. The buyer, therefore, has to find information where she may to help her in choosing between one source of supply and another. This information is given mainly by interested parties—by advertisement and other devices of salesmanship sponsored by the seller. Increasingly, advertisement ceases even to pretend to give information; a whole profession in the art of persuasion has developed.

Market research is partly aimed at finding out what the public (with the money to spend) is likely to want or need, but it is largely aimed at finding out the most effective methods of creating demand for goods which the producer is able to put on the market. Moreover, to ensure an expanding market for consumption goods in general, the press and the mass media (for which advertisement is the main source of revenue) are involved in keeping up the general atmosphere of enthusiasm for new purchases and of prestige attached to possessions. The goods that it is profitable to supply are those that will be bought at the medium and higher levels in the hierarchy of incomes; low incomes do not provide a good market. As general consumption increases, there is less and less motive for catering to the needs of the poorest.

Relative poverty is no less humiliating because the absolute level of consumption has risen; everyone is kept running to stay in the same relative place. It is because of this that firms can always find workers and staff to serve them, and consumers to buy their output at profitable prices.

Here, we can only throw out some hints of major questions which need to be studied, for a hundred years of *a priori* argument about 'maximizing utility' has not contributed much to them.

3. The public sector

The method of supplying goods and services and of distributing incomes through the market, operates in only part of a national economy. A part of the economy is operated by governmental authorities which collect money through taxation and allocate expenditure to various purposes decided by political, rather than purely commercial, considerations. In modern times, there has been a great growth in the sphere of operation of the public sector in all industrial countries.

(a) Public and private expenditure

A broad indication of the influence and importance of the public sector is given by the proportion of public expenditure in the *gross national product* (GNP). The gross national product, for a year, is a statistical measure of a country's total productive activity, both at home and abroad, resulting in the output of goods and services. It thus represents the value of total production at current prices within a country, excluding payments for imports and including income received from abroad.

The value of GNP may be presented in three different ways: (i) As the total costs of production originating in each industry (equal to the net output or value added of that industry) before providing for depreciation and excluding stock appreciation, plus net property income from abroad. Costs of production represent the sum of income from employment, income from self-employment, profit incomes, and rent. (ii) As the value of total output (excluding taxes or subsidies that enter into prices) as declared by the producers of goods and services, less the value of intermediate goods which enters the value of the goods in the production of which they are used. This measure includes provision for depreciation but excludes stock appreciation. (iii) As the total value of sales, at market prices, of goods and services in the domestic market (including stock building) less expenditure on intermediate goods, plus payments for exports of goods and services and property income received from abroad, less payments for imports of goods and services and property income made abroad, less taxes on expenditure, but including subsidies. An omniscient statistician would find exactly the same value for GNP measured from any or all of these three viewpoints. The volume of expenditure is equal to the value of total production, which is equal to the flow of income.

Calculations of GNP are often used to indicate the economic success or prosperity of a country. This measure is unreliable, firstly, because money incomes are an imperfect measure of the value to society of the activities of the individuals who receive them, and secondly, because all unpaid services and free goods (including fresh air) are excluded from the estimates.

The proportion of public expenditure (expenditure of the state, local authorities, and government agencies) in GNP represents the proportion of national income derived from the state. Table 7.2 traces the growth of public expenditure in the UK since 1860. Before the Boer War, state expenditure made up only about 10 per

205

cent of GNP, rising sharply with each period of war. The strains of the inter-war period increased the role of the state, and since the end of the Second World War, state activity has increased continuously until, by 1970, more than 50 per cent of total income in the UK was derived from the expenditures of public authorities.

Table 7.2

The proportion of total government expenditure in Gross National Product 1860–1970, selected years (percentages)

1860	1880	1900	1920	1938	1950	1955	1960	1965	1970
11	10	15	26·1	30·1	39·5	37·3	41·5	45·3	50·3

The government's total expenditure is usually divided into *exhaustive* expenditure comprising purchases of goods and services of various kinds, for use by the public authorities, and *transfer payments*, which involve passing money from the Exchequer to individual citizens in return for no present activity, for example, payments of interest on debt arising from government borrowing, and the government contribution to unemployment allowances. There are some borderline cases, such as the salaries of the highest ranks in the Civil Service.

(b) Activities of the state

In modern industrial countries, there is a large overlap between the public and the market sector. A number of services, such as the mail, are provided at prices designed to cover costs, while nationalized industries, taken over in the past from private capitalists, employ labour and sell their products in much the same manner as the rest.

Two main elements in public expenditure are differentiated from the market. The first is concerned with the apparatus of government, the administration of the law, and the provision of so-called defence. The second type of public activity arises from the conflict between the demands of democracy and the distribution of purchasing power among families thrown up by history and the market. Consumer choice, in a well-to-do family, gives education and medical help a high priority; these are provided free or at subsidized prices, at least to a minimum extent, for the general population. It is in the interest also of the well-to-do that families who could not pay for education and medical treatment at commercial rates can have the benefit, so as to check the spread of infectious diseases and to maintain a literate labour force. There are also a number of provisions to relieve extreme poverty.

206   In both the government and the welfare spheres, the allocation of national resources between objectives comes about through a political process which requires a different kind of analysis from that which is appropriate to the market.

(c) Taxation

Historically, the main concern of the state in economic affairs was connected with taxation. As Adam Smith put it:

> Political œconomy, considered as a branch of the science of a statesman or legislator, proposes two distinct objects: first, to provide a plentiful revenue or subsistence for the people, or more properly to enable them to provide such a revenue or subsistence for themselves; and secondly, to supply the state or commonwealth with a revenue sufficient for the public services.[4]

Intricate and detailed problems, which we shall not enter into here, are raised by the effects of different taxation systems: the relative merits of *direct* taxes, assessed on income or wealth, and *indirect* taxes levied on the production or sale of goods, from the point of view of the Exchequer and that of the taxpayer; and the whole problem of the relation of nominal tax liabilities to what is actually paid. We can make only some general observations.

Taxation involves important questions of social policy. It is a generally accepted principle that taxation should be progressive, taking a larger proportion from higher incomes and placing taxes on what are regarded as luxuries rather than necessities. However, tax systems in force for many decades, in countries like the UK, which, on paper, seem extremely progressive, have had only a slight effect on inequalities in ownership of wealth, which is the main source, directly and indirectly, of inequalities in income.*

In the UK, there seems to have been some shift, since before the last war, from the share of the highest incomes towards the upper-middle range, but the proportion of the total going to the half of the population with the lowest incomes is no higher, (see Table 7.3).

There are many minor conflicts between social policy and the Exchequer that lead to anomalies. For instance, a habit-forming commodity such as tobacco provides a convenient object of taxation because the demand of addicts is very inelastic. Just as a monopolist can get more revenue by raising his price where demand is inelastic, so the Chancellor of the Exchequer can rely on getting more revenue every time he adds to the tax on cigarettes. When it is discovered that smoking is deleterious to health, it is hard for a government to give quite whole-hearted support to a campaign to stamp it out. But public opinion would be deeply shocked if a government proposed to get revenue from some new kind of vice.

Every fiscal system is necessarily a compromise between expediency and principle. Many taxes produce unintended side effects; in particular, taxes on business profits

4. *Wealth of Nations*, book IV, *Introduction*.
* See Table 7.1.

and high incomes have brought into existence whole professions of accountants and legal advisers who assist taxpayers to minimize their liabilities.

Table 7.3

Distribution of personal incomes, after tax, in the UK,
1938–39 and 1966–67

Percentage of persons receiving incomes	Percentage of total personal income	
	1938–39	1966–67
Bottom 10	5	4·2
Bottom 50	30	31
Top 50	70	69
Top 25	54	40
Top 10	33	20
Top 5	25	13

Source: *Annual Abstract of Statistics*, 1955 and 1969.

Every kind of tax is felt to be a burden and is resented as unfair, but ideas and habits adapt to a system once it has been established. Hence the saying: An old tax is a good tax.

The fiscal policy of any government is influenced partly by traditional notions of what is acceptable, and partly by the interest of the classes from which it draws support. There are no 'purely economic' aspects of government policy that can be fenced off from wider social and political problems and discussed in terms of strictly economic considerations alone.

(d) Government borrowing

The expenditure of the state may be covered by taxation or by borrowing. When tax revenue falls short of expenditure, the government must borrow. When revenue is greater than expenditure, it can take the opportunity to pay off debt accumulated in the past.

Traditional economic doctrine frowned on borrowing. From the time of Adam Smith to the mid nineteen thirties, the government financial policy advocated by the orthodox theory of taxation was a direct extension of the successful financial policy of a household; expenditure should not exceed income. When a particular amount of expenditure was dictated by political necessity, the problem was to devise ways to raise the amount of tax revenue necessary to *balance the budget*.

In certain circumstances—say, in preparation for a war—it might be desirable that revenue should exceed spending, so that state savings are built up to provide for

the future. In normal circumstances however, this policy was held to impose unnecessary burdens on the people. In any case, expenditure ought not to exceed
revenue, for as in the case of a household, this was the road to ruin. Not only would
'unsound finance', in the form of debts incurred by government borrowing, disturb
the financial and monetary system, but also, borrowing would shift the burden of
repayment to future generations who received none of the benefits of the expenditure. An unbalanced budget was not just unsound, it was immoral.

These ideas were still dominant during the great slump. Keynes was trying to
establish the view (which now seems obvious) that, when an economy is suffering
from unemployment and low profits, government expenditure financed by borrowing
increases real income through the effect of the multiplier,* even when the objects of
expenditure are not useful in themselves, and that, when they are useful, it cannot
be a burden on future generations to provide them with more houses, productive
capacity, or transport facilities than they would otherwise have had.

After the experience of full employment in wartime, these ideas generally prevailed
over the old doctrines. Nowadays, the accepted view of public finance is that the
budget is primarily an instrument for regulating the level of effective demand. When
there is unemployment, it is now agreed that the government should increase
expenditure and cut taxes to bring about an upswing in activity. (The argument is
always phrased in terms of employment, but it is acceptable to business opinion
because an increase in employment is accompanied by an increase in profits.†) A
boom that is so strong as to create an all-round excess of demand for labour is
regarded as inflationary and calls for an increase in taxation to check it. (Budgetary
employment policy is bound up with, and hampered by, problems connected with
a country's balance of international payments, which we will discuss later.)

As we now see, the purpose of taxation is not to raise money to pay for expenditure,
but to deflect demand from private to public ends. Thus, the politician's cry: 'We
cannot afford it!' is not a reasonable reply to a demand for socially beneficial expenditure. The employment of idle resources costs nothing. When resources are
fully utilized, such a plea can only mean something like: 'The government cannot
afford to build more hospitals as this would involve taking scarce building resources
away from the construction of luxury flats and motorways.'

The idea that the government of a country is concerned with the level of employment of its labour force, makes a great breach in *laissez-faire* orthodoxy and brings
public policy into every sphere of economic life.

(e) **The burden of the National Debt**

The accumulated result of past deficits (less any repayments) remains as an outstanding obligation from the government to its citizens; this constitutes the *National
Debt*. (Here, we consider only *internal* debt. Foreign obligations will be discussed

* See **2** 3 §2(a).
† See **2** 3 §2(b).

later.) The notion that the National Debt is a burden on the community went out of fashion with the acceptance of the Keynesian view of finance. Obviously, the existence of the National Debt does not reduce the real productive capacity of the nation in a direct way. The government undertook to pay interest when it borrowed; this is taken from taxpayers and passed to the holders of government obligations. The citizens of the state, as a whole, are paying themselves. The situation is unlike that of a family obliged to pay interest to its creditors (or of a nation making payments to meet foreign obligations).

Nevertheless, the existence of a large National Debt is a great nuisance. All taxation causes anomalies and discontents, and most has unwanted side effects. The greater the total value of revenue to be raised, the worse these are likely to be. When a government is committed to a large flow of taxation purely for interest payments, it is harder to raise taxes for desirable purposes. Moreover, however progressive the tax system may be on paper, payment of interest on the National Debt must involve, to some extent, taxing the poor to pay the rich, and taxing the active to pay the idle.

(f) The budget and effective demand

We have observed that it is not legitimate to treat complex quantities like the flow of national income or the level of full employment as though they can be represented by numbers of some simple unit. However, provided we do not allow ourselves to be misled into thinking that formulae mean more than they can, it is helpful to set out the Keynesian argument schematically. We confine the formulae to a closed system, i.e., an economy without foreign trade.

Net national income for a year represents the value of the production of goods and services during the year, that is, GNP *minus* the allowance for amortization deducted from profits. We take national income net of depreciation because we are interested in the flow of disposable income. The ambiguity in the concept of net profit which we discussed above need not bother us in this context.* Furthermore, we assume that amortization can be taken as a correct representation of the part of gross investment that is making good the depreciation of the stock of capital. Then, when Y is net national income for a year, and I is net investment, Y corresponds to the flow of earned and unearned income of all households and the undistributed net profit of firms.

Now, looking at Y, net income, from the viewpoint of how it is earned, it can be exhaustively divided into that derived from production of consumption goods and services, C, from net investment, I, and from government expenditure, G. And looked at from the viewpoint of how it is disposed of, it is spent on consumption, saved, S, or paid in taxes, T.

$$Y = C + I + G$$
$$Y = C + S + T$$

Therefore,
$$S = I + G - T$$

* See **2** 6 §2(a).

That is to say, the total net saving by the public is greater or less than net investment according to whether there is a deficit or a surplus on the budget. When there is a deficit, which represents negative saving by the government, the private sector is saving more than the value of investment.

Now let s be the overall proportion of private saving in total income and t the overall proportion paid in taxes with a particular pattern of tax rates. Then,

$$(s + t)Y = I + G$$

With investment constant, an increase in government expenditure increases income, and increases both total saving and the yield of taxes. The addition to the National Debt caused by a round of government expenditure is less than the expenditure, because of the extra tax revenue that it generates. This was an important part of the case for public investment to combat unemployment in the slump.

Now, suppose that tax rates have been increased; t is higher. Then, if everything else, including I and G, are the same, Y must be lower. This comes about because higher taxes restrain consumption. In so far as a higher t means a lower s—the payment of higher taxes reduces saving—the reduction in Y is that much the less.

This argument leads to a striking conclusion. Imagine a government that adopted a policy of ensuring enough outlay to maintain near-full employment while keeping its annual budget balanced. In a given situation, this government would have to make more expenditure than if it maintained the same level of employment with a deficit, for there has to be enough expenditure to make up for the restraint on consumption by higher taxes. The government therefore has to think of more things to spend money on. Unless it all goes on armaments and the moon, this must mean a greater involvement of the public sector in social policy. Moreover, the fruits of investment carried out under this policy would belong to the nation as a whole, without any associated debt requiring payments of interest in the future.

Thus, when near-full employment is to be guaranteed, the policy of maintaining a balanced budget is far more radical than the so-called Keynesian principle of allowing a deficit whenever effective demand needs a boost.

4. The price level

So far, all our discussions have been carried on in terms of prices relative to money-wage rates. We must now turn to the problem of wages and prices in terms of money.

(a) Money wages

One of the most important elements in the Keynesian revolution was the realization that, in an industrial economy, the main determinant of the general price level is the level of labour costs—money-wage rates relative to output per head—and that the level of money-wage rates, at any moment, is more or less an historical accident, depending on experience over the recent and remote past.

211

In the teaching prevalent before Keynes, problems connected with production of goods and distribution of incomes were discussed in 'real' terms. Money was conceived to be a veil through which the economist had to peer to see the underlying relationships. The general price level was treated as a separate subject, in terms of various elaborated versions of Hume's simple-minded quantity theory of money.* Keynes broke down this dichotomy and treated the monetary system as one element in complex reality.

As we have observed, a non-monetary market economy is a contradiction in terms.† Some unit of generalized purchasing power is necessary for even the simplest kind of exchange between independent specialized producers. It is an even more indispensable prerequisite for a system of production based on wage labour. For Marx, capitalism is the system in which labour itself has become a commodity, an object of exchange. Wages have to be agreed and paid in terms of money. The money-wage rate then becomes the chief determinant of costs for every producer. As we have seen, relative wage rates for different types of workers are subject to long-run influences of technology and the requirements for entry into various occupations. In any particular situation, relative earnings are remarkably stable; in any one country, under normal conditions, industrial wage rates move closely in step with each other. The general level of money-wage rates sets the general level of prime costs of production of all manufactures, and proportionate margins relative to prime cost, overall, are fairly constant. Thus, the general level of prices is governed by the level of money-wage rates.

It is much easier to bring about a rise of money-wage rates when employment and profits are high, than a fall when they are low. Thus, there is a general tendency over the course of history for money-wage rates to rise. For manufactures, this is partly offset by technical progress raising output per head, but personal services, such as hairdressing, in which productivity cannot much increase, become more and more expensive relative to goods.

This is a general phenomenon in all industrial countries. (The relative rates at which wages rise and productivity increases in different countries have repercussions on international trade, which we shall discuss later.)

(b) Inflation

When near-full employment is established after a long depression, it is necessary to raise the relative wage rates in trades where they have been formerly kept low by exceptionally severe unemployment. For instance, in England, when there were vacancies in industry it was necessary to raise agricultural wages, or the farmers would have lost their labour force. When this happens, there is a rise in purchasing power which gives a further boost to effective demand, and there is often pressure

---

* See **1** 3 §4.
† See **2** 5 §2(b).

from higher-paid workers to restore their traditional differential rates. Thus, an inflationary movement may be started from the side of wage rates.

Inflation may also be started from the side of prices. A sharp and sudden increase in effective demand raises prices of primary products, including food. Industrial employers, who are also benefiting from increased activity, cannot refuse to raise money-wage rates to compensate for the rise in the cost of living. Then there is a rise in prime costs, due to higher wages, over and above any rise due to raw-material prices. To keep profit margins constant involves a rise in the price of manufactures. Real wages are then once more lower than before the rise of primary-product prices began, and pressure for higher money wages is resumed.

Further, when a rise in effective demand has led to an increase in output of manu-factures without a rise in their prices, profits have increased all the same—there is a higher level of utilization of plant and a reduction in overhead cost per unit of out-put. Therefore, trade unions regard it as their right and duty to demand an increase in money-wage rates to preserve the share of wages in the value of output. Employers do not put up much resistance as they want to be able to take advantage of the favourable market conditions. But with higher wage rates, prime costs have gone up; prices are raised, the original bargaining position is restored, and (apart from reper-cussions on foreign trade) there is no reason why the spiral of rising money incomes and rising prices should not go on indefinitely.

These are purely short-period reactions. We must also consider the effect of accumulation and technical change. At any moment, some firms are reducing costs and expanding output much faster than others. The firms in which output per man employed is rising have no particular objection to raising money wages to an extent that permits them to keep their prices more or less constant. Indeed, they may be happy to do so, for less-progressive rivals in the same markets have to pay the same wage rates, which may drive them out of business.

Rising money wages for some groups of workers pull up wages for the rest. The more backward industries and services are forced into mechanizing production to raise output per head to a level that makes it possible to continue in business with the higher wage rates, but they cannot do so sufficiently fast to prevent their costs from rising. The unevenness of technical change between different lines of produc-tion thus leads to continuous upward drift in the price level as a whole.

When an inflation has been going on for some time, conventions based on a stable value of money begin to break down. Once an expectation of rising prices takes hold, it becomes a cause of inflation itself. Speculation in old masters and building land begins and huge sums of money accrue to dealers. Then, though the movement may have started through a rise of effective demand, a recession is not enough to check it.

Trade unionists very much resent being told that inflation is all the fault of rising wage rates, and businessmen dislike being scolded for raising prices. Neither party is to blame. Each is behaving correctly according to his own lights. The speculators are following the proper rules of the free market system. The trouble lies, not in anyone's bad behaviour, but in the mechanism of the private-enterprise market economy.[5]

The argument in Keynes' *General Theory*, which showed that there is no meaning to be attached to the idea of an equilibrium price level, was even more shocking to orthodox opinion than the observation that there is no natural tendency in a private-enterprise economy to maintain full employment. It seems to have been left out of the neo-neoclassical reconstruction of pre-Keynesian theory, so that present experience of inflation is as disconcerting for modern orthodoxy as massive unemployment was for the orthodoxy of the 'thirties.

5. Another story: 'consumers' sovereignty'

(a) A harmonious society

To understand the role of consumer choice in neoclassical theory, let us return to our well-run kibbutz. Certain physical resources—labour time and means of production—are available for providing for current consumption, and there is a list of specified consumer goods. The problem is to allocate resources between the commodities in the most desirable way. The committee in charge works out the *production-possibility surface*, showing the maximum amount of each combination of the commodities that the given resources could produce.

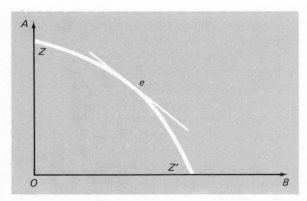

FIG. 7.2   Quantities of commodities *A* **and** *B,* **expressed in physical terms, are measured on the axes. All points between the axes represent combinations of** *A* **and** *B.* **All those within and on the line** *ZZ'* **are producible. All combinations outside the line cannot be produced. All points on** *ZZ'* **are** *efficient* **in the sense that it is impossible to produce more of** *A* **without producing less of** *B,* **and vice versa. The slope of the tangent at** *e* **represents the price of** *B* **in terms of** *A.*

In the simple case of only two commodities, this can be shown in a two-dimensional diagram. The axes represent quantities of two commodities, *A* and *B*. The curve shows the maximum quantity of each that can be produced together with a given quantity of the other. This illustrates two concepts which may be important in con-

5. See D. Jackson, H. A. Turner, and F. Wilkinson, *Do Trade Unions Cause Inflation?*

nection with problems of planning.* The first is the concept of *efficient production*. A quantity of the commodities represented by a point inside the production-possibility frontier represents inefficient production, since more of one or both commodities could be produced with the given resources.

The second concept is *opportunity cost*. At any point on the frontier, it is impossible to produce more of A without producing less of B. At any point, the opportunity cost of each commodity in terms of the other is shown by the slope of the tangent to the frontier at that point.

The committee intend to produce commodities in the proportions that correspond to the tastes of the members of the cooperative. How is purchasing power allocated among them? This subject is sketchily treated in neoclassical theory. Let us suppose that each member is issued with a number of tickets that corresponds to his 'fair share' of consumption. Then a price ratio corresponding to a point on the frontier is called out, and each member is asked to say how he would allocate his tickets between the commodities. If the total tickets cast for A are in a higher ratio to those cast for B than the ratio of production shown at that point on the frontier, a point is chosen at which the price of A in terms of B is higher, and so on. By trial and error, a point is found at which the ratio of the production of the two commodities corresponds to the ratio of the allocation of tickets. Commodities are then produced in these proportions, and passed to the members in exchange for tickets. (With more than two commodities, of course, the whole process would be extremely complicated.) The ratio of demand is an average of the demands of individuals (weighted by the tickets allotted to each) and does not necessarily correspond to the preferences of any individual. However, at this point, no one individual would be able to have more of a commodity that he prefers without depriving someone else of what *he* prefers. This is said to be a 'Pareto optimum' because the name of Pareto is associated with the proposition that perfect competition in a Walrasian market necessarily leads to a point on the production-possibility surface.†

(b) Some difficulties

This argument purports to show that the competitive market brings about an efficient allocation of scarce resources between alternative uses, but it does not even pretend to say anything about the allocation of investible resources between various projects when accumulation and technical progress are going on.[6]

Even on its own static ground, the argument is limited to one narrow sphere of so-called welfare economics—the distribution of goods bought by households at retail. It leaves out the operations of the public sector. It obviously has nothing to say about the 'allocation of resources' to the military, but it does not seem to be able to deal with beneficial public expenditure either. General access to education

* See **2** 11 §2(a).
† See **1** 3 §2(a).
6. See Janos Kornai, *Anti-Equilibrium* II, 11.   **215**

and a reliable health service must surely be a more important contribution to welfare, in the ordinary sense of the word, than most of the goods distributed through the shops.

Finally, the argument takes no account of the distribution of wealth and income between families. The concept of a Pareto optimum is defined purely in physical terms without regard to the human beings involved. When purchasing power is unequally distributed, a position on the production-possibility surface might be reached where some consumers were overeating, and some starving. This would satisfy the Pareto condition perfectly well, for the starving men could not get any more without at least one of the overeaters getting less.

Appendix: Accounting identities and causal relations

There is often some difficulty in bringing theoretical insights to bear upon statistical information. For purposes of theoretical argument we are interested in causal relationships, which depend on behaviour based on expectations, ex ante, whereas the statistics necessarily record what happened, ex post. Moreover, the figures have to be set out in categories for which it is possible to find statistical information, rather than in categories that are significant from an analytical viewpoint. In particular, there is a difficulty connected with the distinction between gross investment, $\bar{I}$, and net investment, I, and between net saving, S, and total saving including amortization allowances, A. The statistics of gross national product for a year necessarily include the value of gross investment, without attempting to allow for the depreciation over the year of the pre-existing stock of equipment, buildings, etc. The corresponding flow of income includes amortization allowances. We can derive a figure for net national income, Y, and net investment, I, by subtracting amortization allowances, A, from gross investment. But the relation between amortization allowances and real depreciation is not precise. It is only by an accounting convention that we can define I as $\bar{I} - A$. Thus, when we write: net national income is composed of the value of net investment and consumption in the form $Y \equiv I + C$ we must use the symbol $\equiv$ which indicates an accounting identity, in which the elements are equal by definition, not $=$ which indicates a causal relationship.

In the early days of the exposition of Keynes' General Theory, it was usual to argue as follows:

$$Y = C + I$$
$$Y = C + S$$

Therefore, $I = S$

But, since net investment and net saving are accounting identities, this was not a legitimate argument; it allowed hostile critics to create confusion.[7] An ex-post accounting identity, which records what has happened over, say, the past year, cannot explain causality; rather, it shows what has to be explained. Keynes' theory

7. See Joan Robinson, *An Introduction to the Theory of Employment* 2nd edition, 1969, pp. xiii–xiv.

did not demonstrate that the rate of saving is equal to the rate of investment, but explained through what mechanism the equality is brought about.

In the argument in §3(e) of the foregoing chapter, it is legitimate to take I and S as net investment and saving, for we are interested in the effect of changes in G and T, while $\bar{I}$, I and A may be taken to be unaffected by them.

In our simple model (**2** 2 §2), the problem of distinguishing gross from net profit did not arise; there were no amortization allowances because there was no physical wear and tear or obsolescence of machines.

Chapter Eight

Finance

Every process of production (except gathering wild fruit) requires some pre-existing materials and equipment, and production takes time, so that the people concerned must have the means to live until the product emerges. In the economy depicted by the Physiocrats, the peasants owned a sufficient stock to provide for a year's productive consumption, and Ricardo's capitalist farmer held next year's wage fund in his barn after the harvest. In a modern economy, a stream of production is going on all the time. An individual who commands purchasing power can buy the inputs required for production, and pay wages in money which permit the workers to support their families by buying goods ready before their own product is available for sale.

Furthermore, there are stocks of all kinds of products in the economy at various points in the pipeline, so that a general increase of expenditure in setting production going, up to a limit which is rarely reached, can take immediate effect; supply is elastic in response to demand. A wage fund does not exist in the form of a bundle of ready-made goods but as a potential flow of production. An increase in effective demand resulting from an increase in payment and spending of wages, calls forth an increase in the flow of output of the goods that workers buy. Similarly, there is a flow of production of the inputs, say, steel or cement, required for construction and the creation of equipment, which increases or contracts with the level of investment.

Finance is purchasing power—sums of money—that is available to be spent before getting a return, so as to make investment possible.

1. Money and finance

(a) The revolving fund

As we have seen, outlay by firms in excess of current receipts or by government in excess of revenue—net investment and a budget deficit—generates a corre-

218

sponding amount of saving through the process of the multiplier.* But, obviously, a particular scheme of investment cannot be financed by the savings that it itself generates. Expenditure has to be made in advance to set the multiplier going. When a steady rate of investment exists, there is a corresponding steady rate of saving but each successive round of investment needs to be financed in advance.

In a situation in which the budget is balanced and industrial and commercial investment is at a steady rate from month to month, let us imagine that we can see the flow of expenditure that arises from a particular scheme of investment. We stain the money pink, so to say, and watch it passing from hand to hand. A firm borrows or draws on its own funds and pays out wages and buys materials. The workers buy goods from the shops, and distributed profits are spent by rentiers. The shops place orders to renew their stocks of goods. As the money passes from hand to hand, we observe here and there a leakage from the flow of payments into un-distributed profits and household saving. In the end, the whole of the original outlay has come to rest as an accumulation of wealth somewhere in the system, for until it has leaked into saving it is continuing to flow and generate more income and expenditure.

When investment is at a steady rate, savings are accumulating at the same rate. As they accrue, savings renew the funds of firms, or are added to the wealth of households, and are thus available to provide finance for further investment, if their owners so wish. Thus investment is continuously drawing on the supply of finance and savings are continuously re-creating it.

The finance needed for a constant flow of investment represents a revolving fund. An *increase* in the rate of investment or deficit spending, from one month to the next, requires an increase in the fund of finance, and generally, an increase in the stock of money in circulation. We must now see how this comes about.

(b) Bank money

In the provision of an elastic fund of finance in a modern economy, a special part is played by the banking system. There used to be an argument as to whether banks 'create money', or whether they are merely 'cloakrooms' where a member of the public leaves money for a time and calls for it when he wants it. Each of these views is true in a certain sense. What for any individual depositor is merely a temporary holding that he may soon withdraw is turned by the banking system into a source of finance.

The essential nature of bank money can be understood by considering its origin. As we have seen, money is anything that is acceptable as money.† When the organization of credit was primitive, gold coins were the main acceptable medium of exchange. Since it was dangerous to keep gold at home, wealthy individuals deposited what they had with goldsmiths to keep in their strongrooms. Then the receipt representing

* See **2** 3 §2(b).
† Cf. **2** 5 §2(b).

the gold owned by an individual could be used to make payments. Debts were settled between individuals with pieces of paper, and the goldsmith kept note of the change of ownership of the gold in his strongroom. Then notes were printed, representing a claim on gold, which provided a convenient kind of currency. From this, followed the emergence of the *banking principle*. Notes could be printed and lent out to finance business. A borrower used notes to pay his suppliers, the recipients used them in turn, and so they continued in circulation, rarely coming back to the bank to be cashed in gold. Thus, claims to the same gold could be outstanding ten or twelve times over, yet the bank remain solvent.

Now the banks were 'creating money'. A medium of exchange had come into existence which was acceptable because, to each individual, it represented gold, though if all of them had asked for gold at once they could not have had it. So long as the credit of the bank was maintained, the original owners of gold were no worse off, while the economy was enriched by the real production that the borrowers were able to carry out. But if for any reason, true or false, a bank was suspected of being unable to pay, a *run* would occur, everyone trying to get his own notes cashed before the others. The bank would close its doors, and the notes become valueless.

In most countries, nowadays, the provision of currency notes has been taken over by the government, and notes are official money, given the status of legal tender, which means that they cannot be refused in payment of a debt, so that they are endowed with general acceptability. The notion of gold backing for these notes has gradually withered away. They are money because they are money. (They are acceptable so long as the state retains its legal and political power. If this were to disappear, the national monetary system, as we know it, would collapse.*)

Banks now hold reserves of official money instead of gold, but the same banking principle applies. Deposits which can be drawn on at will (by writing cheques), or at short notice, are a convenient medium of exchange, and banks (like the goldsmiths) can use them as a source of finance.

A salary earner gets paid at long intervals and spends day by day; a shop or a bus company gets cash day by day and makes payments at intervals. Neither thinks of the cash held between receipts and payments as saving, but what, for each individual, is a mere pause before making payments, for the banks is a permanent fund; some individuals are paying in what others are drawing out. This fund, which represents a large part of the medium of exchange, is partly used by the banks to make loans to businesses and households. When a borrower draws on a bank loan to pay for goods and services, the sums which he spends are paid into the bank accounts of the recipients, and can be used by them to make payments. In this way, bank loans 'create money'.

(c) Consumer credit

Bank loans are made to households as well as to business. Anyone whose credit is good, or who has means to pledge collateral security, can usually arrange for an

* See **2** 5 §2(b).

overdraft or a bank loan when he wants to make payments in excess of his income.

Hire-purchase is a method of lending to households who have no credit, for the object that is sold on this system is itself the security for the loan. In case of default, it is taken back. Not that a part-used washing machine or bedroom suite is of much value, but the threat of losing it is a powerful incentive to keep up payments.

The leading example of a durable consumer good that can be purchased in this way is a house. An important part of house building is financed by loans to households on mortgage, that is, with the house itself as security. Another part is organized through borrowing by local and other authorities which have a concern for providing for the needs of families who have not the means to finance themselves, and part is carried out as a profit-seeking investment in speculative building. The whole of housing is best treated as a special kind of investment with characteristics different from those of industrial investment.

(d) Other borrowers

Many institutions besides local authorities, such as colleges and charitable foundations, have occasion to borrow to carry out their activities. Their income from endowments and subscriptions permits them to pay interest and establish their credit. The cost of financing investments made for such worthy purposes is set by the rate of interest that profitable investments can pay.

(e) Financing finance

The finance for hire-purchase, house building, local authority investments, and so on, is partly provided direct by banks and partly by specialist institutions which work on bank credit. This is an example of the existence of *financial intermediaries* (in addition to the banks themselves) between the lenders and borrowers. Side by side with the development of industry went the development of financial institutions which facilitate lending in a great variety of ways. Moreover, a huge apparatus and many flourishing professions have grown up around the business of bringing lenders and borrowers together, and a great deal of finance is committed to handling finance.

(f) Liquidity

Besides making direct loans to businesses and households, banks also hold securities —obligations representing second-hand debts of the government or of other institutions and businesses. In this way, they are 'creating money' in the sense of providing liquidity, that is, a vehicle for carrying purchasing power that is a more or less close substitute for cash. A deposit in a reputable bank is much safer to hold, and no less liquid, than a bundle of notes. Thus, by holding bills and other less-liquid assets, and providing the owners of wealth with deposits instead, the banks make it possible for them to hold their wealth in liquid form.

221

In the strict sense, the liquidity of a financial asset reflects the ability of the asset to be turned into a sum of money at will. Keynes mixed into the concept of liquidity the concept of uncertainty about the expectation of future value. Thus, for him, liquidity accounts for the preference which individuals or institutions may have for a means of holding wealth which can be changed into money at any time in the future at a foreseen price. The interest that banks offer on deposits is low or negative (through service charges). The interest foregone by holding wealth in the form of money, instead of in placements that yield higher returns, is therefore regarded as the measure of *liquidity preference*.

(g) The basis of credit

Money is essentially a matter of credit. The system depends on the reputation of the banks as reliable creditors. When a bank lends too rashly, and its debtor fails, it has lost money deposited with it. When a boom breaks, losses are widespread, and in former times, the whole banking system might be in danger of collapse. For this reason, every modern country has provided itself with a legal framework and with authorities (reserve banks and Treasuries) responsible for preserving solvency of the monetary system. Banks are obliged to hold a reserve in the form of a deposit with a central bank or some equivalent authority, and by controlling the total amount of reserves, the authorities have some control over the total amount of bank money in existence.

In the traditional British banking system, apart from notes and coins held ready to meet the demands of depositors, the banks held their reserves in the form of deposits with the Bank of England, which are reckoned as *cash*. They were obliged to maintain a certain ratio of cash to total deposits. Formerly, this was a matter of custom; it is now systematized in a set of rules which are recast from time to time.

A bank receives interest on its loans and on the securities that it holds, but cash earns none. The banks, therefore, do not want to hold an unnecessarily large amount of cash. At the same time, they must not allow their ratio of cash to fall below what is required by the rules. This gives the Bank of England power to bring about changes in the total quantity of bank money. The cash reserves of the banks are known as the *basis of credit*. Its amount can be regulated by the Bank.

Let us take a simplified example from the days when the cash ratio was 1:9. Say, the Bank of England buys securities worth £100 from a member of the public with a cheque drawn on itself. The previous owner of the securities deposits the £100 in his bank account. His bank finds its total of deposits increased by £100, and its assets increased by an addition of £100 to its cash. To prevent its cash ratio from rising unnecessarily high, it uses £90 from this £100 to buy securities or make advances, thus, restoring the ratio of cash to other assets to the required figure, 1:9. But the £90 which it expends in this way now appears as additional deposits and additional cash in the accounts of other banks (a part may come back to the same bank) which, consequently, buy securities to the extent of £81. And so on, until the original increase of the cash base has led to an increase in the total deposits of £1000, against which the banks hold £100 more cash and £900 more earning assets.

The rules at present in force are more complicated, but the same principle prevails. The banking system provides a link between the provision of a medium of exchange and a supply of finance for active use, which can be expanded when required, to 'meet the needs of trade'. This does not mean that banks, taken together, can make loans to an extent limited only by their reserve requirements. Proper banking practice requires a high ratio of safe securities, such as short-term government debt, to other assets. In effect, this 'liquidity ratio' was always more important than the traditional cash ratio, in limiting the activity of the banks. Subject to this, the amount of loans that a respectable bank can make depends on the number of sound and reliable borrowers that present themselves, and the collateral security they can provide against the possibility of default. Thus, the proportion of loans to securities in the bank's assets depends, to a large extent, on the general state of business and the prospects of profit.

(h) The supply of money

The amount of money in existence at any moment cannot be expressed as a precise quantity. The narrowest definition of money is legal tender but, in a modern economy, the most important element in the supply of means of payment consists of bank deposits, and these are of various types, such as current accounts—on which cheques are drawn—and time deposits that require notice for withdrawal and may receive interest. Moreover, for any individual or business, undrawn overdraft facilities are more or less equivalent to deposits. There are many institutions, such as savings banks, that make loans and receive deposits which are almost equivalent to ready money for their owners. The power of the authorities to control the banks, therefore, does not give them a tight hold over the quantity of what, from the point of view of business and households, is the supply of money.

Indeed, the demand for money by the public is the main influence on the amount in existence. It is the connection between lending and the provision of currency that makes the monetary system responsive to the requirements of business. The banks lend when they can find sound borrowers. When prospects are bright, banks expand advances and when slumpy conditions set in, contract them. Thus, as activity grows, the supply of money expands. Similarly, as prices rise and wage bills grow, bank loans expand correspondingly. Over the long run, as wealth accumulates (even if prices are not rising) the economy requires a larger amount of currency to carry out transactions and hold balances in a liquid form; this is automatically provided by a growing volume of bank money. The supply of official money expands correspondingly, for every owner of a bank deposit has the right to ask for notes and coins as he pleases. The management of the National Debt, also, is carried out with the requirements of the banking system in mind.

(The fact that, on any reasonable definition, the amount of money in existence in any country grows more or less in step with the money value of the incomes and wealth of its citizens, led to the theory that the quantity of money controls national income. The trouble with this theory is that no one has been able to provide a comprehensible explanation of how an increase in the quantity of money can increase national income, while it is quite easy to understand how an increase in national income brings about an increase in the quantity of money. This matter is discussed below.*)

As we have seen, the authorities have some hold over the total supply of the medium of exchange, but it is much easier for them to allow it to increase than to restrict it. When they attempt to limit the increase in the quantity of money that accompanies buoyant activity, the financial community can make use of forms of credit among themselves that provide substitutes for legal money, such as the extension of trade credit from seller to buyer. Institutions outside the direct control of the authorities may tempt deposits away from the banks by offering a higher rate of interest and make loans (at still higher interest rates) for building, hire-purchase, and other forms of investment. There are many such loopholes in a restriction of credit, which provide the means of evading controls that come between a willing borrower and a willing lender.

The authorities, moreover, are necessarily national, and as we shall see later, the problem of providing an adequate and reliable international monetary system presents great difficulties. Furthermore, management of internal monetary affairs cannot be easily separated from its international context.

2. The market for placements

Apart from bank loans, the main way in which firms raise finance is by selling *securities* —paper representing an obligation to make certain payments in the future. Also, as we have seen, the National Debt represents obligations created by government borrowing. Securities (like the bills in our simple model) can be dealt in at second hand; at any moment, there is a large amount of securities in existence, corresponding to finance raised in the past.

(a) Bonds and shares

There are two main classes of business securities, each with many subdivisions: *bonds*, which represent an acknowledgement of debt and carry a promise to pay a certain sum of money per annum, and *shares* which give a claim on the profits of the business. (This terminology is a mixture of English and American usage, chosen for its perspicuity. In England, bonds are called 'debentures' or 'government stock', and in America, shares are called 'stocks'.)

The National Debt, apart from short-dated bills mainly held by banks and other financial institutions, is in the form of bonds. The bonds of a respectable government

* See **2** 8 §4.

are called *gilt-edged* because there is no danger of default. The ability of other institutions and of businesses to borrow by issuing bonds depends on their credit-worthiness.

For business, bonds and shares are legally quite different; a bond represents a debt, so that the payment of interest is a legal obligation, while a share represents part ownership of the firm. Legally, the shareholders collectively own the capital of the business and have a right to appoint a board of directors who hire managers to operate it, but shareholders are not owners in the full sense that they are responsible for the debts of the business. If a business goes bankrupt and cannot pay its creditors, its shares become worthless but a shareholder has no further obligation.

As a result of this principle of *limited liability*, shares have become merely a con-venient kind of placement for rentiers, and over a hundred years and more under this legal system, the typical limited company has developed into a particular type of institution, controlled by a self-co-opting board and managed by salaried staff. Managers aim to make profits, for without profits a firm cannot flourish and grow, but they are not really making profits for the sake of the shareholders, they are making them for the sake of the company, with which their own interests are identified. The need to pay out a *dividend*—a share of net profit—is not very different from the need to pay interest on bonds. Despite their different legal status, bonds and shares are in normal circumstances best thought of, from a firm's viewpoint as alternative ways of raising finance, and from the rentier's viewpoint as alternative types of placement.

(b) The Stock Exchange

A stock exchange is a market in which securities can be dealt in at second hand. The finance that they represent was long ago expended by government, or embodied in earning capacity by a firm. A firm is committed to some particular line of activity. The securities can pass from one owner to another every day, without having any effect on the business that they represent. Securities, therefore, are a much more liquid form of wealth than real investments.

The Stock Exchange is primarily a convenience for rentiers. A large and well-paid profession has grown up in the business of dealing in second-hand securities. New issues are initially dealt with by specialist institutions. But, indirectly, the Stock Exchange performs a service to industry, making securities attractive by increasing their liquidity and so keeping down the cost (in terms of interest and dividends) of raising finance. For established companies, however, the main source of finance for new investment is, as in our simple model, retention of profits. The amount of new finance that passes through a stock exchange is very small compared to the great volume of dealings at second hand.

As a result of the system of limited liability, retention of profits has led to a peculiar system of property. The managers of firms are continually reinvesting amortization funds in new equipment, and they also retain a large proportion of net profit to finance the growth of their productive capacity. All the new capital which is created

225

in this way legally belongs to the shareholders. Provided that the investments are successful, the flow of earnings corresponding to a share is continually rising; the stock-exchange value of the share goes up correspondingly. Thus, the wealth created by the workers, managers, and designers employed by the firms is dropping into the laps of the rentiers without their contributing anything to production. As Professor Galbraith has pointed out: 'No grant of feudal privilege has ever equalled, for effortless return, that of the grandparent who bought and endowed his descendants with a thousand shares of General Motors or General Electric'.[1] The main economic role of a stock exchange is the preservation and expansion of rentier wealth, rather than the provision of finance for industry or government.

(c) Instability

Placements are held simply as a form of wealth, without other considerations such as may attach to real estate or old masters. The holders of placements are always on the look-out to make a gain and avoid a loss. *Bulls* are buying shares which they expect to rise in price, and *bears* are holding money as they wait for shares to fall in price. Expectations of changes in prices have a tendency to be self-fulfilling; there is a movement to buy securities that are expected to rise and so they do rise, and contrariwise.

The influence of expectations on stock-market prices, and the consequent importance of feelings of optimism or pessimism which may have little objective basis, makes the market for securities unstable. Self-fulfilling expectations will generate waves of buying or of selling, creating sharp fluctuations in prices.

The instability of the market for placements exaggerates the instability of industry. When there has been a rise in the level of profits of firms in the recent past, expectations of earnings per share have gone up. On the basis of the old prices of shares, there has been a rise in yields, i.e., the ratio of earnings to stock-exchange prices, but the old prices are raised, and the rise is likely to more than offset the actual rise in earnings, so that yields are reduced. Borrowing is now easier, which assists the rise in investment. At the same time, the wealth of rentiers has increased so that their expenditure goes up. The combined effects of increased investment and increased rentier expenditure will increase actual profits, and therefore expectations of profits, all the more. The rising spiral continues till something happens to check it; then expectations are reversed and a cumulative fall of share values sets in. The instability of the market for placements has a disruptive effect on industrial investment. 'When the capital development of a country becomes a by-product of the activities of a casino, the job is likely to be ill-done.'[2]

The institutions providing consumer finance also have a tendency to accentuate fluctuations of effective demand. When incomes are rising, household borrowing for expenditure on durables increases. When income ceases to grow, households are

1. *The New Industrial State* p. 394.
2. Keynes, *General Theory* p. 159.

burdened with payments on what they have already bought; they cannot enter into new commitments, and the demand for durables falls abruptly.

The instability of the Stock Exchange may develop to a pathological extreme, as in the great bull market in Wall Street which broke in 1929.[3] Then it may become an independent source of instability, over and above fluctuations in industrial activity. When share prices are rising for no other reason than that they are expected to rise, the market is heading for disaster. Sooner or later, something will happen to undermine expectations that have no basis except in expectations; as soon as share prices cease to rise, they crash. The shock to confidence then reacts on investment, and a real slump is precipitated by the slump in paper values. The great disaster of 1929 illustrates, in an exaggerated form, the nature of the relations between finance and industry in the modern private-enterprise system.

3. Interest rates

(a) Long-term rates

The level of prices that obtains in the market for placements is the main influence on the level of interest rates at which new finance can be raised. A high price of bonds means a low rate of interest on new borrowing. Suppose an irredeemable bond were issued when the rate of interest for that type of security was 5 per cent. A face value of $100 carries a promise to pay $5·00 per annum for ever—the bond has no redemption date. When the corresponding rate of interest is 4 per cent, the bond is worth $125, since 5 is 4 per cent of 125. A new bond of the same type can be issued at $100 with an obligation to pay only $4 per annum.

In this case, a simple inverse relationship exists between the price of a bond and the rate of interest. In general, the relationship is influenced by differences in the date of redemption and other elements in the terms of the original loan.

The income from a share is a much more vague conception. Expectations of the performance of particular firms are involved, and expectations about the value of particular shares in the future have a more important influence on the choice of placements than do current dividends. Usually, however, the same principle applies as with bonds. A rise in the general level of share prices reduces the yield—that is, income, however defined, expressed as a percentage on the market value of shares. This corresponds to a fall in interest rates and creates conditions favourable for making new issues.

(b) Stock and flow

The total of finance potentially available to industry, at any moment, can be regarded as a large pool representing all private negotiable wealth. Into the pool, flows day by day a stream of new saving looking for placements, and from time to time, new securities are thrown in by firms raising finance or repaying loans from banks.

3. See J. K. Galbraith, *The Great Crash.*

227

Household saving is largely in the form of contributions to pension funds and insurance of all kinds. These funds are held in income-yielding securities by the businesses that manage them. So long as the total volume of saving in this form is growing, there is an excess of payments into the funds over disbursements so that the total demand for placements that they represent is growing as time goes by. There is also some saving by wealthy households which is placed directly on the Stock Exchange.

The flows per annum, both of demand for placements and of new issues representing addition to supply, are necessarily small compared with the total stock of financial assets in existence at any moment, which represent the cumulative results of flows for a century or more. *A fortiori*, changes in the relation between flows of demand and supply, that would alter the level of the pool of placements, are likely to be very small in relation to the mass of the pool. Thus, the level of prices in the market is influenced only to a minor extent by the flows of demand and supply of new borrowing and lending; the main influence is the state of expectations in the market. (In our simple model, the stock of bills in existence was small relative to the flow of new lending. For this reason, the demand for loans, governed by the expected rate of profit, had much more influence over the level of the rate of interest than it has in a modern stock exchange.*)

The pattern of relative interest rates for different types of securities varies with the state of the market. When profits are high and share prices rising, the rate of interest on bonds has to be high. The prices of old bonds has to be low enough to make the return on them high enough to compete with shares. The yield of shares may be low because their prices have recently increased more than in proportion to their earnings, but an increase in price gives capital gains to shareholders, which are added to dividends in reckoning the return on shares. New bonds can be sold only if they promise a correspondingly high return. This is reinforced by the operation of the banks. When prospects of profit are good, they make more loans and hold fewer bills and securities. Thus, an increase in bank loans tends to reduce demand for bonds, so pushing up rates of interest. Thus, the banks help to influence the movement of interest rates, upwards in a boom and downwards in a slump.

(c) Monetary policy

The authorities have considerable power over the level of interest rates. Firstly, there is an official rate (in the British system, for centuries, this was called Bank Rate) at which short loans, on prescribed security, are offered by the central authority. The rate for various types of bank loan is set in relation to the official rate. This has an influence throughout the market for securities. For instance, a reduction in the short-term rate of interest makes it profitable to borrow in order to buy securities carrying a higher rate of interest. Such purchases raise the price of bonds somewhat, lowering the

* See **2** 3 §3(b).

bond rate of interest, which makes shares more attractive and pushes up their price, lowering yields. The converse applies when short-term interest rates rise.

Secondly, as we have seen, the authorities can manipulate the quantity of bank money by buying and selling securities from the public, so affecting the total of bank deposits. Then, in order to take securities from the public, the banking system has to push their prices to the point at which the public is willing to part with them and hold money instead. Thus, in a given general state of liquidity preference, an increase in the quantity of money, relative to the amount required for current transactions, leads to a fall in interest rates.

Thirdly, a large part of the total volume of placements is represented by the National Debt. Its structure can be manipulated by issuing more short-dated bills to buy long-dated bonds, or vice versa. This has an important influence on the liquidity of the banking system, and so on the whole complex of interest rates.

(d) The economist's day dream

The power of the authorities to influence interest rates has led to the conception that, by means of this instrument, the government of a country can regulate its economy. A fall in effective demand could be offset by a reduction in interest rates which would stimulate investment and increase purchases for consumption by discouraging saving. When an upswing was leading to inflation, a rise in interest rates would check it. Full employment with constant prices could thus be guaranteed.

Unfortunately, there are some serious difficulties about this conception. First, the rate of interest, though having some influence on investment, is too weak an instrument to control effective demand. Second, stability of effective demand does not guarantee that money wages will rise only enough to offset rising productivity and keep prices constant. Third, no country has autonomy in respect to its own level of interest rates, for through the international monetary system, it is connected with the level elsewhere, as we shall see below.*

4. 'Monetary theory'

In the doctrines inherited from the neoclassics, which were still dominant during the great slump, there was a sharp distinction between 'real' and 'monetary' forces influencing the operation of a market economy. 'Real' forces determined the relative prices of commodities and the commodity earnings of 'factors of production', while 'monetary' forces determined the general price level. The 'real' forces had a strong tendency to establish equilibrium (including full employment), while 'monetary theory' dealt with phenomena such as the trade cycle, inflation, and 'lapses from full employment'.

The central tenet of monetary theory was expressed in the formula

$$MV \equiv PT$$

* See **2** 10 §3(a) and **3** 1 §3(a).

T represents the volume, measured in some kind of physical unit, of transactions carried out during a year, with the use of money as a medium of exchange; P is the average price of the physical unit, thus, PT represents the money value of transactions per annum. M represents the quantity of money in existence, and V the average time that a unit of money is used in transactions during the year. Thus, MV also represents the money value of a year's transactions. The formula is an identity, not an equation.*

'Transactions' in physical terms was rather a vague concept. There were also difficulties about the meaning of MV. On the one hand, if M is narrowly defined as the stock of legal tender, then V is mainly determined by the amount of bank balances and other media of exchange available for carrying out transactions. To make the identity hold, V must be defined as PT/M. On the other hand, if M includes all means of payment that can be used in transactions, a large part may be idle in any year, with zero velocity. V is then a weighted average of the velocities of idle and active balances.

There were a number of variants of the theory, but all had the same general drift. T was taken to be fixed by the 'real forces' and V depended on habits such as whether wages are paid weekly or monthly; it followed that there must be a direct relation between M and P. This led to the conclusion that the quantity of money determines the level of prices.

Keynes began life as a 'monetary economist', but in his *General Theory* he broke down the division between the two departments of economics; he showed how so-called monetary disturbances are rooted in the 'real' behaviour of a private-enterprise economy. In the language of the formula, he showed how changes in T come about (through movements in output and employment) with changes in expectations of future profits, and he pointed out that the main influence on P is the level of money-wage rates.†

An increase in PT, due to a rise in activity or in the level of money-wage rates, normally leads to an increase in M, through an increase in bank advances, but if the authorities try to prevent M from increasing, they bring about a rise in the rate of interest, which tempts some idle balances into active circulation, so that V rises.

It is sometimes argued that the possibility of raising V is limited, so that ultimately the authorities could stop an increase in PT by refusing to allow M to increase. But, in fact, they cannot do so. Since depositors have a right to draw out notes and coins when they like, the total of official money in circulation is determined by what the public require. If the total of bank money were limited, other kinds of credit would be devised among the business and financial community. The authorities can retain their influence over the monetary system only so long as they use it with moderation.

On the other tack, an increase in M (however defined) may have some influence in encouraging activity. When expectations are gloomy, an increase in M will run to waste in reducing V. (This is called a 'liquidity trap' by the quantity theorists.) But, in general, a reduction in the level of interest rates, which puts up the value of

---

* For use of the symbol $\equiv$ see **2** 7 appendix.
† See **1** 3 §6(c).

securities on the Stock Exchange, stimulates investment and, by making rentiers feel richer, may stimulate consumption. Thus, Keynes was in favour of manipulating the quantity of money for good purposes, while denying that it was the all-powerful instrument of policy that the Quantity Theory seems to suggest.

Keynes' theory, though—as he said—'moderately conservative', had implications inimical to *laissez-faire* doctrine. Professor Milton Friedman attempted to bring about a revival of pure *laissez-faire* in the guise of 'monetary theory'.[4] He restored the dichotomy between 'real' and 'monetary' forces and, taking for granted that 'real' forces tend to equilibrium, concluded that only incorrect monetary policy prevents the maintenance of full employment and steady growth.

The argument is supported by the historical observation that there is generally a fairly high correlation (as we have seen) between the quantity of money in circulation in a country and the money value of its national income, over a run of years. But, while it is easy enough to see how changes in national income induce changes in the quantity of money, no one seems able to explain how changes in the quantity of money cause changes in national income—except by exaggerating the importance of Keynes' point that a temporary spurt in investment and consumption might, in favourable circumstances, follow a fall in the rate of interest.

4. See, for example, *The Optimum Quantity of Money and Other Essays.*

Chapter Nine

Growth: firms, industries, and nations

The modern study of economics began with an inquiry into the nature and causes of the wealth of nations, but even in Adam Smith's day, the 'wealth' of Britain was partly drawn from goods produced overseas. With the worldwide spread of capitalist industry, and the ramifications of finance spilling out over continents and penetrating frontiers, the boundaries of a national economy have grown still less clear. Nevertheless, the existence of nations, politically defined, of various shapes and sizes and various degrees of independence, is still a feature of the greatest importance in economic life. Here, we consider, in broad terms, the behaviour of capitalist firms in general and then see how national government policy may interact with it.

1. Behaviour of firms

The firms in our simple model were endowed with the main characteristics of industrial business—they operated plant and employed labour to produce output, they provided rentier income, they carried out accumulation and made use of changing techniques of production—but all this was in the simplest possible guise.

Reality, of course, is much more complicated. In a modern economy, there is a great variety of types of business engaged in the pursuit of profit in industrial, commercial and financial activity. Over the last two hundred years there has been a rapid development and evolution of forms of business; today, change is going on more rapidly than ever. At each stage, as new forms emerge, older ones continue to exist. To study the internal structure and the behaviour of firms of all kinds, we need the approach of a naturalist observing animals in the jungle, rather than of the pure theorist manipulating formulae.

232   Nonetheless, the basic characteristics of capitalist business remain the same,

though forms of organization change. Some observers suggest that the modern corporation is a completely different animal from the old family business. But the fact that each is employing labour to make profits out of selling goods means that they have similar problems, similar criteria for success, and a similar attachment of their leading personalities to the system in which they are able to flourish.

(a) Rentiers

It might be said that the position of rentiers is completely different nowadays from what it was before the introduction of limited liability. Certainly, this is true from a legal viewpoint, but it is our contention that, generally, relations between managers and shareholders in a modern corporation are not very different from the relations between an old-fashioned businessman and his wife.

The wife says, 'Now you are so prosperous, you should buy me a fur coat.' 'No,' says he, 'the business needs the money.' 'But,' she replies, 'Mrs Jones has a new fur coat. You would not like people to think that you're not doing as well as Jones and Co.' Just so, the management of a limited company has to refrain from investing part of its profits and pay out dividends to keep up its credit on the Stock Exchange. For this reason, we felt justified, in our simple model, in regarding rentiers as merely receiving a dole paid out of the profits of firms.

(b) The process of growth

We have remarked that it is a feature of any business that, once established, it has to make profits to survive and to grow. Like all generalizations, this is subject to exceptions. There are always a number of spivs who jump into a market to make a quick gain and jump out again, and there are businessmen who are content to limit themselves to a small scale of operations and have no ambition beyond it, but capitalism could not have grown as it has if either of these were the usual type. In general, a successful firm is one which has a longer life than an individual business-man, and increases its capital and scale of operations from generation to generation. Those which fail to grow, most often shrink and disappear or are swallowed by successful rivals.

Our model exhibited a number of firms already in existence, already in possession of productive capacity. They must have come into existence, in the first place, by getting command over finance to carry out the initial investments. Access to finance is on the principle: to him that hath shall be given. Credit means belief. A borrower has to be able to inspire the lender with a belief that he will be able to pay, and the best way to inspire that belief is to have property to pledge. Business is not a democracy. At any moment, there are only a few individuals in a position to start a new business, even on a small scale, and it becomes progressively harder to start a new business, or to survive for long after a business has been started, as old-established firms grow, and spread their tentacles into more lines. It follows that, in an active and prosperous private-enterprise economy, the number of independent firms is falling and the size of the typical corporation growing, although as the giants conquer more and more of the market they throw up opportunities for 'small men'—for instance, in service trades, or in highly specialized production of components for complex products such as motor cars.

Marshall resisted the idea of the tendency towards oligopoly in industrial production. He emphasized the prevalence of economies of scale—the reduction in the cost per unit of output as a firm grows in size and gains experience—but, at the same time, he wanted to believe that the number of firms serving any market would always be large enough to maintain competition. (This is known as 'Marshall's dilemma'.[1]) He tried to combine these incompatible ideas by basing the argument on family businesses. The grand old man who founded a firm is followed by heirs who have grown up in luxury and have not the ability and the ambition that led to his success. Thus, firms will not continue to grow after the third generation. In Marshall's famous simile, an industry is like a forest in which each individual tree grows to only a certain height and then decays.

There are, it is true, a great number of family firms which have followed this history, but there are others—in each of the industrial nations—which continue to flourish for many generations. And a successful family business can turn itself into a joint-stock company, selling its earning assets to shareholders, investing the proceeds in further productive capacity, and so continuing to grow. Marshall was aware that this was a serious objection to his theory, and he met it with an answer that has turned out to be remarkably mistaken: he said that joint-stock companies tend to stagnate. It may be true that huge corporations tend to suffer from technological hardening of the arteries, so that the best new ideas are developed by individuals but, then, corporations can buy them up. It is precisely the principle of limited liability, which enables joint-stock companies to command huge masses of finance, that keeps them expanding. Fish in a pond, where the big ones eat up the little ones, would be a better metaphor than trees in a forest.

(c) The technostructure

Marx foresaw the process of concentration of capital in ever fewer hands, and the growth of monopoly power, but he was wrong in thinking that this would make it easier for the workers, when the time is ripe, to 'expropriate the expropriators' and take over the management of the economy. A great corporation cannot be controlled by an individual capitalist. It is run by a hierarchy of executives; it requires a bureaucratic apparatus and it employs a great number of specialists—designers, engineers, salesmen, accountants, lawyers, and a research staff both for sales and for produc-

1. See G. L. S. Shackle, *The Years of High Theory*, chapter 3–5.

tion. The specialization of individuals and the complexity of the business deprive them of independence. The salaries and prospects of all these are involved in the success of the firm; they become attached to it and develop a feeling of loyalty to it. The sharp division of interest between workers and capitalists in Marx's vision is muffled by these layers of intermediate interests.

Professor Galbraith has coined the term 'technostructure' to describe the apparatus of management in the great corporation.[2] There has been some dispute as to whether the view that corporations are run by the technostructure means that they are not dedicated to the pursuit of profit. This seems to be an unreal argument. Individuals who make up the technostructure have just as much dependence as an old-fashioned capitalist on the success of the business for which they work. They have had an expensive education which is generally agreed to give them a right to a position of superiority and to a higher level of earnings than the rest of the labour force. This they could not enjoy unless business was profitable. It may be that they attach a high value to security, for if the firm they work for gets into trouble they will be in trouble themselves, but this is just as true, or more so, of the management of a family business.

Since members of the technostructure have to be, to some extent, intellectuals, they provide a link with the educational system and the media of propaganda, which helps to form a public opinion congenial to the system in which they flourish. By this means, the forms of political democracy can be made compatible with a very undemocratic distribution of economic power.

(d) 'Maximizing profits'

Traditional theory is summed up in the proposition that firms seek to maximize profits. This phrase is sometimes to be understood in a loose way to mean that the object of business is to make money. In general, it is clear enough that the system works, as Adam Smith said, by the appeal to self-interest; it is in the interest of anyone who owns wealth to increase it. But there must be something more involved. If profit were the only motive, why should anyone take the risks of industrial investment? If nothing but making money were the motive, it would be easier, and more secure, to buy shares in successful corporations than to commit capital to some particular type of productive capacity.

There is another point to be considered. If profit is the only criterion by which behaviour is to be judged, there is no distinction between an honest man and a crook. Now, it is true that crooks flourish in a private-enterprise economy, and it is true that many highly respectable businesses make profits in an unscrupulous manner; scandals break out from time to time, and legislation is often changed to check them. All the same, there is a distinction in the minds of business executives between proper and improper conduct that is not based merely on legality. Profit cannot be their sole and exclusive aim in life.

2. See *The New Industrial State*, chapter VI.

Rather, it seems that the private-enterprise system creates a great sphere in which ambition, the love of power, and the vanity of success can be satisfied through making profits or through taking part in an organization which flourishes best when it is most profitable.

In this sense, it is true that profit must be the aim of business. The firms which are surviving, at any moment, are those that have succeeded in the pursuit of profit and those which are most ruthless in the pursuit set the pace for the rest.

(e) The profit criterion

In a more precise sense, maximizing profits means that the conduct of a firm is governed by the choice of the most profitable alternative in view, in all circumstances. But business is carried on in changing conditions. It can never be known in advance what the most profitable course will turn out to have been. *Maximizing* is a mathematical operation performed with specified quantities under specified constraints. It can be applied to the description of equilibrium conditions in an abstract model, not to the multifarious influences playing upon business decisions.

The management of a manufacturing business has to consider, all the time, what productive capacity to install, what new commodities to produce or old ones to drop, what advertising and sales effort to undertake, what prices to charge, what workers and staff to employ, and what offers of pay to make. For some of these decisions it has wide freedom of choice; for others it is narrowly constrained by the situation in which it finds itself. In no case can there be a clear and obvious indication of what combination of policies will be the most profitable; the situation does not remain stable for long enough to find out by trial and error what the consequences of a particular policy will be.

Where management is in the hands of an individual, the alternatives are weighed up in his head by a process of which he cannot give an exact explanation. In the case of the great departmentalized corporations, a system of bureaucratic rules has to be instituted and organization often gets itself tied up in its own red tape.

The concept of maximizing profits, therefore, cannot be taken in a precise, mathematical sense, but it remains true that all business decisions are taken under pressure of the need to maintain profits and avoid losses.

(f) The authority of finance

The high-minded spokesmen of industry maintain that Management has a threefold responsibility: to the shareholders that provide finance, to the workers who are employed, and to the customers who buy the goods produced. In this balance of responsibilities, it is finance that has the final say. The management of a powerful firm may indulge a fancy for providing amenities for the workers, or experiment with democratic methods of control; in the internal conflict of forces within a business, the engineers may prevail over the salesmen, so that technical excellence becomes an end in itself. But if these aims are pursued at the expense of profitability, the supply of finance for expansion dries up or actual bankruptcy may threaten.

A particular way in which finance asserts its power over industry is through the instrument of the *takeover bid*. The value of a firm's shares on the Stock Exchange depends on the market's assessment of its earning capacity. From the viewpoint of the general run of shareholders, the company as such is of no importance; they are interested only in the money value of their placements. It is therefore possible for a firm with finance available for investment to take a business over by offering to the shareholders a price above the current market value of the shares, though less than what the 'taker-over' considers the potential value of the business to itself. It can then proceed to absorb or throw out members of the old management and bring into the growth of its own activities whatever it wants of the equipment, the labour force, and the market connections of the original business.

A potential victim can sometimes defend itself by telling a plausible tale to its shareholders about future growth; or it may pay out more dividends and so raise the price of its shares immediately, though this makes it all the harder to grow to a size at which it will be out of danger.

Finance has the whip hand. When the workers or the customers want to press for their interests to be considered, they must do so over as wide an area of business as possible, by united trade-union action or by advocating legislation, so as not to put particular firms at a competitive disadvantage and make them a prey to more tough-minded rivals.

Each firm in existence today must have originated in one country or another. A kind of patriotism, or the hope of support from their government, may influence the policy of managements to some extent, but if it comes to a pinch, the need for profits must override all other considerations.

2. Industries
(a) Demarcation

The textbook concept of perfect competition required a large number of independent sellers of a single homogeneous commodity. A group of firms producing the same commodity was called an industry, and they were supposed to be constrained by competition to sell their output at a uniform price.* This is an unnatural concept. Some industries are described in terms of the market that they serve, for instance, agricultural machinery or medical supplies, but they produce a wide range of distinct commodities. More often, they are described in terms of the main material being processed, say, steel or petrochemicals, or the type of technique required. Then, their products are being sold in many markets. At the same time, a single market may be supplied with commodities which are close substitutes for each other, produced by quite different industries.

But an industry is not merely a convenient category for the statistical description

* See **2** 5 §7.

of an economy. It has a life of its own. An industry consists of a group of firms which have some technical characteristics in common and employ a labour force with the requisite know-how and skills. Even when they think of themselves as keen competitors, such firms are willing to combine in a number of ways to support their collective interests.

Nowadays, however, large corporations often operate plants belonging to a number of distinct industries. It is generally easier for a business to expand in lines in which it has grown up, but, when it wants to expand faster than the markets for the commodities it is already producing and its proportionate share of those markets is limited by powerful rivals, it may branch out into some completely different line. Moreover, diversification may be a deliberate policy to spread risks. This kind of expansion often takes the form of the kind of takeover described above, so that the growing firm acquires access to markets and a ready-made labour force in its new line.

(b) Supplies

Manufacturing is essentially processing. The heavy concentration of industry in Western Europe (and now Japan) has to be fed with materials from overseas; North America, though a main source of supply for many primary products, is also a great importer of them. The lands peopled by the so-called white race developed their own capitalism (in the first instance, with the aid of European finance); in the rest of the world, production of raw materials and exotic foodstuffs was mainly organized by both finance and management from the industrial countries.

In one sense, the Marxist view that the main motive for the export of capital was to find labour to exploit, was clearly true, but the direction of investment was mainly determined by the search for minerals and other natural resources; where the local population would not provide a labour force, slaves or indentured workers were brought in to replace them. Thus, industrial capitalism spread out and organized the world economy to suit its needs. Its dominance is, nowadays, challenged both by the secession of the socialist nations and by the attempts of ex-colonial countries to get control of their own resources, but over most of the world it still persists.

Where the natural resources of a region have been taken over and developed by a single corporation or a monopolistic consortium of firms, the production and marketing of the commodity in question, on which the economic life of the region depends, is controlled from outside and—even if it has a nominally independent national government—so is its political life. The 'banana republics' of Central America have become proverbial.

So long as the world demand for the commodity in question keeps up, the profits to be made from this kind of business are generally much greater than high-wage manufacturing industry can yield. When demand slackens, attempts are made to curtail supplies to prevent a crash in prices.

238   Where a would-be developing ex-colonial country can influence the production

of its export commodity, it is anxious to push sales to earn foreign exchange. When the same commodity is produced by several countries in this situation, they are apt to cut each other's throats by overproduction on a falling market. Their conflicting interests make it difficult to organize a restriction scheme to keep up prices. The industries purchasing materials from them have no interest, at least in the short term, in helping them to do so.*

(c) Markets

An industry which consists of a number of plants in a particular location, producing a particular range of commodities, has to sell its products outside the immediate neighbourhood. It is often easier to sell within a region covered by the same language and laws, that is, within the same country. When the area and the wealth that happen to be under one national government is very large, the greater part of the output produced within its bounds is sold there, but industries situated in small nations have to export.

Exports of manufactures are partly to regions where the industry in question has not yet developed, and partly between industrial centres, where ever-finer subdivision and specialization take place within industries, and where technical developments and a growing level of consumption give opportunities for introducing new commodities.

As a successful firm grows and plans to enlarge its productive capacity, it looks round for markets. As we have seen, the great oligopolistic corporations, controlling large numbers of plants, are not necessarily confined to one industry or range of products, but, at the same time, it is easier to expand in lines in which the technostructure of the business has experience. Thus, expansion nowadays takes place largely by setting up subsidiary companies in different countries, particularly in those that attempt to defend their home market by tariffs. In them, local businesses are bought up or a new plant erected, to supply the same range of commodities produced in the original country. Local workers are employed while the top management is entrusted to home nationals. Key elements in technical know-how are kept secret, and often, components are exported from the home-based plants to be assembled for sale by the subsidiary. This kind of investment from industrial centres to the outside world, which is seeking markets rather than developing supplies, is growing rapidly. This is by no means confined to investment in what is called the Third World. Proud nations that once controlled empires of their own now see an appreciable part of their labour force and the personnel of their technostructures earning income from subsidiary branches of foreign corporations which dictate employment and investment policies from headquarters, and play off one host country against another in the pursuit of their own interests.

---

* Cf. **2** 5 §3(c).

3. National policy

There are many ways in which the existence of separate national governments influences the economic development of the world. The relations between the developed industrial nations is somewhat analogous to the relations between independent firms in an industry. They are competing with each other, yet they have a common interest and they support each other, in face of both the socialist countries and the ex-colonial world, in trying to keep as wide an area as possible open to profit-seeking enterprise. This raises major questions in which the military and political aspects dominate the purely economic. Here we must confine the argument to narrower lines.

(a) Free-trade theory and protectionist practice

At the start of the Industrial Revolution in England, Ricardo diagnosed a conflict of interest between capitalist industry and landed property. He supplemented his argument against the Corn Laws with a general case against the prevalent system of protection. He analysed an imaginary example of trade between England and Portugal, in which both countries produce both wine and cloth. To make the story as striking as possible, he assumed that output per man employed was higher, in both commodities, in Portugal than in England, thus ruling out the case for protecting high-cost industry. The point of the argument was that productivity was higher in Portugal by more in wine than in cloth. Trade permits each country to move labour out of its inferior use (wine in England and cloth in Portugal) into its superior use.

In Ricardo's example, a unit of cloth in England requires the labour of 100 men for a year; a unit of wine, 120 men. In Portugal, the same quantity of cloth is produced by 90 men, and of wine by 80. Prices in each country are proportional to labour cost. Cloth in England can be exchanged for wine at the ratio of $1:\frac{5}{6}$ and in Portugal at the ratio of $1:1\frac{1}{8}$. It is, therefore, advantageous to England to send cloth to buy wine in Portugal and advantageous to Portugal to send wine to buy cloth in England. England then gets its wine at a lower cost by exporting cloth than it could get it by producing at home, and Portugal gets its cloth at a lower cost by exporting wine.

The case for free trade was adopted and became an article of faith in British politics, not because of the economists' theory but because, so long as British manufacturers dominated world markets, they did not need protection. Imports of raw materials were not competing with home products, and the rapid expansion of population and wealth provided a growing market for British agriculture despite free imports of foodstuffs.

Free trade was imposed over the British Empire, ruining ancient handicrafts and impeding the growth of industry to rival the metropolis. Independent nations, in particular Germany and the USA, realized that protection from cheaper and superior imports would permit industries to grow up, accumulate capital, build up a labour force and acquire know-how, until they became superior in turn. (This used to be

240

known as the 'infant industry' case for protection, but it was treated as a rare exception in free-trade doctrine, not as the normal case.)

The tradition of free-trade policy remained strong in Britain after powerful rivals had grown up, for the Empire still provided sheltered markets. Even today, the tradition is powerful, though a number of 'invalid industries' are now protected, in direct or indirect ways, from industrial rivals and the products of low-wage labour in ex-colonial countries.

(b) Beggar-my-neighbour

Besides helping to promote industrialization and defending particular groups of firms from competition, the third main motive for a national policy of protection is to combat an overall decline in effective demand which reduces profits and increases unemployment. In a country in this situation, there is general pressure (from the public as well as business) to keep out foreign goods to preserve a market for home products.

In the great slump, all trading nations (except the USSR) found themselves with falling investment, business losses and high unemployment. Each tried to get as large a share as possible for itself in the shrunken level of world activity. Tariffs and other restrictions to keep out imports, subsidies to exports, restriction schemes to keep up prices of primary products, pressure to lower money wages, especially in export industries, and exchange depreciation (which we will examine later) were used in a general competitive scramble. Each move by one country made the situation worse for others. This was known as 'exporting unemployment'. Each move by one drove the others to try to export the unemployment somewhere else. World trade went into a declining spiral. Total world employment could not be increased by such means; if the end of the scramble left some countries better off than they would have been without it, it was only the result of making others still worse off.

(c) Rules of the game

Competitive restrictions for the trading world as a whole are a great nuisance (particularly, of course, to the country which expects to gain most from the removal of barriers to its exports). Governments may therefore enter into agreements to restrict restriction. The lowering of tariffs has to be carried out by a process of detailed bargaining, setting off the losses to be expected from increased competition in one line against the gains to be expected from freer competition in another. (The ex-colonial nations are generally in a weak position to secure advantages for themselves in the process.)

Along with reduced protection, national governments may agree to accept certain rules of the game, such as to refrain from subsidizing exports.

For a trading nation, it is an obvious and immediate advantage that *others* should reduce protection. When it is in a strong position to expand exports, removal of

241

protection from its own markets is also an advantage, for then, its most profitable industries can expand and draw labour and finance away from inefficient home industries that cannot keep going without protection, while their place is taken by imports. Imports of a variety of consumption goods give pleasure to households, and imports of investment goods promote specialization. Thus, a country whose volume of exports is growing can take progressive advantage of the 'international division of labour' which Adam Smith and Ricardo praised.

For a country whose industries are in a weak competitive position, with antiquated plant and self-satisfied businessmen, the advantages of general free trade are more dubious. In the short run, the country may lose from reduction of protection of home industries more than it gains from a reduction of foreign barriers to its exports. At the same time, to rely on protection to keep its industries going will lead to more and more loss of competitive power as technical progress and capital accumulation go on in the rest of the world. To refuse to accept the competitive rules of the game might seem to be a policy of despair, unless the country's industry is preparing itself by modernization to enter the game later on.

The advantage to each country of adhering to the rules depends on others observing them. But there are no sanctions. Agreements of this kind are kept by the nations which find that they seem to be on the whole favourable to their commercial interests, but a powerful nation may break them at any time that its government or its public opinion turns against them. Whether the long-run results will be advantageous to that country or not, it is bound to be upsetting for the rest.

(d) Planned trade

The trade of the socialist countries is developed on different principles. A planned economy ought to be able to secure full employment of its own labour force and develop its own natural resources without regard to the problems of effective demand. Its industries produce the commodities that planners believe to be needed. They make exports to get purchasing power to buy imports. For them, exports are a cost, a sacrifice of resources that could have been used at home, and imports are a benefit for which the sacrifice is worth making. They do not have the love of exports for their own sake which is the paradox of capitalist economies.

Since separate planning organizations have been set up within historic national boundaries, the socialist countries have some difficulties, in organizing trade among themselves, to find an acceptable manner of sharing the benefits, but they have no need to play beggar-my-neighbour with each other merely to keep up effective demand.

4. The neoclassical model

242

The so-called theory of international trade was built on Ricardo's argument against protection but, as it developed, it became more and more remote from real problems.

The argument is set out in terms of a country in static equilibrium, with given resources, fully employed. Outputs and relative prices of commodities are determined by supply and demand, as in a Walrasian market.

Now there is another country, representing the rest of the world, in a similar position. This country has a different pattern of resources but produces and consumes the same range of commodities. (If the two countries produced different commodities, neither would have a motive for protecting its own from competition; there would be no need to argue the case for free trade.)

The argument then jumps to an equilibrium position with trade going on. The value of imports for each country is equal to the value of its exports. Each country is exporting commodities which have the lowest opportunity cost in terms of its resources, relative to demand, and importing those which have the highest opportunity cost. Thus, for each, the average value of output per unit of resources is higher than before. The two countries taken together are producing and consuming a larger volume of commodities than they did in isolation, with the same total of resources.

This model rules out all the objectives of protection. There is full employment, and trade is somehow always balanced. There are no losses or painful readjustments to change; only equilibrium positions are discussed. 'Given resources' rule out accumulation and technical change. True, the orthodox argument allowed for protection of 'infant industries' but this was only because common sense would break in. The static model cannot really accommodate it.

Even then, it was not possible to demonstrate that one country could not gain at the expense of the rest of the world by restricting trade. In a Walrasian market, if the sellers of one commodity could get together and reduce sales, price per unit of their commodity in terms of other goods would be higher. They could make a monopoly profit and share the swag. Similarly, a group of buyers who agreed to buy less of a particular commodity would get it cheaper. One of the trading countries, by reducing both imports and exports to a certain point and switching resources into home production, could turn the terms of trade in its favour and increase its total income. It is objected that, by doing so, it might provoke the rest of the world to retaliate. Thus, even in this fanciful model, the case for free trade depends on the case for observing rules of the game that are on the whole beneficial to all, though they may be more so to some than others.

In the neo-neoclassical theory a still more abstract model is used. The countries are exactly alike in all natural, human, and technological characteristics. The only difference is that they are endowed with 'factors of production' in different proportions.[3]

When the 'factors' are land and labour, it is at least possible to see what these assumptions are intended to mean. One country is sparsely populated, so that rents are low relatively to wages; in the other, land is scarce and rents high. But what can be said when the 'factors' are labour and 'capital'? What is meant by a quantity of

3. See P. A. Samuelson, 'International Trade and Factor-Price Equalisation', *Economic Journal* June 1948.   **243**

homogeneous capital? And if equipment per man employed in different countries could be roughly compared in terms of, say, dollars, or horsepower, or tons of steel, would we expect to find that the country where it is highest (say, the USA) has the lowest rate of profit?

With all these modern refinements, Ricardo's original insight has been quite refined away.

Chapter Ten

International balances

One element in national sovereignty that has an important influence on world trade is the existence of independent currencies. Each more or less developed country has its own unit of official legal tender and has authorities, such as a Treasury or a central bank, concerned with maintaining good order in its monetary system. To see what difference this makes, we must first try to find an answer to the old examination question: Why is there a problem of the balance of payments for the UK but not for the county of Oxfordshire?

1. Trade of a region

We can draw an imaginary boundary line round any geographical area we choose. Then if we had complete information, we could set up the accounts for trade and payments between the inhabitants of the region and those outside. It may not always be easy to decide which individuals should be regarded as inside the boundary line, but this applies also to a nation; residence and citizenship are complicated legal concepts. Let us suppose that we have drawn the boundary in such a way that the households, business establishments, local authorities, etc., within it can be listed unambiguously. (We are dividing the economy vertically into regions rather than stressing the horizontal divisions of classes and types of income within it.) Part of the income of the region's population is derived from activities or property within the boundary, and part comes from outside. Part of their expenditure falls on goods and services or local taxes within the boundary, and part falls outside. All the employees of establishments within the ring are regarded as insiders, while businesses make profits from sales both inside and out.

(a) The foreign balance

We can observe, say over a year, the receipts of firms and of households derived from selling goods and services across the boundary; these are the export earnings of the region.

In national accounts, exports and imports of goods constitute *visible trade*, while payments for services such as transport, and fees of all kinds, are *invisible items*.

There are also receipts such as interest and dividends representing income from property held outside. When the region is part of a larger fiscal system, there may be payments to it from the Exchequer for government servants and for social security benefits, etc. All these constitute the *foreign income* of the region.

Similarly, payments to outsiders for goods and services are the import bill of the region; remittances of interest and dividends, profits of local branches passed to the headquarters of corporations outside, and payments of central taxes are made to meet its *foreign obligations*.

From these, we derive the regional balance on *income account*, showing the excess of receipts over payments or of payments over receipts, as the case may be.

(b) Home activity

A surplus on income account (an excess of receipts over payments) represents the *foreign investment* of the region over the year. It has a relation to the level of home activity similar to that of home investment. Receipts from the sale of exports are similar to outlay on investment in that they represent incomes which generate spending without providing a corresponding flow of goods or services available to spend income on.* This boosts demand at home. At the same time, payments for imports represent a leakage, like saving, from the circular flow of home income and expenditure. Payments for imports are generating income outside the boundary, as receipts from exports for the rest of the world. The level of effective demand at home is supported by home investment and export earnings (including foreign income of residents), while payment for imports (and to meet foreign obligations) depress effective home demand.

At the same time, changes in home activity react on the foreign balance. Any increase in home activity is likely to increase imports, partly for ingredients going into home products and partly as an object of expenditure from increased home income. The incremental *propensity to import*, that is, the increase in imports induced by an increase in home activity, thus depends partly on technical relationships, partly on the amount and the composition of the increment of consumption that accompanies an increase in home income, and partly on the competitive relations between home and foreign products. The net effect of a change in the value of exports on the foreign balance of the region tends to be less, the greater the propensity to import. Similarly,

* See **2** 3 §1(c).

a change in home investment will make less change in the level of home income when there is a greater propensity to import.*

(c) Accumulation

A net surplus on income account is analogous to investment also, in that it contributes to accumulation of wealth. It represents assets that households and firms inside the boundary have acquired, over the year, in the form of claims on those outside.

The net saving made in the region, plus amortization, (abstracting from government activity), is equal to its gross investment plus or minus the surplus or deficit on its foreign income account. If we could calculate the amount of amortization allowances and use it to estimate the difference between gross and net investment, we could write:

$$S \equiv I + B$$

where S is net saving, I is net investment, and B is the balance on income account. B may be positive or negative.

As we have seen, an increase in home investment may be a cause of a reduction in the balance. Here, we set out the net effect of what happened over the year. Net saving of the region over the year is equal to net investment plus or minus the balance on foreign income account:

$$Y \equiv C + S$$
$$\equiv C + I + B$$

where Y is net income of the region, and C is home consumption of home-produced goods and services.

These formulae are ex-post accounting identities, not causal relationships. Net values are the result of bookkeeping calculations, while ex-ante decisions are necessarily made in terms of gross expenditure. The identities are useful in keeping track of the overall consequences of individual behaviour rather than explaining them.†

(d) The capital account

Besides receipts and expenditure on income account, there are transactions across the boundary which involve lending and borrowing and purchase and sales of property. The distinction between the income and capital accounts is not always unambiguous. Should the sale of an old master from a British stately home to an American collector be regarded as an export or a depletion of capital? Is it worthwhile to disentangle repayment of debt from current interest, with which it is often combined? For the present argument, however, fine points of definition are un-

* See appendix.
† Cf. **2** 7 appendix.

important so long as every transaction across the boundary is listed under one head or the other.

In this context, 'capital' means finance or property rights, not stocks of machines. *Capital outflow* or *foreign lending* comprises loans, purchases of outside securities, whether new issues or second hand, funds passed from headquarters to an outside branch, and so on; *capital inflow* or *foreign borrowing* are the corresponding transactions in the opposite direction. The capital account is concerned with financial movements of a more or less long-term character.

(e) The balancing factor

Recording the year's transactions over the boundary under these heads (smoothing the ragged edge due to time lags overlapping the end of a year), we can set the balance on income account against the balance of lending and borrowing. To simplify this cumbrous terminology, let us amalgamate foreign income and payments due to foreign obligations with sales and purchases of goods and services, so that we call a positive balance on income account a *current surplus* and a negative balance a *current deficit*, or simply, a surplus and deficit for short.

Now, when the insiders taken as a whole have a net outflow of foreign lending less than their current surplus, or a net inflow of foreign borrowing greater than their current deficit, net payments are due to them from outside. Similarly, when they lend more than their surplus or borrow less than their deficit, net payments are due from them. How are these payments made?

Here, it makes an important difference whether we draw the boundary round a small district in a large country or round an independent nation with its own currency and monetary institutions. The difference is bound up with the existence of national monetary spheres. Within a country, its national official money is accepted without question, and deposits with respectable banks, nominally convertible into official money, provide a large part of the currency in which transactions are made. But the acceptability of a currency depends, in the last resort, on the authority of the national state and is coextensive with the operation of national law. As we shall see, transactions between national currencies are much more complicated.

When insiders and outsiders share a common currency and banking system, the balance of payments between them passes unnoticed. (Indeed, it would not really be possible, with the statistics normally available, to record their transactions in the way we have imagined.) Some imports into the region may come from overseas, or part of its exports of services may be made to citizens of other nations visiting its hotels, but all its transactions take place in terms of home currency, the acceptability of which is not in question.

(f) The balance of payments

The balance of payments of the region, for a year, emerges from all the transactions, **248** to and from the region, that have passed over the boundary during the year, showing the combined effect of the income account and of lending and borrowing. When it is *favourable*—when there is a net outflow on capital account less than the current surplus or an inflow greater than the deficit—there has been a net inflow of cash (notes and coins) and bank deposits, in terms of a single national currency, coming into the hands of households and businesses inside the boundary.

It may be that in the next year the region requires a larger stock of money. This would happen if money incomes and the value of transactions inside the region is higher than before, if the velocity of circulation is slower (say, there has been an increase in payments made quarterly relative to those made weekly), or if some households have added a recent increment of wealth to a hoard of cash. Part of the surplus may provide for an increment in the stock of money. For the rest, the excess of home saving over foreign lending goes into deposits with local banks, which provide their headquarters with means to make loans and purchase securities outside the region.

Similarly, a deficit in the balance of payments, in excess of any reduction in the stock of money within the region, is matched by an increase in bank loans and overdrafts or in sales of securities across the boundary.

Looking at the story from the standpoint of monetary movements, part of the savings corresponding to a current surplus may be used to build up money balances held in the region, the rest is matched by foreign lending; part of the current deficit may be offset by a reduction of money balances instead of an increase in indebtedness.

A current deficit that is associated with households getting into debt and businesses making losses, obviously must cure itself over a run of years, by reducing capacity to purchase imports, but an excess of purchases of outside securities by means of a current surplus can go on indefinitely, since securities provide backing for bank loans.

For a region inside a nation, the total balance (including monetary movements) automatically balances from year to year without anyone being aware of it. When the region is a nation with its own currency, the situation is different. The official money which is legal tender at home is not legal tender abroad. Thus, from international trade, the need arises for an internationally acceptable medium of exchange.

(g) International money

Trade gives rise to exchanges of national moneys. An exporter wants to receive payment in his own currency which he can use for meeting his expenses at home, while an importer has only his own currency to pay with. Trade and financial transactions involving different currencies require markets in which one kind of money can be changed into another. As in any market, some medium of exchange is adopted by common consent, providing a unit of account to facilitate calculation, an intermediary in three-cornered transactions, and a vehicle for carrying purchasing power into the future. For long periods, gold has served as international money, supplemented by bank deposits in terms of whichever national currency was the most acceptable at the time. A favourable or unfavourable balance of payments, for a nation as a whole, means an increase or reduction in its holdings of international money. Their ebb and flow is closely watched and, as we shall see, has an influence on many aspects of national policy. Here lies the difference between the balance of payments of the UK and that of Oxfordshire.

(h) Other differences

Another important difference between a region and a nation is that a region (even a State in the USA) has little control over its propensity to import, while a national government may use protective measures to reduce the ratio of imports to home expenditure.

This apart, the distinction between regional and international trade is a matter of degree. The larger and more diversified a geographical area, the smaller is the dependence of its inhabitants on income from outside and the larger the proportion of all their transactions that takes place among themselves. However, some small and specialized nations are less self-sufficient than some regions in a large nation.

A region may suffer, as much as a nation, from a loss of competitive advantage. Indeed, the level of unemployment in a particular region in an industrial country may exceed the national average by far more than the differences between averages among developed nations. Similarly, a change in the level of investment for a nation will usually take place first in some particular region and will affect that neighbourhood more strongly than other parts of the country.

A prosperous region will attract workers from elsewhere, and a pleasant one, well-to-do families, but this is also true of nations.

There is a distinction, however, in respect to wages. The differences between money-wage rates in districts within a country are generally much less than differences between national levels. Trade unions are organized nationally and, within each country, there is a strong tendency for sympathetic movements in money-wage rates which does not cross national frontiers.

When we are discussing national economies, it is important to distinguish in what respects (apart from patriotic sentiment) they really are, or are not, distinct economies.

(i) A national account

The income account of a nation is set out under conventional heads. As well as visible trade, other items in a nation's income account are those that we have distinguished for any region. For many countries invisible earnings—shipping services, expenditure of visiting tourists, remittances from family members working abroad, and so on—are more important than exports of goods, and for some, the contrary items are a considerable addition to payments for imports.

250   There are also large flows of payments in respect of unearned income. Foreign

placements owned by home citizens bring interest and dividends. Subsidiaries overseas remit profits to their parent company. These elements in a nation's income
account are affected by the tax system of the countries concerned. Mutual arrangements to avoid taxing the same income at both ends have been instituted.

For a few countries, an important item is overseas military expenditure, and
subsidies to allies or clients. (There is also some aid for benevolent purposes.) This
might be classed as a special kind of import or foreign obligation, but it is better to
treat it as a separate heading in the income account. An example of the current
account of a country in a year in which it was in deficit is given in Table 10.1.

Table 10.1

Current account (£ million)

1. *Visible trade*			
Imports		5044	
Exports		4779	
Visible balance			− 265
2. *Invisible trade [net, credit (+), debit (−)]*			
Government expenditure: civil	− 179		
military	− 200		
		− 379	
Shipping		− 19	
Civil aviation		+ 24	
Travel		− 44	
Other services		+ 243	
Interest, profits, etc.		+ 342	
Private transfers		− 8	
Invisible balance			+ 159
3. *Balance of payments on current account*			− 106

2. Current balances

The pattern of surpluses and deficits in the income accounts of the various nations,
over any year, depends on accidents of geography and history, population, wealth
and tastes, and the evolution of technology. It is influenced also by imperial and

military relationships between nations, and modified, as we have seen, by commercial policy.*

Changes in activity also have an effect on the pattern of balances. A country which increases home activity ahead of the rest will generally increase imports relative to its exports. When there is a general upswing, trade increases all round, and some countries get more of the benefit than others. The pattern of surpluses and deficits is, thus, continually changing both for long-run and short-run causes. This was, for the most part, ignored in the traditional theory of international trade, for it operated generally on the assumption that 'exports pay for imports', and each country's trade is normally in balance.

(a) Gold flows

Ricardo's discussion of the overall balance of payments was very offhand. He treated the income account only in terms of imports and exports of commodities, and maintained that they must necessarily balance, for he ruled out foreign lending. Ricardo maintained that differences between the profits obtainable in one region or another within a country are quickly ironed out by movements of investment:

> Experience, however, shows, that the fancied or real insecurity of capital, when not under the immediate control of its owner, together with the natural dis-inclination which every man has to quit the country of his birth and connexions, and intrust himself with all his habits fixed, to a strange government and new laws, check the emigration of capital. These feelings, which I should be sorry to see weakened, induce most men of property to be satisfied with a low rate of profits in their own country, rather than seek a more advantageous employment for their wealth in foreign nations.[1]

A current surplus would mean a favourable balance of payments and an inflow of international money, which in Ricardo's day was mainly gold, from the rest of the world. Relying on the Quantity Theory† he supposed that this must cause home prices to rise and world prices to fall. Since the same commodities are produced (actually or potentially) at home and abroad, competition reduces exports and increases imports until their values are equal, and gold movements cease.

This story sounds cheerful enough when told from the standpoint of the surplus country. By treating the case of falling prices due to a deficit as perfectly symmetrical with rising prices due to a surplus, the theory suggested that the monetary mechanism for regulating the balance of payments was automatic and painless. But we know from sad experience that to cure a deficit in the balance of payments by driving down prices requires unemployment and losses.

When the exports of a deficit country are highly specialized—say, a primary

* See **2** 9 §3(a).
1. *Works* vol. I, pp. 36–7.
† See **1** 3 §4.

commodity for which demand is inelastic—a fall in prices sets up a vicious spiral of reduced export earnings; the whole weight of readjustment has to fall on reducing imports, which may not be possible without total ruin.

In any case, the relationship between the stock of gold in a country and its price level was a good deal more complicated than Ricardo's story requires, even when gold was the basis of internal currency as well as the international medium of exchange.

(b) A substitute model

Among industrial countries, movements of the price level and the pattern of relative prices, within each, are determined mainly by movement of the overall level of money-wage rates relative to output per head in various lines. (This is modified by differences in proportionate profit margins but these cannot vary much, while differences in money-wage rates are without limit.) By appealing to relative changes in money-wage rates, we can construct a model that would behave according to Ricardo's theory as follows.

There are no long-term capital movements. The currency of each country is exchangeable with gold so that fixed exchange rates are taken for granted. In the competitive world market, there is a single price level of tradable goods, modified by transport costs. There are a number of countries each producing and consuming a number of tradable manufactures, some of which are in common while some are specialities. The level of money-wage rates in any one country rises when there is a high demand for labour and is constant or sagging when there is unemployment.

Each country has near-full employment of its labour force when its trade is balanced. In a position of balance, each country is exporting goods for which the value of output per head at home is higher than the average at home (we are neglecting differences in profit margins) and importing those for which it is lower. For each country, at the base date, the annual value of imports and exports are equal.

Now, suppose that one country enjoys an increase in productivity which leads to a surplus of exports. Foreign lending and borrowing are ruled out. It therefore has a favourable balance of payments and is receiving an inflow of international money. The main point, however, is that it now has super-full employment (the basic postulate of the model is that there is full employment when trade is balanced.) Consequently, money-wage rates rise in the surplus country while they are constant, or even falling, in the rest of the world.

In the surplus country, the costs of all those goods for which productivity has not increased have now risen. The relative rise of costs for a speciality with inelastic demand (such as Scotch whisky), increases the value of exports, but for the most part, the country is subject to competition. It loses competitive advantage in export markets. Its imports increase because some home-produced goods are now more expensive than foreign substitutes, and since the purchasing power of an hour's work at home over foreign goods has risen, it also increases imports of consumption goods which it does not produce at home.

253

The contrary effects in the rest of the world increase exports there, and reduce imports.

There is a new position of balance with a different pattern of trade, once more balanced for each country. The advantage to the country where productivity increased remains in the form of a higher level of real wages in terms of tradable goods. Part of this advantage may have been passed to other countries which experienced a current surplus during the transition towards the new balanced position, increasing the deficit for others, for the burden of the readjustment is not likely to be evenly spread over the rest of the world.

(c) Imperfect adjustments

In a broad way, over a long run of years, a mechanism somewhat like this does work between the developed industrial countries. There is, certainly, a tendency for competitive advantages to be offset by movements of relative money-wage rates so as to keep current surpluses within bounds. Looking round the world, we see great differences in output per man between nations in terms of their production of tradable goods, but these differences are largely offset by differences in the level of money-wage rates. The countries with high productivity tend to have a more or less correspondingly high cost of labour in terms of commodities, and high purchasing power of an average week's earnings over tradable goods. But, as a mechanism for redressing balances of trade, it is unreliable and far too slow; the process of adjustment may be spread over decades. A country in which productivity in industries producing tradable goods is rising faster than the rest of the world, is tending to gain a competitive advantage which may be less than offset by a relative rise in its level of money-wage rates. A nation which has exceptionally active capitalists and deferential trade unions is gaining competitive advantages over the rest, while one with complacent capitalists and vigorous trade unions is losing. It is by no means unknown for the country with the largest deficit to have the fastest rate of inflation. Moreover, from time to time, international relations are drastically upset by political events. As the kaleidoscope of history is shaken, changes in relative advantages may be too great and sudden to be overcome by the mechanism of changes in money costs. Current surpluses and deficits can persist for long stretches of time.

3. The balance of payments

In the overall balance of payments of a country, the capital account and the current account cannot be treated separately.

When we discussed the balance of payments of a region we drew a sharp distinction between movements of long-term lending or borrowing and short-term movements taking place in the banking system. This was not quite accurate, even for a region, because nowadays there are other institutions besides banks that accept deposits and make loans. For a nation, financial flows are still more difficult to distinguish sharply. However, without being precise about definitions, we can discuss the principles underlying these flows.

(a) Foreign lending

An outflow of capital from a country may take the form of portfolio movements—purchases of new or second-hand securities (bonds and shares)—and *direct investment*, which occurs when a firm buys a business abroad with a view to controlling it, or supplies finance out of profits received at home to a branch or subsidiary operating abroad. (In so far as a foreign subsidiary is financed by bonds sold locally, the capital controlled by the parent company, and its right to profits, are increased without a corresponding outflow of finance emanating from the particular home country.)

Flows of finance of this kind respond to differences in the prospective profits in various countries; they are also influenced by the interest rates ruling and the facilities for dealing in various financial centres.

The need to keep interest rates in line with those in other centres sets narrow limits to the power of each national authority to pursue an independent monetary policy.*

Short-term financial movements arise from the existence of the balances held by traders, international corporations, dealers in finance and dealers in foreign exchange. There is a large amount of money controlled by businesses of all kinds which can be held temporarily in one centre or another. It moves about in response to differences in short-term interest rates or expectations of changes in exchange rates.

Finally, there are the reserves of the central monetary authority. A favourable overall balance of payments (including short-term finance) means an excess of demand over supply for the currency concerned and tends to push up its value on the foreign exchange market. When the policy of the authorities is to keep the rise in exchange value below a pre-ordained ceiling, the central authority sells home currency and allows its reserves of international money to rise. This is easy and pleasant. When there is an overall deficit, to prevent the exchange rate from falling, it must sell foreign currencies and let its reserves run down. The key factor in monetary policy is the need for an authority to maintain reserves which it regards as adequate to fulfil this requirement.

(b) A balance of payments

The overall balance, of which the current account was given above, is shown in Table 10.2 overleaf.

---

* See **2** 8 §3(d).

Table 10.2

Overall balance of payments (£ million)

3. *Balance of payments on current account*	−106	
4. *Long-term capital account*		
[purchase of assets overseas (−)		
sales of assets (+)]		
Official investment (net)	− 81	
Private investment (net)	−137	
	――――	
5. *Balance of current and long-term capital transactions*		−324
6. *Balancing item**		+105
7. *Monetary movements*		
Short-term capital movements (net)	−104	
Changes in account with IMF	+499	
Changes in gold and convertible currency reserves	−176	
	――――	
8. *Balance of monetary movements*		+219

* The balancing item is a 'catch-all' for errors and omissions. Since the overall balance of payments must balance, any discrepancy must be due to a failure to record certain transactions. The balancing item merely records the size of this failure (− 324 + 105 + 219 = 0).

(c) Harmonious movements

Some types of relationship between a country's income and capital balance may be regarded as harmonious, in the sense that they do not set a strain on its monetary system.

(i) A current surplus permits a net outflow of long-term lending without causing a deficit on the balance of payments. It is clearly advantageous to rentiers to be able to place their wealth overseas, and to firms to invest there, as they please, and provided they are successful, they increase the net foreign income of the country for the future. (For the welfare of the home population as a whole, more home invest-ment or socially beneficial consumption, with a smaller current surplus and less foreign lending, might well be more advantageous.)

(ii) A current deficit matched by borrowing may also be acceptable in certain cases. The leading example is a country with potentially rich natural resources which has the capacity neither for the saving nor the organization of finance required to develop them.

The story may run as follows. Finance is raised by selling bonds abroad, which provide an attractive placement for foreign rentiers or financial institutions. This represents an inflow on capital account. Part of the ingredients required for development are imported (say, steel rails for building a railway). The main part of home investment is the work done by labour on the spot. Expenditure of wages and other incomes generated by this investment falls largely on imports, since the capacity to produce consumption goods at home is limited. Thus, there is a large deficit on current account. This represents negative foreign investment. Part of the savings of the outside world are being drawn on to supply a deficiency of saving at home; the net increment of wealth for the country is equal to its home investment minus the current deficit.

Part of the investment is matched by home saving (including amortization allowances which will not be needed for replacements for some time), while the whole finance for the investment was borrowed abroad. The net inflow on capital account exceeds the current deficit over the period while the investment boom lasts. There is a favourable balance of payments, and the country's reserves of international money increase.

The natural resources that have been developed provide for a flow of exports, at a later stage, that is more than sufficient to provide for the foreign obligations of interest and amortization on the original loans, and the debt can be paid off.

When the home resources are developed through direct investment by foreign firms instead of by selling bonds abroad, the equity belongs to foreigners; the obligation to remit profits is perpetual. When this has been going on for some time, local businessmen and the public generally begin to realize what is happening, and the government and monetary authorities—which have been basking all the while in a favourable balance of payments—find that they have lost control over their economy.[2]

(d) Disharmony

(i) When, through bad luck or bad management, a country has lost its former competitive advantages, or has suffered a large decline in its net foreign income, so that it is continually running a current deficit, it is not attractive to foreign lenders (and any borrowing it can do further weakens its prospects for the future). It suffers a continuous tendency to a deficit on the balance of payments, which requires remedial action. The authorities feel obliged to check investment and allow unemployment, so that imports are reduced. This does not remove the basic difficulty unless it induces a sufficient relative decline in money-wage rates, while underutilized capacity and low profits are retarding innovations and making the competitive position of the country worse.

(ii) A country with a current deficit matched by an inflow of finance devoted to investment—not to build up exports in the future, but merely to provide for sales

2. Cf. Kari Levitt, *Silent Surrender.*

in the home market—is incurring foreign obligations which tend to make the current deficit grow. It is heading towards national bankruptcy.

(iii) A country which has a large and continuous current surplus which is not offset by lending, is imposing a deficit in the balance of payments on the rest of the world. Sooner or later the rest of the world will try to defend itself.

The most important rule for monetary harmony is that a country which has a current surplus must either lend it or get rid of it by increasing imports. But a surplus country is in a strong position; the system imposes sanctions only on the weak.

(iv) A country whose currency is widely used as international money can run an overall deficit on its balance of payments to the extent that the rest of the world is increasing the stock of that currency that it holds. This system requires that the country which provides international money should be politically dominant and should hold a powerful position in world trade. Sterling could not function well as world currency when the trading position of the UK weakened considerably after 1914, and it progressively lost standing as the British Empire was wound up.

A struggle for hegemony between two or more national centres is reflected in chronic unease, erupting into occasional crises in the world's financial system. A particularly awkward situation arises when the country whose currency is most widely used develops a deficit in its balance of payments that greatly exceeds the requirements for world currency. The central banks of the other countries are then in a dilemma. They must either accept a favourable balance of payments that they can use only to lend to the deficit country by allowing its currency to flow into their reserves, or they refuse to accept its currency, cause their currencies to appreciate in terms of it, and so put their country's traders at a competitive disadvantage.

After 1918, economists and bankers looked back to the harmony of balances that appeared to have existed before 1914 under the hegemony of sterling, as though it were 'normality', but ever since, disharmony has been the normal state.

4. The foreign exchanges

When so-called harmony existed in the pattern of balances for the main trading nations, it was possible for them to maintain a system of stable exchange rates between their currencies, and the harsh discipline of credit restrictions could be imposed on the rest. But, when large-scale disharmony developed among the financially powerful countries after the First World War, the system could not be maintained, and with experience, exchange rates became an instrument of policy.

(a) The gold standard

The role of gold metal in the gold-standard system was due to its enormous historical prestige—going back to antiquity—which gave it acceptability as international money. The essence of the system was nothing to do with the properties of the metal; it worked because all the main currencies had a declared value in terms of gold.

258

National monetary authorities were charged with the duty of maintaining the rates of exchange between currencies closely in line with their relative values in terms of gold. A depreciation of one currency, say sterling, made it profitable to buy gold for export to buy, say, dollars at the official rate, then with dollars to buy sterling, and so make a profit on the round trip. If an outflow of gold persisted, it would mean a loss of reserves that the authorities could not permit, but so long as the main pattern of current and capital accounts was harmonious, so that there was no one-way trend in the balance of payments for any major country, such a system could be maintained. Minor discrepancies were ironed out by flows of short-term capital, for while there was unquestioned faith in the maintenance of exchange rates, speculation worked in this way: An adverse balance of payments, from day to day, led to a fall in the price of the currency in question, in terms of others, on the foreign exchange market; there was then a profit to be made by buying it, since it was confidently expected to rise again. Similarly, a rising currency was sold. Thus, a fall or rise could never go far. The movement of balances from one centre to another operated, like the movement within a unified banking system, to provide a counter flow of short-term lending to make up any discrepancy between the current and capital accounts and to keep overall balances of payments balanced.

Once the financial world has learned that an authority in charge of one or other of the major currencies may, from time to time, find itself unable or unwilling to prevent its exchange rate from falling, faith is destroyed and speculative movements may become perverse. In one sense, the gold standard was a state of mind; once it was lost it could never be recovered.

(b) Depreciation

A depreciation of a currency means a fall in its price in terms of other currencies. It operates at two levels, on the overall balance of payments and on the balance on income account. The immediate effect is to stop an outflow of short-term speculative lending or to attract an inflow, so reversing an unfavourable balance of payments. (This is subject to the proviso that the amount of the depreciation is not less than financial opinion was expecting. If it leaves the market expecting a further depreciation, the last state is worse than the first.)

The immediate effect on the current deficit is likely to make the position worse, for bargains entered into at the old rate have to be discharged at the new, and it takes a long time for changes in prices to bring about changes in the volume of trade. But after a time, a depreciation may be expected to have a favourable effect on the income account.

It is often said that depreciation makes home goods cheaper to foreigners, and foreign goods dearer at home, so that there is a tendency for home goods to be substituted for the rest in the total world market. This is a rough way of putting the case, and we must consider it more exactly. In the first instance, if home costs—say, in sterling—and world prices—say, in dollars—are unchanged, there is a sharp

259

increase in terms of sterling in the profit margin that exporters receive. This encourages them to seek more sales, to switch output from home to foreign markets and to press exports of commodities that it did not seem worthwhile to export before. In doing so, they may cut their dollar prices somewhat to get more business, and they are likely to find that sterling costs of imported materials have risen, so that profit margins are not raised fully in proportion to the rise in the sterling price of dollars. However, a sufficient increase in margins may be expected, so long as relative money-wage rates are constant, to encourage an increase in the physical volume of exports, without too much fall in dollar prices, so as to bring about an appreciable rise in the total value of exports in terms of dollars.

We must look at the effect on imports of two classes: those that are a necessary ingredient in home production, and those which are substitutes for home-produced commodities. The first class consists largely of primary products of the type for which prices rise with an increase in demand.* Thus, if the devaluation is successful in increasing home output, the dollar prices of these commodities may rise. Then, when both the quantity imported and dollar prices are higher, the import bill in dollars is correspondingly greater and the import bill in terms of sterling rises more than in proportion to the devaluation.

The second class of imports are substitutes for home products. These now tend to be dearer in terms of sterling and may be so much so that less of some of them is bought and, consequently, the import bill in terms of dollars is reduced. But industry in the capitalist world is always somewhat in a buyer's market, with productive capacity for more than can be sold. Just as exporters may cut dollar prices to get more business, so foreign exporters may not raise sterling prices much, in order to avoid losing business. This limits the gain in competitive advantage for home goods, but it means that the cost of imported goods in terms of dollars rises by less than in proportion to the depreciation in sterling.

Putting the two classes together: in terms of dollars, the value of exports is expected to rise (if this were not so, a devaluation would not be an appropriate remedy for a current deficit); the dollar value of imports may either rise or fall. In terms of sterling, receipts from exports rise, when the dollar value has risen, more than in proportion to the depreciation. The bill for imports in terms of sterling rises by more or by less than in proportion to the devaluation, according to whether the bill in terms of dollars has risen or fallen.

(c) Money wages

An extremely important proviso was made above. A depreciation may be expected to raise the dollar value of exports provided that the relation of the levels of money-wage rates at home to those abroad is constant.

The theory of the relation of exchange rates to the current balance was pioneered in the 'thirties, when there was heavy unemployment everywhere. It was natural

* See **2** 5 §3(a).

to assume that money-wage rates were more or less constant and that supplies, both of manufactures and of materials, were highly elastic. These assumptions are inappropriate at a time of near-full employment. Moreover, nowadays even when there is unemployment, a rise in the cost of living combined with an increase in profits leads to a push for rises in money wages which cannot easily be resisted.

A rise in money-wage rates at home, relative to the level in competitive countries, has an effect on the current balance similar to that of an appreciation of the home currency. Thus, if a depreciation sets up a tendency for a relative rise in money wages it soon wipes out the benefits that were expected from it.

(d) World currencies

An appreciation of a currency can take place when the balance of payments is continuously favourable. An appreciation, however, is rarely accepted voluntarily. The authorities generally like having a favourable balance of payments from the monetary point of view, and they like to have a current surplus to keep up effective demand. Moreover, the interest of the industrial firms making profits from exports is much more influential than the interest of consumers in cheaper imports. We saw above that the reluctance of central banks to cease taking in unwanted reserves is due to dislike of having appreciation forced on them.*

A depreciation of one currency (in relation to relative wage rates) is to some extent an appreciation of the rest. The national authorities, nowadays, are extremely conscious of each other's exchange rates and, from time to time, an attempt is made to set up rules of the game, and to realign currencies by consent, forcing some to appreciate and allowing others to depreciate. However, so far, the rules of the game amount to no more than each country agreeing never to depreciate its currency except when it does.

A disharmonious pattern of world balances may be partially counteracted for a time by an alteration in the pattern of exchange rates, but the underlying causes of disharmony must always be expected to reassert their influence before very long. The best that can be hoped for is a history of 'muddling through'.

5. The myth of normality

The discussion of exchange rates, not only among economists but also in public affairs, is generally conducted in terms of an equilibrium situation that ought to be established. This idea was written into the Bretton Woods agreement which set up the International Monetary Fund: 'A member shall not propose a change in the par value of its currency except to correct a fundamental disequilibrium.' But no one declared what a state of equilibrium might mean.

Discussion is often carried on in terms of over-valued and under-valued exchange rates. An exchange rate is said to be over-valued when exports appear to be dis-

* See **2** 10 §3(d).   **261**

couraged and imports encouraged, by a high value of the currency, so that the balance of payments can be kept in balance only by unemployment. The exchange rate of a country is said to be under-valued when competition from goods produced in it is proving embarrassing to other countries. Appeal is made to some mythical 'correct' exchange rate which ought to be established.

For an individual country, a state of equilibrium might mean that it has near-full employment with as large a current surplus as its authorities regard as adequate (taking into account the amount of overseas military expenditure it is carrying out). But every major country wants to have a current surplus, and those which have it, with rare and brief exceptions, would like to have more. How can all have a surplus when none has a deficit?

The gold-standard system worked as it did because no one was concerned about unemployment. It was regarded as perfectly right and natural that a country which was losing gold should impose credit restrictions, check investment, and reduce employment. Nowadays, when national governments are concerned about the level of employment, they cannot accept the rule of fixed exchange rates when it requires an adverse balance of payments to be met by an induced depression. No pattern of exchange rates can be freely acceptable to everyone at once. Political pressure and horse-trading come in to settling what it shall be.

The myth of normality lies at the basis of arguments in favour of 'free-market' exchange rates. The idea is that market forces of supply and demand will somehow find the correct exchange ratios between currencies, and will adjust these ratios as is required by 'underlying economic forces'. Even apart from the effects of the uncertainty engendered by fluctuating rates of exchange, there is no such thing for any country as the 'correct' exchange rate which will balance the conflicting aims of different sections of the community—reflected in the trade in particular commodities, or in international flows of capital, and in the desire of the authorities to maintain full employment or to limit the rate of inflation. Still less, is there a 'correct' pattern of exchange rates which will reconcile the interests of various groups in all countries at once.

Appendix: The multiplier and the propensity to import

A formula for the multiplier to be applied to home income in an open economy can be set out as follows.

Symbols apply to values at constant prices over the period in which the initial effect of a change works out. (This may be somewhat less than a year, or as much as two years or more.)

$\overline{Y}$ = Gross national product
$\overline{I}$ = Gross investment
E = Value of exports
C = Home consumption

s = Proportion of saving in an increment of GNP
m_i = Proportion of imports in an increment of $\bar{I}$
m_e = Proportion of imports in an increment of E
m_c = Proportion of imports in an increment of C

The proportion of saving, s, in an increment of GNP includes the change in private-sector saving and in the (positive or negative) excess of tax receipts over government expenditure. (This is $\Delta s/\Delta Y$, not s/Y as in **2** 2 §2(d).)

Now, $\Delta C = (1 - s)\Delta\bar{Y}$. The proportion of ΔC produced at home is $(1 - m_c)$. Thus, the increase in home consumption of home-produced goods accompanying an increase in GNP is $(1 - m_c)(1 - s)\Delta\bar{Y}$.

The increase in home production directly due to an increase in exports is $(1 - m_e)\Delta E$, and for investment, $(1 - m_i)\Delta I$.

For a closed system, the value of the income multiplier is $1/s$, so that $\Delta\bar{Y} = (1/s)\Delta\bar{I}$. (This corresponds to the employment multiplier of 4 in the example in **2** 3 §2(b).) In an open system, the formula is:

$$\Delta\bar{Y} = \frac{1}{s + m_c(1 - s)} \{(1 - m_i)\Delta I + (1 - m_e)\Delta E\}$$

The elements in this formula depend on technical relationships and the conditions of demand for particular commodities; it summarizes complex relationships which are liable to change from period to period. The formula can be only a rough guide to the expected consequences of a change in activity.

Chapter Eleven

Socialist planning

We have seen in the foregoing chapters that the neoclassical theory of equilibrium and harmony in a market economy is inapplicable to modern capitalism. It is often claimed, however, to provide a useful approach to problems that arise in a socialist economy.

When a revolution has got rid of capitalist firms, other organs have to be developed to carry out the functions that they formerly fulfilled. The main lines of the distribution of income between families, the direction of investment, the choice of technique, the pattern of prices, and the terms of trade between agriculture and industry are now determined directly by a political process instead of indirectly through the distribution of property, power and knowledge among individuals, groups, and institutions.

A revolution made in the name of Marxism takes over from Marx the main categories of economic analysis. But the labour theory of value was designed to diagnose the nature of exploitation under capitalism. It is not directly applicable to the problems of designing a more efficient and equitable set of rules of the game. On the other hand, the neoclassical system—which tried to describe an ideal economy that never existed in fact—might contain some valuable suggestions. In what follows, we examine the concepts of planning that the two kinds of theory suggest.

1. Prices and incomes

In the philosophy dominant in the USSR, the regulation of production and distribution by means of values expressed in terms of money is a hangover from capitalism which will gradually disappear on the way to *communism*. Then, the principle: 'From each according to his ability, to each according to his need' will prevail and there will be no use for calculations in terms of money. Meanwhile, in the transitional phase of *socialism*, a system of incomes and prices in terms of money is necessary, but, in this view, the principles on which it operates are of little interest. In the neo-classical philosophy, on the other hand, the system of prices is the central concern, and the purchasing power of an individual's money income is the main index of his 'welfare'.*

The neoclassical discussion of welfare is concerned largely with the types of goods sold to the public at retail. It does not throw much light on the provision of housing, education, medical services, and amenities of all kinds, a certain amount of which are provided partly or wholly outside the price system, even in the most *laissez-faire* of contemporary economies.† However, the purchase of commodities to consume is a large element in the standard of life in all except very simple, unspecialized economies. As long as incomes accrue in the form of money, to individuals or families, the level and pattern of the prices of consumption goods in terms of money is an extremely important feature of the economic system.

(a) Costs and surplus

In a planned economy without private property in the means of production, the volume of money income derived from the socialist sector (excluding cooperative agriculture and self-employed professionals) depends on the size of the labour force (including all who work in any capacity) and the rates of pay for various activities, along with pensions, scholarships, etc. The flow of money demand for goods to be bought by households is determined by the total of money incomes less net private saving. (There is no rentier wealth. Saving is almost entirely saving up to spend later; the flow of expenditure at any time is reduced by current saving, and swollen by dis-saving of money retained from incomes received in the past. The flow of net saving is the excess of total positive saving over dis-saving.)

From this expenditure, the government must recover the costs of production of the goods sold, plus a sufficient surplus to provide for the rest of its expenditure. (Net saving out of household income permits the state to cover part of its expenditure by borrowing through savings banks, or by increasing the note issue to correspond to the addition made to private hoards. Thus, net saving makes the surplus required to be extracted from the sales value of commodities so much the less, and the price level can be correspondingly lower.)

Here, we are ignoring direct taxes, which are an anomaly in a socialist economy in which all earnings are derived from the state. We assume that the whole of the surplus funds required for government expenditure, including investment, are col-lected (like profit margins in the market economy) by means of mark-ups contained in the prices of commodities sold to the public. (In the Soviet system, there is a small income tax—partly due to a hangover from the past and partly to deal with self-employment—which we shall not discuss here.) The first principle of pricing in a

* See **2** 7 §5(a).
† See **2** 7 §3(b).

planned economy is to set the overall level of prices for the goods sold to households, in relation to the level of money incomes, in such a way that the value of sales will yield the necessary surplus over costs of production.

Decisions as to how much and what kind of consumption goods to produce must be taken before setting prices. The planner's freedom of choice (apart from foreign trade) is limited, on the one hand, by availability of primary products—food and raw materials—as well as by specialized productive capacity, and on the other hand, by the needs and habits of the population which he aims to provide for. There may be a feedback from prices onto decisions about production for the future, but at any time, the flow of output of goods of all kinds has already been planned.

The flow of goods to be sold is produced by one part of the labour force and purchased for consumption by the whole labour force. The prices of consumption goods must be such as to yield a surplus over the wage bill for producing them; this surplus must equal expenditure on them out of the wages of all the workers engaged in other lines—the general administration of the country, investment, the armed forces, scientific research, etc.—as well as expenditure from non-wage incomes such as pensions, and from earnings derived from the production of all goods and services, such as education, medicine, and grand opera, which are provided to the public free or at subsidized prices. This determines the total amount of the necessary surplus in the total money value of sales.

The surplus may be collected by means of a turnover tax, by planned profits included in the ex-factory prices that enterprises receive, or partly by each. (The surplus over costs per unit of sales value of output corresponds roughly to the net profit margin in capitalist industry plus any indirect taxes entering into prices.) It remains to consider how the total surplus is distributed over the various elements in total consumption, i.e., how the mark-ups enter into the pattern of prices of commodities.

(b) Classical prices

To follow a policy of setting labour-value prices would require the surplus to be allotted in a uniform ratio to the labour time required, directly and indirectly, to produce each element in total output. This raises the question of different types of work and levels of skill. Is every individual to produce the same 'value' in an hour of work? The Marxian concept of 'abstract labour' has never been reduced to operational terms.* In practice, an allowance for differences in skill could amount only to reckoning the value of different hours of work according to whatever happened to be the relevant wage rates paid for them, which makes the whole calculation arbitrary.

A system of 'prices of production', which yields a uniform rate of profit on invested capital, such as we exhibited in terms of Sraffa's model† is even less applicable in a

---

* See **1** 2 appendix.
† **2** 6 §3(d).

socialist economy. It would require all the stocks of means of production in existence to be given a value in terms of money, and then, prices to be set in such a way that the sales of each commodity would yield a uniform return on the value of the stock of means of production directly and indirectly involved in its output. What would be the point of such a calculation?

But there is no reason to expect that either labour value or a uniform rate of profit would yield a practicable set of prices; prices set according to long-period costs would fail to correspond to requirements for two sets of reasons. First, prices involve social considerations, as we shall see in a moment. Second, prices have to correspond to scarcities relative to demand. With prices governed only by costs, some commodities of which the rate of output was limited—whether by availability of supplies of materials, productive capacity, or specialized labour—would be too cheap. They would disappear into a black market to be resold at prices corresponding to the demand for them. Others, of which supply was relatively plentiful, would be too dear and remain partly unsold.

The conception both of labour-value prices and of prices corresponding to a uniform rate of profit on capital ignores the question of matching demand to available supplies. It was derived from a model of competitive capitalist industry in which the supply of means of production is already adjusted to the flows of output that profit-seeking firms choose to produce. This has no bearing on the price policy appropriate to socialist industry.

In fact, in Soviet economic parlance, the belief that prices ought to correspond to Marxian values is reconciled to the fact that they have to adjust demand to supply, by changing the meaning of the 'law of value' and using it to signify something like a balance of demand with supply in the market.

(c) Neoclassical prices

The neoclassical prescription would be to find the level and the pattern of prices that equates demand to available supply of each commodity. This would automatically yield the required surplus, for the excess of the sales value of consumption goods over their cost of production would necessarily equal the volume of expenditure coming from incomes earned in ways other than producing consumption goods. There are, however, objections to this prescription.

Neoclassical prices mean rationing by the purse. This is less arbitrary in an economy without unearned income than it is in the capitalist world. Differences in rates of pay under socialism are intentional (on whatever principle they are set) and are meant to result in differences in real income. But still there are inequalities, and when average real income is low, inequality means poverty for the lowest income group and may result in undernourishment for the children of large families. Until inequality has disappeared it is more desirable to keep the prices of basic necessities low and to ration them. At the other end of the scale, when only a small trickle of output of consumer durables is produced, while all families with above-average income are anxious to make a first purchase, the demand is much higher than it will be when the stock in the possession of the public has been built up. Here, an organized system of queueing by delivery date may be preferred to very high prices that will be lowered in the future.

Furthermore, wider considerations are often involved in the setting of prices. There are many forms of consumption that social policy aims to promote, such as those connected with approved sports; these must be provided cheaply. There are some, such as hard liquor, which it aims to restrain, and limitation of supplies must be matched by high prices.

After all these exceptions have been made, there is a certain range of products to which the principle of free choice for the consumer can be applied. For these, it is appropriate to charge prices that fit demand to the planned supplies, so that the market regulates itself without unnecessary rationing or administrative control.* But this does not mean that it would be sensible to imitate the flexibility of prices depicted in neoclassical textbooks.

(d) Changing prices

A system in which prices are sensitive to shifts in consumer taste could work smoothly where the price elasticity of demand for most commodities was very high. Then, in principle, the appropriate changes in relative prices could be made by watching the movement of stocks of finished products. According to the textbook prescription, when stocks of a commodity are falling, its price is raised. This reduces sales and deflects purchasing power to be spent on other things. When stocks are silting up, price is reduced, sales increase, and purchasing power is drawn away from other lines to this one. Thus, consumption is continuously steered away from the commodities that are most scarce relative to demand, and towards those that are most plentiful. But when demand is inelastic to price,† this system does not work. A rise in the price of a scarce commodity then leads to a small reduction in its sales, and a large reduction in sales of other things from which purchasing power is attracted away.

Within groups of commodities meeting the same need, say, different kinds of textiles, there may be sufficient substitutability to make demand respond in the right way to differences in relative prices, though habit and snobbery (even under socialism) have to be taken into account. As between groups of commodities, there is no reason to expect substitution. To lower the price of textiles may reduce the amount of money spent on them and increase demand for, say, leather shoes or wooden furniture. The phenomenon of inelastic demand is particularly awkward in connection with habit-forming consumption. A rise in the price of vodka may reduce demand for everything else.

A further difficulty with the neoclassical scheme is the problem of timing. In a

* See **2** 7 §2(a).
† See **2** 5 §3(a).

Walrasian market, the equilibrium is found by the process of shouting offers and demands before trading begins. This is a phantasy. When the pattern of prices is arrived at by an actual process of trial and error, goods must be sold at some price or other before the final pattern is found (in Walrasian language, trading takes place at 'false prices'). The real purchasing power of incomes of people with different needs and tastes is variously affected by the prices that they have to pay, and so the imaginary position of equilibrium, which would be established if the final prices were set at once, is no longer there to be found.

In a planned economy, the problem of price policy does not present itself in this way. At any moment, there is a pattern of prices that, in the broad, adjusts demand to supply. People have got used to it and regard it as normal. Apart from changes dictated by social policy, it is better to hold prices constant and allow changes in demand, as far as possible, to influence the composition of output. When stocks are silting up in some line, the planners should cut down the flow of output of that particular item, instead of cutting the price, and offer a different quality or design, or perhaps deflect resources into some other line of production. This is the correct principle: the manner in which it is carried out depends on the administrative system, which differs very much from one socialist economy system to another. (The Chinese system of state wholesaling seems to be run on these lines.*)

(e) Purchasing power and shopping power

There is one moral that can be drawn from experience rather than theory. That is, that (provided basic needs can be met) rationing by the purse is preferable to rationing by queues. This means that basic necessities should be kept at low prices and rationed specifically if demand exceeds supply, while inessential goods should have sufficiently high prices (relative to money incomes) to create a moderate buyer's market. Prices are then such as to keep demand for each line from exceeding supply. Stocks are never exhausted and everyone can spend his money on what he prefers. When prices are set too low (which has been the traditional pattern in the Soviet sphere) there is a general excess of demand for everything, and shortages frequently occur, with a great loss of time and temper in searching for goods to buy. The busiest workers have the least shopping power so that idle members of the community gain an advantage. Moreover, in that situation, shop assistants are apt to be brusque, and manufacturers careless of quality, unless they are actuated by the Chinese motive to 'serve the people'.

These considerations ought to be taken into account when planning is first instituted. Once a seller's market has become habitual, it is very difficult to change. Sellers, of course, find it convenient, and dislike the idea of having to be more subservient to their customers. The customers, also, having got used to a certain level of prices, that is, to a certain purchasing power of money, would very much dislike having prices raised. A promise of a great economy in shopping power would not seem to compensate for an immediate loss of money purchasing power.

* See **3** 2 §3(b).

2. Efficiency

The market system is a system of devolution of economic control. In each enterprise, the need to minimize costs in terms of money tends to bring about an efficient use of resources to the extent that resources are valued in terms of money. But, for the economy as a whole, the neoclassical claim that the market produces efficient allocation of scarce means between alternative uses is subject to the major objection that money values provide an imperfect way of evaluating the benefit to society of uses to which means may be put. In a planned economy, when the broad outlines of production have been decided, the notion of *efficiency* comes into play. An efficient plan is such that it would not be possible, with given labour time and given physical resources,.to produce any more of one thing without producing less of some other.*

(a) Production possibilities

In principle, with complete and detailed information, planners could work out the production-possibility surface corresponding to given resources, with given specifications of goods and services to be produced. They could then choose the combination of products that they regard as the most desirable, and give instructions for production to take place accordingly. Of course, in reality this is impossible. The required detailed information does not exist, and if it did, it would take too long to analyse. Production possibilities would shift faster than a plan could be devised. Much more rough and ready methods have to be used.

In small sections of a plan, however, the concept of efficiency is useful. L. V. Kantorovich, one of the leaders of the school of mathematical economics in the USSR, worked out the theory of *linear programming* in order to find how to produce the maximum flow of a specified product from a given set of machines of various types.[1] The essence of the argument is the same as that we met in Ricardo's theory of rent—that the maximum output of a single crop ('corn') is produced from a given area of land of various levels of fertility when work is distributed over the cultivable area in such a way that the marginal productivity of labour is everywhere equal.†

The analysis can be extended to the case of several commodities (each homogeneous within itself), provided that the desired output is specified in fixed proportions. Furthermore, it is possible, in principle, to find the opportunity cost of the components of output in terms of each other, and some rough kind of estimate of this might be used; the proportions of the commodities in the bundle can then be modified if it seems desirable to do so. For instance, where two commodities are substitutes from the point of view of the user, a larger total of use value would result from expanding the output of the commodity estimated to have the lower opportunity cost.

---

* See appendix I.
1. See L. V. Kantorovich, 'Mathematical Methods of Organising and Planning Production'. English translation, *Management Science* July 1960.
† See **2** 1 §4(c).

The scope of this method of allocating resources is narrowly limited. It applies only to cases in which the available resources and required outputs are strictly specified in physical terms. It could not be used to lay out a plan for the whole of industry, or even for the consumption-good sector. The method cannot tell the planners what demands ought to be met. Nor can it indicate the right distribution of resources between, say, education and sport, or even between footballs and hockey sticks.*

The so-called mathematical economists in the West produce theorems about maximizing 'utility' for society as a whole, and even in the USSR, some mathematical economists have been tempted to make exaggerated claims for their theoretical apparatus.[2] Maximization is a mathematical concept that can be applied only to quantities of strictly uniform and measurable units. To apply it to social relationships or moral values is merely a deception.

(b) Allocation of materials

In one sphere, the problem of scarce means with alternative uses is very important for socialist planners, that is, in the allocation of raw materials between end products. Extractive industries have limited productive capacity, and foreign purchasing power for imported inputs is always a scarce resource.

Apart from special skills which need long training, the labour force is versatile. It sets a limit to total production but not to production of particular commodities. The limiting factor for each broad line of production is availability of materials.

Each material has a range of uses, and every use can be provided for more or less satisfactorily by several materials. To maximize overall productivity, each material should be allocated to the use for which its superiority over substitutes is greatest. Copper and aluminium can both be used for electric wiring and for making kettles and saucepans. Copper may be absolutely superior in both uses, while its superiority over aluminium in wire is greater than in kettles; moreover, the output of electric apparatus is more important to the development of the economy than is the output of kettles.

The greatest merit that can be claimed for the market system is that it brings about the allocation of scarce materials between uses through the price mechanism. An increase in demand raises the price of a material which is in inelastic supply, and causes profit-seeking firms to look for cheaper substitutes. The supply then goes to the firms for which substitutes are the least eligible.

The market mechanism steers supplies of materials to their most profitable uses, which may not correspond to their most important uses in a planned economy, but the principle is the same. The planners need to make use of materials in the most economical way possible, taking into account the importance in the plan of the products into which they enter.

* See appendix 1.
2. See Michael Ellman, *Soviet Planning Today* p. 26.   **271**

To devise a means of meeting this requirement, whether by central allocation or some kind of devolution of decision making, is one of the main requirements for organizing a planned system. Certainly, there is something to be learned here from the neoclassics about the nature of the problem, but their theory does not provide a ready-made solution.

(c) Rent

There is another concept in neoclassical theory which is useful in a planned economy, that is, what Marshall called 'cost at the margin' in extractive industries.*

In agriculture, mining, fisheries, and forestry, where resources are given by nature, it is generally true that some sources of supply are easier to work than others and give a higher output per man employed. This is the case of land of different degrees of fertility which we examined in Ricardo's model.†

In production of this kind, when management is instructed to produce at minimum cost, or to maximize output per head, only the best-quality, highest-yielding sources are used, until they become exhausted. There may be a sharp rise in the real cost of production when labour has to be moved to poorer sources. This method of working underestimates the true cost of the product at first, and encourages too lavish a use of it, by failing to allow for its overall scarcity. Moreover, the labour cost of the whole output is raised by inefficient working. This problem may be dealt with by charging something like Ricardo's differential rent on different sources, and instructing enterprises to minimize cost including rent. By this means, an approximation is made to the Ricardian position of equal marginal productivities of labour applied to sources of different quality.

In practice, however, it is not easy to distinguish the true economic rent, chargeable as a result of purely natural advantages of particular sources, from that accruing from superiority due to investments in equipment, skill and diligence of the labour force, or successful organization of management. Here again, a neat theory can be applied only in a clumsy way.

3. The rate of accumulation

Up till now, we have been discussing short-period problems—those concerned with the use of existing resources and the disposal of their output. We must now consider the determination of the level and content of investment designed to increase available resources in the future.

(a) The schema of reproduction

In Marx's vision of socialism, the workers expropriate the expropriators when capitalism has fulfilled its historic task of accumulation and technical development. Some

---

* See **1** 3 §3(c).
† See **2** 1 §4(a).

investment would still be necessary, but it would not be of central importance. As it turns out, revolutions are made in relatively backward economies while capitalism is still powerful. The most urgent of all aims for the planned economies is accumulation and increased productivity.

The Marxian analysis of accumulation in capitalist industry, in terms of the schema of 'expanded reproduction', provides the starting point for the discussion of investment policy.[3] Department 1 is identified with the production of equipment, and department 2 with necessary consumption goods. Investment consists of the net output of department 1 and the addition to stocks made by department 2. A continuous process of accumulation requires the proper balance between them. Department 1 is divided into two parts, that which produces equipment for its own enlargement—broadly, basic industry—and that which provides equipment for department 2, broadly, light industry.

The overall rate of accumulation may be accelerating, decelerating, or steady as time goes by.[*] This can be seen in terms of our simple model with one kind of machine, in which the machine sector increases its own stock of machines at the same time as it produces machines to equip labour in the corn sector.[†] While accumulation is accelerating, the proportion of investment carried out by department 1 (our machine sector), in expanding itself, must be greater than the proportion of investment for the corn sector.

For instance, suppose that, initially for every 80 machines in the corn sector, there are 20 machines in the machine sector, producing 10 new machines a year, and suppose that 6 new machines are put back into the machine sector. Next year, 26 machines produce 13 new machines (taking a year as the gestation period of a machine). The output of machines has risen by 30 per cent, while the output of corn has risen only by $\frac{4}{80}$ or 5 per cent.

So long as the ratio of machine-sector machines to total machines is growing, accumulation is accelerating, i.e., the proportionate growth from year to year of the total stock is greater each year than in the year before. The output of corn (consumption goods) is growing, but its share in total output (measured in labour value) is shrinking from year to year.

The rate of growth is decelerating when the proportionate growth in the number of new machines allocated to the machine sector is falling from year to year. So long as the number is more than in proportion to the existing stock in the machine sector, the ratio of investment to income is still growing from year to year, but now at a decelerating rate.

When a plateau of steady growth is reached, the allocation of new machines to each sector every year is proportionate to the numbers in each, and investment is a constant proportion of output. The output of corn for consumption is then rising from year to year at the same steady rate as total output. In the above example,

3. See *Capital*, vol. II, chapter 20.
* See appendix 2.
† Cf. **2** 2 §5(c).

when eight machines are added to the corn sector, and two to the machine sector, the whole stock is growing in proportion at 10 per cent per annum.

Our model of corn and machines makes the Marxian schema easy to grasp though, of course, it is too simple to be of much use to the planners.[4]

At one time, the official Soviet view was that acceleration was the 'first law of socialist accumulation'. Such an heroic programme puts a great strain on the community, and generates mounting inflationary pressure through the rising proportion of the surplus to be extracted from the sales value of commodities. After a sufficient basis of heavy industry had been laid down, the Soviet doctrine was changed to the reasonable view that acceleration is no more than a necessary phase in the early stages of industrialization.

(b) The neoclassical view

The coherent body of neoclassical theory was worked out in terms of comparisons of stationary states; treatment of accumulation was scrappy and vague. The neo-neoclassical reconstruction of the pre-Keynesian model admittedly works properly only in a one-commodity world, with a 'well-behaved production function' in terms of labour and stocks of that commodity. However, this does not affect the basic neoclassical conception that accumulation takes place through decisions of households to save, and that saving means a sacrifice of present consumption for the sake of greater consumption in the future. The experiences of a family which saves part of its income to accumulate wealth, and places its wealth in interest-bearing securities, is used to account for the behaviour of the economy taken as a whole.

Now, we know that there is generally a sufficient amount of slack in a private-enterprise economy (except in wartime or during an exceptionally strong boom), for an increase in investment to be accompanied by an increase in consumption. Here, saving as a sacrifice does not make sense.

All the same, it is true that if near-full employment is going to be maintained in any case, then a faster rate of accumulation must be associated, in a given technical situation, with a lower level of consumption. In the market economy, this is brought about by a higher share of profits in the value of output; those who are saving and adding to their wealth are, therefore, normally consuming more than they would be if profits were lower. Abstinence from consumption is not required from the savers, but from the workers who are receiving lower real wages. They have to abstain not only enough to allow for higher investment but also a bit extra to allow for the higher consumption of the savers.*

4. See G. A. Fel'dman (1928), 'On the Theory of Growth Rates of National Income', in *Foundations of the Soviet Strategy for Economic Growth*, ed. Spulber, 1964.
* See **2** 6 §4(f).

(c) Socialist accumulation

For a socialist economy, certainly, accumulation requires a sacrifice of present consumption for the sake of the future, but it works out in a more complicated manner than can be expressed in terms of the Marxian schema of reproduction.

Firstly, the underlying conception of the schema is appropriate only to industrial development. The most important element in the supply of consumption goods—foodstuffs—as well as much of the raw materials for light industry, such as cotton, comes from agriculture. The relation between investment and expansion follows its own rhythm in agriculture and cannot be relied on to keep up the same pace as in industry.

Secondly, the growth of consumption depends on the form that investment takes. Once full employment has been organized, no increase in provision of goods to buy, of housing, sport and entertainment, or social services, can take place without prior investment in equipment, construction, and training of personnel. The choice is not between consumption and investment, but between quick-yielding investment and long-range investment.

Thirdly, the timing of accumulation depends a great deal on what sacrifices the planners can call upon the community to make. A policy of allowing a large share of investment in light industry and agriculture would raise consumption fast at first but at a decelerating rate later, while (leaving aside armaments and sputniks) a high proportion of investment in basic industry restrains the growth of consumption at first and permits it to expand faster when capacity for investment has been enlarged. But to restrain consumption and postpone too long the enjoyment of benefit from investment may damage morale, and end up producing slower growth after all.

4. Choice of technique

The notion of a ready-made 'book of blueprints' is not of much use in the discussion of investment in the leading industrial countries where innovations are being embodied in each generation of new plant.* Overall investment planning, however, was evolved in the context of a deliberate policy of industrializing a mainly agricultural economy. Then, all the techniques that have been used in the course of capitalist development are known, so that something like a book of blueprints is available to the latecomer. Consequently, a problem of the choice of technique arises in terms of the objectives and costs of the various forms in which investment can be embodied.

(a) Objectives

The aim of an investment plan is an increment in the bill of goods that is to be produced. When the armed forces, education, house building, and so forth, have

* See **2** 4 §4.

been given their allotted share, there remains a particular amount available to increase the output of consumption goods. As we have observed, no amount of mathematics will tell the planners what they ought to want. The composition of the increment of output must be decided in advance. It may be modified as production goes on; when more than the expected quantities of some goods can be produced, part of the labour force can be deflected to producing something else; when too little, output must be reduced where labour can best be spared.

Since the object of the plan is a heterogeneous bundle of goods and services, there is no way to reduce it to homogeneous terms. The prices that a household pays for consumption goods are a very unreliable measure of the benefit they offer. Even in neoclassical theory, relative prices measure only relative *marginal* utilities. There is no theory to deal with the benefit from discrete increments of consumption. Besides, selling prices are influenced by social policy. If we went by prices, an increment in the supply of vodka would be more valuable than anything else. The object of the plan must be set out in terms of future outputs of particular commodities, not of a flow of values.

The time-pattern of future outputs is also a matter of great importance. Flows of goods to households have to fit with each other. (It is no good offering electric irons before supplies of domestic power.) The rate at which consumption of various types of goods is to be allowed to rise has to be decided in the plan, on general principles. There is no way of setting out the analysis of planning in terms of a general 'productivity of investment'. All the same, as we shall see, the cost of investment plays an important part in the argument.

(b) Labour as a cost

Under capitalism, the choice of technique is supposed to be governed by a desire to maximize profits. The cost of labour comes into the argument as the future wage bill that will have to be paid to operate equipment that is to be installed. Under socialism, wages are not a cost. Society is responsible for providing for all its members; no one ceases to be a responsibility because he is unemployed.

Labour is not a cost, but a potential resource to be used. The whole labour force, now and in the future, is to be organized to produce something or other. Unemployment occurs only as the result of faulty administration (including a failure to provide useful occupations for the rural population in the slack seasons of agriculture). But labour time is a cost in the sense that it is the ultimate scarce resource. The aim of investment is to reduce the labour cost of particular commodities, by increasing output per head. Thus, the choice of projects must be made in terms of future labour saved per unit of current investment.

As accumulation goes on and experience is acquired, output per man hour of labour rises. The part of the benefit of this that goes to the consumer-good sector may be distributed by raising money incomes or by lowering prices. The real-wage rate is then rising. This certainly does not mean that the cost of employing labour has gone up. The scarce commodity to be allocated between different uses is labour time, not the goods consumed by workers.

However, provided that this is recognized, it is legitimate, simply for convenience, to reckon the cost of labour time, both today and in the future, in terms of given wage rates, provided that we can allow adequately for differences in the scarcity of different kinds of skill.

(c) Material resources

The resources required for investment exist in particular concrete forms, say, capacity to produce steel, coal, and electric power. Labour is the ultimate bottleneck for all production but there are also separate bottlenecks for particular outputs. For purposes of discussing the cost of investment, this difficulty can, to some extent, be overcome by assessing the relative cost of different materials in terms of the labour time required (with normal working hours) to make a small increase in the output of each. The materials that are most scarce are those that have the highest 'cost at the margin', and so require the greatest amount of work to increase the current rate of output. Thus, in a rough and ready way, we can reduce investible resources as a whole to terms of labour time in the investment industries.

(d) Allocating investible resources

The choice of technique comes into the argument after the bill of goods has been decided. For a future flow of output of a particular commodity, there may be several possible techniques; one which requires a greater cost of investment to equip a man for future employment must offer a higher level of future output per head.

When the time-patterns of inputs and outputs are alike, techniques can be compared simply in terms of the future output per head of a particular commodity obtainable per unit of today's investible resources (measured in labour time), i.e., the return per unit of investment in terms of saving future labour time. (This is the same conception as the *degree of mechanization* that we met with in the discussion of technical change.*)

Now, just as the criterion for the choice of technique for any line is expressed in terms of the saving of future labour time per unit of investible resources devoted to it, so, in the plan as a whole, investible resources should be allocated between lines according to the saving of future labour time that a unit of investment makes possible in each.

A mechanism to implement this principle might be as follows: a premium is attached to the labour cost of investible resources at so much per cent per unit; a plan is then designed to minimize the cost of the flow of each type of output in terms of future labour time (at current wage rates) together with the charge for the premium.

* See **2** 4 §3(d).

(This charge is purely notional. As we have seen, the prices at which goods are sold to households are arranged on different principles.) Then, when costs are correctly worked out and the correct design of plant chosen, the saving of future labour time per unit cost of investment will be the same, at the margin, for each line of production, so that there would be no advantage in switching a little more investment to one line from another. (Here, we are appealing once more to the principle of *efficiency* developed in neoclassical theory.)

The premium measures the scarcity of investible resources relative to future labour time. It is intended to steer investment into the lines and into the forms which bring about the greatest saving of future labour time that planned investment can make possible. The level at which the premium must be set depends on the labour force in the part of the investment industries devoted to providing equipment for the consumption-good industries, relative to the labour force becoming available for employment in them. If the premium were set too low, investments would be planned to use too much equipment per head, and there would not be enough plant to offer employment to all available workers. If it were set too high, investments would bring too small a rise in output per head in many lines, and there would be a scarcity of labour.

When it is set just right, at each phase of investment there is continuous full employment, with the maximum technically possible saving of future labour time, or, to put it another way, for a given amount of labour time, the maximum rate of rise in total output of the commodities which the plan is designed to offer.

It must be emphasized that this analysis is restricted to the case of simple time patterns of production which are the same for all techniques. In fact, the choice of a technique cannot be separated from the choice of its time pattern. Often, the more mechanized technique will require a longer delay between starting investment and beginning to produce. (Hydropower plants have a heavier investment per man, and a longer gestation period, than thermal plants of the same capacity.)

Obviously, a technique that required a high cost of investment today, for a smaller saving of labour in the future, would be *inferior** and should be rejected. Similarly, an investment that involves more delay before output begins to be available—a longer gestation period—without a higher rate of output when it is completed would be inferior to one that begins to yield sooner. A technique requiring a longer delay to get a sufficiently increased future output may be eligible, but the benefit from it cannot be expressed simply in terms of saving future labour time in general. It is going to offer specific outputs at specific dates. A theory of the choice among techniques of different time paths would be extremely complicated and impossible to apply in practice. When calculation has gone as far as it can, the planners have to decide somehow, and hope for the best. Indeed, the conception of an optimum choice of technique could not be made operational in a precise way. All the same, it points in a direction which is important in reality.

* See **2** 4 §3(d).

(e) 'Walking on two legs'

When a process of industrialization is beginning, there is an enormous mountain of equipment that it is desirable to create, and a very small amount that can be installed in one planning period. A choice, then, has to be made among the various commodities that it is desirable to produce, to see which should have investment allocated to it first. The difference that is made to output per head by investment in equipment differs very much from one line of production to another, and different lines differ in importance for further development. Thus, the correct policy is to look over the bill of goods, and find where the greatest difference is made to output per head by installing new equipment. A small part of the labour force is then to be provided with equipment, in the most modern and superior form, needing very high investment per head, while the rest are provided with only enough to permit them to produce by the old labour-using methods, improving their equipment by their own efforts as best they may. Year by year, the number of highly mechanized installations is increased until, in some far-distant future, everyone is equipped with the best.

To work out precisely which projects should be undertaken on this principle requires detailed information, including estimates of possible future improvements in technique. It could not be represented in a premium measuring the scarcity of investible resources. We could not really pretend that an optimal programme could be worked out mathematically. Chinese experience, however, offers some obvious examples. Railways are built for long-distance heavy traffic while donkeys, or even men, pull carts for short hauls; the great iron and steel complexes supply the main construction and machine-making industries, while small forgings in the country produce farm tools. These examples illustrate the principle of using investible resources selectively while maintaining full employment, or as the Chinese say, walking on both legs.

5. Another story: 'the rate of return'

The concept of the productivity of 'capital' plays an important part in neoclassical theory. It is often confused with the concept of the productivity of investment or the 'rate of return' on saving for the community as a whole,* as it were, the benefit of accumulation to a socialist economy.

Various schools of neoclassical thought have tried in various ways to equate the 'productivity of capital' with the rate of profit accruing to capitalists on the finance invested in business, or the rate of interest accruing to rentiers on their placements. This involves a confusion, first, between the total value of capital of all firms taken together, and the increment to the stock of capital made at any moment by investment; and second, between the means of production which enhance productivity, and property which gives its owners a claim to a share in the money value of the product.

* See **2** 4 §4.

We have seen that the level of the rate of profit on capital depends, broadly, on the state of technology and the level of real wages, and that the level of interest rates is mainly determined by the state of opinion in the market for placements—the Stock Exchange—and the manipulations of monetary policy. What has the 'productivity of capital' to do with either of them?

There remains the concept of the productivity of investment from the standpoint of society as a whole. Certainly, to accumulate more means of production embodying superior techniques is a benefit to society in the sense that it increases output from a given labour force, i.e., reduces the labour time required to produce a given output. But, as our discussion of the problems of a planned economy has shown, this benefit is not something that can be reduced to a 'rate of return'. The proportion of investment in total activity, the allocation of investment between broad sectors, and even the composition of output within the consumption sector, have to be decided by a political process. There is no way of reducing to a uniform measure the benefit to society of the various objectives of investment.

The only element in the neoclassical scheme that we can find of use in discussing planned investment is the concept of a premium charged for investible resources as a determinant of the degree of mechanization of technique, to be chosen after both the rate of investment and its objectives have been decided. Even in this narrow sphere, the notion is useful only as a vague general indication of the right policy, for the calculations involved in working it out would require more precise data than are likely to be available. Planning has to proceed by much rougher means.

Appendix 1: The search for efficiency in Soviet planning

The basic character and direction of long-term investment in the plan can be determined only by the general political and economic decisions.

At the same time, in the process of working out the plan, resulting from the general line [of the party], the calculation of efficiency should play a very important role, in particular in the consideration of more partial, but also important questions such as the choice of which raw materials and technological processes to use, the type of enterprise, the degree of concentration and specialisation and so on. Of course these questions also must be solved taking into account the general plan.

L. V. Kantorovich[5]

In the years immediately following the Soviet revolution of 1917, there was a great deal of lively and creative controversy about economic matters, but between 1929 and 1956 the orthodox view prevailing in the Soviet Union was that the function of economists is to provide ex-post rationalizations of government economic policy. Economists had nothing useful to contribute either in the field of the techniques of economic planning or in the organization of economic institutions. After 1956, the obvious need to improve the techniques of planning encouraged a reappraisal of

280   5. *The Best Use of Economic Resources* p. 184.

the economists' potential contribution, and in consequence, a number of new ideas have been debated and, to a certain extent implemented.

1. Traditional techniques

(a) Input norms

Traditionally, the main technique used in the attempt to achieve efficient socialist planning was that of *input norms*. An input norm is a number assumed to describe an efficient process of transformation of inputs into outputs. For example, suppose that the norm for the utilization of coal in the production of one ton of steel is x tons. Then the efficient production of z tons of steel is assumed to require zx tons of coal.

The method of norms is widely used in Soviet planning, and considerable effort is devoted to updating them. But the method is incapable of ensuring efficiency. The norms used in planning calculations are simply averages of input requirements, weighted somewhat in favour of efficient producers. Actual technologies show a wide dispersion in input–output relations. Further, given norms take no account of the possibilities of substitution of inputs for one another in the production process, non-constant returns to scale, and the results of technical improvement. Thus, in general, the method of norms does not make it possible to calculate efficient input requirements, and plans calculated in this way are always inefficient.

(b) Consistency

A more modest requirement than efficiency is *consistency*. Consider a farm which can produce corn and potatoes by three different techniques. The inputs available are such as to give the production-possibility area shown in Fig. 11.1. Any output plan on *PQRS* is efficient.* Any output combination in the shaded area is inconsistent

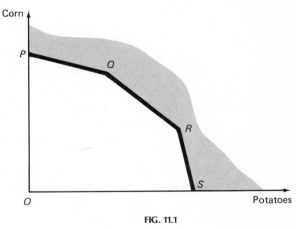

FIG. 11.1

* Cf. **2** 7 §5 (Fig. 7.2).

with the input plan, and cannot be produced. Any output inside *OPQRS*, though inefficient, is at least consistent with available inputs.

(c) Planning and counterplanning

The method to ensure that the plans for each enterprise are at least consistent (not in the shaded area) is that of planning and counterplanning. If the plan were simply handed down to the enterprises from above, in accordance with the planners' view of national economic requirements but in ignorance of the real possibilities of each enterprise, then clearly, such planning would be inconsistent. Conversely, if plans were simply drawn up by each enterprise, they might fail to use resources in accordance with national economic requirements. The process of planning and counterplanning involves a mutual submission and discussion of planning suggestions, designed to lead to the adoption of a plan which is feasible for the enterprise and ensures that the resources of each enterprise are used in accordance with national requirements.

Unfortunately, the bureaucratic complexity of this procedure militates against both efficiency and consistency.

(d) Material balances

The method used to ensure that plans for each commodity are consistent is that of *material balances*. This involves drawing up balance sheets for particular commodities, showing on the one hand, the economy's resources and potential output, and on the other, the economy's need for a particular product.

Normally, at the start of planning procedures, the anticipated availability of a commodity is not sufficient to meet anticipated requirements. To balance the two, the planners seek possibilities of economizing on scarce products and substituting for scarce materials; they investigate the possibilities of increasing production or importing raw materials or equipment, or in the last resort, they determine the priority needs to be fulfilled by the scarce commodity.

But, even with great efforts, achieving a balance is difficult. The complexity of an economy in which a great variety of commodities are produced by different processes, all of which are subject to continuous technological change, is too great for the attainment of anything other than broad consistency.

The harmful effects of inconsistencies in planning have been limited by the relatively small changes that planners impose on the economy at any time. They tend, rather, continuously to make small changes in the existing structure of production. Mistakes are seldom so large as to be impossible to rectify. Nonetheless, the traditional planning system has the appearance of a rather pragmatic attempt to muddle through.

2. Innovations in planning

In the mid 'fifties, it became apparent that traditional planning methods were unsatisfactory, particularly in view of increasing diversity of the economy and attempts being made to develop the consumption-goods sector.

(a) The recoupment period

The first new method of economic calculation put forward by economists concerned the problem of choice of technique. The recoupment period is a method used to compare different techniques for production of a given output. The comparison is made in terms of the reduction in future running costs that can be attributed to higher initial investment costs. A technique with greater investment cost, compared with another requiring less investment, is chosen only if the additional investment cost can be covered by savings on running costs within a period equal to, or shorter than, the recoupment period officially prescribed for that sector.

A longer recoupment period permits higher initial investment per man, i.e., a higher degree of mechanization,* and vice versa. This method is an attempt to find the appropriate degree of mechanization to fit available investible resources to available labour, but since the calculation is in terms of more or less arbitrary prices, instead of costs in terms of labour time, it cannot be very satisfactory. Moreover, the problem of comparing time-patterns of investment and output is dealt with very sketchily.

Furthermore, this method is only useful in determining the degree of mechanization in each sector separately. The division of investible resources between sectors is conducted by the *ad hoc* procedures described above. There is nothing like the Chinese method of 'walking on two legs' which links the allocation of investment between sectors to the rise in productivity in the plan as a whole.

The recoupment period, input norms, and material balances are still the main techniques used in the planning of Eastern European economies. In the 'sixties, however, experiments were made with new techniques, such as input–output analysis and linear programming.

(b) Input–output

The first set of national accounts providing data on production relationships between industries was compiled by the USSR Central Statistical Administration in the 'twenties. Most of the development of the technique has been done by Professor W. Leontief, in the United States. Here again, the use of arbitrary prices impairs the precision of any calculation in value terms,† but Soviet planners have also compiled input–output tables in physical units and labour units. The method is useful in directing attention to the interrelationships of sectors, particularly in terms of the direct and indirect inputs required in production of a given output.

* See **2** 4 §3(d).
† See **2** 6 §3(c).

The first major study of the influence of the composition of final output on the overall structure of production was made in connection with the 1966–70 Soviet five-year plan. It became clear that increasing the share of investment in national income would increase the rate of growth of national product but have little effect on the rate of growth of consumption for some time. This follows the line of Fel'dman's model,* but the input–output technique improves on it, since it requires an examination of the effects of different strategies at industry level, rather than merely in terms of aggregates.

(c) Linear programming

Perhaps the most important innovation in planning techniques has been the introduction of linear programming. This technique involves the maximization (or minimization) of a linear function (such as the sum of outputs of cement from different factories or the time spent by trucks making deliveries to different points), subject to constraints in the form of linear equations (such as the relationship between the availability of lime, etc., and the potential output of cement). A number of problems in economic planning may be given this type of mathematical formulation, and methods exist for finding precise numerical solutions. The solution to a linear-programming problem yields the best magnitudes for the physical variables (the output of cement by each plant) and also provides a measure of the opportunity costs of different combinations of outputs and inputs.

In his classic study, *Economic Calculation of the Best Use of Resources*, L. V. Kantorovich introduced linear programming by means of a simple example. Two outputs are required, α and β. The needs for them are unlimited, but it is necessary that twice as much of α be produced, as of β, and this proportion is fixed whatever total output may be. Each of these goods may be produced at factories of types A, B, C, D, and E, each type having a different output capacity. The number of factories of each type and the production capacity per month for α and β are shown in Table 11.1.

Table 11.1

Type of factory	Number of factories	Production capacity if all capacity is devoted to		Opportunity cost of α in terms of β	Opportunity cost of β in terms of α
		α	β		
A	5	100 000	15 000	0·15	6·7
B	3	400 000	200 000	0·5	2
C	40	20 000	2 500	0·125	8
D	9	200 000	50 000	0·25	4
E	2	600 000	250 000	0·42	2·4

* See appendix 2.

It is assumed that combinations of outputs from any one factory are possible under conditions of constant returns to any one output. Thus, to attain one more unit of α from factory A will involve giving up 0·15 of a unit of β. The opportunity cost of α in terms of β is 0·15 of a unit.

The production possibilities can be expressed graphically. From factories of type A, we may attain 500 000 units of α or 75 000 units of β, or any proportionate (linear) combination of the two. This is shown by the line AA' in Fig. 11.2. Similar lines are shown for the other factories.

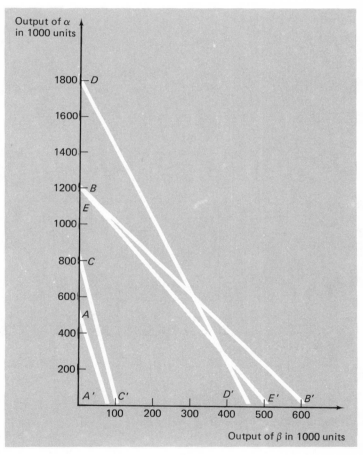

FIG. 11.2

If only α is produced, total output equals 5 500 000 units of α. Suppose we wish to produce 1 unit of β. Then, part of the capacity of the factory which has the lowest opportunity cost of β in terms of α will be used to produce 1 unit of β. In our example, this is a factory of type B. Greater output of β will all be produced by type B factories up to the maximum capacity of type B factories, 600 000 units of β. If more β is required, then capacity of factories of type E will be used to produce it, and so on.

The maximum potential outputs at each particular ratio of α output to β output form the production-possibility frontier shown by $PQRSTU$ in Fig. 11.3. The required ratio of α output to β output, 2:1, is shown by the line OO'. Thus, the optimal plan, giving the maximum amounts of α and β in the ratio 2:1, is at a. What a involves in terms of the output of each type of factory is shown in Table 11.2.

One type of factory, D, produces both α and β. For factories of type D, the opportunity cost of β in terms of α is 4, as may be seen from the slope of RS in Fig. 11.3.

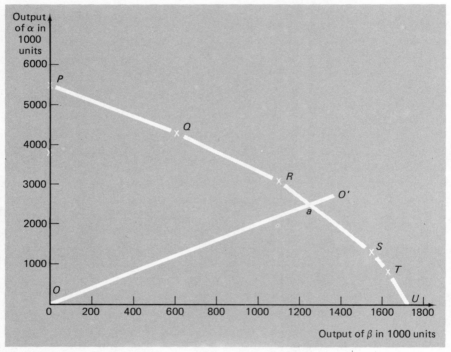

FIG. 11.3

(d) Application of linear programming

Although linear programming was developed by a Soviet mathematician, its first large-scale applications were in the USA, where the technique was discovered independently a few years later. Some American applications have been in the scheduling of iron and steel production, in the paper and oil industries, and in transport (to minimize freight costs).

In the USSR, the application of linear-programming techniques to the production of steel tubes is estimated to have increased output of tubes in 1970 by 108 000 tons.

Table 11.2

Type of factory	Article α		Article β	
	Number of factories	Aggregate output	Number of factories	Aggregate output
A	5	500 000	—	—
B	—	—	3	600 000
C	40	800 000	—	—
D	6	1 200 000	3	150 000
E	—	—	2	500 000
		2 500 000		1 250 000

A further important improvement has been attained in the combination of fuels used in production of electricity, particularly in the choice of fuel for new generating stations. In the latter example, the calculation of opportunity costs gave different results from those originally attained by using the conventional prices at which fuels are sold.

A great deal of attention has been focused on the use of programming techniques in investment planning. The planned development of the cement industries in the late 'sixties was based on programming results. The problem was to minimize the total cost of producing given outputs of cement in particular locations in the Soviet Union. The variables in the problem were the existing enterprises, the capacity and location of new enterprises, and the transport scheme. The results of the calculation were a list of enterprises which should be closed, a list of enterprises which should be maintained at existing capacity, and a list of places where new enterprises of particular capacities should be built. The result of linear-programming calculations indicated that it was desirable (taking account of transport costs) to concentrate the production of cement in a small number of large factories, rather than to treat cement as a 'local' commodity, production of which should be sited in different parts of the country. This was contrary to influential opinion in the cement industry and, presumably, to many local interests.

These examples show the way in which mathematical techniques, of which linear programming is only one, may be used to solve well-defined economic planning problems. The technique cannot determine what is produced or what social policy may be (for example, 'inefficient' plants may be kept open for a while to avoid throwing men out of work), but it can contribute to the efficient use of resources.

Appendix 2: The first law of socialist accumulation

Our simple model describing the production of corn and machines by machines and labour may be used to illustrate Fel'dman's adaptation of Marx's schema of reproduction into a theory of accumulation.* From this theory was derived the 'first law of socialist accumulation', which has played a major role in the formation of economic policy in the Soviet Union and East European countries.

In our model, the machine sector produces machines for itself and for the corn sector. Once machines are allocated to one use they cannot be moved to another. To simplify matters, we will no longer assume that machines have a long gestation period. Machines and consumption goods are produced by means of machines and labour in one period, say, a year or 18 months. There is always enough labour available to man the entire stock of machines. Machines do not wear out and there is no technical progress.

The economy can be characterized as comprising two 'departments', the first of which, the machine sector, is, itself, divided into two:

Department 1
a Work with machine hours produces machines for department 1
b Work with machine hours produces machines for department 2
Department 2
Work with machine hours produces corn (consumption goods)

(a) Steady growth

Suppose that, at the beginning of our story, there is a stock of 10 000 machines in department 1a and the same number in department 1b, and that there is a stock, of equal size, of 20 000 machines in department 2. In department 1, five machines with the appropriate complement of labour produce one machine in one period. With each machine in department 2, one unit of corn is produced per period. Thus,

1a Work with 10 000 machines produces 2000 machines for department 1
1b Work with 10 000 machines produces 2000 machines for department 2
2 Work with 20 000 machines produces 20 000 units of corn

The manner in which development goes on depends on the allocation of the output of department 1a between 1a and 1b. If a large proportion of these new machines is given to 1b, then the production of corn-sector machines (and, ultimately, of corn) will increase rapidly. But the growth of capacity for machine production will slow down, and eventually the proportionate growth of capacity in all sectors of the economy will be reduced.

When the larger proportion is given to department 1a, the growth of capacity in all sectors of the economy will eventually be increased, though production of corn may temporarily be retarded.

* See **2** 11 §3(a).

The proportionate distribution of the output of department 1a is, therefore, the central element in the pattern of accumulation adopted by the economy. We will call the proportion retained in department 1a, α. Suppose, in the above example, that $\alpha = 0.5$. Then the output of department 1a is divided evenly between departments 1a and 1b which were equal to start with. In the next period

1a Work with 11 000 machines produces 2200 machines for department 1
1b Work with 11 000 machines produces 2200 machines for department 2
2　 Work with 22 000 machines produces 22 000 units of corn

Output in all sectors of the economy has been increased by 10 per cent. If α remained at 0.5 in succeeding periods, then output in all sectors would rise by 10 per cent in the next period, and so on, *ad infinitum*. The economy will remain on a steady-growth path at 10 per cent per period, so long as the ratio of investment to the stock of machines remains constant, and α remains at 0.5.

This result is due to the coefficient α being equal to the ratio of the stocks in the two departments with which we began the story.

(b) Accelerated growth

To achieve levels of output of corn higher than those attainable by means of the steady-growth rate, the capacity of department 2 must be increased more rapidly. This, in turn, indicates that the capacity of department 1b must be increased more rapidly. An increase in the capacity of department 1b may be achieved quickly by reducing α towards 0, and allocating a larger part of the output of department 1a to department 1b, or more slowly by increasing α, thus increasing the output of department 1a, and eventually increasing the rate of growth of capacity in department 1b. The first strategy will bring about an immediate increase in the capacity of department 1b, but the growth rate of the economy will then steadily diminish. The second strategy will eventually shift the economy to a permanently higher growth path.

Suppose that, at the end of period 3, α is increased to 0.75, and thus, of the output of 2420 machines from department 1a, 1815 machines are retained in department 1a, and only 605 machines added to the capacity of department 1b. This investment policy is maintained for the next 30 years. The effect on the growth rate of corn is shown in Table 11.3.

The switch of capacity to department 1a initially reduces the rate of growth of corn output. But, after period 12, the overall effects of rapid growth capacity are reflected in an increasing growth rate of corn output. The 10 per cent growth rate of the steady-growth path is exceeded by period 22 and, 30 periods after the change in α, corn output is rising at 13 per cent per period, and the rate of increase is still accelerating.

The effect on absolute levels of corn output is shown in Fig. 11.4. Despite the acceleration of the growth rate of corn output, the absolute level of corn output on the steady-growth path is not overtaken until period 33.

289

If α were maintained at 0·75, the rate of growth of corn output would continue to accelerate until settling down to a new steady-growth path of 15 per cent. Further acceleration could then only be attained by a further increase in α.

Table 11.3

Period	α	Rate of growth of output of corn on accelerated growth path (%)
1	0·5	
2	0·5	10
3	0·5	10
4	0·75	10
5	0·75	9·6
6	0·75	9·2
:		
10	0·75	8·5
11	0·75	8·46
12	0·75	8·47
13	0·75	8·52
:		
20	0·75	9·6
21	0·75	9·9
22	0·75	10·1
23	0·75	10·4
:		
32	0·75	12·6
33	0·75	12·8
34	0·75	13·0
35	0·5	13·2
36	0·5	15·0
37	0·5	16·3
:		
39	0·5	17·5
40	0·5	17·6
41	0·5	17·5
:		
49	0·5	14·7
50	0·5	14·4

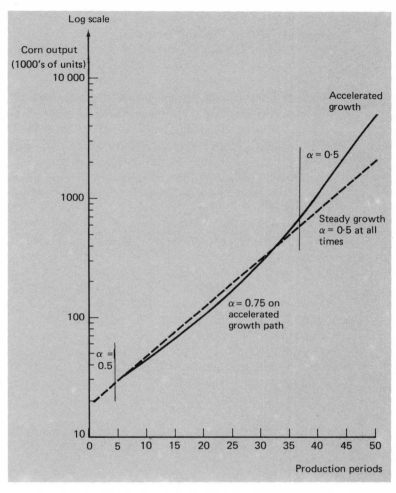

FIG. 11.4   Corn output, steady growth, and accelerated growth.

(c) Decelerating growth

Once high levels of capacity have been built up, it may be decided that the restraint on present consumption involved in a high rate is no longer necessary. A reduction in α will give a rapid boost to the growth of corn output, as a larger proportion capacity is allocated to department 1b. Ultimately, the rate of growth of corn output will decelerate as the growth of capacity in department 1 slows down, and the economy will again tend towards a steady-growth path of 10 per cent. But this new 10 per cent path will involve a much higher absolute level of corn output than would have been the case if steady growth had been maintained all along.

The process of deceleration is illustrated in Table 11.3 and Fig. 11.4, in which the value of α is reduced to 0·5 in period 35.

(d) Generalization

Fel'dman's departments may be generalized to correspond with broad sectors of a complex economy. The model contains some important clues to the nature of industrial growth. The empirical conclusions of the model can only be regarded as indicative of the direction of change, rather than its magnitude, since too many important factors in economic development are omitted. Nonetheless, the ideas contained in Fel'dman's model, particularly with respect to the role played by investment in machine-making capacity, had a considerable influence on Soviet planning in the 'thirties.

Book Three

Modern problems

Introduction

Before 1914 and even up to the 'thirties, economic doctrines used to be pronounced with great confidence. The duty of a national government was to keep its budget balanced, maintain the gold standard, eschew protection, and observe the rule of *laissez-faire* in its dealings with industry. Some economists, nowadays, content themselves with trying to find assumptions on which the old doctrines would have been correct, but those who concern themselves with what goes on in the world cannot maintain the serene complacency of earlier generations. Whether they discuss the problems of contemporary life in tones of apology or indignation, they have to admit that there are many problems for which the solution is not obvious.

The emphasis in the following notes is on problems and difficulties and the conflict of interests in attempts to solve them. There are few problems in economics to which a solution can be found that 'does good to at least one individual without doing harm to any other'. Once the veil of *laissez-faire* doctrine has been torn aside, every economic problem is seen to have a political aspect, and *laissez-faire* itself is seen to have been one kind of political programme.

Economic reasoning, alone, cannot offer a solution for any economic problem, for all involve political, social, and human considerations that cannot be reduced to 'the lore of nicely calculated less and more'. The object of an introduction to analysis should be, not to propound solutions, but to suggest to the reader what he must take into account in trying to make up his own mind about the issues presented to him by the age in which he lives.

Chapter One

Capitalist nations

After 1945, the era of *laissez-faire* was found to have come to an end. The governments of all the capitalist industrialized countries, tacitly or openly, accepted responsibility for management of their economies. To the traditional concern of the authorities with military affairs and the international balance of payments was now added a third—to maintain a high and stable level of employment. But since, as we have seen, success in maintaining near-full employment sets up a tendency to inflation, a fourth preoccupation developed—to keep rising prices within bounds. The aims of national economic policy became crystallized in the conception of 'growth'. This gives an important role to statisticians who provide the measure of GNP,* average income per head, and the level of real-wage rates.

Problems of the management of a modern economy are all interconnected; as we take up each in turn, we shall be looking at one complex of relationships from several angles.

1. Armaments

It would not be appropriate here to raise the question of the necessity, or success, of a crusade against communism as a defence of freedom in the capitalist world, but it is impossible to discuss modern economic problems without glancing at the role of investment in armaments.

(a) The USA

The policy of the cold war was firmly established before there was any lack of buoyancy in effective demand in the postwar situation in the United States. There

* See **2** 7 §3(a).

is no reason to suppose that it was adopted primarily as a prophylactic against recessions. But once the need to build up the military might of the nation had been accepted and the postwar arms race had begun, expenditure on armaments provided an easy and unobjectionable means for underpinning full-employment policy. What President Eisenhower described as the military–industrial complex provided an insatiable demand for funds. The self-styled Keynesian economists had undermined the objections of 'sound finance' to budgetary deficits. Military expenditure was a ready remedy for a tendency to a recession in business activity and a rise in unemployment that would be politically damaging to the government in power. This does not mean, of course, that outlay on armaments is necessary for government employment policy. If the outlet through armaments had not been available, the spectacle of the USSR apparently enjoying continuous full employment while the USA fell into a slump would have called for a remedy of some other kind. But once military expenditure was available, it was the line of least political resistance to make use of it.

The development of armaments industries is detrimental to the rest of the national economy. (If it is necessary for national survival, the sacrifice has to be made, but who is to judge the necessity?)

The first disadvantage is the obvious one, that if the sums being spent on armaments were devoted to civilian uses they would be making a contribution to increasing productivity or providing amenities for the population. Keynes argued that, as a remedy against unemployment, paying men to dig holes in the ground and fill them again was much better than doing nothing, for the wages would be spent on goods and services that would otherwise not be produced; but he pointed out that it would be much more reasonable to provide employment in doing something useful. He maintained that, in other ages, building pyramids or cathedrals or great mansions had maintained effective demand:

> 'To dig holes in the ground,' paid for out of savings, will increase, not only employment, but the real national dividend of useful goods and services. It is not reasonable, however, that a sensible community should be content to remain dependent on such fortuitous and often wasteful mitigations when once we understand the influences upon which effective demand depends.[1]

The palaces and tombs at least leave some splendid monuments for posterity to admire, which cannot be said for the manufacture of weapons that (let us hope) become obsolete before they are used.

The second drawback is, perhaps, even more detrimental to the national economy. The conduct of research, in conditions of secrecy, devoted to devising ever-new means of annihilation (quite apart from its effect on the morality of the intellectual elite) deprives industry and developments favourable to human life of the services of a great part of scientific manpower and the fruits of education.

The dominance of the United States in the world economy after the war was so great that it took another ten years for the force of President Eisenhower's warning

1. *General Theory* p. 220.

to be generally recognized. Meanwhile, the influence of the USA had fostered the power of the military, and investment in armaments, not only in the supposed national enemy, but also in allies and clients all over the world.

It is often claimed that military developments, or projects due to national vain-glory such as landing a man on the moon, lead to a spin-off of discoveries of scientific importance and to invaluable technological innovations that would never otherwise have been made. This is no doubt true, but the argument is political, not techno-logical. The point is that such drive and such large funds are never available for useful or humane research. If they were, we should expect that research directed towards particular ends would be more successful than unintended by-products of something else.

(b) UK and France

Neither Britain nor France had any need to 'dig holes in the ground' to maintain economic activity. There was plenty to do in reconstructing, expanding and modern-izing industry, and much less resistance than in the USA to socially beneficial government expenditure. But both countries were burdened with dissolving empires and dreams of past glory which kept them from devoting all their resources to civilian reconstruction.

Despite two disastrous wars and an independent atom bomb, the French emerged with less damage to their economy than did the British. Before 1939, the greater part of British overseas military expenditure was paid for on the Indian budget. After the last war, it was a heavy burden on the UK balance of payments, and it accounts for a large part of the troubles which we shall be discussing under that head.

(c) West Germany and Japan

The defeated nations were not, at first, allowed to rearm. They could put all their investment and all their patriotism into a drive for economic development. Both were helped by American loans and subventions until they could build up an export surplus. When West Germany was called on, after all, to rearm to make a contribu-tion to the defence of freedom, she did so largely by importing weapons. This had the double benefit of gratifying her allies, who are always anxious for exports, and of leaving her own heavy industry free for civilian uses.

In Japan, the economy is strictly disciplined and susceptible to central direction. In West Germany, under cover of the slogans of *laissez-faire*, the economy is much more subject to control (through the banking system) than in Britain, which has adopted the slogans of Keynesian policy.

West Germany and Japan had another characteristic in common. Both had a considerable reserve of potential industrial workers in agriculture (West Germany also drew in refugees from the German Democratic Republic and, later, immigrant workers from underdeveloped countries), and both (partly for that reason) had a   **297** somewhat tame and undemanding labour force. It was some time before either began to suffer the inflationary effects of continuous near-full employment, so that each had a strong competitive position in international trade. Energetic businessmen and compliant workers made it possible for the defeated nations to take full advantage of the bonus that the victors gave them. It is now generally admitted that the burden of armaments on the US economy, and the absence of that burden on her two greatest rivals in manufactures, is an important contribution to the crisis that broke out in 1971.

2. Employment policy

The aims of employment policy are not at all simple. A recession, raising unemployment, is regarded as an evil, but a very low level of unemployment is not an unmixed blessing. It is convenient for business to have a pool of available labour to draw on. Discipline in industry is easier to maintain when the loss of his job is a serious threat to every worker. (Humane methods of management may be efficient in the long run but brutal methods are quick and easy.) Inflationary pressure speeds up when profits are high. A boom tends to encourage rash speculations that can be successful only so long as the boom continues to accelerate; when it slows down, there is a crash, with losses and bankruptcies that give a painful shock to confidence for the future. Policy is involved in damping activity at some times, as well as in boosting it at others.

Employment policy cannot be separated from the concern of governments with international balances. This is less true for the United States than for other countries. International trade plays a much smaller part in total income for the USA than any other capitalist country, merely because of its large size and diversified resources. Moreover, for twenty-five years after the war, unquestioned dominance in the world's financial and monetary affairs made problems connected with the balance of payments seem unimportant. For the rest of the world, American economic policy was a matter of anxious concern but in the United States it appeared to be a domestic matter.

Here, we first discuss the instruments available for influencing employment at home and, later, the international aspects of the problem.

(a) Confidence

An important contribution that a government may make to maintaining effective demand, perhaps in practice the most important of all, is to inspire confidence in the leaders of industry that a slump will not be allowed to occur. This promotes expectations of profitability so as to encourage large-scale investment and innovations that would be much too risky in fluctuating markets. Thus, accumulation and technical development keep going because they are expected to keep going. Moreover, when a recession does occur, the belief that recovery is bound to come makes it easy to bring about.

298

(b) Fiscal policy

All government activities involve expenditure, covered either by taxation or by borrowing, and all exert an influence on the state of business. The most powerful instrument that a government has for affecting activity is to vary expenditure, but expenditure cannot be determined entirely by the requirements of effective demand, for it is bound up with other aspects of policy and involves the conflicting interests of powerful groups that influence government. We have seen how employment policy facilitated the growth of the military–industrial complex in the United States but, once its power was established, it went far beyond the requirements of employment and is now accused of ruining the economy with cold and hot wars.

At the same time, the requirements of employment policy may frustrate other aims, as when a sudden 'national crisis' calls for cuts in expenditure on the social services.

However clumsy and imperfect it may be, regulation of government expenditure has played a great part in employment policy, and indeed, the great increase in the sphere of government activity in all capitalist countries was a precondition for the very concept of controlling employment as an aim of public policy.

The second aspect of fiscal policy—taxation—is also an instrument for influencing effective demand. A cut in taxes is a means of encouraging household expenditure, and this, by increasing current sales, helps to encourage investment as well. The most powerful influence is exerted by cuts in taxes on the lowest incomes. Proportional cuts give the largest benefit to the highest incomes and so are generally partly wasted in increased saving.* (Just as an increase in taxation designed to dampen a boom is partly wasted in reducing saving.) It might be thought, therefore, that budgetary policy aimed at increasing employment would be the most effective if it were combined with a policy of reducing inequality but, generally, proportional reductions in taxation are preferred to those that give the greatest relief to the group of tax-payers whom it would most benefit.

(c) Interest rates and investment

The second main instrument of employment policy is much less powerful—control over credit. Various types of investment are susceptible to monetary influences in different degrees. The great corporations generally hold liquid reserves, partly in bank deposits and partly in readily marketable securities. Moreover, they have sufficient weight and influence over financial institutions to be able to borrow when they wish. They are, in general, independent of financial control and can make investment plans as they please. It is true that the terms on which new issues can be made, whether of bonds or shares, depends on the state of the market for placements, but for large firms the timing of investment is not tied to the possibility of borrowing. New issues are made when the market seems favourable; then reserves used up in investment are replenished, or bank loans paid off. To carry out large investment

* See **2** 7 §3(f).

projects, it is not necessary to wait for a favourable state of the market, nor does a favourable state of the market promote investment except in so far as it is a symptom of good prospects of profit.

In any case, the level of the rate of interest plays only a small part in the calculation of the prospects of profitability in industrial investment. When the riskiness of a venture is reckoned on the basis of a three-year pay-off, it has to promise gross profits at an annual rate of $33\frac{1}{3}$ per cent of the investment over the first three years. Compared with this, even a large difference in the rate of interest, say, between 5 and 10 per cent per annum, does not have much effect. Thus, for risky projects, the cost of borrowing (or the return to be got on unused reserves) is not an important influence on investment decisions.

The situation is different for small businesses that depend on bank loans. The rate of interest that they have to pay is an important part of their costs; new starts, or extensions of existing businesses, depend on being able to satisfy a bank that the proposition is creditworthy. Here, the control of the monetary authorities over the basis of credit has some influence on the level of investment.

The influence is limited, however. When prospects of profit are low, easy credit cannot do much to get business going, and when prospects of profit are high, a restriction on bank lending will be offset by other institutions taking over the business of supplying finance, using their reserve funds to make loans instead of holding them as bank deposits.*

The most important domestic influence of monetary policy is on house building. The demand for houses by consumers is largely independent of the state of trade, while what a family of given income can afford depends very much on the rate of interest they have to pay for a loan. Building as an investment is also influenced by the rate of interest. The demand for housing is fairly reliable, particularly in a country of increasing population and increasing wealth. The pay-off in terms of future rents may be reckoned on the basis of ten or fifteen years. Compared with a gross return of 10 per cent per annum, a difference of even one point on the rate of interest (say, between 5 and 6 per cent) makes a great difference to the eligibility of investment.

(d) Monetary boosters and dampers

An increase in the basis of credit promotes bank lending and tends to bring down interest rates. As a remedy against a recession, this has some favourable influence, provided that confidence has not been too badly shaken. It allows the banks to make loans for small businesses that formerly they were refusing; it promotes house building; it puts up the value of securities on the Stock Exchange, which encourages rentier expenditure, and it eases hire-purchase terms. It may also encourage investment by the big firms, which take it as a sign that the authorities are not going to allow the recession to go too far.

300   * See **2** 8.

As a check to what the authorities regard as an excessive boom, a credit squeeze is not very effective unless applied at a moment when the boom is just about to break, or unless accompanied by other measures calculated to restrict activity, for so long as prospects of profit are buoyant, investment will continue, loans can be got from one source or another, and Stock Exchange prices will continue to rise despite higher interest rates. In so far as a credit restriction does work, it works on house building and consumer credit and on small businesses.

A sufficient check to expenditure, however it is produced, may react on the large investors by dimming prospects of profit. Then, what was intended by the authorities as a mild dampening of the boom may turn into a serious recession. Experience has shown that monetary policy cannot be a nice regulator of an economy. It cannot have an appreciable effect without having too much.

(e) Stop-go

A serious drawback to every kind of anti-cyclical policy is the time that it takes to act. First, the authorities have to make up their minds that some action is necessary. While they are brooding over the situation, either a boom is building up or unemployment is rising to an alarming extent. Then the remedies decided take time to be effective. Once effective, they are followed still later by the secondary consequences of a change in the rate of investment on consumption expenditure and of a change in consumption expenditure on investment (via current profits, and so expected profits), so that, from time to time, the authorities are obliged to kill off a boom which they began by encouraging, or to pump out expenditure to check a recession which followed from their own success in killing a boom.

All the same, though compared with the promise of a high and stable level of employment, performance has not been perfect compared with the devastating experience of the great slump, postwar capitalism can claim credit for a very remarkable change in its behaviour.

3. Open economies

Until now, we have discussed employment policy from a purely internal point of view, but not even the United States is entirely free from external influences, and for all other capitalist countries, international problems are the main preoccupation of policy.

(a) The balance of payments

The monetary authorities in each country are concerned with the overall balance of payments. Under a regime of fixed exchange rates, the authorities commit themselves to maintaining their national currency at a particular parity. An adverse balance of payments means an excess demand for foreign currency, so that the exchange rate can be maintained only by allowing an outflow from the reserves of internationally acceptable money (say, gold and dollars) that the authority holds. The authorities are obliged to try to reverse the outflow, otherwise they must admit defeat and allow the exchange rate to fall.

A favourable overall balance of payments, bringing an inflow of reserves, is usually welcome to the monetary authorities of the country enjoying it, but as we shall see, circumstances may arise in which it is embarassing.

We distinguished above, three elements in a national balance of payments, the surplus or deficit on income account, the net flow of long-term capital, and inflow and outflow of short-term borrowing and lending.* Traditional banking policy evolved from the control of short-term flows. Once the gold standard was firmly established, there was never any doubt about the exchange rate of a respectable currency. Then the balance of payments could be regulated by movements of interest rates. Movements of short-term funds (which were, in those days, much smaller than now) were made from one centre to another in response to small differences in the interest rate they could earn. An outflow of gold from London was checked by a rise in Bank Rate, influencing interest rates generally, which made sterling a more attractive currency in which to hold balances. An inflow permitted an expansion in the basis of credit, which brought interest rates down.

The influence of relative interest rates on the movement of short-term lending is still an element in the international monetary system, though no longer the most important.

In a period when there are no particular expectations of changes in exchange rates, funds move from one centre to another on the basis of the relative attraction of the interest rates obtainable. Each country has to keep up with the level of interest rates offered elsewhere. The authorities in a country with a weak balance of payments dare not let its level of interest rates fall, however beneficial it might be to home employment to do so, while the authorities in a country with a strong balance of payments do not often feel compelled to bring their rates down.

Any one country finds its interest rates pulled up or allowed to slip down according to what is happening in other financial centres, without regard to the requirements of its own domestic policy. (This spoils the economists' day dream of the interest rate as the regulator of effective demand.†)

Nowadays, the most important influence on short-term flows arises from expectations of changes in exchange rates. Whenever there is a belief (whether well- or ill-founded) that a particular exchange rate will be depreciated, there is an outflow of short-term funds, and when there is an expectation of appreciation, an inflow. Grieved politicians complain of speculation, but the phenomenon is produced by traders, financial institutions, and owners of wealth prudently trying to avoid losses and make profits, according to the proper rules of the private-enterprise system, which the very same politicians, in other contexts, often extol.

* See **2** 10 §3(a).
† See **2** 8 §3(d).

When the monetary authorities are trying to maintain the exchange rate for their currency in face of a general and well-founded belief that they will be unable to do so, they are bound to lose, for there are indefinitely large funds in the financial world that can be devoted to what appears to be an almost safe bet. To meet this situation, the device of 'floating' the currency is sometimes used. When the authorities allow the exchange rate to go up and down under pressure of supply and demand, a weak exchange rate may fall too far and rise again, or a strong one, rise too high and fall again. Bets on the exchange rate over the immediate future are no longer safe; the one-way movement of funds is checked.

The international monetary system resembles the game of solo whist in which the strongest call is *misère*—an undertaking to lose every trick. The authorities in charge of a weak currency can usually gain an advantage by allowing it to fall.

It is disconcerting that, since 1971, the dollar, which provides the greater part of internationally acceptable currency, has called *misère*. The US authorities have found that an unfavourable balance of payments does them no harm, since the authorities in the surplus countries have to buy dollars so long as they want to prevent their own currencies from appreciating, while if they cease to do so, the dollar will be depreciated, in practice if not in name, which will help to give a boost to the US economy. The traditional lore of central bankers gives no guidance in this situation and they are obliged to look for new ways of dealing with it.

(b) Competitive success

The scope of employment policy for each country depends on its position in world trade. A country which is in a strong competitive position can follow a consistent path of 'export-led growth', while a country in a weak trading position is driven to use short-period expedients that often make its basic situation all the worse.

The authorities of a country for which the value of exports is continuously growing can permit and encourage imports, home investment, and home consumption to grow at the same rate without having to place a periodic 'stop' to a policy of 'go'. Continuous home investment devoted to industrial development involves technical progress and keeps up the original competitive advantage over other trading countries.

Export-led growth is certainly to be preferred to import-led stagnation, but there are problems and difficulties that arise even for a country in this situation.

Firstly, it is not immune from inflation. A long-run of near-full employment sets up the spiral rise of profits, wages, and prices. The rate of inflation is less than in the world market as a whole, partly because output per head is rising faster than in other trading countries. Exports are not yet much impeded by it, but it still is a great nuisance at home. (This is discussed further below.)

Secondly, a continuous surplus of exports may be a wasteful use of resources from the standpoint of the national economy as a whole. A current surplus permits a corresponding capital outflow to take place without the authorities needing to try to curb it. This is convenient for firms that wish to make investments abroad, or for rentiers who want to acquire foreign placements. But while the long export-led boom goes on, firms and rentiers may prefer to keep money at home. The current surplus, not offset by foreign lending, brings an inflow of reserves. Thus, all the labour, technical ingenuity, and salesmanship which goes into the surplus of exports is earning nothing for the home economy, considered as a whole, except unnecessary foreign exchange reserves. More imports or more socially beneficial home investment might be considered preferable.

But it is rare for the monetary authorities really to object to a favourable balance of payments, and the workers as well as the capitalists in export industries have a powerful vested interest in their profitability. Imports are increasing but protection may still be necessary for backward elements in the generally prosperous economy. The argument that resources could be better used than in an export surplus will not find influential backers.

Pressure comes from outside. The current surpluses of one country are matched by the deficits of others. But the government of every industrial nation regards it as right and normal to have a current surplus. A deficit calls for strenuous efforts to correct it. Capitalist industry is always somewhat in a buyer's market, with capacity to produce more than can be profitably sold, and the nations are always in danger of falling into a beggar-my-neighbour scramble, each to safeguard its own share in the limited world market. (This situation arises, not from a general slump as in the 'thirties, but from the competitive strains set up by unequal rates of growth.) The United States uses political means to curb exports from the surplus countries and obliges them to appreciate their currencies. It does not do to be *too* successful.

The Mercantilist policies of the seventeenth century were largely concerned with fighting over trade (and loot) in what is now the Third World. The New Mercantilism is more concerned with trade among the industrial nations themselves, so that the competitive struggle takes more devious forms. At the same time, there is a growing threat from some parts of the so-called underdeveloped world as well, where a labour force with an Oriental level of wages is being equipped with Western techniques. So far, the rich countries have succeeded in limiting imports from these countries while continuing to make pious pronouncements about aiding development.

(c) Competitive weakness

A country in a weak competitive position (of which the UK in recent years has been the leading example) suffers from a tendency to develop an unfavourable balance of payments that has to be corrected. The policies available to correct an unwanted current deficit are to increase protection, either selectively or by an overall surcharge on the value of imports; to depreciate the currency (by a single step or 'floating' downwards); and to dampen effective demand and cause unemployment. (A fourth policy, advocated by those who argued in favour of the UK joining the Common Market, is to *reduce* protection in the hope that the cold wind of competition will improve the performance of home industry.)

304

Protection invites retaliation. Depreciation is an immediate remedy against an adverse balance of payments, by reversing movements of funds made in expectation that the exchange rate is going to fall. Its effect on the balance of trade depends very much on the general situation in the world market. It may do the trick soon, it may bring slow or partial relief, or it may be swamped and made irrelevant by an upswing in world activity.

It is to be observed that floating the exchange rate is a useful device against speculative flows of short-term balances; it cannot be relied on to keep the balance on income account in good order. Firstly, the exchange rate reacts to the overall balance of payments, not the balance of trade alone. The authorities in a country in a weak position want the exchange rate to float downwards to stimulate exports but, if at the same time they raise interest rates to restrain home activity, an inflow of short-term loans may make the exchange rate float upwards. Secondly, when a depreciation is brought about, it cannot be relied on to correct a deficit in the balance of trade quickly, even if it will do so within a year or two. Finally, the immediate rise in home prices of imports (particularly if these include foodstuffs) may lead to such pressure for raising money-wage rates that the depreciation will be offset before it has had time to be effective. To think that a floating exchange rate could be a perfect regulator of the balance of trade, as opposed to the balance of payments, is another economists' day dream.

To postpone a devaluation that, in the end, turns out to be inescapable and to fight against it by deflation and unemployment can be clearly seen after the event to have been stupid, but it is not always clear in advance what ought to be done.

The immediate effect of unemployment produced by monetary and fiscal dampers is to reduce imports of raw materials and ingredients of investment. (There is an extra fall for a time, while stocks are running down. Thereafter, imports recover to the lower level appropriate to the reduced home activity.) Reduced home income also checks sales of imported consumption goods. Firms finding the home market shrinking may be more eager to export. Thus, an artificial recession in one country sets up a tendency to improve its balance of trade.

It used to be thought that unemployment brings a more fundamental remedy. If it slows down the rate of rise of money-wage rates, while in other countries the rise remains rapid, the basic competitive disadvantage of the weak country is lessened. (The effect is similar to devaluation.) With lower relative costs, it should be able to return to a higher level of employment without recreating the deficit.

Nowadays, it sometimes seems that advertising unemployment as a remedy against inflation pours oil on the fire of trade-union intransigence, and causes wages to rise all the more.

The traditional mechanism for correcting imbalance is the rise of money-wage rates in the countries where productivity is rising fastest.* This does occur (after the 'reserve army' of labour has been absorbed into employment) but wages rise also in a slow-growing country. Recent British and American experience shows that there

* See **2** 10 §2(b).

may be a long run of years during which the labour cost per unit output remains higher in the industries of the weak countries compared with that of their stronger competitors.

An important consequence of differential movements in costs is to bring about changes in the share of profits within the various trading countries. We have seen that, in relation to home production for home sales, gross margins are generally held fairly constant. Prices move closely with prime costs, so that the overall share of wages in the value of output is little affected by movements of money-wage rates, but international competition is not softened by the mutual forbearance of a group of oligopolists sharing a growing market. Firms competing with foreign rivals cannot automatically raise prices when home costs go up. Thus, in the less successful countries, profit margins are squeezed. The resulting rise in real wages at home increases consumption, but a large part of this falls upon imports.

A decline in profits depletes the liquid reserves of firms which provide finance for investment and, at the same time, impairs the prospects of profit which provide the motive for investment. A decline in the rate of investment exacerbates the basic trouble—a relatively low rate of technical progress.

The situation is full of contradictions. Firms in the weak country may be anxious to invest abroad, which increases the haemorrhage of industry at home, and at the same time, weakens the balance of payments. Exchange depreciation brings temporary relief, but only by raising the home cost of living and so making the demand for higher money wages harder to resist. In an attempt to keep up the inducement to invest, the government may succeed in shifting the burden of taxation from profits to wages. 'Incomes policy' is advocated as a way of checking the rise of money-wage rates, or a once-for-all 'freeze' is decreed in order to break the momentum of inflation. There is an outbreak of class war against a labour force that has come to expect a continuously rising level of real-wage rates by capitalists who are no longer able to provide it.

A country which is in a weak position in the world market, but strong in political power, brings pressure to bear on too-successful competitors, both the faster-growing industrial nations and those struggling to emerge from 'underdevelopment'. It makes exceptions for itself in the rules of free trade and fixed exchange rates, which it imposed on the world when its own competitive position was unchallenged. This creates great confusion in world trade, as well as in the teaching of the economists for whom the doctrine of the universal benefits of the free play of market forces is an article of faith.

4. Growth

(a) Economic miracles

Over the twenty-five years following the end of the Second World War, some nations were less successful than others in managing effective demand, but for the capitalist economy as a whole it was a period of a long boom, interrupted by only minor set-backs. Accumulation, embodying technical innovations, was maintained at an unprecedented level. The great growth of scientific manpower, much fostered by the rivalry of the big powers, generated new knowledge at a vertiginous rate, accelerating the pace of technical development. Much has gone into extravagant or horrible forms but there has been a spin-off into a growth of mass consumption which puts formerly middle-class luxuries, such as private cars, washing machines, and foreign travel, at the disposal of most of the population. The very success of this experience is producing side effects which are a cause of anxiety as the decade of the seventies unrolls.

(b) Inflation

It was obvious from the first that continuous near-full employment, without other change in institutions and attitudes, would lead to a continuously rising price level. The only way to combine high employment with stable prices would be to control the growth of incomes in money terms, but there were too many difficulties in the way of doing so, and too many powerful interests opposed to the attempt. (Only the Netherlands ran a successful incomes policy for some years, and when it broke down, their rate of inflation was higher than anywhere else.) Apart from the strains in international trade discussed above, inflation has serious internal consequences, especially when it has been going on long enough to have become habitual. Firstly, it favours property at the expense of earnings, for when an expectation of rising prices in the future has become normal, the money value today of an income-yielding asset is raised by the belief that its money value will be higher in the future. Purchasing power is continually falling into the lap of owners of shares in successful businesses, land, houses, and old masters; this can be realized at any moment, and used to purchase goods and services today. Furthermore, all kinds of property then become a vehicle for speculation; finance is deflected from productive investment to buying pre-existing property for resale.

Secondly, among earnings, pensions, and payments to relieve poverty, inflation is continuously redistributing real income in favour of groups in the strongest bargaining position from those in the weakest. At any moment, the majority of households find that prices have risen since the last time that their money income was raised, while a minority are enjoying a recent rise of money income that, for the time being, surpasses the rise of prices. This sets up a game of catch-as-catch-can, played in an atmosphere of bitterness and mutual recrimination, in which the old and the poor and families with young children always lose out.

Once the inflationary process has taken hold, it cannot be checked by an artificial recession. Those countries where effective demand was damped in the early 'seventies found themselves in the worst of both worlds. Unemployment rose and the growth of real income was checked, but prices went on rising all the same.

In Britain, the authorities plead with the trade unions to exercise restraint in their demands for money wages, and appeal to patriotism by pointing out that the trade of the nation is crippled by rising costs. Moreover, it is said that if profits do not recover, British firms will invest abroad instead of at home; the salaries of top executives must be kept up, otherwise the 'best brains' will leave the country. In short, the workers should be patriotic, but the capitalists need not be. It remains to be seen whether voluntary agreements to limit the rise of wages and prices, or a statutory 'freeze', can be made to work without some more thoroughgoing change in attitudes on both sides of the wage bargain.

(c) Poverty in the midst of plenty

To make growth in statistical GNP the main criterion of economic success is often justified by the argument that a rise in the total level of consumption (or rather of purchases) of goods for the population as a whole will eliminate poverty. Twenty-five years of unprecedented 'growth' still leave the elimination of poverty to the future. In every capitalist country (except perhaps in Scandinavia) there are many individuals and families living below the level of subsistence, in the sense that they cannot provide for the basic physical needs for food, shelter, warmth, and decency.

There does not seem to be much prospect that *more* growth would be a better remedy for this situation than the growth we have already had. In a competitive system there are bound to be losers as well as winners, and so long as there is not really full employment there are bound to be 'unemployables' in industry and the professions, for the least-clever or least-conformist individuals fail to get jobs and then appear not to be worth employing at current levels of pay.

The very lowest incomes, of the destitute, the unemployed, the aged, and so on, are maintained in most countries by social security payments. The argument is often used that if only GNP grew faster, these payments could be increased. But, here also, there is a contradiction; growth depends, for each country, on its position in international competition; each must be careful not to put too great a burden on its industry in the attempt to eliminate poverty, for fear of hampering the 'growth' on which the elimination of poverty is believed to depend.

For those with low earnings, or none, the purchasing power of what money they have is kept down by the very fact of average affluence, for the type of goods that are offered for sale, the packaging, advertising and price, are designed to appeal to the mass market. As growth goes on, more and more simple and cheap products disappear from output for, obviously, there is least profit to be made out of providing for the poorest.*

'Growth', so far, has not eliminated absolute poverty in the richest nations. Obviously, it cannot be expected to eliminate relative poverty. Everyone's idea of a reasonable standard of life is set by people somewhat better off than themselves. A rise in the average level of consumption increases physical comfort but, in the nature of the case, cannot increase satisfaction.

* See **2** 7 §2(c).

'Poverty in the midst of plenty' was a slogan of the great slump. Then, it pointed to potential output running to waste in unemployment. It has a different meaning for a family today, goggling at television advertisements for ever-new commodities that they cannot afford to buy.

(d) Migration

The relatively high level of real wages provided by capitalist industry attracts workers from the less-developed fringe of southern Europe and from the Third World. Some come for a few years and take a large part of their earnings home. Others settle and bring their families. The native population treats them as inferiors and resents their presence. Where colour is involved this attitude is especially pronounced, but as Italians in Switzerland and Catholics in Ulster can testify, colour is by no means the only source of ill feeling.

Looking at the matter from the migrants' viewpoint, no doubt it would be better if they could get a good living at home but, as things are, it is clearly a benefit to them to be able to earn abroad, even if the social conditions are unpleasant.

From the point of view of workers in countries receiving immigrants, the situation is more complicated. On the one hand, an influx of cheap labour permits capitalist firms to grow all the faster and to pay higher wages to their native labour force. The immigrants take heavy and unpleasant jobs and keep down the cost of services that better-paid workers as well as rentiers can enjoy. On the other hand, if the cheap labour were not available, production and services would have to be reorganized in such a way that they could pay wages at the native level. It is noticeable that, in Australian cities, the necessary services are provided somehow or other, without the help of low-wage immigrants, and that the statistical measure of the share of wages in the value of output in recent years was higher in Australia than in any other capitalist country.[2]

From a political standpoint, the existence of immigrant workers is generally bad for the labour movement; native workers allow their protests against unemployment, inadequate housing, and so on, to be deflected into protests against the immigrants. Enlightened self-interest of trade unions requires them to organize the immigrants, and help them to raise their wages and conditions, but it is hard for this policy to make head against the xenophobia of their native rank and file. All this, *mutatis mutandis*, is true of the home-born non-white population of the USA.

(e) Pollution

At the beginning of this century, Pigou pointed out that it is a serious defect in the system of *laissez-faire* that producers bear only the costs that they pay for.* The production of commodities throws costs upon society that are not paid for and do

2. *Patterns of Industrial Growth, 1938–58* UN Department of Economic and Social Affairs, 1960.
* See **1** 3 §6(a).   **309**

not enter into prices. He took the mild example of the smoke nuisance. In recent times, the poisoning of air and water, destruction of amenities, and consumption of irreplaceable natural resources have reached such a stage that even the most complacent apostles of *laissez-faire* have had to take notice of them.

Once the problem is recognized, the technical difficulties of dealing with it could be overcome. The scientific discoveries and technological ingenuity that have created modern industry could be applied to cleaning it up. Where some process cannot be used without emitting poison, another process may be found to replace it; if not, the product could be dispensed with. The difficulties are political and economic rather than technical.

The main difficulty arises out of competition. Producers compete with each other by making innovations to save costs and to make their commodities attractive in variety and packaging. To frame rules that would check deleterious production, not only that exists already, but that might be produced under pressure of competition in the future, would be far from easy, and every rule that is introduced is bitterly resisted. A public outcry can be raised against some gross abuse, such as dumping cyanide where children play, or destroying the fish in rivers to which anglers are devoted, but the general population, as motorists and shoppers, support pollution by making a market for it even when, as citizens, they may disapprove of it. Workers, also, are suspicious of the cry against the firms that employ them, fearing that if they are prevented from making profits, employment and rising wages will be endangered.

The strongest card the polluters can play is always international competition. Any country that hampers the activities of its industry will be in danger of losing exports.

Pollution and the irreparable loss of resources, both for production and pleasure, provide the most obvious and notorious objection to the doctrine that the free play of market forces in a regime of *laissez-faire* leads to beneficial results for society as a whole. Some economists try to recapture lost ground by advocating that a price be put upon the damage that pollution does, and industry be obliged to pay it. This would mean that firms who found it sufficiently profitable to poison us could buy the right to do so.

The whole argument is obfuscated by the conception of 'growth'. In recent years, it has been fashionable to measure the success of a national economy by its rate of growth of GNP. GNP is a statistical measure of the sales value of goods and services at the prices ruling at some base date.* The index, in the nature of the case, cannot take account of any values not expressed in money. It is necessarily an imperfect measure of what used to be called the 'moral and material progress of the nation'. It is, at best, a measure of the growth of economic power in the world market. The British have given themselves an inferiority complex because their rate of 'growth' has been relatively slow in the postwar era. Now the cry is raised that growth causes destruction and ought to be stopped. A better argument for the anti-pollutionists would be that, if the true costs of production were included in the calculation of

* Cf. **2** 7 §3(a).

GNP, growth might very well be negative, so that it is really they who are in favour of positive growth.

But even this argument would imply accepting total *national* product or *average* income per head as a measure of economic success. The neoclassical economists were obliged by the logic of their own argument to admit that the total utility obtained from a given flow of goods and services depends on its distribution among consumers. The principle of falling marginal utility of income points to complete equality of distribution as the ideal. The neoclassicals managed to tone down this conclusion by arguing that some people have a greater susceptibility to pleasure than others, so that to maximize total welfare they should be provided with pro-portionately higher incomes.* But they could hardly maintain that susceptibility to malnutrition and disease are not much the same for everyone. Today, the uncounted costs of pollution are highest (in city slums) for families with the lowest level of consumption of goods and services; the inequality of distribution of income measured in human terms is much greater than in terms of shares in GNP.

Proposals for policy necessarily run into conflicts of interest and incompatibility of judgements. Every participant in the debate has his own prejudices. But there is one prejudice which is fairly widespread, that is, in favour of bringing up healthy children. The best hope for the anti-pollutionists is to enlist this sentiment on their side of the case.

(f) What now?

Long-range economic predictions are never fulfilled. Marx was the boldest prophet, and much of what he foresaw has come to pass, but he certainly did not expect capitalism to be flourishing as never before, 125 years after the *Communist Manifesto* was published, and he did not expect that socialist revolutions would succeed best in the least-developed economies.

Looking forward in the 'seventies, an optimist might predict that the great corpora-tions, at least in Western Europe, will adopt a policy of enlightened self-interest, and develop a Swedish type of welfare capitalism that will be sufficiently satisfactory, or perhaps sufficiently soporific, to keep their populations from asking for anything more; and that in the United States, cynicism and brutality will be overcome by a revival of the ideals of democracy and peace.

A Marxist may still be looking forward to a revolution raised by the industrial working class, and arguing that it will establish a more progressive kind of socialism than the USSR has been able to achieve.

A pessimist may expect future crises to lead to unsuccessful revolts that will be harshly repressed and leave the last state worse than the first.

Perhaps elements of all three scenarios may mingle in a long, uneasy period of confusion.

* See **1** 3 §2(a).

One prediction that can be made with some confidence is that the governments and corporations in the capitalist sphere will be slow and reluctant to heed the warnings of the biologists about the effect on the capacity of the planet to support a life of 'growth' in the wealthy nations, and that the state of the world will certainly get worse before it begins to get better.

Chapter Two

Socialist states

The most interesting and important questions raised by the existence of socialist economies in the world today are concerned with politics and morality. Here, we can touch only on some points on which economic analysis can hope to throw light. The nations (and two half-nations) that call themselves socialist are very various, and each is deeply marked by its former history and its modern experience; all they have in common is the fact that their economies are not dominated by private enterprise and therefore have to be centrally controlled. When production is planned by a single authority there are two kinds of problems: one, how to plan what ought to be produced, the other, how to see that the plan is carried out. This raises a number of problems that do not appear in a capitalist economy, and eliminates many that do.

1. Another set of problems

As we have seen, in the modern world the government of a capitalist country is concerned with the level of employment, the balance of payments, the balance of trade and the price level, without having sufficient instruments to control them all. These problems take a very different form in a planned economy.

(a) Employment

A planned economy is not subject to fluctuations in effective demand. The overall ratio of investment to consumption is settled by the plan. Industrial enterprises, which are organs of the socialist state, recruit workers to fulfil their planned assignments, and so distribute the labour force between sectors as the plan requires. The rate at which workers are drawn out of agriculture depends primarily on the rate at which investment is expanding industry, creating jobs for them.

313

The geographical distribution of the labour force and the training of recruits with various types of qualifications are designed to fit in with planned developments, instead of being left to the decisions of profit-seeking firms. The fit will never be exact. So long as rapid industrialization is going on, there is an excess demand for every kind of skill; the educational pipeline is widened to meet it and when the pace of development slackens, too many, or the wrong types, of qualified personnel are trained. However, these problems are less severe and more easily remedied in a fully planned system than under a regime of stop–go.*

In Soviet industry, there is a great deal of what a capitalist employer would regard as wasted labour. A socialist enterprise is not allowed to declare any of its workers redundant. Once they are on the payroll, management has to find them something to do. Moreover, an enterprise may be obliged to take on workers who happen to be available in the neighbourhood, whether more hands are needed or not. The revolution was made in the name of the working class; the principal benefit that they have got from it is a guarantee against unemployment.

(b) International trade

The attitude to trade in the planned economies is different from that of the New Mercantilism. They want to export only to be able to pay for imports (apart from some loans and subventions to allies and supporters).

For any country (even a huge one), foreign exchange is more valuable than home resources, for with foreign exchange it can go shopping among the varied resources of the world. This is especially important for a latecomer among sophisticated industrial economies. Exports, therefore, are highly desirable, but at the same time they involve a sacrifice, a sacrifice of home resources and labour time, which however, is worth making to get something that can contribute more to home development than what is given up.

This is more rational than Mercantilism as a general point of view, but trade has to be managed by some kind of bureaucracy so that it may often be irrational in detail. Moreover, in the Soviet sphere (though not in China) commercial expertise is despised as unworthy of socialism so that opportunities for a good bargain are often missed.

The greater part of socialist trade is arranged bilaterally. Each country aims to balance the imports taken from each other country against exports made to it.

Even among themselves, the socialist countries of Eastern Europe have not gone very far, despite considerable efforts to develop a system of trade that would enable them to enjoy the advantages of specialization and international division of labour.

In this respect, socialist economies are more nationalistic than capitalist ones, perhaps because the trade of each is controlled by its own bureaucrats, while the personnel of a capitalist firm owes its loyalty to the business rather than to a nation.

Deals between socialist countries are carried out at world prices, and their

* See **3** 1 §2(e).

officials take a good deal of trouble to find out what the appropriate prices are. The reason for this is not that they want to measure their own costs by capitalist standards, but that it is convenient for them to have some outside criterion to settle bargains among themselves. This system of trading limits the benefits to be got from international specialization; at the same time it keeps a planned economy, in the main, free from the perturbations of the world market and insulates it from the influence of international finance.

(c) Inflation

In socialist industry, grades of wages and salaries are set in money terms, and the prices of goods to be sold to the public are fixed centrally. An excess of the flow of money demand over the money value of the goods offered to meet it leads to shortages, and distribution by shopping power in the manner described above.* A rise of prices can follow only to a limited extent in permitted or illicit second-hand sales. This situation may be described as suppressed inflation. An enterprise suffering from a shortage of labour may sometimes upgrade workers so that they can be paid more, and succeeds in being allowed to draw a larger wage fund. This generates a mild degree of open inflation. But there cannot be the kind of general and persistent inflation of money wages, profits, and prices that is familiar in latter-day capitalism.

One clear and indisputable advantage of socialist industry over private enterprise is that it can continuously maintain a 'high and stable level of employment' without suffering from inflation.

(d) Public finance

Personal taxation provides a small part of the state revenue in the USSR and Eastern Europe, and none in China. The great bulk of the funds required for government expenditure, including almost the whole of investment, is raised by turnover taxes and the profits of industrial enterprises, which enter into the selling prices of manufactures,† and from the profit on sales of agricultural products.

To pay indirect taxes in the normal course of shopping is less irritating than to have to part with an equivalent amount of purchasing power to the tax gatherer. Furthermore, this system obviates most of the undesired side effects of taxation.‡ It does not involve a large amount of expensively educated personnel in the activity, on the one side, of enforcing taxation and, on the other, of legally avoiding it. Moreover, this system leaves little scope for outright illegality.

In the capitalist world, the system of taxation has at least to appear to make some correction of the unequal distribution of purchasing power between families which offends democratic sentiment. In contemporary socialist societies, the dream of

* See **2** 11 §1(e).
† See **2** 11 §1(a).
‡ See **2** 7 §3(c).   **315**

Communism—to each according to his need—is still far distant. (The Chinese accuse the Soviets of receding from it rather than moving towards it.) There are considerable inequalities in earnings and privileges, but since there is no property in the means of production, there are no private fortunes and no legal means of making money by speculation. If it were not so, the simple method of collecting the revenue from all alike through a mark-up in prices would not be tolerable.

Another important difference between the socialist and the capitalist system is that, in the socialist system, the funds representing the whole surplus of production over consumption are pooled under a single authority. In the private-enterprise system, the greater part of the funds for industrial investment accrue, in the form of retained profits, to individual firms and another part is drawn from household savings. Under socialism, the funds for investment are controlled by the same authority as is the rest of the revenue. This, of course, is a necessary condition for central planning of investment. It also has the effect of removing the distinction between private and public expenditure on education, medical assistance, and other social services.

In the private-enterprise economy, taxation to pay for these services is felt to be a burden, particularly by households well-enough off to purchase them for them-selves. In a planned economy, there is no such resistance to any beneficial outlay that social policy dictates. To put it at no higher level, a healthy population, trained for all necessary tasks, is the greatest asset of the national economy.

At the same time, the monolithic system of finance for cultural life supports the power of obscurantists and philistines in authority to persecute and suppress originality.

(e) Alienation

In one respect, Soviet industry is more like capitalist industry in practice than it is supposed to be in theory. In theory, the equipment that Soviet workers operate belongs to them as members of the 'state of the whole people'; wages are not a payment for work but a share in the product of the national economy. But, in daily life, industry may be no less tedious and inhuman in a socialist factory than in a capitalist one, discipline may be no less irksome, and the pay packet no less the main inducement to put up with it. Once management has lost the goodwill of the workers, neither the stick of harsh penalties nor the carrot of bonus payments can elicit efficiency.

The greatest problem for all countries in the Soviet sphere is to find some way to get the workers to work; it is made all the more difficult by the cynicism which has been generated by years of sanctimonious official propaganda.

When Yugoslavia broke out of the Stalinist orbit, a system of workers' control was introduced which, in effect, gave property in each enterprise to the labour force that happened to be operating it. This gave workers the same strong motive to run the business profitably that the technostructure has in a capitalist firm. At the same time, it brought other characteristics of capitalism in its train. The most successful

316

groups, which made the most profit, were interested in building up their own businesses, not in contributing to development in parts of the country that needed it more. Unemployment persisted and inequalities developed to a point that threatened to discredit the whole experiment. The Chinese seek to overcome alienation by political education and by consultation between management, technicians and workers, giving everyone a feeling of concern for production.

Meanwhile, the most advanced capitalist management has come to the conclusion that work would be more efficient if it were more interesting. Perhaps they will soon be giving the Soviets a lead.

2. Agriculture

The problem of inducing the workers to work is even more acute in agriculture than industry. It is easier to organize and supervise production in a factory than on the land and industrial technique is something that can be studied and learned, while the lore of the cultivator is largely an inarticulate tradition. For agricultural production, the socialist countries mainly rely on some kind of cooperative system or on independent peasants, so that the income of the individual is closely related to the work he does.

(a) Extracting the surplus

The development of industry depends on the existence of an agricultural surplus— an excess of the net output of food over what the cultivators eat. (Agricultural products are also important as raw materials and for export.) The manner in which the surplus is extracted from agriculture has a great influence on the manner in which a socialist economy develops.

The physical product that workers can produce by cultivating the soil depends on its fertility as well as on the technique in use and the hours of work put in. The share which the cultivator can keep for himself of the product he wins from the land depends on the manner in which he is induced, or compelled, to part with the rest. So long as there is property in land, the surplus is extracted by means of payments of rent in one form or another. A socialist revolution abolishes rent and allocates land to particular groups of cultivators. Then taxation in kind or delivery quotas are substituted for rent. The prices of agricultural products in terms of industrial products are fixed partly in relation to the degree of compulsion that can be exercised—the lower the price, the more the force required to get the cultivators to produce and deliver—and partly in relation to political considerations: the relative benefits to be offered to agricultural and industrial workers. The theory that prices are, or should be, determined by labour value has no application, for here, the value that each man produces has no meaning apart from prices to be attached to his particular product.

317

(b) The terms of trade

In a capitalist economy, to leave the terms of trade between agriculture and industry to be determined in a free market leads to continuous fluctuations, with generally an average level below the long-run supply price of agricultural labour. For this reason, all developed industrial nations have some form of political control over agricultural prices, and it is generally aimed at supporting incomes in that sector rather than depressing them.*

In economies which try to industrialize in more or less free market conditions the opposite problem arises. An increase in urban employment leads to an increase in demand for food. The supply is inelastic, so that prices rise (whether the benefit goes mainly to cultivators or landlords); consequently, it is necessary to raise money-wage rates in industry; the money demand for food goes up, and so on round. The textbook notion of market prices tending to establish equilibrium between supply and demand is not much use in either situation.

(c) Political prices

In the USSR under Stalin, there was a strong drive to develop heavy industry. Whatever consumer goods were produced were put at the disposal of the rapidly growing labour force in industry. Very little could be offered to cultivators to spend money on. The surplus from agriculture had to be taken by force. Attempts to improve productivity at the same time did not have much success. A similar formula was followed in most of the East European socialist countries, though in a less brutal manner. After industry in the USSR had recovered from wartime destruction, the terms of trade were turned somewhat in favour of agriculture, and a flourishing market economy developed on the private plots which collective farms allowed for peasant cultivation. All the same, it seems that agriculture has not got over its bad start and that it sets a drag on the development of countries in the Soviet sphere.

In China, collectivization was carried out in a manner that helped the cultivators to help themselves, and it brought an immediate benefit to the majority—'the poor and lower-middle peasants'. The surplus is taken partly in the form of a tax and partly in the form of quota sales at fixed prices. Quotas are allocated on the principle that each group of cultivators should keep enough to feed themselves. The surplus, therefore, is taken from those who can best afford to part with their crops. Learning by the mistakes of the Soviets, the Chinese planners arrange that the cultivators are provided with attractive things to spend money on, so that they are glad to earn it. As industrial production develops, the terms of trade are shifted appreciably in favour of agriculture.

Economic analysis can help us to examine the consequences of these various types of price system, but the reasons for them must be found in political history.

* See **2** 5 §5(b).

3. Projected reforms

At present, an urgent problem in the Soviet sphere is how to use the productive capacity that has been accumulated with such heroic efforts, to raise the standard of life of the population. During the great drive for accumulation, the feeling prevailed that only heavy industry was important; consumption goods were not serious. Now the emphasis has changed, but institutions and ideology cannot easily be adapted to fresh objectives.

(a) What is an enterprise?

One element in the attempts at reform which petered out in Poland and were crushed in Czechoslovakia was concerned with the degree of independence and initiative of an enterprise. In the Soviet system, the director of an enterprise is an officer of the state. He has been put in charge of a particular installation, permitted to draw a certain wage fund from the bank, and instructed as to what materials to use and what output to produce. Since the instructions that he is given and the criteria according to which he can claim bonuses are detailed and sometimes inconsistent, he has to wangle and bend the rules, whether he is sincerely concerned with production or only with his own career.

To cut through the red tape and encourage initiative, the reformers proposed to introduce some form of imitation profit system into the management of enterprises. Instead of innumerable directives in physical terms, an enterprise should be given a single instruction. In one variant, this is to maximize the excess of the money value of sales over costs; in another, to recover from the market the costs of production of the flow of output, in which should be included a tax on the wage bill and the assessed value of capital equipment. The enterprise is not to earn profits for itself, as in Yugoslavia, but earnings are to be taken as a criterion of success.

The concept of using the profit criterion without the profit motive raises a number of difficulties. The first concerns the prices at which goods are to be sold by an enterprise. If an enterprise is free to set its own prices, each manager has an incentive to organize his group of workers to exploit the public—the workers in general—by allowing themselves higher margins or by being more slack about costs; this allows the profit motive to creep in behind the profit criterion.

On the other hand, if prices are to be centrally fixed, there are bound to be anomalies. When a price list is first rationalized, there are striking improvements, for the old prices were completely arbitrary, out of touch both with costs of production and with consumer demand, but a new price list will soon become ossified again.

Some of the would-be reformers advocated making prices flexible, so as to maintain equilibrium between demand and supply in the manner depicted in Western textbooks. As we have seen, the textbooks are misleading on this point.*

The second layer of difficulties is concerned with the meaning of efficiency. What

* See **2** 11 §1(d).   **319**

is supposed to be the relation of the management of an enterprise to its labour force? One of the drawbacks of the system is said to be a wasteful use of labour. Is an enterprise, then, to be charged with getting rid of redundant workers—and who will arrange for them to be re-employed? Is it the business of management to speed up production´ and to insist on quality? How is this to be done if the workers do not agree? Indeed, does an enterprise consist of its whole personnel or of an employer whose business it is to get the best possible bargain in the labour market?

Thirdly, the profit criterion does not give sufficient guidance in the day to day management of an enterprise. The decisions that have to be taken, at every level, are concerned with people and with things. The calculation of costs and profits is a post-mortem examination of what has been done. It can show how the last lot of problems that came up were dealt with, but the next lot will not be the same.

The main obstacle to reforms, however, comes from the objections of the bureaucracy to giving up the power that it enjoys over industry and allowing more independence and initiative to managers, technicians, and engineers.

(b) Political consciousness

Chinese Communists have made a careful study of the Soviet system in order, as they say, to learn from its achievements *and* its mistakes. The main point, of course, is concerned with agriculture but there are also some interesting differences between Chinese and Soviet policy concerning manufactures.

The Chinese early discovered the secret of controlling production at the wholesale stage. Those capitalists who remained after Liberation in 1949 (mainly in the textile industry in the coastal cities) were encouraged to carry on production. They were supplied with materials and their output was bought, at prices which allowed a margin reckoned to be sufficient to cover the wage bill and a reasonable profit. (These enterprises were finally absorbed into socialist industry in 1956, and their owners paid 5 per cent on the assessed value of their assets for the next ten years.)

The whole supply of consumption goods is organized on this system. The Department of Commerce, in every locality, arranges contracts or buying agreements with producers, and passes commodities to the shops. Prices to the public and to the enterprises are fixed, and the assortment of goods to be produced is regulated according to the rise or fall of stocks, so that demand has a direct and immediate influence on supply.

The various enterprises in each line dovetail their plans to secure the flow of materials; the shops keep the Department of Commerce in each locality informed of what the public seems to want; enterprises also keep in direct touch with department stores and village shops to fit their designs to the wishes of their customers. The system of production on contracts also controls the relations between investment-good industries under the national and regional plans. An enterprise has no concern with sales, only with production; prices are fixed, and individual bonuses for plan fulfilment, and so forth, have been abolished. Each enterprise has its allotted labour force and staff. The workers, as much as management, are taught to feel concerned about efficiency, quality, technical progress, and economy of materials and power. The system is not controlled by profitability or by any one-dimensional criterion of success, but by self-respect, or as the Chinese put it, by the high level of political consciousness of the workers.

When the original ideals of socialism have been worn down by years of cynicism and discouragement, they cannot be restored merely by making some alterations in the directives given to industry. No doubt, there will be important changes in the Soviet sphere, but no one can guess today what form they are going to take.

Chapter Three

The Third World

A large number of countries do not fit into the category either of fully developed capitalism or of socialist planning, the majority being successor states of former empires, from which they have established some degree of independence. For want of a better term, these countries are referred to as the Third World.

They are extremely various in history, geography, social structure, and traditions. The three continents—Asia, Africa, and Latin America—each have their own characters, marked by historical evolution, and within each there is a wide variety of political and economic situations. In so far as all these countries have a characteristic in common, it is that they have been left out of the development that accompanies the growth of modern industry or that they have been forced into the position of 'hewers of wood and drawers of water' for the great capitalist powers. Now that they are nominally independent (apart from those that are fighting for freedom from an old-fashioned colonial regime or kept peaceful in thinly disguised neocolonialism), their spokesmen have adopted the conception that they are 'developing countries', implying that it is possible and desirable for them to catch up and enjoy some of the advantages of wealth and power that the industrialized nations have attained.

Here, even more than in the other two groups of countries, politics dominate over economics, for in each of these emergent states, economic policy is involved with the type of society that it is building up. Is development intended to aim primarily at feeding the people and overcoming the grossest misery, or is it primarily to make room for a prosperous middle class, or to defend the privileges of landed property? Is the objective to establish national independence and power that will be taken seriously in the world, or is the position of a satellite acceptable? The political issues are the most interesting, and the most important, but once more, these notes must be confined to the points at which economic analysis is relevant.

1. Underdevelopment

Countries which lack the conveniences and the inconveniences produced by modern industry are generally described as underdeveloped. Underdevelopment, in this sense, has been the normal state of all human societies apart from the few which, in the last two centuries, have applied scientific technology to production and warfare. A basic characteristic of a developed economy is that technology, equipment, and political power enable it to get food and other primary products with a small proportion of its manpower, so that a large proportion is available for industry and other activities. Underdevelopment means that most of the population has to be engaged in producing food; the rest live on the surplus of the cultivator's product over what his family must eat, so that the whole development of society depends on the level of output per head in agriculture.

To rise out of this situation, industrialization is necessary, for industrialization means the application of power to production and transport, to supplement human and animal muscle. The Chinese have shown how much can be done by mobilizing the population to work 'with their bare hands', but output (and therefore consumption) per head cannot begin to rise towards modern levels without mechanical aids. 'Development' is, therefore, rightly identified with industrialization, in the general sense in which it applies as much to agriculture as to manufactures.

Once the industrial revolution has happened anywhere in the world, the situation for all the rest is radically changed. On the one hand, the application of science to technology in the leading countries pioneers the way to high productivity, which can then be followed elsewhere when the political situation allows. On the other hand, the economic and military power that industrialization develops in the leading countries can be used, in brutal or subtle ways, to frustrate attempts to imitate their achievements. At present, the various countries of the Third World are in different phases of pre-capitalist underdevelopment, colonial-distorted development, or incipient modern development.

(a) Landlord and peasant

In some tribal societies, the agricultural surplus is shared by the community and there is no compulsion on any family to produce more than it wants to consume. The superstructure of what is known as 'civilization' has been built on compelling the cultivator to work for others. Many countries of the Third World today remain at the stage at which there is a class of landlords who extract rent and usury from peasants, more or less in the manner described by the Physiocrats,* or who employ labour on their estates at subsistence wages. Since landlords enjoy a traditional style of life, they have no need to bother about productivity. They may, indeed, be positively hostile to improvements which would raise the living standard of the peasants and make them less abject.

* See **1** 1 §2(a).

This method of organizing agriculture keeps the surplus low, and at the same time, consumes a great part of what there is in supporting the households of the land-owners, so that little or none is available to the rest of the economy. Here, Ricardo's view of landed property as an incubus on development still applies with full force.

To tax rent is a way of collecting the surplus for investment to get development going, and at the same time, of putting pressure on landlords to increase productivity, but this method is not used by governments whose political existence depends on the support of the landed interest.

(b) Land reform

In a number of would-be developing countries, some in Asia and a few in Latin America, an attempt has been made to improve the situation of the cultivators by legislation. In some cases, the effect of land reform has been the opposite of its intention. For instance, when the law allows a tenant who has cultivated the same holding for three years running to have some rights in it, the landlord moves tenants around every two years. Sometimes a law has been ineffective, for instance, putting a maximum to the area that one man may own prompts a landowner to distribute his estate nominally among his relatives, and then to carry on as before.

To make a genuine distribution of land to former tenants does not, by itself, solve the problem of low productivity, for as we have seen,* a cultivator needs stock as well as ground to work on. The landlord and moneylender kept the peasant's family alive from harvest to harvest, at however low a level; when he is given a right to the land, he still needs credit. The moneylender, and the dealer who buys the crop cheaply just after the harvest and sells it at prices that rise over the year, appear to the peasants as bloodsuckers, but they are financing a necessary service. Without a source of loans, the peasants may be even worse off than before.

A land reform which is combined with provision of credit may greatly improve the life of the rural population by letting them keep more of their products for themselves. But then they eat more, and less is available to feed the urban population, so that the development of industry is inhibited.

To produce an agricultural surplus without having to rely on the extreme misery of the cultivators, it is necessary to increase productivity, and at the same time, to provide the cultivators with the means and the motive to part with a considerable portion of their products. One way of extracting a surplus from independent peasants is by instituting a tax. The other is by organizing marketing and providing some commodities or services that the rural population want to acquire.

It is not usually much use to try to improve technology before providing an outlet for the available product, but as soon as the peasants have sufficient security to make it worthwhile to improve the land and to take some risks in diversifying produc-tion, they become receptive to new methods of cultivation or new crops, provided that the advantages claimed for them can be demonstrated convincingly.

324   * See **2** 1 §1(b).

To carry out land reform in a quasi-feudal economy without a thoroughgoing revolution invokes opposition not only from the landlords who are to be deprived of their rents and privileges, but from the moneylenders and dealers who have been making a living for themselves by investing finance in the handling of the agricultural product. Some schemes of reform have been rather in the nature of trying to make an omelet without breaking eggs—they aim to help the peasants without injuring anyone else.

In some African countries, however, land reform has been successful in giving the peasantry a stake in the economy, and making them into a reliable conservative force in the political system.

There have been some experiments in land reform and cooperative organization of peasant agriculture which have been more or less successful in overcoming the external difficulties, but then they often run into internal conflicts. In every village, some families are in a better position than others to take advantage of the benefits offered, and a scheme of reform is likely to end up in a situation such as we analysed in the story of the kulak and the poor peasants.* It is not easy for cooperative agriculture to be established except in the framework of a government policy genuinely directed to the interests of the peasantry.

(c) Capitalist farming

Modern methods of irrigation, scientific development of new varieties of crops, and mechanization of cultivation make it possible to take agriculture out of the hands of the old-style landlords and peasants and transform it into a sphere for capitalist investment.

There was already a considerable development, in the colonial period, of cash crops for export.† In some regions, such enterprises are being modernized; in some, more or less successful peasant cultivation continues, while in others, the political situation in a would-be independent country discourages investment by the old plantation owners without putting anything in its place.

A new development of capitalist agriculture in some parts of the Third World has taken over formerly uncultivable land. The deserts of northern Mexico, for instance, have been made highly productive and provide a large surplus for export and to feed cities. The old rural population is left out of this development and continues to exist on low-level subsistence farming.

When capitalist farming is introduced into a densely populated area, as in some parts of Asia, tenants are displaced as the land is bought up to create farms of a convenient size. There is an increase in employment of wage labour to some extent, but the new farmers find tractors easier to manage than men. There is a serious dilemma in this type of development. The new style of farming can be profitable and attract investment only so long as the prices of the main crops—food grains—are

---

* See **2** 1 §2(f).
† See **2** 5 §3(a).

kept up. This means that a continuous increase in agricultural output, from year to year, can be disposed of only if there is a continuous increase in income to be spent on food. If output increases but income is inadequate to provide demand for it, the market will break and high-cost farming will cease to be profitable. But income will not be adequate so long as industry finds it unprofitable to employ workers at a wage high enough to permit them to eat.

(d) Food importers

There are a certain number of countries where an economy has grown up round a single export commodity, such as oil or sugar, which are accustomed to import practically all they consume. Some are situated in deserts. In some, the original inhabitants were long ago wiped out; a population descended from a transplanted labour force has grown beyond the capacity of the cultivable land to support them. So long as the demand for their export commodity keeps up, the people can live and can support a wealthy class—statistical GNP per head in the oil sheikdoms is the highest in the world—but when resources are exhausted, or demand is withdrawn, they are in a hopeless situation.

2. Unemployment

To the authorities in a planned economy, men and women capable of work are, from one point of view, people who must be provided for, and from another, a valuable resource to be used to contribute to economic wealth. In a would-be developing economy in the Third World, unemployed workers are a reproach and a nuisance which, if neglected, may become a political menace. The authorities view their problem as an obligation to try to provide employment, rather than as an opportunity to get something useful done.

(a) Keynesian unemployment

In any mainly private-enterprise economy there is normally some Keynesian un-employment, in the sense that when a chance rise in the level of expenditure occurs, some employers find it profitable to take on more hands and produce more output. Furthermore, in the cities of the Third World, there are great numbers of people living in *disguised unemployment*, offering their services as shoeblacks or porters and trading at street corners, in tiny lots of, say, matches or buttons. A general increase in income and expenditure puts more business in their way.

However, there are narrow limits to the possibility of increasing output merely by increasing effective demand. There is a mass of non-employment due to the fact that the amount of equipment and finance to employ workers is much less than adequate for the potentially available labour force.*

326   * See **2** 3 §4.

A substantial increase in expenditure, through a budget deficit or a burst of outlay on investment, increases demand beyond the capacity of agriculture, transport, and industry to supply consumption goods. Either imports are sucked in or prices rise sharply and set the inflationary spiral of profits and wages spinning.

Keynesian remedies were devised as a short-period cure for under-utilization of productive capacity already in existence; they will not create capacity that is not there.

(b) Under-employment

A man who can eat every day can work every day but, as we saw with the poor peasant family, the amount of productive work that a man can do in agriculture depends on the area he has to work on. There are three elements in enforced idleness in peasant agriculture; the first comes about through what may be called an absolute deficiency of cultivable land. Over the course of history, agricultural technology has adapted to the pressure of population. (In some parts of southern China, in ancient times, holdings were too small to support animals; there, human muscle was the only source of power, while in India, even today, a pair of bullocks is the minimum necessary equipment.) But in any tradition of technology, there is some upper limit beyond which increasing the intensity of cultivation yields no increase of product. When the density of population has passed this point, there is not a full day's work for all, even at the peak season. Where holdings are fairly evenly distributed among families, there are not necessarily any individuals who are unemployed outright, for everyone has a claim on the product of some land, and most share in the work; but taken as a whole, they would prefer to do more work if more work would add to the product. (The typical family is in the situation of the poor peasant depicted in Fig. 1.6 in **2** 1 §5.) This situation may arise among tenants or share croppers, or among peasant proprietors whose holdings have been divided and subdivided as numbers have grown from generation to generation.

So long as there is no other productive work for the cultivators, it cannot properly be called 'uneconomic' for them to crowd on to the land, however wasteful of labour it may appear, for all can share the work and the income instead of some being driven off to live on crumbs in the cities. The waste lies in the lack of alternative employment rather than the inefficient scale of farming.

The second element in rural under-employment arises from an unequal distribution of holdings among families. Our analysis of the kulaks and the poor peasants was very much formalized but it corresponds to the actual situation in peasant agriculture in many countries.

Consider a region where there is not an absolute scarcity of land of the kind described above. If all the work were spread over the cultivable area in such a way as to get the maximum possible total product, the marginal productivity of labour would be positive, i.e., there would be an appreciable loss of output if a man year of work were withdrawn, which would not be true when there is an absolute

327

scarcity of land. But work is not evenly spread over the area. Some holdings are so small that the marginal productivity of the family's labour is zero; others are so large that a family can live comfortably with little effort. The enforced idleness of poor peasants may be reduced if a kulak hires them to cultivate his land, but at first they dislike working for wages, which is undignified and involves submitting to a boss. Pride keeps them idle until they are forced to swallow it. Once they have got used to working for wages, additional income may compensate for the loss of independence.

The third element in enforced idleness is the seasonality of agricultural processes. In many regions, at rush seasons of a week or two once or twice a year, there is no excess of labour—indeed, some scarcity. In between, there are long spells with little or nothing to do at home and no possibility of earning wages.

The phenomenon of rural under-employment and seasonal idleness is sometimes subsumed under the expression 'disguised unemployment' but this is a misnomer. The characteristic of disguised unemployment in the original sense is that it could be cured by an increase in effective demand; rural under-employment requires some basic reorganization of the conditions of production.

It is technically possible, as the Chinese have shown, to make good use of the idle time of the cultivators (once they have enough to eat all the year round) to improve irrigation, check erosion, build roads, and so on, but individual property in land is an impediment to such schemes because of the problem of who is to get the benefit from them.

(c) Choice of technique

The would-be developing countries import industrial technology from the developed countries, partly directly, when branches of foreign firms are set up within their territory, and partly indirectly, as investments are made by their own capitalists or governments following foreign models, at first importing equipment, and later reproducing some elements in it. The technology evolved in the developed economies under pressure of rising real-wage rates generally requires a high cost of investment per man employed, which is obviously inappropriate to the situation of an economy with massive non-employment of labour, limited investible resources, and an ill-organized supply of finance.

It seems to follow that industrialization should be carried out with less labour-saving technique so that each round of investment would provide more future employment.

This sometimes slips over into the view that the object of investment is to give employment, so that the most labour-intensive technique—with the lowest output per head—is to be preferred. But the object of development is, firstly, to give more people something to eat, and secondly, to provide more surplus for further investment. The object is more output per unit of investment, not more work. Low output per man is not a merit in itself. Where there is a choice between known techniques, any that gives a lower output per unit of investment *and* a lower output per man should be rejected.

328

When there is a variety of eligible techniques for producing a given output—say, cotton cloth—they can be compared in terms of the concept of the degree of mechanization which we discussed above (though, as we saw, differences in the time-pattern of inputs required and outputs offered by each technique complicated the argument).* A more-mechanized technique requires a higher cost of investment per man employed and offers a higher output per head.

When the choice is guided by the principle of preferring the technique that offers the highest future output per unit cost of investment, a lower degree of mechanization must be preferred to a higher degree, for a lower degree means a smaller cost of investment per man and a larger future output per unit cost of the investment undertaken today. Incidentally, this offers a higher level of employment as well.

But, now, the concept of wages as a cost comes into the argument.† Comparing one technique with another, choosing that with the lower degree of mechanization will involve a higher future wage bill. Depending on the level of wages ruling, and the levels of output expected from the two techniques, it will often be found that a higher degree of mechanization is the more profitable. It offers a smaller future output per unit of investment, less employment and therefore a smaller wage bill. When the saving on the wage bill is greater than the value of output forgone, a profit-seeking capitalist may be supposed to avoid the technique that offers the larger output per unit of investment, and prefer the one that offers a higher profit per unit of investment.

In this situation, it is sometimes claimed that the most profitable technique is, after all, the most advantageous to the national economy, because it will yield a higher surplus. The less-mechanized technique offers the higher output and calls more men out of miserable non-employment, but they will eat up the wages that they earn. The more-profitable technique offers less employment now, with more surplus to expand investment in the future. If there is no other way to get funds for investment, and if the profits are sure to be invested, not spent by the capitalists on their own consumption, the more-profitable technique may be preferred, but in general, the argument in its favour sounds rather like an extension of capitalist ideology to a sphere where it is inappropriate.

Apart from known techniques, there are indefinite possibilities of devising techniques suited to the capacity of various economies. What are called 'intermediate technologies' have been introduced here and there; these involve methods and equipment more productive than primitive handicrafts but require very much less investment per man and per unit of output than modern Western production. However, the capitalists prefer ready-made techniques and, in any case, they are often working in with foreign firms who regard their own techniques as the best. Moreover, the governments of would-be developing countries often have a predilection for large, impressive schemes which are by no means the most efficient way of using their limited resources. A drawback of imported highly mechanized technology is not

* See **2** 11 §4(d).
† See **2** 11 §4(b).

only that it requires more investment to provide employment but that it starts on a scale and level of sophistication that it is hard for workers, technicians and managers to understand, so that they remain dependent on foreigners and cannot learn the know-how for themselves.

3. Foreign trade

We observed above that, to the economy of any country, foreign purchasing power is more valuable than home resources because it commands a wider range of products.* This is especially true of the would-be developing countries which have embarked on industrialization by importing equipment and know-how from those that are already highly developed.

Not all the foreign exchange available is used for development. In a number of countries, a great part has been used to import armaments, sometimes under the guise of an alliance with a great power, to be deployed against a neighbour or for the repression of the home population. Some is used to import foreign consumer goods to which a growing middle class is addicted, some to salt away in hoards of gold or in foreign bank accounts, and some is used from time to time to relieve famines. But whatever the purpose to which it is to be put, foreign exchange is greatly desired.

(a) Exports of primary products

In many countries of the Third World, sources of supply were developed during the colonial period which now provide them with exports to earn foreign exchange, though, as we have seen, markets are undependable.† Where these resources were developed by capitalists from the old imperial countries, they now have attached to them an obligation to remit profits, and in many cases, part of the salaries of expatriate managers are also allowed to be remitted. Imports of consumer goods have to be allowed for the expatriates and for their local imitators. This reduces the contribution that, at best, the foreign earnings can bring to development. The reasons that would-be developing countries allow themselves to continue in this situation are, first, that their authorities fear that their own people would not be able to manage the production as well as the foreigners can; second, that local capitalists are in sympathy with the foreigners, gain from arrangements with them, and therefore, give them political support. Finally, to challenge the developed countries is highly dangerous. If they do not go so far as to resort to force (directly or through internal subversion), they can block the outlet to world markets of a country that offends against the rules that they have imposed.

Not only does a great part of the production of ex-colonies remain in a dependent relationship with the ex-imperial nations, but new voluntary colonial relations are

---

* See **3** 2 §1(b).

330   † See **2** 5 §3(a).

entered into by would-be developing countries inviting foreign capitalist firms to develop new sources of supply in their territories.

(b) Manufacturers

Low-wage labour is not necessarily cheap labour, for undernourished and illiterate workers do not provide much of a surplus, however low their own share in the value of the product, but there are a number of lines in which low wages permit highly labour-intensive technology to compete successfully with the products of the most advanced industries.

When this type of production is organized by local capitalists, the rhythm of development depends a good deal on their style of life. When they have a taste for foreign-style luxuries and insist on being allowed to import them, or to import the ingredients for producing them at home, development is running up a blind alley. When their profits are mainly saved and reinvested, first in expanding their production of exports and then working back into producing investment goods, they are following the path of capitalist development as it originally took place. The very essence of the process involves a low share of wages in the value of output, that is, a high rate of exploitation of labour. All the same, workers who are being exploited by capitalists are better off than those who are existing at near starvation in disguised unemployment in the cities and as landless labour in the countryside.

The countries attempting to develop on these lines complain that they are frustrated by the protectionism of the developed countries, who do not want their own industries to be undersold. According to the orthodox theory of free trade, they should accept cheap imports of those goods in which labour-intensive techniques are most efficient, and transfer their own resources into more sophisticated industries in which their comparative advantage is greater. But such a transition involves loss for capitalists, and unemployment for workers, in the industries suffering from competition, without any guarantee that other industries will expand to take their place. Free-trade doctrine was all very well when it justified British manufactures ruining handicrafts in the colonial world. It does not have so much appeal when the boot is on the other foot.

(c) 'Import substitution'

Since foreign exchange is always in short supply, the first rule for development should be to economize on imports, that is, to aim for the greatest possible home production per unit cost of imports. This involves eliminating, by prohibitions or tariffs, the import of goods that can be done without or substituted by home production, and allowing in only those that contribute to the programme of development.

This point is not always well understood. Some foreign advisers to the would-be developing world deprecate 'import substitution' as being somehow in contradiction to the proper doctrine of free trade, though all the industrial nations now flourishing began their development under a policy of protection.

Even when the principle of economizing on imports is accepted, it is not always well applied. It is not unknown for protection to increase imports, as when an industry is set up, under shelter of a tariff, that is found to require imported materials to keep it going which involve a higher bill in foreign exchange than importing the finished product. To avoid this kind of error does not need free-trade theory, but technical information, common sense, and an honest administration that does not do favours to business at the expense of the national interest.

The success of a policy of industrialization depends on the markets that are protected. In many Latin American countries, protection has been an invitation to the great oligopolistic corporations to set up branches inside the tariff walls but such installations are often merely assembly plants using foreign components, so that only a part of the value of imports is really saved.

In any case, the imports which protection is aimed to save are usually of a type which only a small part of the population can afford to buy. For instance, investment may be promoted by a high tariff on motor cars, with the result that a number of industries have been set up, working on a small scale and therefore at high cost. The market is narrow so that the firms concerned can expand only by producing some other costly item for sale to the small wealthy class. For such firms to carry on, there must be protection of successive new ranges of commodities, each to be sold on a scale at which the techniques imported from advanced industrial countries cannot be efficient. Along this path, it is not possible to find the rhythm of rising real wages and mass consumption which is the secret of the success of capitalist development.

The objection to this policy is not the one that free-traders raise—the high cost of the protected products. The comparison between home cost and world prices is not relevant, for to buy at world prices involves using foreign exchange, which is scarce relative to home resources. If protection were removed, everything else remaining the same, the middle-class consumer would get cheaper, imported motor cars, there would be more unemployment (as well as lower profits) at home, and there would be an acute crisis in the balance of payments. The objection is not to protection as such, but to the type of investment that the protection is encouraging.

4. Capital inflow

To get a process of accumulation going, whether in a capitalist, a socialist, or a mixed economy, requires three ingredients: finance, the purchasing power available to be spent on investment; saving, the restraint on consumption that permits resources to be used for investment; and imports to supplement the resources available at home. Until a country has acquired a sufficient market for its exports (if it ever will), foreign loans or subventions that permit a surplus of imports are a great assistance in speeding up development. Many countries in the Third World have become accustomed to rely on foreign funds to supply the other two ingredients as well.

(a) Finance

Investments may be financed directly, without needing any borrowing, when, say, a wealthy landlord takes it into his head to spend part of his rents on improving his estate or setting up a factory. The very fact that the Third World is underdeveloped shows that such investment has not happened on a sufficient scale to get development going.

A general process of industrialization requires the owners of wealth to transfer purchasing power to those who will undertake investment and employ labour on production. In a modern industrial economy, the business of bringing lenders and borrowers together is highly organized, and we are inclined to take it for granted, but in an underdeveloped economy, credit is underdeveloped; owners of wealth prefer land or gold to a bank deposit or a share in a business. Also there may be a considerable amount of finance committed to moneylending and to trade, which is earning a high rate of interest that untried industrial investment cannot afford.

A weak government that is unwilling or unable to tax its citizens has poor credit and is also unable to borrow.

For lack of finance, a process of industrialization cannot get started, however urgent the need for it may seem to be. Can the deficiency of finance be made good by foreign borrowing? Foreign banks may operate in an underdeveloped economy, picking out the most promising prospects to lend to, and the government may receive loans or subventions. When the finance is used to import consumption goods or armaments, development is no further on. But suppose that the government, now able to spend in excess of its revenue, undertakes some useful investment, say, in improving the transport system. The expenditure increases incomes, employment, profits, and savings. Apart from any leakage to increased imports, there is an addition to wealth in the country. In so far as the addition to wealth is in the form of business profits it is available to finance further investment, but in so far as it has come into the hands of those who put their savings into gold or foreign exchange (whether legally or illegally) it is lost to the financial circulation. To keep up a steady rate of investment would require a continuous inflow of finance and an ever-mounting foreign debt.

The development of a local banking system and market for placements, in which owners of wealth have confidence, is a prerequisite for accumulation in conditions of private enterprise.

(b) Saving

The argument is often used that income per head in the countries of the Third World is so low that it is impossible for them to save. This argument is sophistical, for income is not equally distributed; everywhere a surplus, in one form or another, is extracted from workers and cultivators. To say that accumulation is held up for lack of potential saving would mean that the necessary consumption of a worker drawn out of non-employment absorbs the whole addition to his output, so that there is no surplus available to increase employment further.

It may happen that a process of accumulation is brought to a halt by lack of goods on which wages can be spent. When there is an addition to employment in industry there is an addition to demand for food. When supply from agriculture is inelastic, the additional demand coming from the expenditure of money wages earned in industry drives up the price of food, which makes it necessary to raise money-wage rates in industry, which drives up the price of food all the more, and so sets a vicious spiral turning. This cannot be attributed to a lack of saving in itself. It is due, rather, to lack of balance between the development of agriculture and industry. The difficulty can be overcome by importing grain, but this may be a palliative that puts off tackling the basic problem.

The problem which goes under the name of a lack of saving is not really a lack of a potentially investible surplus, for an increase of employment in industry is always accompanied by an increase in profits. The difficulty is to ensure that the growing surplus is continuously channelled into increasing the production of necessaries for consumption and the ingredients of investment, so as to make it possible for employment to continue to grow. The problem of saving, that is to say, is the problem of preventing an increase in profits from leading to an increase in luxury consumption.

In so far as foreign loans and subventions are spent on the ingredients required for investment—say, steel or machinery—they supplement home saving in a direct way. The home investment involved is offset by a deficit in the balance of trade (a surplus of imports). Savings from the donor country (which has a surplus of exports) are transferred to the recipient.

But, when the whole cost of the investment is paid for by the donor, including the costs incurred at home, the excess of the import surplus over the investment goods imported takes the form of consumption goods. Foreign saving is substituted for home saving. Assuming that necessary consumption is provided for from home sources, this means that imports are providing for consumption out of profits.

In so far as these imports are paid for out of loans, there will be a burden of future interest payments against which there is no offset in increased productive capacity in the country; in so far as they are paid for out of aid, the benevolent intentions of the donor are being frustrated.

This suggests that the countries which most deserve help are those which nationalize their industries, preventing profits accruing to private families who consume them, and which prohibit the import of luxury goods. However, countries pursuing such policies are the least likely to receive aid.

(c) The morning after

Even when the inflow of foreign funds is used strictly for investment, loans create a problem for the developing economy. Loans are made on terms requiring repayment and interest. The investment that they make possible may be extremely valuable for the general development of the economy without helping to increase export earnings. As the debt mounts, interest payments absorb more and more of available foreign exchange. So long as the country hopes to go on borrowing, it dare not default; after a time it finds itself using a large part of the proceeds of new loans to pay interest on the old ones.

Another form of capital inflow is direct investment by a foreign corporation that sets up a branch in the would-be developing country.

The corporation often provides only a small part of the finance of the investment that it makes, for it can borrow funds locally by selling bonds. It organizes a business, employs labour, and brings in equipment and know-how (which may not be of the kind most appropriate to the country). Against this, it has the right to remit profits in perpetuity. This is generally a more expensive form of borrowing than loans. When the corporation reinvests profits made in the country, to expand its operations, it is organizing development there, but the extra capital created in this way belongs to the parent company and will require more profits to be remitted in the future.

Sometimes a developing country is in a strong enough position to make a bargain with an international corporation that it allows to set up in its territory, according to which the country keeps part of the equity, so that a share of the profit stays at home, along with some other advantages. But many would-be developing countries compete with each other by offering tax concessions and other favours to attract the corporations to come and make profits out of them.

5. Population

Despite these difficulties and contradictions, development does go on. Production and income in the Third World are growing, but at the same time, numbers are growing everywhere, and in some regions, growing appreciably faster than employment and production, so that the mass of destitution and misery is increasing at the same time as development.

(a) Food supply

Agronomists are fond of calculating the possibilities of feeding the population of the world. Some are fairly complacent and some threaten mass starvation within a generation. However that may be, there are great numbers of people near starvation today, and a great number of children growing up half-alive because of under-nourishment in infancy. The overall supply of food for the total potential population of the world is not relevant to the problem of getting the actual population fed today.

(b) Investment

Once modern technology has come into being, it seems obvious that growth of numbers must be a disadvantage to those who are already alive. The proportion of

335

the labour force, and of other resources, that can be devoted to investment (including education), in any economy, is necessarily limited. The smaller the growth of numbers to be provided for, the greater the amount of equipment, housing, and amenities that it is possible to provide, per head of population. 'With every mouth God sends a pair of hands' but not a tractor, a power station, or a schoolroom. Growth of numbers is a drag on the standard of life even in the most wealthy countries and it is a heavy burden in the poorest.

(c) Policy

The great explosion of population in recent years has come about principally through a fall in infant mortality. Historically, a fall in the birth-rate follows a fall in the infant death-rate. Whatever technical facilities are available, it is not easy to get the habit of birth-control established until people have some degree of security and control over their own lives. In China, a campaign for late marriage and small families was not begun until the standard of health and diet had been greatly improved, full employment and social security provided, and everyone imbued with an optimistic view of the future.

In every country, now, in which the authorities and educated public have some concern that all their fellow citizens ought to be fed, housed and educated, the need for birth-control is admitted and efforts made to popularize it, with varying success.

Other regimes regard a plentiful supply of cheap labour as a support for landed property or as an attraction for a rapid expansion of capitalist business. They take advantage of religious prejudice to put obstacles in the way of family planning except for the privileged class.

6. Conclusion

The orthodox doctrines of the theory of equilibrium and of free trade, which are disseminated among the intellectuals of the Third World, are not relevant to their problems. Equilibrium theory is an exposition of the presumption in favour of *laissez-faire*, but the very concept of development as an objective of policy is incompatible with *laissez-faire*. The case for free trade is expressed in a model in which imports and exports always balance, while every country in the Third World is suffering from a deficiency of foreign exchange.

A different approach to economic analysis may enable the intelligentsia of the Third World to see their problems in a clearer light but economics alone cannot tell them where to find the answers.

Bibliography and Index

Bibliography

Chamberlin, E. H., *The Theory of Monopolistic Competition*, Harvard UP, Cambridge, Mass., 1933.

Dobb, M. H., *Theories of Value and Distribution since Adam Smith*, Cambridge UP, Cambridge, 1973.

Ellman, M. J., *Soviet Planning Today*, Cambridge UP, Cambridge, 1971.

Friedman, M., *The Optimum Quantity of Money*, Macmillan, London, 1969.

Galbraith, J. K., *The Great Crash*, Hamish Hamilton, London, 1955.

Galbraith, J. K., *The New Industrial State*, Houghton Mifflin, Boston, 1967.

Jackson, D., Turner, H. A., and Wilkinson, F., *Do Trade Unions Cause Inflation?* Cambridge UP, Cambridge, 1972.

Kahn, R. F., *Selected Essays on Employment and Growth*, Cambridge UP, Cambridge, 1972.

Kalecki, M., *Selected Essays on the Dynamics of the Capitalist Economy, 1933–1970*, Cambridge UP, Cambridge, 1971.

Kantorovich, L. V., *The Best Use of Economic Resources,* English translation, Pergamon, Oxford, 1965.

Keynes, J. M., *The Collected Writings of John Maynard Keynes,* 25 volumes, Macmillan, London, 1971– . (Vol. VII: *The General Theory of Employment, Interest and Money*. Vol. X: *Essays in Biography*. Vol. XIV: *The General Theory and After: Part II Defence and Development*.)

Kornai, J., *Anti-Equilibrium*, North-Holland Publishing, Amsterdam, 1971.

Levitt, K., *Silent Surrender*, Macmillan, Toronto, 1970.

Marshall, A., *Principles of Economics,* (1st edn., 1890) 8th edn., Macmillan, London, 1920.

Marx, K., *Capital*, 3 volumes, Lawrence & Wishart, London, 1970–1972.

Marx, K. and Engels, F., *Selected Correspondence 1846–1896*, Marxist-Leninist Library, London, 1934.

Myrdal, G., *The Political Element in the Development of Economic Theory,* English translation, Routledge & Kegan Paul, London, 1953.

Neumann, J. von, and Morgenstern, O., *The Theory of Games and Economic Behaviour*, Princeton UP, Princeton, 1944.

Ricardo, D., *The Works and Correspondence of David Ricardo*, (Sraffa edn.) 11 volumes, Cambridge UP, Cambridge, 1951–1973.

Robinson, J., *The Economics of Imperfect Competition*, Macmillan, London, 1933.

Robinson, J., *Economic Philosophy*, Penguin, London, 1966.

Robinson, J., *Exercises in Economic Analysis*, Macmillan, London, 1960.

Robinson, J., *Introduction to the Theory of Employment,* 2nd edn. Macmillan, London, 1969.

Schumpeter, J. A., *Capitalism, Socialism and Democracy*, Allen & Unwin, London, 1943.

Shackle, G. L. S., *The Years of High Theory*, Cambridge UP, Cambridge, 1967.

Smith, A., *An Inquiry into the Nature and Causes of the Wealth of Nations,* (Cannan edn.) Methuen, London, 1961.

Spulber, N. (ed.), *Foundations of the Soviet Strategy for Economic Growth,* Indiana UP, Blooming-
     ton, 1964.
Sraffa, P., *Production of Commodities by Means of Commodities*, Cambridge UP, Cambridge
     1960.
Veblen. T., *The Theory of the Leisure Class*, Macmillan, New York, 1899.

Index

341

Printed in Great Britain by
William Clowes & Sons, Limited, London, Beccles and Colchester